D1622124

Addressing Social Issues in the Classroom and Beyond

The Pedagogical Efforts of Pioneers in the Field

a volume in
Research in Curriculum and Instruction

Series Editor:
O. L. Davis, Jr., *The University of Texas at Austin*

Research in Curriculum and Instruction

O. L. Davis, Jr., Series Editor

Addressing Social Issues in the Classroom and Beyond

The Pedagogical Efforts of Pioneers in the Field

edited by

Samuel Totten
University of Arkansas, Fayetteville

Jon Pedersen
University of Oklahoma, Norman

INFORMATION AGE
PUBLISHING

Charlotte, North Carolina • www.infoagepub.com

Library of Congress Cataloging-in-Publication Data

Addressing social issues in the classroom and beyond : the pedagogical efforts of pioneers in the field / edited by Samuel Totten, Jon Pedersen.
    p. cm. — (Research in curriculum and instruction)
 Includes bibliographical references and index.
 ISBN-13: 978-1-59311-566-1 (pbk.)
 ISBN-13: 978-1-59311-567-8 (hardcover)
 1. Educational sociology—United States. 2. Educators—United States. 3. Education—United States—Philosophy.
 I. Totten, Samuel. II. Pedersen, Jon E., 1960-
 LC191.4.A33 2007
 370.11'5—dc22

2006032370

ISBN 13: 978-1-59311-566-1 (pbk.)
ISBN 13: 978-1-59311-567-8 (hardcover)
ISBN 10:   1-59311-566-0 (pbk.)
ISBN 10:   1-59311-567-9 (hardcover)

Copyright © 2007 IAP–Information Age Publishing, Inc.

All rights reserved. No part of this publication may be reproduced, stored in a retrieval system, or transmitted, in any form or by any means, electronic, mechanical, photocopying, microfilming, recording or otherwise, without written permission from the publisher.

Printed in the United States of America

DEDICATION

We, Samuel Totten and Jon E. Pedersen, dedicate this book with the greatest of appreciation and gratitude to Dr. O. L. Davis, Jr. in honor of his outstanding career in education, his sterling achievements in the fields of curriculum theory and social studies education, and his remarkable mentorship of his graduate students at the University of Texas, Austin, along with former students and young professionals in the field of education who have sought his counsel and advice.

CONTENTS

FOREWORD

"When kids enter school, they leave the real world and enter into a contrived, imagined child's world." Marshall McLuhan dropped this sentence onto a small group of us during the early morning hours of an informal seminar now almost fifty years ago. His sentence was a part of—or, perhaps, a kind of verbal footnote to—his rapidly streaming commentary about schooling and media. He did not repeat his sentence; each of us present immediately had engraved it in our separate memories. Across the years, I frequently access this timeless, timely observation. I thought of it again as I read the chapters of Samuel Totten's and Jon E. Pedersen's *Addressing Social Issues in the Classroom and Beyond*.

McLuhan was right, of course. We may not admit at once the veracity of his claim, but we recognize the discomfort of his comment. Our common experience as one-time pupils, as parents, and, for some of us, as teachers is that we recognize the distance of schooling from what many of us call "real life." We recognize the oft-time artificiality of classrooms, certainly our own, and the curriculum with which we want our students to engage. Which one of us adults commonly leaves home or office in order to go to an institutional setting or a site that serves many others at the same time in order to read a novel or to ponder a historical or scientific narrative? Who among us in a citizens' policy group does not seek a hasty conclusion to our consideration of public issues, not unlike we did in our school civics discussions, rather than *to deliberate toward a decision upon which we will act*? Who among us does not recognize the raw impersonal character of classrooms (and beyond) as well as our routine marginalization or dismissal of the "person-hood" of individuals within those classrooms as well as the persons and groups about whom pupils study? The evidence that supports McLuhan's judgment is overwhelmingly apparent and convincing. On the other hand, McLuhan was optimistic: he believed that this impoverished and immoral situation need not continue.

Optimism that social issues *can* be addressed in school, not simply that they *should* be addressed, is a shared attribute of the individuals' lives that are portrayed in Totten's and Pedersen's notable book. For some of these properly identified "pioneers," they did much more than to advocate that social issues be part of the grist of the classroom curriculum.

A number of these educators became actively and publicly involved in the resolution of quite a number of prominent social issues of their times. As "public intellectuals," they wrote letters to elected officials; they wrote articles, op-ed essays, and articles for a public readership as well as spoke their commitments and advocacies on radio and television programs. As activists, some marched and button-holed legislators in open protest of racial injustices such as closed voting booths and restrictive neighborhood covenants and segregated, unequal provisions for schooling. They also kept silent and candle-lit vigil against capital punishment, rallied against lynching and in support of adequate pensions for elderly persons and of child labor restrictions.

Variously, they received both praise and rebuke and some lost income or position or reputation. Beyond the school, they served as their own illustration of a teacher who addressed social issues.

Some of these major educators lived and worked before I launched my career. How I wish that I could have known and listened to John Dewey and Gordon Hullfish, and Jesse Newland and Rachel Davis DuBois, four of this volume's featured persons. I did not, but I can read what they wrote. On the other hand, I had the good fortune to meet or listen to or interact with some of the other pioneers like George Counts, Harold Rugg, Paul Hurd, and Donald Oliver. Others have been or are dear professional and personal friends, for example, Alice Miel, Shirley Engle, and Maxine Greene. No matter if I did not know them or knew them well, I learned from reading this book something that I had not known about each of these outstanding teachers. Consequently, I am better off having read each essay in this book. So, I believe, will be other readers.

Our generation, in our times, stands upon the shoulders of these pioneers, these giants. Additionally, we can be informed and motivated by their efforts, their failures—and they surely did fail at times, but also by their successes. Among other contributions, they sought by both action and thought to open schooling to the study of social issues of their times. Their lives and their advocacies are their pedagogical legacies to the future.

Now is our time to act such that we may open further the classrooms of our own days, to help convert at least some of the contrivances of an imagined child's world called the school into dimensions of the real world. We surely must invent means in this era of high-stakes testing by which social issues are as welcome sources of academic content as is the subject matter specified in the state standards. That task, however difficult or adventuresome, can be accomplished. For inspiration and, as need exists, for stories about how other teachers addressed social issues in the "everydayness" of classrooms, we can turn again to the chapters in Samuel Totten's and Jon E. Pedersen's impressive book.

O. L. Davis, Jr.
Catherine Mae Parker Centennial
Professor of Curriculum and Instruction
The University of Texas at Austin

INTRODUCTION

Samuel Totten and Jon E. Pedersen

There is a long and rich tradition of professors of education in the United States addressing, in one way or another, the vital link between social issues and the educational process. They, in turn, have contributed to the incorporation of the study of social issues into the curriculum of our nation's schools. From the early part of the twentieth century onward, many educational leaders have addressed the critical need, both in oral presentations and in their writing, to assist young people to think about and wrestle with the crucial issues facing society, as well as their own lives. In the early years, this group included such luminaries as John Dewey, the Rugg brothers, George Counts, among others. A generation later, it included many noted social studies educators (e.g., Lawrence Metcalf, Maurice Hunt, Richard Gross, Donald Oliver, and Shirley Engle), science educators (Joseph Piel and Paul DeHart Hurd), and curriculum theorists (Alice Miel). This illustrious group also included Maxine Greene, whose efforts have spanned several generations and who has examined social issues and the impact they have on the lives of individuals, teachers and students through the lens of philosophy.

The aforementioned individuals, as well as many other educators who addressed social issues in one way or another, have made remarkable contributions to the field of education. Among their major contributions are: the development of strong rationales for introducing the study of social issues into the extant curriculum; the publication of key theoretical work vis-à-vis educating about social issues; the development of models and strategies for addressing social issues within various curricular areas; and research regarding the efficacy of teaching about social issues at both the elementary and secondary levels.

Addressing Social Issues in the Classroom and Beyond: The Pedagogical Efforts of Pioneers in the Field comprises essays that delineate the genesis and evolution of the thought and work of pioneers in the field of social issues and education. The authors (many of whom, themselves, are noted professors of education and who have done significant work in the field of social issues and education) delineate and analyze the efforts (e.g., theoretical work, research, curriculum development, and teaching) of such pioneers within the larger framework of their life-story. As a result, the reader is not only introduced to the significant work of each pioneer but valuable and often fascinating insights into how his/her life experiences informed his/her thinking, beliefs, goals and work.

The individuals selected for inclusion in *Addressing Social Issues in the Classroom and Beyond: The Pedagogical Efforts of Pioneers in the Field* are those who, in one way or another, helped to establish the foundation for teaching about social issues in our nation's public and private schools: John Dewey, George Counts, Harold Rugg, Jesse Newlon, Theodore Bramweld, Alice Miel, Rachel Davis Dubois, Alan Griffin, Lawrence E. Metcalf, Maurice P. Hunt, Richard Gross, Donald Oliver, Shirley Engle, Paul DeHart Hurd, Joseph Piel, and Maxine Greene.

In order to assure a semblance of continuity, each author or group of authors was asked to address the same set of questions: (1) What led this individual to initially begin thinking, teaching, writing, and/or speaking about the place of social issues in the extant school curriculum; (2) What were the fundamental problems and issues that drove the individual to study/address social issues? (3) What was the individual's primary aim as a teacher educator and/or scholar in this field?; (4) What individual(s) (both on a personal as well as a professional level) most influenced the individual in his/her work vis-a-vis social issues, and how?; (5) Which scholarly works, if any, influenced the individual in his/her work?; (6) Was there a persistent and consistent focus in the individual's thinking and writing about the place of social issues in the extant curricula?; (7) Did his/her thinking evolve over time, and if so how?; (8) Did the individual face any major obstacles in his/her work; and if so, how did he or she fare against them?; (9) Was the individual a social activist?; and (10) What were the individual's major contributions to the field?

Authors were also informed that, in addressing the aforementioned questions, it was imperative that they approach them in a way that revealed the personality, passions, and insights of the individual being written about. It was also conveyed to the authors that it was equally significant--indeed, a must--to include the most powerful and revelatory personal stories they could in order to illuminate the individual's thinking, experiences, and work in this field.

The biographical essays in this book, then, are threefold in nature: informative, instructive, and engaging. We are, in fact, very pleased with the hard work and effort that each and every author (or team of authors) put into the writing of his/her/their chapter. Due to such diligence and dedication the individual pioneers come alive on the page. As a result, this book is a far cry from the often dry, if not sterile, writing that one comes across in far too many texts on education. The combination of a biographical approach along with the delineation and analysis of each author's life and efforts makes for fascinating reading; and, at one and the same time, provides significant insights into the foundation of what has become an important field within the discipline of education: teaching and learning about social issues.

Ultimately, this book constitutes a rich and unusual record of the thinking and accomplishments of those luminaries who worked tirelessly in the belief that a well educated and well-informed populace was absolutely imperative in a democracy if the latter were to remain healthy and vibrant.

Beyond current scholars and students, we believe that this book will be of great interest to a wide spectrum of individuals: teacher educators who perceive the need to avail their students of the rich history, rationales and methods for incorporating the study of social issues across the curriculum; professors who teach history of curriculum courses and/or history of education courses are likely to be drawn to the book, both for the rich stories as well as the bounty of information found in each chapter; those who specialize in autobiographical studies in the field of education are likely to find the book to be remarkably rich and valuable both for their own research as well as in their teaching; secondary level teachers in science, social studies, and English who are interested in incorporating the study of social issues into the courses they teach will glean incredibly rich insights into why and how to go about such an endeavor; and future scholars and students who care deeply about how society impacts education, education impacts society, and how individuals and groups can have a positive impact on society through their collective efforts are bound to find the book both fascinating and instructive.

We wish to offer a heartfelt thanks to all of the contributors for their hard work, many of whom revised their essays two, three and more times. They were wonderful to work with, and we would be pleased to work with them again.

We also wish to sincerely thank Dr. O. L. Davis, Jr. for his initial interest in this book and his incredible support and outstanding advice and suggestions throughout the development of the book. We have discovered, through our work on this book with many of O. L.'s former and current graduate students, that O. L. is the epitome of what it means to be a mentor. Indeed, it is our belief that there are probably few professors in any field anywhere who are more enthusiastic or more supportive mentors than O. L. Davis, Jr. It is no wonder that current and former graduate students share a special love for him.

Finally, we hope that readers of this book, now and in the future, find it stimulating, and we also hope that it encourages them to follow, *and build-upon*, the giant footsteps left by the pioneers highlighted herein.

CHAPTER 1

JOHN DEWEY AND SOCIAL ACTION

Mark David Dietz and O. L. Davis, Jr.

INTRODUCTION

On July 2, 1894, John Dewey wrote to his wife, Alice,

The other night I met a young fellow about 28 or 30 who was out organizing railway unions. He was quite willing to talk, as quick as he had sent out his telegrams ordering the men out at midnight.... He had been in the business 8 mos.; was a store-keeper on the Great Northern railroad; was told by the Co[mpany] not to join a Union; up to that time had had no special interest in "Labor"; then he went to work to organize a Union in that place. I only talked with him 8 or 10 or 15 minutes but when I got through my nerves were more thrilled than they had been for years; I felt as if I had better resign my job teaching & follow him round till I got into life[.] One lost all sense of the right or wrong of things in admiration of his absolute almost fanatic sincerity & earnestness, & in admiration of the magnificent combination that was going on. Simply as an aesthetic matter, I don't believe the world has seen but few times such a spectacle of magnificent, widespread union of men about a common interest as this strike evinces. (Letter, John Dewey to Alice Dewey, 2 July, 1894, cited in Martin, 2002, p. 161)

Addressing Social Issues in the Classroom and Beyond: The Pedagogical Efforts of Pioneers in the Field, 1–30
Copyright © 2007 by Information Age Publishing
All rights of reproduction in any form reserved.

Dewey had arrived in Chicago just in time to witness the famous Pullman Strike of 1894. Dewey did not quit his job, nor follow this anonymous young man around helping him to organize unions. Nevertheless, readers should not conclude from this passage that Dewey failed in the end to "get into life."

This letter provides a glimpse into a side of Dewey not often seen. Here is an unabashedly romantic account of social action. Anyone, in fact, who has dipped into Dewey's personal correspondence knows that he was quite as capable as the most unexceptional to express the robust sentimentality that domestic life so easily extracts. Even in Dewey's formal writing sudden flashes of passion are apparent. Dewey was not the unemotional, unimpassioned, philosophic observer, forever sitting on the sidelines, that a quick glance at his writings might suggest. If the Pullman Strike was not his to take part in, many another broad and important avenue for social action—for "getting into life"—would come his way in the year's ahead, and in many an instance he would not hesitate to step forward and do what he could.

Born on October 20, 1859, in Burlington, Vermont, to Archibald and Lucina Dewey, Dewey was raised in a household where social action, at a local level and as an expression of Christian charity, was a distinct part of his early life. In his recent biography of John Dewey, John Martin (2002) suggests that Dewey was greatly influenced by his mother's "liberal devotion to public service and her stress on intelligence and experience in interpreting the Bible—concerns that turned her outward to the world" (p. 24). Undoubtedly, Dewey's earliest expressions of social action were extensions of his religious beliefs. That said, Dewey's personal relationship to Christianity was more ambiguous than that of his service-oriented, Christian mother. Still, Dewey's public-spiritedness must clearly date from the early experiences he had with his mother caring for the youth and the poor of the local Burlington community. For example, in his early years he had assisted his mother in her church work, and later established a bible class through the Student Christian Association at the University of Michigan (Martin, 2002, p. 88).

Dewey attended the University of Vermont from 1875 to 1879. Upon graduation, he taught high school in Pennsylvania and Vermont, without much success. Subsequently, he entered Johns Hopkins University to study philosophy at the graduate level. By way of his mentor at Johns Hopkins, George Sylvester Morris, Dewey came under the influence of German idealists like Kant and Hegel. G. Stanley Hall, another noted professor, provided an alternative influence. Hall had received the first doctorate in psychology in the United States and went on to establish experimental psychology as a university discipline. Through Hall, Dewey saw the potential impact of a scientific approach to social and psychological phenomenon. A third imminent scholar was also among the faculty of the philosophy department at Johns Hopkins, C. S. Peirce, who coined the term "pragmatism," or, as he would later fashion it, "pragmaticism," in an effort to distinguish himself from Dewey. Dewey ranked the three in the following order of importance to his growth as a scholar: Morris, Hall and Peirce. Later scholars have been more inclined to invert that order (Ryan, 1995, pp. 62-71).

Morris's personal crisis of faith coupled to his estrangement from the empiricism of Mill seems to have had a strong impact on Dewey. Early on, Dewey wrote of Morris, "I have a feeling that his lectures betrayed the fact he never quite forgave the English empiricists, 'externalists,' and mechanical philosophers for having, for a time, led him astray" (quoted in Ryan, 1995, p. 67).

All crises of faith, of course, are not the same. Today's philosophers, whose own crises of faith are possibly the product of their romanticization of an experience like that which Morris went through, may well be forgiven for overdramatizing Dewey's own crisis of faith which seems to have emerged slowly and tenuously finding its apogee at some unknowable point between his arrival at the University of Michigan in 1884 and his move to the University of Chicago in 1894. Indeed, Dewey's crisis of faith seems to have been more focused on throwing off the idealism he had inherited from Morris, than on rebelling against the Christian activism of his mother. At the very least, Dewey's mature philosophy rather stridently rejected Hegelian idealism, but his involvement in social action, as will be recounted in this chapter, never fully rejected his mother's activism. In the end he would say, in *A Common Faith*,

> I would remind readers in conclusion, it is the intellectual side of the religious attitude that I have been considering. I have suggested that the religious element in life has been hampered by conceptions of the supernatural that were imbedded in those cultures wherein man had little control over outer nature and little in the way of sure method of inquiry and test. The crisis today as to the intellectual content of religious belief has been caused by the change in the intellectual climate due to the increase of our knowledge and our means of understanding. I have tried to show that this change is not fatal to the religious values in our common experience, however adverse its impact may be upon historic religions. Rather, provided that the methods and results of intelligence at work are frankly adopted, the change is liberating. (Dewey, 1934, p. lw.9.38)

Graduation from John Hopkins left Dewey needing to find employment in his chosen field of philosophy. Through Morris, Dewey received a junior position on the faculty of the philosophy department at University of Michigan in 1884. Excepting one year at the University of Minnesota,

Dewey stayed at the University of Michigan until 1894 (Ecker, 1997). In 1886, Dewey married Harriet Alice Chipman. By all accounts the marriage was a positive step for Dewey. The loss of two children, however, took its toll on Alice. Her last years were beset by fits of depression. She died in 1927 of a cerebral hemorrhage (Martin, 2002).

During the early years of Dewey's career he wrote, taught, and engaged in the democratic life of the college campus. As George Dykhuizen (1973) in his biography of Dewey pointed out, "democracy in all its phases—political, economic, social, cultural—came to claim Dewey's strongest allegiance and to command his deepest loyalties; interest in social aid and social reform groups began to replace his interest in the Church" (p. 73).

In 1894, Dewey was asked to lead the Department of Philosophy at the University of Chicago. During the summer of that year, Dewey found himself alone in Chicago, while his wife and children traveled to Europe for a vacation tour. The letter that begins this chapter (and the letter which will end it) come from this summer, a summer that saw Dewey, perhaps unknowingly, at the dividing point of his career. He arrived at Chicago a respected scholar, and would leave Chicago in 1904, a noted actor on the national stage of social action.

Dewey's departure from the University of Chicago was somewhat acrimonious. At the University of Chicago, Dewey founded his famous Laboratory School, but unfortunately, Dewey was not a particularly able administrator. His wife's role as Principal of the Laboratory School, and her dismissal from that role by William Harper, the university's president, no doubt exacerbated the difficulties of the situation (Martin, 2002; Ryan, 1995).

Dewey's years at Columbia University, which followed those at the University of Chicago (until 1930, and again until 1939 as a professor emeritus), would see Dewey solidify his position as a distinguished philosopher. In New York, his social activism also increased and broadened. Not even retirement could abate his activity or his writing. Indeed, he continued an active member of society through his final years. In 1952, he died, active in writing and speaking until very near his end (Ecker, 1997).

SOCIAL ACTION IN DEWEY'S LIFE AND WRITINGS

"Social action" was central to Dewey's intellectual concerns. The phrase appears often in his collected writings (including making an appearance in the title of his 1935 volume *Liberalism and Social Action* (1935)). Social action was both an essential element of his philosophy of education and a recognized mechanism for the intelligent ordering of societal change. In *Education and Experience* (1938) he asserted the following: "It suffices to say that in general the school has been the institution which exhibited with greatest clearness the assumed antithesis between purely individualistic methods of learning and social action, and between freedom and social control" (Dewey, 1938, p. mw.9.310).

The above statement shows Dewey's notion of social action in its philosophical and educational dress. However, in its active and "getting into life" dress, social action for Dewey was something more like this: "I should not have appeared at all, were it not that it gave me the opportunity to express my sympathy with the purpose of this gathering" (Dewey, 1909, in Boydston, 1991, 2005, p. mw.4.156). This expression comes from the Dewey of 1909 speaking before the National Negro Conference (which later would become the National Association for the Advancement of Colored People). Although he did not mention the phrase "social action" in this brief sentence, its presence is nonetheless palpable. "Appeared," "opportunity," "express," "sympathy," "purpose," and "gathering" are Dewey's terms for social action at its moments of engagement with life.

The politeness and gentility of these words, however, did not always carry the day. Dewey engaged in his share of intellectual debate and two "epic confrontations."

> The two epic confrontations of Dewey's career—epic because both parties were writing at the top of their form, were fully engaged, and understood exactly what they were replying to—were those with Randolph Bourne in 1917 and 1918 and with Walter Lippmann in the 1920s. It was no accident that the confrontations concerned democracy and war, though Bourne and Dewey fell out over the war, while he and Lippmann were first of one mind over the war and then at odds over postwar democracy and the possibility of "outlawing' war" (Ryan, 1995, p. 159).

Dewey's support for the "war to end all wars" was unpopular with many of his friends and peers. He was attacked roundly for what was seen as his shortsightedness. "Four years later [Dewey himself] believed that he had been taken for a ride and the American people duped by the imperialist ruling classes of Britain and France" (Ryan, 1995, p. 159). Nonetheless, he had, in the heat of battle, as it were, used his prominence to keep Bourne out of the *New Republic* and remove him from the editorial board of the *Dial*. He had treated Jane Addams appeals boorishly, to say the least. In all, he had not behaved particularly well, and any assessment of his character must take this brief if significant period of his life into account (Ryan, 1995, p. 203). Be that as it may, he still held some goodwill with the public. In that age of post war reappraisal, to have an unblemished character was as much as having no character at all.

Dewey's debate with Lippmann, however, ran deeper than the war, to the very essence of democracy itself. Lippmann had been one of Dewey's allies in former times, but the legacy of the war and the realities of the League of Nations caused both men to rethink their political philosophies. Dewey sided earnestly with the outlawry of war movement. Lippmann attacked the movement; Dewey defended it. Then Lippmann published *Public Opinion* (Lippmann, 1922) and Dewey responded with *The Public and its Problems* (Dewey, 1927). Lippmann had come to the conclusion that the public was now so far removed from the complexities and difficulties of the world that it could not be expected to rationally and responsibly govern. Dewey countered this argument in one of his finest polemical efforts. He concluded in *The Public and its Problems* that,

> There is no limit to the liberal expansion and confirmation of limited personal intellectual endowment which may proceed from the flow of social intelligence when that circulates by word of mouth from one to another in the communications of the local community. We lie, as Emerson said, in the lap of an immense intelligence. But that intelligence is dormant and its communications are broken, inarticulate and faint until it possesses the local community as its medium. (Dewey, 1927, p. lw.2.371-2)

How this local community and word of mouth were supposed to function, Dewey did not make entirely clear. Nonetheless, his defense of democracy was notable, and Dewey is credited, not inappropriately, with having done much to keep the cause of democracy alive within the liberal movement. Not only had he stood his ground against Lippmann's elitism, he also took a strong stand against the totalitarianism of Russia under Stalin and Germany under Hitler.

Quite obviously, Dewey did not see a distinct gap between the philosophical and the practical. Much to the contrary, Dewey quite clearly saw philosophy and practice as continuous. Not surprisingly, Dewey appeared to engage the world at both levels, as a philosopher and writer providing the materials that encouraged an intelligent ordering of societal change and as a pair of hands among many other pairs of hands engaging in the work demanded by social action. In essence, Dewey saw in education, voluntary organizations, democracy, journalism, religion, the arts, and even, if begrudgingly so, in party politics and industrial life, both a philosophical social action and a social action of people coming together and "getting into life."

The question, then, addressed in this chapter is: How might both these types of social action be understood in light of Dewey's personal history and his various writings? The combination of Dewey's actions and his voluminous essays and books, particularly from his days at the University of Chicago forward, portray a man, a human being as much as a scholar, who strove to find outlets that would engage life directly in ways that the philosophy he had inherited and to which he contributed no longer seemed able to do. As he said, when nearing the end of his career, "Before reproaching philosophers for failure to agree we should recall that in the present state of the world agreement among them would be proof positive that philosophy is so technical as to be wholly out of touch with the problems and issues of actual life" (Dewey, 1946, p. lw.15.155).

Convention more than Dewey suggests a phrase like "actions and words." Dewey had no interest in the duality of mind and body on which modern philosophy had come to depend. For Dewey, writing was itself a type of social action. In this chapter, some of Dewey's texts and activities are set side by side, as Dewey no doubt meant them to be seen, in the hopes that by so doing, a richer, more robust portrait of Dewey the social activist will become apparent.

Dewey's social action was pluralistic, thoroughgoing ("radical"), formative, occasional, liberal, cooperative, organized, and democratic. The meanings of these characterizations are best seen in context. The subsequent sections of this chapter will attempt to create that context and complete the portrait.

SOCIAL ACTION AS A MANY-SIDED PLURALISM

Dewey approached social action across multiple vectors. Such multiple vectors Dewey would have perceived as pluralistic, a term and a concept that Dewey inherited from William James. The concept is more common in Dewey's writings than the term itself. Much of Dewey's writing can be read advantageously if viewed as a tendency to move away from dualities and to explore the multiple possibilities present in a thought or idea.

Notice, for example, in the following excerpt from *Reconstruction in Philosophy* (1920) how Dewey treats the words "individual" and "social" as pluralistic concepts.

> Just as "individual" is not one thing, but is a blanket term for the immense variety of specific reactions, habits, dispositions, and powers of human nature that are evoked, and confirmed under the influences of associated life, so with the term "social." Society is one word, but infinitely many things. It covers all the ways in which by associating together men share their experiences, and build up common interests and aims; street gangs, schools for burglary, clans, social cliques, trades unions, joint-stock corporations, villages and international alliances. (Dewey, 1920, p. mw.12.194).

The following quotation from Dewey's *Liberalism and Social Action* (1935) more specifically deals with the pluralism of the individual within the context of social action:

When the conclusions of inquiries that deal with man are left outside the program of social action, social policies are necessarily left without the guidance that knowledge of man can provide, and that it must provide if social action is not to be directed either by mere precedent and custom or else by the happy intuitions of individual minds. The social conception of the nature and work of intelligence is still immature; in consequence, its use as a director of social action is inchoate and sporadic. It is the tragedy of earlier liberalism that just at the time when the problem of social organization was most urgent, liberals could bring to its solution nothing but the conception that intelligence is an individual possession. (Dewey, 1935, p. lw.11.34)

Dewey's many-sidedness, however, was not merely an intellectual stance. Lack of detailed biographical information obscures to some degree the personal and very human side of Dewey. Nonetheless, that human side seems to have been as much an aspect of Dewey's social action as was his desire to see action and experience, intellectually, from all sides. For example, in her introduction to *The Poems of John Dewey* (Dewey & Boydston, 1977), Jo Ann Boydston writes that "the public image of John Dewey—educational innovator, philosopher, polemicist, political activist—is that of a reserved, serious, unemotional, almost stereotypical New Englander, even though of course it has been widely known that he was a warm family man who gave generously of himself to friends and students" (p. xxii).

Understandably, many of Dewey's readers prefer to recall images of the middle-aged philosopher hunched over his typewriter smiling benignly while children play noisily about his feet, rather than the hazy, awkward images that Dewey's voice projects in his characteristically casual, often careless prose style. He had nine children, two of whom died in childhood and three who were adopted, perhaps as surrogates for the two lost children. Somewhat unique among educational theorists, Dewey loved children. Dewey's letters and the anecdotes of family and friends reveal how deep and abiding was the love between parent and offspring. These anecdotes often show a Dewey who was absent-minded, bemused, and confronting life's little peccadilloes with all the unassuming charm one might expect from one of those grand Hollywood character actors playing the stereotypical absent-minded professor. One anecdote states that Fred, the Dewey's eldest child, was playing at recreating the biblical flood and caused the upstairs bathtub to overflow. "Finally the water dripped into Dewey's study. Rushing upstairs, he stood silent with amazement until the boy spoke up: 'Don't say anything, John,'" he ordered. "Get the mop" (Martin, 2002, p. 112).

The stereotype of the absent-minded professor seems to sit so well on Dewey's shoulders that deeper and richer character traits are easily overlooked. Dewey was, however, a complex human being. Beside portraits of domestic humor and the hurly-burly of family life, his biographers have drawn images of sadness, anxiety and grief, moments of disillusionment and frustration, a lifelong effort to conform to and free himself from his mother's well-meaning expectations, a possible extramarital affair, the loss of his wife and the mother of his children to heart disease, and a late life romance and marriage. Jay Martin's (2002) biography, *The Education of John Dewey*, may treat some of these aspects of Dewey's life with more melodrama than they might properly warrant, nonetheless, like any modern adult living a full life in the twentieth century, Dewey felt and experienced the pull and push of a frantic, changeful age.

The story of his possible extramarital affair suggests something of the depth, indeed the many-sidedness, of Dewey's response to the world around him. In 1918, Dewey led a study of the Polish community in Philadelphia. His translator and secretary was a young woman named Anzia Yezierska who had already written a few short stories and would go on to write a number of best-selling, semi-autobiographical novels. (In his biography of Dewey, Martin, 2002, ironically entitled this episode "A Philadelphia Story," pp. 287-293). Yezierska, coming out of the poverty of a Polish ghetto in Philadelphia was certainly no Kathryn Hepburn, and John Dewey was no Cary Grant, nor Jimmy Stewart, for that matter. Yezierska recorded her impressions of the affair, if, indeed, an affair had occurred, in the pages of her novels; Dewey recorded his feelings in a handful of poems that he balled up and threw in the back of his desk or the nearby waste basket. These poems were "rescued" by two of Dewey's colleagues at Columbia and in 1977 were edited by Jo Ann Boydston as *The Poems of John Dewey*. In "My Fever" (Dewey & Boydston, 1977, p. 23) we read,

> My body of crowding pains a vase
> Of flaming fev'rish flowers was.
> My bones not mine but a tight mesh,
> A trap, a snare, in which soul slunk
> In kettle of hot seethings shrunk,
> Where boiled and bubbled pulsing flesh.

These lines of poetry show Dewey in a very passionate and emotive mood, trying to make the symbols of poetry work for him and experimenting with a very expressive and personal style. He pursues, as one would expect of a man who thought that the mind and body division was too much emphasized in western philosophy, a way of interpreting this passion through references to his own body; these are then connected to extremes of action and emotion—thus "body" is followed by "crowding," "flaming," and "fev'rish," while Dewy portrays his "flesh" as "seething," "shrunk," "boiled," "bubbling," and "pulsing." He has filled his stanza with objects into which he pours his feelings, transforming them and himself quite zealously, indeed, almost too zealously. Thus his body becomes a "vase" and then, abruptly, a "kettle." A Freudian might perceive a good deal of angst and unconscious sexuality here, but the opposite seems more likely to be the case. Dewey appears, rather, to be toying with the conventions of poetry as a way of expressing some very common, if unpleasant emotions—emotions of which he was, no doubt, painfully conscious. That is to say, Dewey seems in this and much of his other verse to have known both the limits of his own poetic ability and the limits of his own passions and to have turned these into a kind of self-reflective experiment.

"Two Weeks" is a poem that Boydston explicitly associates with Dewey's possible affair (Dewey & Boydston, 1977, p. 17).

> Then take me as I am,
> Partly true and partly sham
> Not from willful choice
> But by too ready acceptance
> Of the constraining work of chance.

So different is this voice from Dewey's prose voice (earlier in the same poem he had confessed, "I told you my diet should be prose") that its very sound takes some getting used to. Nonetheless, it is as much Dewey as those rare flashes of passion and metaphor that occasionally light Dewey's awkward prose.

Truly pluralistic, Dewey the poet did not solely produce love poems. Boydston divides the Dewey poems into four sections: Lyric Poems, Nature Poems, Philosophic Poems, and Children's Poems (Dewey & Boydston, 1977). Not surprisingly, sentiments of social action emerge in some of these poems, metrically stumbling, somewhat artless, or at the least guileless, but clear and forceful, nonetheless:

> Of fraud and force fast woven
> Marched the governments of man
> Of blood with tears deep mixt
> Where drowned the liberties of man
> As wealth and might stood fixt
> To keep the severing span
> That makes unequal life
> Till last shared griefs awake
> The slumb'ring thoughts of man
> An equal life to make
> Upon a common plan. (pp. 56-57)

This quality of many-sidedness, of pluralism in thought, action and character, seems to dictate a path for Dewey that could never be wholly satisfied sitting at a typewriter while the children played around his feet.

The sections that follow seek to display not only the many-sidedness of Dewey's thought and action, but also to note the other qualities that he brought to his understanding of social action. The resultant portrayal should demonstrate the richness and variety of his social sensibility and lead to a better understanding of how he perceived the interrelationship of life, social action, and democracy.

SOCIAL ACTION AS FORMATIVE AND RADICAL

Anyone familiar with Dewey knows about his many writings on education (e.g., *The School and Society,* 1900, *The Child and the Curriculum,* 1902, *Democracy and Education,* 1916) and that singular public work with which Dewey is most commonly associated, the University of Chicago's Laboratory School. The history of the latter activity needs only a short retelling here, for it is generally well known and well developed in the works of others (e.g., Mayhew & Edwards, 1936; Tanner, 1973).

The name of the Laboratory School suggests that it was to be a laboratory for the study of pedagogical technique, or as Dewey stated in an interview in 1896, "the development of method in psychological experiment and observation as applied to the child-study movement" (quoted in Martin, 2002, p. 198). But as Ryan (1995) points out, the aims soon became quite confused: "… the school became a sort of site for the pedagogical demonstration; visitors could see Dewey's ideas about elementary education in operation.… It also provided an excellent, if unintended, base for training elementary school teachers" (p. 120).

Whatever the Laboratory School's actual purpose and results—setting aside the administrative problems that harried Dewey who, to be honest, was no administrator—the Laboratory School was a highly visible and important public activity. In fact, social action could not find a more visible and noteworthy vehicle in Dewey's long career than it does in the University of Chicago Laboratory School. A separate task is now demanded: How to characterize Dewey's experience with the Laboratory School and his many writings on education in terms of social action?

In the first chapter of *The School and Society* (1900), which constitutes Dewey's most direct statement on his work at the Laboratory School, Dewey quotes Horace Mann, "Where anything is growing, one former is worth a thousand re-formers" (cited in Dewey, 1899, p. mw.1.5). Dewey interprets the quotation to mean that the enterprise of education must be formative in every essential: "Only by being true to the full growth of all the individuals who make it up, can society by any chance be true to itself. And in the self-direction thus given, nothing counts as much as the school" (Dewey, 1899, p. mw.1.5).

Dewey also suggests that not only is the school itself formative, but so too should be the thought and action that contribute to transforming the school into the social instrument that it should be: "Whenever we have in mind the discussion of a new movement in education, it is especially necessary to take the broader, or social, view. Otherwise, changes in the school institution and tradition will be looked at as the arbitrary inventions of particular teachers; at the worst transitory fads, and at the best merely improvements in certain details—and this is the plane upon which it is too customary to consider school changes" (Dewey, 1899, p. mw.1.5).

Individual readers may argue about whether or not Dewey really "formed" a new school. Still, the nature and quality of its formation rather than any reformation seems to echo throughout Dewey's thoughts on social action. For example, Dewey wrote,

> In short, liberalism must now become radical, meaning by "radical" perception of the necessity of thoroughgoing changes in the set-up of institutions and corresponding activity to bring the changes to pass. For the gulf between what the actual situation makes possible and the actual state itself is so great that it cannot be bridged by piecemeal policies undertaken ad hoc. The process of producing the changes will be, in any case, a gradual one. But "reforms" that deal now with this abuse and now with that without having a social goal based upon an inclusive plan, differ entirely from effort at re-forming, in its literal sense, the institutional scheme of things. The liberals of more than a century ago were denounced in their time as subversive radicals, and only when the new economic order was established did they become apologists for the status quo or else content with social patchwork. If radicalism be defined as perception of need for radical change, then today any liberalism which is not also radicalism is irrelevant and doomed. (Dewey, 1935, p. lw.11.45)

What seems to be particularly striking is his use of the word "radical." Dewey recognizes two definitions of the term. In the paragraph quoted above, he focuses on "thoroughgoing changes" and sets "radical" in opposition to "piecemeal" and "ad hoc" changes. In the paragraph that follows the aforementioned excerpt, Dewey clearly states that he does not mean by "radical" the use of violent means. Indeed, in the final pages of *Liberalism and Social Action* (1935), Dewey asserts, with no equivocation, his opposition to the use of violence as a means of social action. Dewey's opposition to violence is certainly a significant characteristic of his approach to social action.

Still, a third and more subtle issue emerges from his use of the word "radical." In this usage, Dewey remains somewhat ambiguous. Radical may mean thoroughgoing, a condition affecting all of society. Of course, it could mean violent. In this reading, however, Dewey appears to accept the first meaning and jettison the second. The third meaning acknowledges change of great significance, even a revolutionary (as opposed to evolutionary) change. In *Liberalism and Social Action* (1935), Dewey rejects revolutionary change, but still insists that social action produce change.

Only on the topic of violence is Dewey clear and unambiguous. On the other two meanings of radical, his pluralism creates possibilities from what are apparent extremes. Ultimately, the social change Dewey portrays and advocates is radical and formative; nevertheless, it insists on certain inevitable caveats. It must be radical, but not violent. It must be formative, but nonetheless evolutionary. It must be thoroughgoing, but gradual.

To attempt to understand Dewey without accepting his contingencies is to mistake the very nature of Dewey. Ruthlessly opposed to dualisms (see, for example, the first chapter of *Experience and Education*, 1938), Dewey can be a forceful thinker, one whose writings if read in single, isolated sentences will entirely or crudely misrepresent the essential qualifying thoughts that inevitably follow. His qualifying thoughts are not only necessary; arguably, they are essential to Dewey.

Another aspect of Dewey's educational work merits some attention. From the 1910s to 1930s Dewey was active in the New York City Teacher's Union. Like many of Dewey's social activities, Dewey's work with the teacher's union has been passed along by way of a handful of writings and a few miscellaneous activities in the received chronology of his life (Southern Illinois University, 2003). That is to say, the active side of his work with the union commonly comes to attention in a somewhat muted fashion. His correspondence conveys an elliptic picture of thought and action. Here, for example, is an excerpt from a letter written February 23, 1913, to Dewey by Henry R. Linville (who would later become president and executive of the New York City Teacher's Union, 1916-935): "Dear Prof Dewey: I suppose you are expecting a letter from me reminding you of your part in the meeting of the Teachers League on the evening of Friday, February 28, at Milbank Chapel, Teachers College" (Letter from Henry R. Linville to John Dewey, 1913, in Hickman, Levine, Sharpe, & Simon, 2005, 1913.02.23 (03312)). Dewey's "part" in the meeting was the delivery of a speech, "Professional Spirit Among Teachers." The letter can be found in *The Correspondence of John Dewey* (Hickman, et al., 2005); the full text of the speech is available in *The Collected Works of John Dewey* (Boydston, 1991, 2005). Entirely absent from both is commentary about the meeting itself with its audience reactions, friendships, camaraderie, small talk, and all the other ineffable qualities that are an essential part of social action and "getting into life."

A few anecdotes of Dewey's social activism do, however, survive. One such anecdote indicates something of Dewey's approach to such social activism. In December 1917, three teachers were dismissed for "disloyalty." Dewey read the transcripts of their trial closely and concluded, "I don't know what this is called in 1917, but I know what it used to be called. It used to be called the Inquisition" (quoted in Martin, 2002, p. 274). Accordingly, Dewey chose to deliver a public speech on "Democracy and Loyalty in the Schools."

One question that must be raised is, Why did Dewey spend so little time in actual schools? He and his daughter, Evelyn, of course, studied a small group of mainly independent, progressive schools the report of which they published as *Schools of Tomorrow* (1915). However, Dewey confessed that Evelyn did all the field research (Martin, 2002, p. 155). Many educators and others would have expected that *the* philosopher of American education would have delighted in spending time in school rooms (that is to say, beyond the lecture halls of higher education). He did not. Consideration of this point is not to carp, particularly given the quantity and diversity of activities in which Dewey engaged. Moreover, the question is notable mostly because it verges upon the rhetorical. Perhaps no satisfactory answer to the question is possible. However, as do some of the other asked and unanswered questions offered below, this question suggests, in its own way, something of the character of Dewey's approach to social action.

SOCIAL ACTION AS THE OCCASION PRESENTS ITSELF

A key question that must be considered is: How did Dewey address such varying social issues as race relations, juvenile delinquency, the role of women, crime, poverty, labor relations, indeed, the whole panoply of domestic social issues that are at the core of liberal social action? With respect to some of these persistent concerns Dewey was silent. About others, a muted Dewey wrote about "opportunity," "sympathy," "purpose," and "gathering." The real Dewey rather than the received Dewey remains conspicuously silent when most of his readers search for his opinions, analysis, and prompts for specific social actions. Silence, however, cannot be construed, in Dewey's case, as inactivity.

A resonant example of his willingness to act is the part he played in the founding of the National Association for the Advancement of Colored People (NAACP). Earlier noted were some of his introductory remarks to the National Negro Conference in 1909. "I should not have appeared at all, were it not that it gave me the opportunity to express my sympathy with the purpose of this gathering" (Dewey, 1909, quoted in Boydston, 1991, 2005, p. mw.4.156). Dewey, then, proceeded to express the scientific community's general consensus that "acquired traits are not transmittable." His assertion might be understood to suggest, on one hand, that an individual's hard work and learning may not become apparent (biologically or socially) in the succeeding generation, whereas, on the other hand, this realization makes clear that "there is no inferior race." He goes on to conclude,

> For if these race differences are, as has been pointed out, comparatively slight, individual differences are very great. All points of skill are represented in every race, from the inferior individual to the superior individual, and a society that does not furnish the environment and education and the opportunity of all kinds which will bring out and make effective the superior ability wherever it is born, is not merely doing an injustice to that particular race and to those particular individuals, but it is doing an injustice to itself for it is depriving itself of just that much of social capital. (Dewey, 1909, quoted in Boydston, 1991, 2005, p. mw.4.157)

Comparatively, Dewey wrote little on the topic of race relations (as it was then called), nor was he apparently sensitive to the absence of its inclusion in school programs. For example, in his "Introduction" to Elsie Clapp's *Community Schools in Action* (Clapp, 1939), Dewey wrote, "Miss Clapp remarks that 'A great deal is said in calling a school a "community school."' If the school lives up to that name, everything is said" (quoted in Boydston, 1991, 2005, p. lw.14.351). Dewey, however, was not the only observer and advocate of Clapp's extraordinary school in West Virginia who failed to recognize the school's inattention to issues associated with race and class (Perlstein, 1996).

That said, Dewey did not hesitate when asked to clarify his sentiments and to harness his energy and effort toward an activity that he thought necessary. How eloquent, for example, is the small phrase "opportunity to express my sympathy." It seems to stand as a silent motto to that social activity which Dewey engaged and encouraged, but of which he wrote sparingly. True to his philosophy that no real dichotomy exists between the mind and the body, Dewey appears to have believed that to act explicitly was in itself significant and that not all actions needed a typewriter full of words to commend them. A small, but humorous anecdote points out how Dewey's sense of social action could easily trump the immediate effect of words and slogans. "[Dewey] was getting ready to march in one parade, picked up the banner that was thrust into his hands, and was mildly surprised by the number of amused grins he attracted as the column marched down the street. Only at the end did he look to see what he had been carrying: 'Men Can Vote; Why Can't I?'" (Ryan, 1995, p. 161).

No great purpose would be served here in following Dewey into every corner of the social landscape in order to document those actions he took or failed to take relative to general social issues; however, a partial consideration of a few seems sufficient to recognize his personal engagement in a variety of such activities. He was involved in the formation of the New York City Teachers Union and the NAACP. He also actively participated in Jane Addams' Hull House, and was instrumental in the organization or founding, among others, of the following: the American Association of University Professors; the American Federation of Negro College Students (which Dewey helped to create and for which he persuaded Eleanor Roosevelt to chair its Advisory Council); the American Union Against Militarism (an antiwar organization founded in 1916 which later became the American Civil Liberties Union); the League of Independent Political Action; American Association for the Advancement of Science; the Organizing Committee for National Aid to Education; and the Chinese-American Commission (Martin, 2002, pp. 242-250).

The long list of organizations with which Dewey involved himself suggests his commitment to volunteerism or, more properly, to public activity outside governmental action. In 1935, Dewey wrote of this belief. "A liberal program has to be developed, and in a good deal of particularity, outside of the immediate realm of governmental action and enforced upon public attention, before direct political action of a thoroughgoing liberal sort will follow" (Dewey, 1935, p. lw.11.14). The organizations which he helped launch and those with which he allied himself through both word and act reflect Dewey's philosophy of social action.

Dewey's personal volunteerism, in an interesting way, seems to step outside of what may be found explicitly stated in his writings on the character of social action. The issue here is the occasional nature of much of Dewey's activity. His activities can be seen as occasional in that, at times, he seems to have allowed the "occasion" to inform his actions. Although Dewey sometimes engaged in the formative creation of some new social enterprise, much of his social action occurred in groups organized by others. Invited to attend a group's meeting, Dewey would weigh the values inherent in his act of attendance and decide upon a response appropriate to himself. Significantly, he did not attend all the meetings to which he was invited, nor join all the organizations that solicited his participation. Some organizations Dewey considered incompatible, and when he came to that conclusion he quickly discontinued his association with them, doing so, at times, quite publicly. On the other hand, if the occasion were right and the organization was one for which the "opportunity to express my sympathy" was meaningful, Dewey was prepared to affiliate himself and to do his part to make the group's intentions successful.

Dewey's most significant occasional acts, however, were often unique and rather personal gestures. The Gorky Affair is a case in point. In 1906, Maxim Gorky came to the United States seeking support for Russian revolutionaries who were fighting against the czar. At the time, Americans generally were well disposed toward such activities (in Russia). Gorky, however, appeared in the United States with his mistress on his arm while his wife and two children remained at home. His behavior was a breach of social decorum that not even Mark Twain could quite reconcile to his satisfaction. Having spoken favorably of Gorky's effort at a fund-raiser, when the news hit the papers, "Twain reconsidered." Turned away from every hotel, Gorky and his mistress departed New York City for Chicago where Jane Addams welcomed them. When they returned to New York, once again finding no available residence, John Dewey stepped forward with "Gorky and his mistress soon living in Dewey's apartment." The Deweys were, as Max Eastman (1941) wrote, "violently attacked for this act of magnanimity" (p. 684) Dewey's wife Alice provided the touchstone message to this act: "I would rather starve and see my children starve than to see John sacrifice his principles" (Eastman, 1941, p. 684). Administrators of Columbia University, at which Dewey then was employed, simply looked the other way (Martin, 2002, p. 241).

These episodes are not a mere vagary in Dewey's history. Time and again, he let the occasion decide for him. He came to Bertrand Russell's aid not once but twice and in very public ways. In 1921, while visiting China, Bertrand Russell became ill and had to be hospitalized. The Deweys who were also in China, took care of both Russell and his mistress, Dora Black. Russell's mistress had not been well received by both the "American community in Beijing and upper-class Chinese" (Martin, 2002, p. 324). However, once again, this did not matter to the Deweys. "If I can accept Bertrand Russell, why can't I accept Dora Black?" Alice Dewey asked (quoted in Martin, 2002, p. 324). In 1940, Dewey defended Russell from further attacks upon his character when he (Russell) was invited to lecture at City College in New York (Martin, 2002, p 442).

One of the most singular examples of Dewey allowing himself to follow the pull of the current historical moment is the case of the Trotsky Commission. Leon Trotsky had been tried in absentia by Josef Stalin as part of the 1936-1937 show trials intended to shore up Stalin's grasp upon power within the Soviet Union. In 1937, then aged 78, Dewey agreed to head the commission that would review the charges against Trotsky and determine its own verdict. Many of Dewey's family and friends did not want Dewey to participate in the commission. In fact, Dewey pondered whether to accept the position for some time before agreeing to take it on. He was not altogether certain that he was the best man for the job, but the American press quickly agreed that Dewey's presence brought to the commission a prestige it would, otherwise, not have had. The commission contained a veritable who's who of the American left: Max Eastman, James Farrell, John Dos Passos, Reinhold Niebuhr, Lionel Trilling, Horace Kallen, Edmund Wilson, and Mary McCarthy. And that just names a few of its notable members.

Like Wilson, Dewey had a past literary relationship with the Soviet Union. In his *To the Finland Station*, Wilson had demonstrated his disillusionment with the Soviet Union. Dewey, on the other hand, had won the respect of the Soviets by evenhandedly praising the Soviet educational system. If Dewey were to determine Trotsky's innocence, utilizing the same values of justice and evenhandedness, the verdict would be more universally recognized as true. The verdict the commission came to was, indeed, that Trotsky was not guilty, but Dewey's close association with Trotsky resulted in his full rejection of Trotsky's philosophy (Ryan, 1995; Martin, 2002).

In one of his final and most visible public acts, Dewey severed his own social views from those of communism, irrevocably. Yet the act was very much an act of the moment, and Dewey was an actor caught up in the historical threads of his time. Dewey accepted life as it came to him. If that quality is not revealed in his written philosophy, it nevertheless is written indelibly into his actions.

In *Liberalism and Social Action* (1935), Dewey wrote "the alternatives [for a renascent liberalism] are continuation of drift with attendant improvisations to meet special emergencies; dependence upon violence; dependence upon socially organized intelligence. The first two alternatives, however, are not mutually exclusive, for if things are allowed to drift the result may be some sort of social change effected by the use of force, whether so planned or not" (Dewey, 1935, p. lw.11.61). Dewey, of course, directs readers toward the final alternative of "socially organized intelligence." What Dewey meant by "socially organized intelligent" is difficult to say. He clearly meant to contrast this term with the extremes of Marxism and of other more radical (and violent) modes of social action. Dewey regarded his own social action as radical, but he tempered his views with intelligence and forethought. He seems to place social action in the context of both the social organization and the individual intelligence simultaneously. Where either of these modes (the social or the individual) tends toward violence or a too urgent and unthinking impulsiveness, then Dewey shies away and balks like a pensive and determined long-distance runner who had accidentally found himself among the more passionate and feverish sprinters.

Again, a question must be raised. Did these occasional acts fall into the category of "attendant improvisations to meet special emergencies?" Certainly, readers need not criticize Dewey for such acts even if they were ad hoc and, thus, contrary to his stated positions. At the same time, they reasonably might represent another quality, a kind of "forbearance." Lacking the behind the scenes dialog engaged by Dewey and his wife in the Gorky affair, the "occasional" act of housing these two individuals who were such obvious social outcasts can be understood as ad hoc and ill-considered, the very opposite of an act that was intelligent and organized. Alice Dewey's comment, however, suggests that a dialogue had occurred and that the Deweys perceived their actions as appropriate to their mutual philosophies. To be sure, this supposition may be overstated. Still, these occasional acts, ones that seem as much to have chosen Dewey as they were ones that he purposefully chose, occurred throughout his involvement in social action. Dewey was not so precise in the application of his expressed ideas as to set aside the opportunities or necessities that they represented. Whether or not this quality inheres with Dewey's philosophy of social action or merely the native expression of his personality is a matter that readers must decide for themselves.

SOCIAL ACTION AS WORLD CITIZENSHIP

Dewey did not limit his approach to social action to the domestic sphere. When called upon to act on the world stage, Dewey did so. The first world war had turned many American minds toward the realities of other countries. No less had it affected Dewey. Subsequent to the war, the establishment of the League of Nations, with its idealistic promises, proved unable to stem the worst excesses of nations during the 1930s.

When in 1919, Dewey was asked to lecture at Tokyo Imperial University, he was happy to turn his eyes from Europe to Asia. Dewey had been a strong sponsor of Asian students and had an interest in Asian philosophy. Shortly after the invitation to lecture in Tokyo, a similar request came from two of Dewey's former students to teach in China. Dewey spent 3 months in Japan delivering lectures that he would later convert into the book *Reconstruction in Philosophy* (Dewey, 1920). Dewey, however, did more than just deliver the eight lectures to the Tokyo Imperial University. He also visited dignitaries, spoke at private universities, normal schools and teacher associations, and was the guest of honor at many societies (Martin, 2002, pp. 311-313).

China, in 1919, was a country in the midst of change, on the verge of revolution. Dewey noted this situation and wrote home,

I doubt if the Chinese are personally as much a sealed mystery as reported sometimes, but the country is so vast, and the parts of it so different, and the accumulations from the past so enormous, and one would have to live here so long to begin to get hold of even the most important which are needed to understand things.... Here is one incident which personally concerns us, and also seems typical. The other day the Peking univ students started a parade in protest of the Paris Peace Conference action in turning the German interests in China over to the Japanese. Being interfered with by the police they got more unruly and beat up the Chinese minister to Japan who negotiated the treaties that sold China out. Well, in one sense this was a kind of Halloween students spree with a somewhat serious political purpose attached. In another sense, it may be—tho probably not—the beginning of an important active political movement, out of which anything may grow. (John Dewey to the Dewey children, quoted in Hickman et al., 2005, 1919.09.05 (03903); also quoted in Martin, 2002, pp. 316-317)

Having expected to be in China only 2 months, Dewey stayed for 2 years, and lectured to thousands of eager students. His influence was lasting. Many of his books were translated into Chinese and his lectures in China were published there and sold quite well. Dewey's wife, Alice, used the time to study and speak on the role of women in both China and Japan. Alongside John Dewey's career as an intellectual and social activist, Alice was busily constructing her own career. A recent dissertation, "The Unsung Partner: The Educational Work and Philosophy of Alice Chipman Dewey" (Hall, 2005) brings a much needed focus on Alice Dewey's efforts both in collaboration with her husband and in her own right. These trips abroad allowed Alice Dewey significant opportunities to address those issues that were most important to her.

Alice Dewey's concern for the status of women in society was apparent throughout her visit to the Far East. In fact, what was most notable about her time abroad was her persistent focus on three social issues: social inequity, the independence of women, and education. Drawing upon her abilities to make careful observations as well as to analyze and critique, Alice Dewey took pains to blend into local cultures and to seek out direct contact with "ordinary people"—many of these experiences were colorfully related in her correspondence home. A talented writer, Alice Dewey's writing was deeply descriptive, and showed a genuine effort toward understanding phenomenon in context (Hall, 2005, pp. 130-131).

The Deweys' Japan-China excursion was followed by a similar visit to Turkey. At the request of the Turkish government of Ataturk, they traveled to Ankara in 1924 to inspect the country's system of education. They visited schools, interviewed teachers and administrators, and inspected school rooms, equipment and facilities. Dewey concluded in his final report that

> Fortunately, there is no difficulty in stating the main end to be secured by the educational system of Turkey. It is the development of Turkey as a vital, free, independent, and lay republic in full membership in the circle of civilized states. To achieve this end the schools must (1) form proper political habits and ideas; (2) foster the various forms of economic and commercial skill and ability; and (3) develop the traits and dispositions of character, intellectual and moral, which fit men and women for self-government, economic self-support and industrial progress; namely, initiative and inventiveness, independence of judgment, ability to think scientifically and to cooperate for common purposes socially. To realize these ends, the mass of citizens must be educated for intellectual participation in the political, economic, and cultural growth of the country, and not simply certain leaders. (Dewey, 1924/1960, p. mw 15.275; also quoted in Martin, 2002, p. 340)

The year 1926 saw a similar trip to Mexico City for the purposes of evaluating the country's school system and presenting a few lectures at the National University. Dewey published three articles on his experience in Mexico. In the first, he noted the same problem he had seen in Turkey, the clash of new ideas of progress with traditional culture and religion. In the second, however, he was enthusiastic about the community involvement in Mexican schools, but complicating the issue, Dewey states in his final article, is the ill-effects of American economic endeavors (Martin, 2002, pp. 342-344).

A fifth world traveling excursion rounded out Dewey's outward reach in the 1920s. Dewey was invited by the Soviet minister of education to lead a group of educators (including his daughter, Evelyn) to the Soviet Union to study and evaluate Russian methods of instruction. The project was to be nonpolitical and Dewey found himself between avid Soviets on one side and the opponents of the Soviets on the other. Dewey had long been an outspoken anti-Bolshevik, but he took his role as the leader of a nonpartisan investigating committee quite as seriously as he would later approach his role with the Trotsky Commission. In the long-run, he concluded that Soviet education took a practical and commendable approach to technology and industry, and that it undertook such efforts more effectively than had the United States. Dewey distanced himself from Lenin-Marxist views, but that had little impact on his critics on either side. To the Soviets, he was as well received for this particular report as he would be poorly received for the report that came out of the Trotsky Commission's work. To many in the United States, he was simply under the sway of communist propaganda. Dewey saw these responses coming and answered that neither side could really see what would be the results of the great Russian experiment; the future was a great unknown (Martin, 2002, pp. 350-358; Ryan, 1995, pp. 227-228).

SOCIAL ACTION AS PARTY POLITICS AND JOURNALISM

Dewey's relationship to party politics was equivocal, to say the least. A joiner when it came to political organizations outside the realm of party politics, he generally held himself aloof from traditional and even nontraditional political disputes and campaigns. Neither of the two established parties, Democratic or Republican, satisfied his rather singular notions of party responsibility. Early on he soured on Communism and never fully embraced Socialism, at least not as a political party. In 1930, he made an ill-judged effort to form a third party which failed embarrassingly (Ryan, 1995, pp. 245-246). The story of this ill-fated effort is interesting for what it reveals about the character of Dewey, the man. In November 1930, Dewey wrote an open letter to Republican Senator George Norris of Nebraska on behalf of the League for Independent Political Action. Dewey invited Norris, whose recent behaviors suggested a maverick and progressive nature, to resign from the Republican party and to take up the radical cause of the League. Norris responded that he was a "good Republican" and urged only the elimination of the electoral college in recognition that the president owed allegiance to all the American people. "Newspaper comment sided with Norris and against Dewey" (Ryan, 1995, p. 246).

Alan Ryan (1995) has declared rather pointedly, "Dewey was not a 'party man.' He had no sense of the positive value of party systems in modern democracies and not much 'feel' for the realities of political life" (p. 246). Continuing, Ryan (1995) asserts that "it is tempting to say that we have no cause for complaint; he was a professional philosopher, not a professional activist" (p. 246). Ryan's counsel should be taken to heart. Dewey was neither a professional activist nor a professional politician. In some ways, consequently, his social actions become all the more interesting. He was, after all, a philosopher focused upon the active life. Moreover, his amateurism in activism and politics might well appeal to the amateur in most people. Nonetheless, Dewey, the philosopher, was out of his depth in matters of political involvement.

At times, observers have regarded Dewey as the architect of modern liberal thought in America. Architect, as a term, must be used cautiously with reference to Dewey because his thought, quite intentionally, was never so systematic as the word "architect" implies. Nonetheless, in both *Liberalism and Social Action* (1935) and *Freedom and Culture* (1939) Dewey seems to have sought opportunities to craft the political domain for what he called a "renascent liberalism." His antipathy for communism, fascism, and violence in politics, however, led him to develop what others came to call a "middle-of-the-road" liberalism. Dewey defended himself against such charges, but not aggressively:

> [Liberalism's] task is the mediation of social transitions. This phrase may seem to some to be a virtual admission that liberalism is a colorless "middle of the road" doctrine. Not so, even though liberalism has sometimes taken that form in practice. We are always possessed by habits and customs, and this fact signifies that we are always influenced by the inertia and the momentum of forces temporally outgrown but nevertheless still present with us as a part of our being. Human life gets set in patterns, institutional and moral. But change is also with us and demands the constant remaking of old habits and old ways of thinking, desiring and acting. The effective ratio between the old and the stabilizing and the new and disturbing is very different at different times. Sometimes, as at present, change is so varied and accelerated that customs seem to be dissolving before our very eyes. But be the ratio little or great, there is always an adjustment to be made, and as soon as the need for it becomes conscious, liberalism has a function and a meaning. It is not that liberalism creates the need, but that the necessity for adjustment defines the office of liberalism. (Dewey, 1935, pp. lw.11.36-37)

To reframe the apparent mediocrity, blandness, and colorlessness of these "middle-of-the-road" politics as rather an active, constantly adjusting, and essential of politics would, no doubt, be closer to Dewey's brand of liberalism. Nevertheless, as Dewey noted, "the effective ratio between the old and the stabilizing and the new and disturbing is very different at different times" (Dewey, 1935, p. lw.11.36-37). This tendency toward contingency appears to be the real character of Dewey's liberalism. To understand Dewey's notions of social action is not to remake Dewey, but to understand the man as he was.

Dewey appears to contemporary readers through history as a writer of heavy tomes on education, experience, liberalism, and democracy which, sometimes, may seem irrelevant. As a result, one of his chief vehicles for social action in the political realm is no longer so apparent as it was in his lifetime. That vehicle was his journalistic work. Dewey wrote regularly for such popular magazines as the *Nation* and the *New Republic*. Alan Ryan (1995) characterizes his early relationship with the *New Republic*, in this way:

> Dewey was not wholly at home in this environment. He brought to the *New Republic* his prestige as a reformer and the best-known pedagogical thinker in the country. All the same he was not entirely a New Republic "natural." Dewey had voted for Eugene Debs in 1912 and was much less enamored of political power in any shape than were the editors of the *New Republic*. He

was more nearly a lay-preacher looking for a public forum than an amateur politician looking for a government to infiltrate. (p. 190)

Ryan's final sentence underscores an important aspect of Dewey's approach to social action. In his writings, Dewey often understood himself as talking directly to a democratic public and not to a specialist audience of fellow philosophers. Throughout much of his career, Dewey seems to have looked for ways to speak directly and plainly (if not always as clearly as he might have) on matters of importance to as large and as democratic an audience as possible. He spoke and wrote, not out of a desire to grandstand or to display a personally egotistic sense of self-importance, but rather he believed that the role he filled by his public presence was necessary and important for the "socially organized intelligence" that he advocated. Turning again to *Liberalism and Social Action,* Dewey (1935) wrote that "mankind now has in its possession a new method [an alternative to force], that of cooperative and experimental science which expresses the method of intelligence" (Dewey, 1935, p. lw.11.58). Ryan (1995) characterized Dewey's politics as cooperative, but Dewey seems, in his own way, to have been looking beyond party politics toward the mass of the public whom he believed needed the guidance of scientific intelligence to enable them to sort out the active landscape of emergent democracy and renascent liberalism from older forms of democracy and liberalism. If contemporary readers see in his stance a rather overreaching paternalism, they should be sure to remember the moderation and mediation with which Dewey approached his liberalism and politics. Indeed, he seems invariably to have positioned himself within democracy and the public and, very seldom, heavy-handedly above it.

SOCIAL ACTION WITHIN INDUSTRY
AND CORPORATE LIFE

One question nags many readers: Why did not Dewey do more, or act more directly on matters associated with industry and corporate life? No doubt can be placed upon his frustration with industry (e.g., his feeling that industry was failing to meet the full needs of a democratic society). Why, then, for example, did Dewey not join the Pullman picket line or more aggressively attack the corporate and industrial culture that exercised so much influence on the society of his time?

One answer is that Dewey had accepted the legality of many aspects of industry about which he and others were willing to critique. Even more important, he accepted the long-standing moral foundations of property rights within human society.

Because of conditions that were set by the legal institutions and the moral ideas existing when the scientific and industrial revolutions came into being, the chief usufruct of the latter has been appropriated by a relatively small class. Industrial entrepreneurs have reaped out of all proportion to what they sowed. By obtaining private ownership of the means of production and exchange they deflected a considerable share of the results of increased productivity to their private pockets. This appropriation was not the fruit of criminal conspiracy or of sinister intent. It was sanctioned not only by legal institutions of age-long standing but by the entire prevailing moral code. The institution of private property long antedated feudal times. It is the institution with which men have lived, with few exceptions, since the dawn of civilization. Its existence has deeply impressed itself upon mankind's moral conceptions. Moreover, the new industrial forces tended to break down many of the rigid class barriers that had been in force, and to give to millions a new outlook and inspire a new hope; especially in the United States with no feudal background and no fixed class system (Dewey, 1935, p. lw.11.53-54).

Property rights have deep roots, indeed. They were deep enough for Dewey to doubt the efficacy of revolutionary change and to move, instead, toward the slower processes of socially organized intelligence which he believed could achieve his radical (i.e., thoroughgoing) results with consequences consistent with a democratic life. Still, even if some individuals continue to doubt Dewey's belief in the effectiveness of such a slower, more patient process (Stanley, 2005; Williamson, 2005), Dewey pointed out that the alternative cannot be any more appealing. If industry is removed from the private sector, where will it be placed? Can this change be effected by democratic means? And if effected, is the public sector really prepared to handle the responsibility?

Consider, as an example, the argument that since the processes of industry, on the side of both labor and capital, have become collective, ownership and control must also be collective, resulting in elimination of private income from rent, interest, and dividends. From the standpoint of democracy, this end, which is put forward in the interest of maintenance of democracy, raises the problem of the possibility of its execution by democratic methods. Can the change be effected by democratic means? (Dewey, 1939, p. lw.13.113).

And again,

The real problem is deeper. There is no well-defined continuity of political movement because of the confusion that exists in general social movements. That the general trend is toward increase of public control of private industry and finance in the United States as in other countries is undeniable. But the movement is not clear-cut in theory nor are its consequences consistent in practice. In fact, there is one thesis of Herbert Spencer that could now be revived with a good deal of evidence in its support: namely, the economic situation is so complex, so intricate in the interdependence of delicately balanced factors, that planned policies initiated by public authority are sure to have consequences totally unforeseeable,—often the contrary of what was intended—as has happened in this country rather notably in connection with some of the measures undertaken for control of agricultural production. (Dewey, 1939, p. lw.13.107)

JANE ADDAMS AND THE DEMOCRATIC LIFE

Dewey clearly credited Jane Addams with having significantly informed his approach to social action. Consideration of Dewey's Hull House experience toward the end of this chapter rather than at its beginning, where chronologically it normally would appear, facilitates the portrayal of the extent to which Dewey absorbed Addams' unique approach to social action as well as ways that he integrated this approach into his own social action throughout his long life.

Some sense of the influence Addams had on Dewey is revealed in the October 10, 1894 letter that Dewey wrote to his wife, Alice. Readers should note that this letter was written just a few months after Dewey's letter to Alice Dewey (with which this chapter began) in which he wrote about his reaction to the Pullman Strike:

> Miss Addams was evidently feeling rather blue ... I guess I didn't tell you that Miss Addams said she hoped they wouldn't start the settlement from a spirit of ambition, or from a feeling that a settlement was a good thing "let's have a settlement" ... Miss A. also said that she had just received the first personal flagellation she had ever rec'd—She had just been to a Mr. Ayers who had given money rather freely ... & asked him for more money for this winter's relief. He turned on her, & told her that she had a great thing & now she had thrown it away; ... that like an idiot she had mixed herself in something which was none of her business & about which she knew nothing, the labor movement & especially Pullman, & had thrown down her own work etc. etc. And then she went on to say that she had always believed & still believed that antagonism was not only useless and harmful, but entirely unnecessary; that it lay never in the objective differences, which would always grow into unity if left alone, but from a person's mixing in his own personal reactions—the extra emphasis he gave the truth, the enjoyment he took in doing a thing because it was unpalatable to others, or the feeling that one must show his own colors, not be a moral coward.... That historically only evil had come from antagonisms—she kept asking me what I tho't, & I agreed up to this point, but then after the manner of fools, I dissented; then she went on, that if Jesus drove the money changers out of the temple that accounted for the apparent difference between the [later] years

of his ministry & the earlier, & for much of the falsity in [Christianity] since; if he did it, he lost his faith & reacted; that we freed the slaves by war & had now to free them again individually, & pay the costs of the war & reckon with the added bitterness of the Southerner beside &c &c. I asked her if she didn't think that besides the personal antagonisms, there was that of ideas & institutions, as [Christianity] & Judaism, & Labor & Capital, the Church & Democracy now & that a realization of that antagonism was necessary to an appreciation of the truth, & to a consciousness of growth, & she said no. The antagonism of institutions was always unreal; it was simply due to the injection of the personal attitude & reaction; & then instead of adding to the recognition of meaning, it delayed & distorted it. If I could tell you the absolutely commonplace & unemotional way in which she said all these things, it would give some better idea of the most magnificent exhibition of intellectual & moral faith I ever saw. She converted me internally, but not really, I fear. At least I can't [see] what all this conflict & warring of history means if it's [perfectly] meaningless; my pride of intellect, I suppose it is, revolts at thinking its all merely negatively, & has no functional value. But I can also see, or rather dream, that maybe its a mere illusion because we put ourselves in a wrong position & thus introduce antagonism where its all one; & that its sole function is to warn us never to think division. But when you think that Miss Addams does not think this as a philosophy, but believes it in all her senses & muscles—great God. I guess I'll have to give it [all] up & start over again. I suppose that's the subjective nature of sin; the only [reality] is unity, but we assume there is antagonism & then it all goes wrong. I can [sense] that I have always been interpreting the Hegelian dialectic wrong end up—the unity as the reconciliation of opposites, instead of the opposites as the unity in its growth, and thus translated physical tension into a moral thing—As a sample of Miss Addam's intellect, when I spoke of the place tension held in all natural forces & in growth, she said "Of course, there's the stress of action, but that's an entirely different thing." I don't know as I give her the reality of this at all—it seems so natural & commonplace now, but I never had anything take hold of me so; & at the time it didn't impress me as anything wonderful; it was only the next day it began to dawn on me. (Letter, John Dewey to Alice Dewey, quoted in Hickman et al., 2005, 1894.10.10 (00206); also in Martin, 2002, pp. 165-168)

Two days later Dewey wrote to Jane Addams:

Dear Miss Addams—

I wish to take back what I said the other night. Not only is actual antagonizing bad, but the assumption that there is or may be antagonism is bad.... In fact, the real first antagonism always come back to the assumption. I'm glad I found this out before I began to talk on social psychology as otherwise I fear I should have made a mess of it. This is rather a suspiciously sudden conversion, but then it's only a beginning[.] Gratefully yours, John Dewey.

(Letter, John Dewey to Jane Addams quoted in Hickman et al., 2005, 1894.10.12 (00619), n.p.)

The conversation referenced in these letters and Dewey's comments about them are important. They illuminate the seeds of Dewey's distaste for Marx's turn toward the Hegelian dialectic and violent revolution as a mechanism of social reform. In Addams' ambiguous and challenging statement, "the antagonism of institutions was always unreal," thoughtful readers can see the difficulty that Dewey must have experienced when his peers and supporters called upon him to advocate for radical changes in the existing institutions of democratic life. In one way or another, Dewey seems to have been seeking to interpret this comment in his ongoing efforts at social action.

SOCIAL ACTION IN A DEMOCRACY

Dewey's liberalism seems a kind of middle-of-the-road politics. On the other hand, perhaps, Dewey consciously tried not to limit himself to the simple dichotomies of antagonism, to the inevitable synthesis that boils out of a confrontational thesis and antithesis.

Dewey, for example, could not accept the idolatry of the U. S. Constitution. He wrote, "In times of imminent change, our verbal and sentimental worship of the Constitution, with its guarantees of civil liberties of expression, publication, and assemblage, readily goes overboard" (Dewey, 1935, p. lw.11.46). He, also, observed, "It is true that in this country, because of the interpretations made by courts of a written constitution, our political institutions are unusually inflexible" (Dewey, 1935, p. lw.11.31). He could not accept that society and the individual were inherently at odds ("a wholly unjustified idea of opposition between individuals and society has become current" (Dewey, 1935, p. lw.11.60)). These patterns of rivals (e.g., constitutional vs. nonconstitutional, individual vs. society, Republican vs. Democrat) Dewey dismissed as monistic beliefs because they invariably led an individual to accept one or the other, to fall into an either-or pattern of thought. This mode of thinking, he believed, could have a direct impact on day-to-day action, an impact that was not inherently democratic.

His final sentence in *Freedom and Culture* (1939) is instructive: "at the end as at the beginning the democratic method is as fundamentally simple and as immensely difficult as is the energetic, unflagging, unceasing creation of an ever-present new road upon which we can walk together" (Dewey, 1939, p. lw.13.188). Here, Dewey clearly asserts that he has set aside the historicism of Hegel and Marx. The way forward, the route of social action, he believed, cannot be made, it must be found. Theory may inform it, the public may or may not embrace it, institutions can surround it. If they are democratic institutions, however, they are the context, not the enemy. This claim is not the easy route to sustainable social action. It is the difficult route that requires much more energy, much more thought, much more tenacity than do the weak offerings of slogan and conflict and revolution. Indeed, Dewey insisted, the route to social action requires, and is, socially organized intelligence. Ultimately, this tough requirement is what Dewey came to understand as "getting into life."

REFERENCES

Note: All references to Dewey's writing use the page numbering conventions of the Collected Works, [Electronic edition] (Boydston, 1991, 2005).

Boydston, J. A. (1991, 2005). *The collected works of John Dewey, 1882-1953* [Electronic edition]. Carbondale: Southern Illinois University Press.

Clapp, E. R. (1939). *Community schools in action*. New York: Viking Press.

Dewey, J. (1900). *The school and society*. Chicago: University of Chicago Press.

Dewey, J. (1902). *The child and the curriculum*. Chicago: University of Chicago Press.

Dewey, J. (1915). *Schools of to-morrow*. New York: E. P. Dutton.

Dewey, J. (1916). *Democracy and education*. New York: Macmillan.

Dewey, J. (1920). *Reconstruction in philosophy*. New York: Henry Holt.

Dewey, J. (1924/1960). *Report and recommendation upon Turkish education* (1924: typescript). (Published under the title *The John Dewey Report* by the Research and Measurement Bureau of the Ministry of Education in Ankara Turkey, 1960.)

Dewey, J. (1927). *The public and its problems*. New York: Henry Holt.

Dewey, J. (1934). *A common faith*. New Haven, CT: Yale University Press.

Dewey, J. (1935). *Liberalism and social action*. New York: G. P. Putnam's Sons.

Dewey, J. (1938). *Experience and education*. New York: Macmillan.

Dewey, J. (1939). *Freedom and culture*. New York: G. P. Putnam's Sons.

Dewey, J. (1946). *Problems of men*. New York: Philosophical Library.

Dewey, J., & Boydston, J. A. (Ed. & author of Introduction). (1977). *The poems of John Dewey*. Carbondale: Southern Illinois University Press.

Dykhuizen, G. (1973). *The life and mind of John Dewey*. Carbondale: Southern Illinois University Press.

Eastman, M. (1941, December). John Dewey. *Atlantic Monthly*, p. 684.

Ecker, P. (1997). John Dewey: 1859-1992. Retrieved December 28, 2005 from http://www.bgsu.edu/departments/acs/1890s/dewey/dewey.html

Hall, I. (2005). *The unsung partner: The educational work and philosophy of Alice Chipman Dewey*. Unpublished doctoral dissertation, Harvard University, Cambridge, MA.

Hickman, L. A., Levine, B., Sharpe, A., & Simon, H. F. (2005). *The correspondence of John Dewey, Volumes 1-3: 1871-1952*. Carbondale: Center for Dewey Studies and Southern Illinois University.

Lippmann, W. (1922). *Public opinion*. New York: Free Press Paperbacks.

Martin, J. (2002). *The education of John Dewey*. New York: Columbia University Press.

Mayhew, K. C., & Edwards, A. C. (1936). *The Dewey school*. New York: Appleton-Century Crofts.

Perlstein, D. (1996). Community and democracy in American schools: Arthur Dale and the fate of progressive education. *Teachers College Record, 97*(4), 625-626.

Ryan, A. (1995). *John Dewey and the high tide of American liberalism*. New York: W. W. Norton.

Southern Illinois University Carbondale. (2003). Chronology of John Dewey's life and work. Retrieved November 25, 2005 from http://www.siu.edu/~deweyctr/chrono_page.htm

Stanley, W. B. (2005, September). Social studies and the social order: Transmission or transformation? *Social Education, 69*(5), 282-285.

Tanner, L. (1973). *Dewey's laboratory school: Lessons for today*. New York: Teacher's College Press.

Williamson II, D. F. (2005, November/December). Dew-ey (or not Dew-ey): A social reconstructionist? *Social Education, 69*(7), 354-362.

Wilson, E. (1940). *To the Finland station*. New York: Harcourt Brace.

CHAPTER 2

GEORGE S. COUNTS AND SOCIAL ISSUES

Gerald L. Gutek

INTRODUCTION

In the history of American education, George S. Counts (1889-1974) is noted for his ability to relate educational institutions and processes to broad social, political, and economic issues. A pioneering figure in creating the social foundations of education, Counts' scholarship crossed the boundaries of history, political science, sociology, and comparative education to provide an interdisciplinary focus on social and educational issues. As a historian, Counts described the public school as the "American Road to Culture." When he asked, "Dare the School Build a New Social Order?" Counts acted as a catalyst for the Social Reconstructionist philosophy in education. As a comparative educator, his analysis convinced him that the Soviet system posed a serious challenge to American democracy. As a mature scholar near the end of his career, he lauded American education as having the potential of creating a great civilization.

As a graduate student of the history of education at the University of Illinois (Urbana), I first became acquainted with Counts through his publications, especially his much quoted book, *Dare the School Build a New*

Addressing Social Issues in the Classroom and Beyond: The Pedagogical Efforts of Pioneers in the Field, 31–48
Copyright © 2007 by Information Age Publishing
All rights of reproduction in any form reserved.

Social Order? In the early 1960s, I heard him speak at the University of Illinois and recall that his lecture had three or four conclusions. Still a dynamic speaker, Counts would conclude, sit down, and responding to sustained applause, rise, come to the podium, and make a new insightful conclusion. Fortunately, I took the advice of my doctoral director, Professor Archibald Anderson, who encouraged me to analyze Counts' educational ideas as my dissertation topic. Engaged in my research, I traveled to Carbondale in 1963 to interview Counts, then a distinguished visiting professor at Southern Illinois University. Receptive to my questions, he answered them all, sharing his ideas on education with me, and encouraging my work. Completing my dissertation, "An Analysis of the Social and Educational Theory of George S. Counts During the Depression of the 1930s," I received my doctoral degree in 1964. I wrote two books on Counts: *The Educational Theory of George S. Counts* (1970) and *George S. Counts and American Civilization: The Educator as Social Theorist* (1984). My last meeting with Counts was in Chicago, where I introduced him as the featured speaker at the annual meeting of the Midwest History of Education Society.

My commentary on Counts as one of the pioneers of the education of social issues uses various contexts and life phases as organizing devices. A contextual theorist, Counts defined education and social issues as occurring within particular places and times. For him, the American context, with its particular natural environment—geography, climate, topography—and its particular history and political, economic, and social systems shaped social and educational issues. Allied philosophically with John Dewey's Instrumentalism, Counts saw social issues arising from a people's interaction with their environmental context. In this regard, he wrote:

> The historical record shows that education is always a function of time, place, and circumstance. In its basic philosophy, its social objectives, and its program of instruction, it inevitably reflects in varying proportions, the experiences, the conditions, and the hopes, fears, and aspirations of a particular people or cultural group at a particular point in history. Education as a whole is always relative, at least in its fundamental parts, to some concrete and evolving social situation. (Counts, 1934, p. 1)

Though the concept of a context appears commonsensical, it carries important educational implications. Contextual thinking can be illustrated by considering its oppositional educational philosophies. In the western educational tradition, Plato's Idealism and Aristotle's Realism are based on a metaphysical affirmation that universal truth, knowledge, and values transcend and are above contexts. For these traditional philosophies, truth and value, residing in the nature of the universe, do not vary in different climes and places. The Perennialism of Robert Hutchins,

Mortimer Adler, and Jacques Maritain is based on a conception of universal truth and on a general education that is everywhere the same. For these traditionalists, social issues, grounded in universal concepts of human nature and human rights, are the same for people everywhere. The definition of a social issue, in these more traditional educational philosophies, is related to and resolved by its conformity to an abstract higher order principle. In contrast to the Traditionalists, Progressives such as John Dewey, William H. Kilpatrick, Harold Rugg, and George Counts pragmatically rejected philosophical universalism and focused on specific contextual situations, occurring in particular societies at given historical moments.

As previously mentioned, in addition to contexts, my chapter uses the organizing principle of life phases, or stages. Individuals, like the contexts in which they live, change and, hopefully, grow and mature. In this chapter, Counts can be seen at particular stages in his long career. The themes of context and life phases are conceptually integrated in the thought and actions of Counts, an educator who faced changing issues at particular times in his life.

EARLY CAREER

Counts, born in December 1889 on a farm three miles from the town of Baldwin in northeastern Kansas, was the third of six children, and had three brothers and two sisters.

While neither his father nor mother attended college and only went a couple of years into high school, he said they greatly valued reading and the arts. Speaking of his parents and their influence on him, he commented, in an essay entitled "A Humble Autobiography," that,

[P]erhaps the most important thing about my parents was their system of values and their code of ethics. My father would often employ a "hired hand" to work on the farm or a "hired woman" to help mother in the house. ... And some of them were Negroes. In every case the "hired hand," whether white or black, was treated as if he or she were a member of the family. My parents always endeavored to live according to the principles of the Judeo-Christian ethic. They took seriously the second of the two great commandments and believed in the brotherhood of man. As I look back over my life, clear back to my early childhood, I can see how they influenced me. When I was 7 years old, a Negro boy, Johnny Hawkets, a close friend of mine, was attacked by four white boys. Even today I can see blood streaming from his nose. I took his part. (Counts, 1971, p. 156)

Counts earned his Bachelor of Arts degree in 1911 at Baker University, which was located in Baldwin. He majored in the classics, both Latin and Greek, and graduated first in his class. He immediately took a job as a teacher even though he had never taken a course on pedagogy or even thought of entering the profession of education. He began his career at Sumner County High School in Wellington, Kansas, where the taught math and science. A year later he took a job as principal in a high school in Peabody, Kansas, where he also taught biology. Recalling his days as a biology teacher in Peabody, he notes that he taught his students about evolution but was not criticized for doing so even though he was the only employee in the school who believed the theory was correct. In his autobiography he muses that the main reason he likely was not criticized was due to the fact that he regularly attended services at the Methodist Church and also taught a men's Sunday school class.

For his graduate work in education, Counts enrolled at the University of Chicago, a premiere American research institution, in 1913, where he intended to study sociology. His reason for going to the University of Chicago was "that it was regarded at that time as a champion of radical ideas in the fields of biology, social science, philosophy, and theology" (Counts, 1971, p. 158). Ultimately, Counts was convinced by his future brother-in-law, William Bailey, to consider earning his doctorate in the field of education. After speaking with Charles H. Judd, a national leader in the scientific movement in education and dean of the School of Education, Counts chose to switch fields. Still, while at the University of Chicago Counts took more courses in sociology than in education, and, in fact, took every course offered both in sociology and anthropology. He also took numerous courses in economics and political science.

For Judd, who became Counts' program director, education as a professional field was to be studied with scientific objectivity. Free from personal biases, the scientific educator was to arrive at research findings that measured and verified educational outcomes empirically rather than ideologically. For the scientific educator, the school curriculum facilitated effective and efficient instruction in essential skills and subjects rather than open-ended discussions of social issues. Although Counts learned the quantitative and field study methods of the science of education from his mentor, he sought a broader, more socially oriented, approach to educational inquiry. To broaden his graduate work, Counts enrolled in sociology courses taught by Albion Small, a pioneer of modern sociology, and W. I. Thomas, a leader in social theory (Counts, 1971, pp. 151-174). His dissertation, "Arithmetic Tests and Studies in the Psychology of Arithmetic," followed Judd's orientation to the science of education (Counts, 1917). Counts received his PhD in 1916, graduating *magna cum laude*.

Upon graduation, Counts became a university professor, which remained his profession for the rest of his life. Between 1916 and 1926, he taught at Delaware College (which became the University of Delaware), Harris Teachers College in St. Louis, the University of Washington, Yale University, and the University of Chicago.

Following his stint as a member of the Philippine Educational Survey Commission (PESC), which conducted a study of the educational system of the Philippine Islands, Counts was recruited, in 1927, by Teachers College, Columbia University, to serve as the associate director of its International Institute, whose express purpose was "to foster the interchange of ideas among educators, teachers, and students of the world" (Counts, 1971, p. 160). He made the observation that "my acceptance of the invitation certainly marked a turning point in my life" (Counts, 1971, p. 160). Commenting on his new position and its influence on him, Counts (1971) stated that:

> Each member of the staff of the institute was expected to study the language, the schools, and the basic social institutions of some country or region of the earth. Since no one had chosen the Soviet Union and since I had been interested in the Russian revolution through the years, I decided to fill the gap. In the summer of 1927 I made my first trip to the Soviet Union.... In the following years the study of the Soviet Union and communism became a major interest in my life.... After the seizure of power by Lenin and his Bolsheviks in November [1917] I was challenged by the proclaimed goals of the Soviet government to extend educational opportunities to all, to eradicate racial and national prejudices and hatreds, to prevent depressions, and to bring the economy, science, and technology into the service of all the people. At the same time, from the first I had grave doubts and misgivings about the dictatorship which shaped the course of the revolution. I hoped that these evils would weaken and disappear with the passing of the years. But the exact contrary happened. The dictatorship became ever more ruthless and assumed the totalitarian pattern of rule. It also became clear that, in spite of its professions, the Communist movement through the world is profoundly hostile to democracy and human freedom. (Counts, 1971, p. 160)

As a professor at Teachers College, Counts allied with his progressive "frontier" colleagues—William H. Kilpatrick, Harold Rugg, and John Childs—would come to foster a social reconstructionist theory of education. Thus, though he began his career in the scientific camp of Judd and Franklin Bobbitt, Counts moved toward the social foundations approach that used history, philosophy, sociology, anthropology, and economics to examine education. Many of his books—*Selective Character of American Secondary Education*, *The Senior High School Curriculum*, and *The Social Composition of Boards of Education*—incorporated insights from both the science of education and from sociology (Counts, 1922, 1926, 1927). Not content to analyze curriculum according to the science of education's emphasis on social efficiency, he examined the social and economic motives of the dominant classes who controlled the high school. Anticipating the Critical Theorists, Counts often used the concept of social control in describing contested areas in education. Moving to broader structural-functional analysis, Counts, in *Secondary Education and Industrialism*, examined the high school's role in American industrial and technological society (Counts, 1929).

Counts' *The American Road to Culture*, which analyzed the public school's role in transmitting and shaping American culture, unequivocally located him in the social foundations approach to education (Counts, 1930). For him, the school transmitted the culture selectively rather than impartially. As a result, educators faced the ethical challenge of selecting and transmitting the cultural elements that were viable for an industrial society and integrating them with technology, the new material variable that needed to be incorporated into a modern community. Although recognizing the public schools' vital role in transmitting the cultural heritage, Counts believed U.S. citizens had an exaggerated faith in the schools' power to solve all kinds of social problems. Seeing education as a much broader concept than schooling, Counts anticipated Lawrence Cremin's and Bernard Bailyn's critique of the historiography of education that found it to be celebrationist and overly focused on schooling (Bailyn, 1972; Cremin 1965).

THE DEPRESSION OF THE 1930S

The second phase of Counts' career unfolded during the Great Depression of the 1930s. Although he had been examining the relationships between educational policy and social issues throughout the 1920s, the dramatic events of the 1930s moved him to a Social Reconstructionist position. According to Social Reconstructionism, education, particularly schools, should not reflect the social, political, and economic status quo but rather deliberately advocate and engage in democratic and egalitarian social reform. In 1932, Counts delivered two addresses along the latter line: "Dare Progressive Education be Progressive?" to the Progressive Education Association (PEA) and "Dare the School Build a New Social Order?" to the National Education Association (NEA) (Counts 1932a,b). Taking a firm ideological stance, Counts passionately argued that schools and teachers could not remain neutral in the crisis of the Depression. Like a political stump speaker rather than a professor, he pointed out the contradictions facing Americans: industrial and technological development "accompanied by extreme material insecurity"; "dire poverty" by "the most extravagant living that the world has ever known"; hungry "children marching to school past bankrupt shops laden with rich foods"; millions of "strong men" futilely "searching for employment" (Counts, 1932a, pp. 259-260).

Teachers, Counts argued, should join with progressive and liberal forces such as the labor unions and farmers' associations to reach for power and create a genuinely democratic and egalitarian new social order. Teachers needed to oppose the vested special economic interests, challenge the obsolete but still powerful myth of economic individualism, and work to construct a cooperative planning society. He urged them to "come to grips with the problem of creating a tradition that has roots in American soil, is in harmony with the spirit of the age, recognizes the facts of industrialism, appeals to the most profound impulses of our people, and takes into account the emergence of a world society" (Counts, 1932b, p. 36). The "new social order," Counts argued, needed to affirm the democratic values embedded in the American past and recognize the emergence of an industrial-technological society (Counts, 1938, p. 318).

Writing about the criticism he received for his publication of *Dare the School Build a New Social Order*, he said:

> ... I gave particular attention to the thesis that the school should assume responsibility for the improvement of our society, for the fulfillment of the age-long "promise of America."... This philosophy was expressed most vigorously and even militantly in *Dare the School Build a New Social Order?*— published in 1932. Many persons who never read the book have criticized it on the grounds that the school not only should not but could not do this. On page 24 I wrote that "the school is but one formative agency among many, and certainly not that strongest at that." And on page 37 I defined the goals of the school in these words: "This does not mean that we should endeavor to promote particular reforms through the education system. We should, however, give to our children a vision of the possibilities which lie ahead and endeavor to enlist their loyalties and enthusiasm in the realization of the vision. Also our social institution and practices, all of them, should be critically examined in the light of such a vision." (Counts, 1971, pp. 172-173)

Philosophically, Counts operated within the intellectual framework of John Dewey's Instrumentalism. For Dewey, socially intelligent persons continually reconstructed their ideas and values by using the scientific method of problem solving. Intelligent societies, like intelligent individuals, reconstructed their social, political, and economic experience when they faced new social issues. In fact, Dewey's *Individualism: Old and New* and *Liberalism and Social Action* addressed issues similar to those raised by

Counts (Dewey, 1929/1962, 1935/1963). Dewey, like Counts, called for a reconstructed Liberalism that moved it from its *laissez-faire* origins to a revitalized process of social action that could be used to solve the issues facing an increasingly corporate and technological but dysfunctional society.

Counts' call for educators to build a new social order in his PEA and NEA addresses of 1932 provide classic insights into his strategy of relating educational policy to social issues. First, he eschews an objective and neutral approach to education. For him, like Paulo Freire, all education is partial to a particular ideology's interpretation of the past and vision of the future. Second, he addresses issues that arise within a social, political, and economic context and relate to a society's unresolved contradictions. Third, educators, by articulating an ideological perspective, can shape the resolution of these contradictions and in doing so create a new social order. Fourth, the ideological inclination in this new social order should be socially and economically egalitarian, politically democratic, and methodologically empirical and experimental.

Counts' association with Charles A. Beard (1874-1948), the veteran progressive revisionist historian, further developed his strategy for identifying and resolving social issues. During the mid-1930s, Counts and Beard were influential members of the American Historical Association's Commission on the Social Studies (AHACSS). Appointed to the Commission in 1928, Counts became its Director of Research in 1931. Widely recognized for his controversial book, *An Economic Interpretation of the Constitution of the United States,* Beard argued that economic factors shape history and condition social and political control and change (Beard, 1913). Counts enjoyed a close collaborative working and warm personal relationship with the elder Beard, whom he affectionately called "Uncle Charley." As a mentor for the younger Counts, Beard, the veteran historian, and Counts, growing in repute as an educator, operated from a culturally relativist ideological orientation. Just as Counts rejected universalism in education, Beard denied that universal laws governed history. Beard argued that history was conditioned by the social, political, and most importantly economic forces operating at a given time and place (Dennis, 1989, p. 19).

During the 1930s, Counts' critics, noting his research on Soviet education, attacked him for trying to impose a Marxist interpretation on American social education.[1] Although both Beard and Counts used an economic interpretation of history, they rejected Marx's dialectical materialist claim that economic forces—control of the means and modes of production—were the single cause operating in history (Gutek, 1984, p. 14). Counts, influenced by Beard, saw economic forces as largely conditioning but not necessarily determining history. Carefully distinguishing conditioning from determining, Counts stated, "history is neither wholly bound nor wholly free; though always conditioned, never fated. Within the bounds of the possible human preference operates" (Counts, 1938, p. 74).

In devising a strategy to examine social issues and solve social problems, Counts constructed an interpretation of U.S. history. Not a dispassionate historical rendition, his history was ideologically charged and designed to foster social change. In almost dialectical fashion, Counts interpreted U.S. history as falling into two conflicting traditions or strands—one Jeffersonian and the other Hamiltonian. The Jeffersonian tradition, which Counts endorsed, provided the democratic and egalitarian elements needed for reconstruction into the new industrial and technological social order. The Hamiltonian strand represented domination by an economic elite and its special interests over the great majority of the people (Committee, 1933, p. 12). Although not an original interpretation, Counts used the dichotomy of Jeffersonian and Hamiltonian traditions to build his argument for constructing a new society. Jeffersonian democracy and equality, he espoused, needed to be reasserted against the special economic interests.

Believing that American society desperately needed regulation, reform, and centralized planning, Counts and Beard were determined to use history and the social sciences as instruments educators could and should use in creating a new social order. They proceeded to employ their work on the Commission to construct a frame-of-reference to guide teachers in a momentous program of directed social change. In *A Charter for the Social Sciences in the Schools*, Beard (1932) argued that history and the social sciences, functioning in contexts of time and place, were never completely objective, nor neutral, but were "organized around some central philosophy" (p. 34). Teachers needed a frame-of-reference that recognized that U.S. society: (1) was undergoing profound social change; (2) rested on an industrial economy based on science and technology; (3) needed to use rational planning and intelligent cooperation in all social sectors, particularly in industry and government, to solve its problems; and (4) needed to recognize and reassert that representative government requires public discussion, debate, and criticism informed by the social sciences (Beard, 1932, pp. 34-51).

A key argument in Beard's *Charter*, that Counts endorsed, was that schools, like other social institutions, lagged in adapting their programs to technologically-generated change in the material culture. Reflecting Ogburn's (1933) cultural lag theory, Beard argued that social science education needed to reduce the gap between technological change in material culture and social knowledge and ethical values. To reduce the gap, U.S. society, government, and education needed to throw off the residues of *laissez-faire* economic individualism and move rapidly toward a democratic and collective planning society (Beard, 1932, pp. 54-55).

Counts' far ranging *The Social Foundations of Education*, a companion volume with Beard's *Charter*, examined the educational implications of politics, government, religion, science, social class, economics, art, law, recreation, and communication and the media. It virtually encompassed the whole of education—philosophy, administration, curriculum, and instruction. In preparing his proposal for the book, Counts (1932c) wrote to Beard:

> My argument is a simple one. I shall contend that as a people we have received from the hand of Nature and from our European heritage practically all of the favors and advantages that ever blessed any people; that throughout the nineteenth century we held out to ourselves and to the world at large the promise of realizing what James Truslow Adams has called the "American Dream"; that for one reason or another this early promise has not been realized and that something has gone badly askew; that the vast changes that recently have been seeping over America and the world have so altered the terms in the equation that we must restate the problem of life and recast the scale of values by which we are to live; that you and I and anybody else whom we can draw into the hazardous undertaking are to cast caution to the winds and tackle this job of restatement and reformulation; and finally, that schools and teachers must shape their programs with reference to the needs outlined and accept heavy responsibilities for the satisfaction of these needs. I may add that in my judgment the facts will drive us irrevocably from our traditional individualistic professions and in the direction of a society marked by the socialization, integration and coordination of the basic social process. (pp. 1-2)

Counts examined the great transformation of the United States from an agrarian and rural society into an urban, industrial, and technological one. His sketch of the emerging new social order portrayed a society that was interdependent, planned, highly integrated, and coordinated. The question was—would this emergent society be democratic and egalitarian or would it take some other political form, perhaps a totalitarian one? To ensure a democratic alternative, Counts believed that education, especially in the social sciences, needed to be "organized within the frame of reference provided by the idea of a democratic collectivism" (Counts, 1934, pp. 48-49).

Counts alerted teachers to the broad topics and issues that social science education and the social foundations of education should examine. More specifically, he suggested, they should: "(1) examine the social history of ordinary people; (2) examine the development of democratic institutions and processes; (3) examine industry and technology's emergence and socio-economic impact; (4) identify and analyze contemporary society's major contradictions; and (5) critically analyze the important proposals, programs, and philosophies related to social issues, and provide the information people needed to make intelligent and democratic choices" (Counts, 1934, pp. 48-58).

Although a committee of Beard, Counts, and August C. Krey, the Commission's chairman, were to prepare the Commission's "Conclusions and Recommendations," Krey, who was ill, was frequently absent from meetings. In effect, Beard and Counts were the principal authors of the document. In their recommendations, the two collaborators, taking a broad interdisciplinary view, stated that social science content should be derived from physical and cultural geography, economics, sociology, political science and history. It should include both classic and important contemporary works in these fields. Methods of instruction should emulate the great educators of past and present (AHA, 1934, pp. 46-83). More telling than their pedagogical recommendations were their ideological prescriptions that: (1) the social sciences should provide "accurate knowledge" and "informed insight" about the human being and society; (2) social creativity and planning cannot rest "on empiricism alone" but requires "ethical and aesthetic considerations"; (3) the social sciences should affirm the ethical and aesthetic values of individual worthwhile recognizing that the era of *laissez-faire* individualism had ended and that an interdependent and collectivist society and world were imminent; (4) the social sciences should be deliberately committed to democratic processes, to improving living standards for all people, and to creating a sense of toleration at home and abroad (AHA, 1934, pp. 5-9).

The "Conclusions and Recommendations" provoked controversy as Commission members Charles Merriam, Edmund Day, and Ernest Horn refused to sign the final report. Merriam, a distinguished political science professor at the University of Chicago, objected to "collectivism," as an unnecessarily provocative and ideologically biased term. Charging that the "Conclusions" endorsed indoctrination, Day claimed they inadequately addressed the issues of "tolerance of conflicting social studies," "freedom of speech," and freedom to teach controversial issues (Dennis, 1989, pp. 87-88). Judd, Counts' dissertation director at the University of Chicago, caustically wrote:

> Inspired by the idea that schools must contribute in some way to social reform, certain radicals have gone so far as to advocate that teachers assume the role of leaders and direct the reorganization of the economic and political systems. These extremists have misconceived the function of the schools. The duty of education is to prepare people to make intelligent judgments on social problems. (Judd, 1934, p. 268)

Defending the "Conclusions and Recommendations," Counts argued that an "educational program" always involves "imposition on the mind" of the person being educated. He stated, "If you set up a school you set up a system of social relationships and transmit certain values. A certain outlook on life. There is a system of values in anything that is done" (quoted Dennis, 1989, pp. 87-88). Attacking educational neutrality, Counts (1934) argued:

> Any concrete school program will contribute to the struggle for survival that is ever going on among institutions, ideas, and values; it cannot remain neutral in any firm and complete sense. Partiality is the very essence of education, as it is of life itself. The difference between education and life is that in the former partiality is presumably reasoned and enlightened. (p. 535)

In 1934, Counts and other like-minded progressive educators such as Kilpatrick and Rugg launched *The Social Frontier,* an issue-oriented reconstructionist journal. As its senior editor from 1934 to 1937, Counts affirmed that the journal would be committed to "raising of American life from the level of the profit system, individualism and vested class interests to the plane of social motivation, collectivism and classlessness." Focusing on the "class struggle," Counts' editorials urged teachers to join with organized labor and to use the school to improve economic conditions and create the climate for a new egalitarian and democratic social order (Dennis, 1989, p. 118).

Counts' *The Prospects of American Democracy* presented his most developed agenda for the reconstruction of U.S. life and institutions during the Depression period. He urged teachers and other forward-looking individuals to: renew their commitment to democratic processes; disseminate the knowledge people needed to solve the cultural crisis; mobilize for social reconstruction; ensure that fair and effective elections carried out popular mandates; ensure that the popularly elected government controlled military and police power; maintain civil rights; and to analyze and expose political propaganda (Counts, 1938, pp. 176-194).

Counts' educational policy views in the 1930s were influenced by his study of education in the Soviet Union as well as his interpretation of the domestic situation in the United States. As mentioned earlier, as a member of Teachers College Division of International Education, Counts identified Soviet education as his area concentration, and in the late 1920s he traveled in the Soviet Union conducting field research and interviewing leading Soviet educators. In 1929, Counts drove a Model A Ford, sent from Detroit to Leningrad, through the Soviet Union. Within the Soviet Union he drove some 6,000 miles, for the most part by himself and along large swaths of land where there were no roads and where many had never seen an automobile.

When Counts was conducting his research, the Soviet Union was mobilizing all of its social and economic sectors to fulfill the First Five Year Plan. And during this period Josef Stalin was still in the process of consolidating his power. Counts was impressed with the Soviet commitment to total planning which he contrasted with the lack of planning in the United States. He argued that the U.S. government, society, and education should engage in planning; however, he believed that such planning should be democratic and experimental. Counts' critics who alleged that he sought to impose a Soviet-style process on the United States seized upon Counts' recommendations for "a planning society" to discredit his efforts for constructing a new society through education.

Two important assumptions shaped Counts' perspective on social issues in the 1930s: one, U.S. educators needed to become directly and overtly committed to the ideology of Social Reconstructionism and work to create a more democratic and egalitarian society; two, the Soviet experiment in planning could be instructive to Americans. Here it needs to be emphasized that Counts was not calling for Marxist-Leninist Soviet-style planning in the United States; rather, he believed the Soviet model of total planning could be studied in the United States where a democratic approach to planning could be instituted. Educationally, Counts urged educators to become students of planning and to become planners themselves. In defining social issues, Counts projected a view of how the problems related to them could be solved by thorough planning.

WORLD WAR II AND THE COLD WAR

From the prelude to World War II (1938-1940) to World War II (1941-1945), and from the period of Postwar Reconstruction through the Cold War (1946-1960), Counts, still operating as a contextual theorist, gradually moved from the specific context of the United States to the larger world. His preoccupation with the issues of the Depression's economic crisis shifted to the Nazi, Fascist, and Communist totalitarian threat to democratic institutions and processes.

By the end of the 1930s, Counts and other liberals in the United States, especially those identified with Dewey's pragmatism, had grown thoroughly disenchanted with events in the Soviet Union, where Stalin had ruthlessly purged his former Bolshevik comrades and was relentlessly consolidating his power. Counts found that because of the purges many of his friends in Russia had disappeared or had become nonpersons. He wrote that the "Soviet leadership turned against me after my third long visit in 1936. In fact, my closest Soviet friend, Dr. Pinkevich, a leading educator who bid me good-bye at the end of December, was sent to a forced-labor camp in January and died there 2 years later" (Counts, 1971, p. 162). Counts found that Soviet education, growing increasingly doctrinal, slavishly adhered to the official Marxist-Leninist ideology. Ultimately, Counts charged that Soviet schooling had become a form of mind control over the young generation.

COUNTS AS A POLITICAL ACTIVIST

Counts was a political activist as well as a scholar, and was a founder of the American Labor Party and then of the Liberal Party, two significant left-of-center third parties in New York state. He also began a determined struggle against the American Communist Party, which he regarded as a tool of Soviet Communism. The Communist Party, he charged, had manipulated popular causes and had frustrated liberal reform efforts through its Machiavellian tactics. In 1939, Counts, heading an anti-Communist slate, was elected President of the American Federation of Teachers (AFT). During his 3-year term from 1939-1942, he took the offensive against the Communist domination of some AFT locals. Under his leadership, the AFT Constitution was revised to eliminate members who belonged to totalitarian parties, be they Fascist or Communist. Summing up his career as an activist, Counts (1971) reminisced:

> Reared in the tradition of the American frontier, I have always regarded myself as a product and champion of our American democracy as outlined in the Bill of Rights and the Declaration of Independence. Sensing from early manhood the great dangers threatening that democracy due to the rise of our urbanized and industrialized society, I have ever sought to make organized education serve the purposes of democracy—democracy conceived both as social ends and as social means. In pursing this course, I have been bitterly opposed at times by totalitarians of all brands—left and right, foreign and domestic. The Fascist-minded have sometimes called me a "Communist," even as the Communist-minded have called me a "Fascist." In fact, like my people, I regard myself as a cross between a Jeffersonian Democrat and a Lincolnian Republican, struggling with the old problem of human freedom and equality in the age of science and technology. I enjoy surprising my students by telling them that I am a conservative, that I have striven throughout my life to "conserve our radical tradition." I have been a member of the American Civil Liberties Union for almost half a century and a Member of its National Committee for approximately 30 years. (pp. 163-164)

Though known as a radical and condemned as a "Communist" and "red" by the Hearst press, Counts had moved from a sympathetic view of the Soviet Union in the early 1930s to a decidedly anti-Communist stance by the decade's end. In 1943, Counts and his Teachers College associate, John Childs, in a remarkable prescient book *(America, Russia, and the Communist Party in the Postwar World)* argued that the Communist Party would undermine Post War reconstruction and threaten world peace. Counts and Childs urged the Soviet Union to cease exporting its ideology through Communist parties in other countries. They warned that those who looked to the Soviet Union for guidance would meet with severe disillusionment (Counts & Childs, 1943).

Counts post-War works tended to enlarge the context of American education by emphasizing it as part of Western Civilization and as being shaped by the Hebraic-Christian tradition and cosmopolitan humanism. In *Education and the Promise of America*, Counts, calling for a renascent liberalism, urged educators to embrace an inspiring interpretation of U.S. history that examined the democratic potentialities of U.S. industrial and technological society (Counts, 1946, p. 103).

Counts' comprehensive and highly reflective book, *Education and American Civilization*, called upon educators to construct a generous philosophy of education that grew out of and nourished American civilization. America's cultural heritage, he wrote, contained immense possibilities for creating a great and enduring democratic civilization. As in his earlier works, Counts examined both the challenges and the possibilities that technology placed on U.S. society. Optimistically, he identified the positive elements in American culture as the Hebraic-Christian ethic, the humanist tradition, the scientific method, the rule of law, and allegiance to democratic institutions and processes. He called for creating a great humane and ethical system of education that would contribute to preserving individual excellence, social equality, political liberty, a just economy, and enduring world civilization. As Counts broadened his contexts, he also enlarged his conception of the issues facing American society. There were, he stated "issues caused by the major contradictions of freedom and tyranny, of equality and caste, of cooperation and competition, of prosperity and depression, of security and liberty, of beauty and ugliness, of war and peace, of progress and catastrophe" (Counts, 1952, p. 365).

In the 1950s, Counts grew increasingly hostile to Marxist-Leninism, Stalinism, and to Communism in general. Counts' (1957) *The Challenge of Soviet Education* described the Soviet system as a form of mind control in which the Communist Party censored and managed all forms of information and education. He joined the pragmatist philosopher Sidney Hook in organizing the Americans for Cultural Freedom as a counter force to those intellectuals who still believed in the Soviet Union as a progressive force. While opposed to the American Communist Party and recognizing the Soviet Union as a threat to democratic institutions, Counts opposed the constraints on freedom of expression and association generated by the witch hunts of the McCarthy period.

ELDER STATESMAN

Counts reluctantly retired from Columbia University's Teachers College in 1955, at the then mandatory retirement age of 65. After retiring, he was a visiting professor at the University of Pittsburgh, the University of Colorado, Michigan State University, and Northwestern University. Along with several other distinguished retired education professors, such as his Teachers College colleague, John Childs, his last service as a professor was at Southern Illinois University in Carbondale, where he enjoyed a reputation as an elder statesman of American education. In the final stage of his career, from 1955 to 1974, the contexts Counts used to develop his educational ideas, especially in relation to social issues, became broader and more humanistic. He traced the United States' origins to the eighteenth century Enlightenment. He proclaimed that the United States' abundant great natural resources and geographical expanse created the possibility of generating a generous and enduring form of democracy. Like President Dwight David Eisenhower, he feared the rise of a military-industrial-complex might undermine democratic processes. He defined educational leadership as a form of statesmanship in which educators examined the issues they faced from the larger expanses of history, philosophy, and social science.

CONCLUSION

For some historians of education, Counts is framed in time, as the fiery radical of the 1930s, standing at the podium of the NEA convention in 1932 and asking his famous question—"Dare the schools build a new social order?" For Counts, himself, however, this was but one of many significant episodes in a long and ongoing career.

Counts' call for educators to build a new social order still has relevance for contemporary educators. As Counts maintained, schooling is always based on a frame-of-reference rooted in the cultural heritage. Curriculum content always requires selection. He advised educators to determine which elements in the heritage are viable and which are obsolete in the contemporary situation. The selective prisms of viability and obsolescence were (and are) changeable and relative to particular social situations. After a social issue is defined and its problematic conditions identified, the viable elements of the heritage can be used instrumentally to resolve the issue. What was most important for Counts was that the process of inquiry and the resolution of a social issue be democratic and experimental.

NOTE

1. Beard encouraged Counts to develop an analytic strategy based on the American historical experience rather than European models.

REFERENCES

American Historical Association, Investigation of the Social Studies in the Schools. (1934). *Conclusions and recommendations of the commission*. New York: Charles Scribner's Sons.

Bailyn, B. (1972). *Education in the forming of American society*. New York: W. W. Norton.

Beard, C. A. (1913). *An economic interpretation of the Constitution of the United States*. New York: Macmillan.

Beard, C. A. (1932). *A charter for the social sciences in the schools*. New York: Charles Scribner's Sons.

Committee of the Progressive Education Association on Social and Economic Problems. (1933). *A call to the teachers of the nation*. New York: John Day.

Counts, G. S. (1917). *Arithmetic tests and studies in the psychology of arithmetic*. Chicago: University of Chicago Press.

Counts, G. S. (1922). *The selective character of American secondary education*. Chicago: University of Chicago Press.

Counts, G. S. (1926). *The senior high school curriculum*. Chicago: University of Chicago Press.

Counts, G. S. (1927). *The social composition of boards of education: A study in the social control of public education*. Chicago: University of Chicago Press.

Counts, G. S. (1929). *Secondary education and industrialism*. Cambridge, MA: Harvard University Press.

Counts, G. S. (1930). *The American road to culture: A social interpretation of education in the United States*. New York: John Day.

Counts, G. S. (1932a). Dare progressive education be progressive? *Progressive Education, 9*.

Counts, G. S. (1932b). *Dare the school build a new social order?* New York: John Day.

Counts, G. S. (1932c). *Letter to Charles A. Beard* (January 7, 1932) Counts Special Collection, Morris Library, Southern Illinois University, Carbondale, Illinois.

Counts, G. S. (1934). *The social foundations of education*. New York: Charles Scribner's Sons.

Counts, G. S. (1938). *The prospects of American democracy*. New York: John Day.

Counts, G. S. (1946). *Education and the promise of America*. New York: Macmillan.

Counts, G. S. (1952). *Education and American civilization*. New York: Teachers College Press.

Counts, G. S. (1957). *The challenge of Soviet education*. New York: McGraw-Hill.

Counts, G. S. (1971). A humble autobiography. In R. J. Havighurst (Ed.), *Leaders in American education: The seventieth yearbook of the National Society for the Study of Education* (pp. 151-174). Chicago: University of Chicago Press.

Counts, G. S., & Childs, J. (1943). *America, Russia, and the Communist Party in the postwar world*. New York: John Day.

Cremin, L. A. (1965). *The wonderful world of Ellwood Paterson Cubberley*. New York: Teachers College Press.

Dennis, L. J. (1989). *George S. Counts and Charles A. Beard: Collaborators for change*. Albany: State University of New York Press.

Dewey, J. (1962). *Individualism: Old and new*. New York: Capricorn. (Original work published 1929).

Dewey, J. (1963). *Liberalism and social action*. New York: Capricorn. (Original work published 1935).

Gutek, G. L. (1984). *George S. Counts and American civilization: The educator as social theorist*. Macon, GA: Mercer University Press.

Gutek, G. L. (1970). *The educational theory of George S. Counts*. Columbus: Ohio State University Press.

Judd, C. H. (1934). *Education and social progress*. New York: Harcourt, Brace.

Ogburn, W. F. (1933). *Recent social trends in the United States*. New York: McGraw-Hill Book.

CHAPTER 3

HAROLD RUGG

Apostle of the Modern Social Studies Curriculum[1]

Ron Evans

INTRODUCTION

Harold O. Rugg was one of a small group of leaders of the Progressive Education Movement centered at Teachers College, Columbia University, and a leader among the Social Frontier group that emerged in the 1930s to argue that schools should play a stronger role in helping to reconstruct society. He was the author of an innovative and best-selling series of social studies textbooks which ultimately came under attack from patriotic and business groups in the prelude to the United States involvement in World War II. The story of his rise and fall encapsulates a significant and central story in the history of American education. The Rugg story reveals a great deal about the direction of schooling in American life, the many alternative roads not taken, and the possibilities for the future.

Rugg's story remains important today chiefly because it reminds us that social studies as a broad and integrated field of study has potential

Addressing Social Issues in the Classroom and Beyond: The Pedagogical Efforts of Pioneers in the Field, 49–69
Copyright © 2007 by Information Age Publishing
All rights of reproduction in any form reserved.

49

for the development of thoughtful and caring citizens, and that it is possible for a social studies reformer to influence the course of events. Rugg's work had a real impact, not only on rhetoric among theorists but on schools. His work brought an integrated and issues-centered approach to the field and to a large segment of U.S. school children during the 1930s, and thus influenced the education of a generation of U.S. citizens. His textbooks and materials sold millions of copies and ultimately inspired a controversy that changed the course of the curriculum.

More specifically, Rugg created an avant-garde social studies program which was pedagogically advanced, instructive for those with an interest in issues-centered education and/or in teaching for social justice. He developed an approach to social studies instruction that integrated the social sciences and history in an issues-centered program focusing on understanding and social transformation. To this day his program serves as a useful prototype for a unified social studies program focused on issues and societal problems and aimed at education for social justice.

Rugg envisioned an entire social studies curriculum centered around "The American Problem," and aimed at leading a thousand-year march to a "cooperative commonwealth." Rugg's story is a reminder of the potential power of social studies reform—his materials were pedagogically sophisticated and somewhat daring, and they asked tough questions on topics that need to be addressed in a democratic society: the role of business in controlling government, the role of government in regulating business, the influence of men of wealth and property on the constitution and our form of government, the role of government in providing for the general social welfare, immigration concerns, issues related to racial diversity, the role of the United States in world affairs, and a myriad of others. He was an American original, the progenitor of education for social justice in social studies education. Furthermore, Rugg's work was built on a thoughtful rationale that combined student interest with social worth—a powerful combination that still has appeal.

The Rugg story is also important today because social studies as a broad, interdisciplinary and issues-centered field is currently endangered: reports on classroom practice find a pattern of instruction focused on content acquisition and a fact-myth-legend approach to history; the revival of history and a mania for standards and high stakes tests are increasing an emphasis upon traditional history and narrowing the range of issues and questions discussed in schools.

As alluded to earlier, in the late 1930s and early 1940s Rugg was censured by a media storm fed by conservative patriotic and business groups who, in an un-American fashion, did not want school children, or their parents for that matter, raising questions about the basic structures of American life and the capitalist economic system. The attack on Rugg, his ideas, textbooks, and school materials were perhaps the first major battle of what I have termed "the war on social studies" (Evans, 2004). It is a war many educators of progressive mind are still fighting, and, unfortunately, still losing.

Rugg's story also illustrates the point that being a social critic or progressive reformer can be dangerous, especially so in education. To openly declare allegiance to ideas that challenge capitalism and its most basic assumptions can, and has—on many occasions—led to serious repercussions.

Rugg's life and work have great resonance today, in the 21st century. The Rugg story raises serious questions about the rationale and purposes of schooling for citizenship: What kind of citizens and citizen education do we want? How far can and should schools go in providing opportunities for social criticism? What kinds of activities and materials are appropriate in support of education for social justice? What are its limits, if any? And, behind all of these questions, Whose version(s) of the American way should schools support?

Rugg was one of the seminal thinkers in the development of education for social reconstructionism, a forerunner of education for social justice. Teaching for social justice has had many advocates over the years and seems a permanent interest group in the panoply of educational thought. The literature on social justice oriented schooling has mushroomed since the 1970s, an offshoot of critiques of society, and of schooling, developed in many quarters during the 1960s and later (Ayers, Hunt, & Quinn, 1998). To a greater degree than many recent advocates of teaching for social justice, Rugg's work achieved a strong presence in schools. Thus, most important, the Rugg story, his life and work, challenges us to make a difference in schools.

DEVELOPMENT OF THE RUGG SOCIAL STUDIES PROGRAM

Harold Ordway Rugg, born in Fitchburg, Massachusetts on January 17, 1886, the son of a cabinet maker, attended Fitchburg public schools, worked in a textile mill, and, through good fortune and his own initiative, attended Dartmouth College. He studied civil engineering and worked as a railroad surveyor, then taught civil engineering for 2 years and became interested in how students learn. His engineering background would later influence his penchant for social engineering as embodied in his evolving ideas for education. Ultimately, Rugg decided to pursue a doctorate in education, and did so due to his growing interest in questions related to learning, intelligence, and the social context of schooling and because of the potential opportunity to teach at a respected school of education. He earned a PhD in Education at the University of Illinois under the mentor-ship of William C. Bagley in 1915, then held a teaching post in educational psychology and statistics at the University of Chicago, engaging in what he would later describe as "an orgy of tabulation" (Rugg, 1941, p. 182).

Rugg was raised in modest circumstances in Fitchburg, always it seemed, with "not enough" in the way of the material goods of life. As a carpenter and cabinet maker, his father struggled at times to hold a job. Rugg's sense of deprivation was heightened by his observation of the wealthy among Fitchburg—their power, influence, and luxurious lifestyle. Thus, he had grown up holding many mainstream attitudes, with something of a liberal bent, and an exceptionally strong drive for career success.

It was not, however, until he had become a professor of education and was called to serve on the Army's Committee on the Classification of Personnel, which assisted in the aptitude and intelligence testing and sorting of personnel during the Army's large scale expansion, that he went through a transformation in his world view, a transformation to a progressive ideology and his conversion from the field of educational psychology and statistics to social studies. Rugg's dramatic transformation was precipitated by his service on the Army's Committee on Personnel, and through his interaction and friendship with others on that committee, including Arthur Upham Pope (former professor of philosophy at the University of California), John Coss (an educator at Columbia University), and Walter Lippmann (a former editor at *The New Republic* and later a renowned political columnist), and by his introduction through these contacts to contemporary social critics—including Van Wyck Brooks, Waldo Frank, and Randolph Bourne who held an aesthetic orientation and who had written for *The Seven Arts*, a highly regarded literary journal.

Rugg was strongly influenced by the "frontier thinkers" on the cutting edge of modern scholarship. Indeed, he was also profoundly influenced by the work and thought of John Dewey, by various forms of social criticism (though he never professed allegiance with any of the "isms"), by the social experiment of Soviet Russia, and by the movement for Technocracy, especially the thought of Howard Scott, who promoted a vision of a society of shared abundance in which the industrial economy would be run by expert technicians in the interest of abolishing the hardships and class conflict associated with industrialism.

Behind Rugg's conversion to social studies and focus on social issues was a new awareness of the displacement and human suffering caused by industrialism and its allied developments, modern warfare, and colonialism. Rather than focus on any one issue, his orientation focused on the broad nexus of forces, issues, and problems that needed to be understood, and overcome, in order to ameliorate human suffering in the world.

In January 1920, Rugg joined the faculty at Teachers College, Columbia University, where he served as school psychologist for the Lincoln School, one of the leading progressive private schools in the nation, founded with the intention of changing the face of American education. It was at the Lincoln School that Rugg found a laboratory for working out his ideas for the social studies curriculum with a handful of teachers and students. His contact at Teachers College with John Dewey, William H. Kilpatrick, George S. Counts, John L. Childs, Jesse Newlon, R. Bruce Raup and others had a profound influence on his intellectual development, as did his association with the avant-garde in the New York area including creative artists such as Alfred Stieglitz and Georgia O'Keefe in Greenwich Village and his later residence in the arts community of Woodstock, New York, which inspired Rugg's interest in the arts, in imagination and creativity.

Rugg's theory of social studies, which melded history and the social sciences into one continuous course, focused on a deeper understanding of the industrialized world. Given time to read and think as per his agreement with his new employers, Rugg set to work exploring the seminal works in history and the social sciences of the late 19th and early 20th century. He read historians such as Frederick Jackson Turner, Charles A. Beard, and James Harvey Robinson, and social scientists including Thorsten Veblen, Charles Horton Cooley, and John Maynard Keynes. As a result of his reading, "a new vista of possibilities" and a new understanding of the problems of modern industrial society opened up before him. Following this period of intense study, Rugg's conversion to social studies was more or less complete. It was during and shortly after this time that Rugg developed the core of his idea for a unified social studies curriculum, crossing but not obliterating disciplinary boundaries, focused on issues and problems and presenting history and the social sciences through the lens of persistent societal issues. In his initial publication after arriving at Teachers College, Rugg wrote:

> My own procedure would be to ignore the fact that we have today a curriculum in history, geography and civics; and start afresh and define clearly the scope, functions and objectives of the course by the criterion of "social worth." [Thus]—to be included in the course, the material must contribute—to an interest in and appreciation of the outstanding "problems" and "issues" of contemporary civilization. (Rugg, 1921a, p. 189)

During this period, he also began work on the Rugg social science pamphlets which he would eventually develop into a best-selling textbook series. At this time, Rugg's scholarship was devoted primarily to critiquing traditional approaches to social studies, which was dominated by traditional history, and to developing and expounding upon his theory of a unified social studies program.

During his early years at Teachers College, Rugg decided to attempt to improve education through what he saw as its most influential element, school textual materials. He set out to create an alternative form encapsulating his vision for social studies. In 1921 he called for a social studies curriculum that would be entirely problem-centered, and built around, as previously mentioned, "The American Problem." In this regard, Rugg (1921b) argued that:

1. "All units of work shall be presented definitely in problem-solving form."
2. "There should be one continuous social studies course from the first grade to the twelfth."
3. Problems shall be based on "personal appeals" (e.g., what would you do if?; etc.?) or "alternative proposals" in order to force comparison, "intellectual opposition," and "concrete human detail to (generate) interest."
4. "Constant practice shall be given in analyzing, generalizing, and organizing, as material that pertains to the 'problems' is collected and studied."
5. "Problem-situations shall be presented first through current affairs. Only those historical backgrounds shall be developed which … are crucial for clear thinking about contemporary matters."
6. "Problems, or the examples of generalizations and organization which contribute to them, should occur in many grades on an increasingly mature level … (through) some form of 'layer' scheme" (p. 252).

Rugg would later argue that the entire social studies curriculum should be organized around problems of contemporary life. Though not the only experiment in unification in social studies at the time, these ideas were clearly far ahead of their time, and were later to become central guiding principles for reflective and issues-centered approaches to social studies. Rugg hoped to create a fully integrated social studies curriculum, abolishing the artificial divisions among history, geography, political science, economics, and sociology and thus grouping all of the material under the general rubric of social studies. Though his vision for social studies underwent slight modifications, and his rhetoric shifted somewhat during the 1930s, he basically maintained such an approach to the social studies curriculum throughout his career.

Rugg's definition of "problems" and "issues" was shaped by his world view. He saw social problems as structural in origin, rather than piece-meal, and believed that they were an obstacle to building a just and sustainable society. He was not satisfied with academic abstractions or a view of social issues as addressed through the academic disciplines, but believed that a broad synthesis of knowledge and a critical understanding of the social world was necessary for the proper education of thoughtful and forward-looking citizens.

He contacted former students and asked them to subscribe, sight unseen, to the social science pamphlet series that he and his entourage had developed experimentally at the Lincoln school. The response was overwhelming. By June 1922, he had received orders for 4,000 copies of each (see Appendix). The second edition of the pamphlet series resulted in about 100,000 copies of each unit shipped to schools (Nelson, 1977; Kay, 1969).

The pamphlets were problem-centered and pedagogically advanced: virtually every topic was introduced through a contemporary issue or problem connected to students' lives; open-ended discussion questions were prominently featured in "open forum" and "group discussions"; the pamphlets made frequent use of photos, drawings, and cartoons; and, provocative topics were given full coverage, including potentially contro-versial topics such as the influence of business on government, and the influence of men of property on the development of the U.S. Constitu-tion.

THE RUGG TEXTBOOK SERIES

The Rugg-developed pamphlets were revised and published in textbook form, two texts per grade (seventh, eighth, and ninth) for use in junior high schools, beginning in August 1929, by Ginn and Company. The pub-lication of additional volumes in the series were published every 6 months thereafter. The series became a huge financial success, and represents the zenith of issues-centered social studies materials entre into classrooms in the twentieth century.

During the 1930s, sales of Rugg's textbook series skyrocketed. For the 10-year period from 1929 to 1939, the series sold 1,317,960 copies at approximately $2.00 each, and more than 2,687,000 workbooks. Rugg and his associates had created a unified social studies program and his books attracted worldwide attention and imitation. Through force of will, brilliance, hard work and fortunate timing he had clearly become the leading social studies educator in the United States (Winters, 1967).

The content organization of the Rugg textbooks was centered around guiding principles distilled from the "frontier thinkers" discussed above, including the growth of modern cultures, development of loyalties and attitudes for decision-making, and the synthesis of knowledge from history, the social sciences, and other areas of study relevant to developing a critical understanding of the modern industrial world. The methodology for introducing this content included the dramatic episode, planned recurrence of key concepts, practice in skills of generalizing, and learning by doing.

The six volumes of the junior high school program were "designed to provide a comprehensive introduction to modes of living and insistent problems of the modern world" (Rugg, 1931b, p. vi) with the purpose of "introducing young people to the chief conditions and problems which will confront them as citizens of the world" (p. vi), through a unified course in social studies. Rugg defended his development of a "unified" course by alluding to students' need to "utilize facts, meanings, generalizations, and historical movement" (p. vi) in understanding modern institutions. He also cited the need to tie various factors "closely together in their natural relationships" (p. vi) to help students understand the modern world. In this regard, he asserted that,

> Whenever history is needed to understand the present, history is presented. If geographic relationships are needed to throw light upon contemporary problems, those geographic relationships are incorporated. The same thing has been done with economic and social facts and principles. (Rugg, 1931b, pp. vi, vii)

Though the books contained a great deal of historical narrative, not unlike many other texts, the overarching aim was to make the study of history and the social sciences relevant, interesting, and meaningful to students in service of the ultimate goal of social melioration. In both the pamphlet series and the textbooks, material from history and the social sciences was frequently framed with issues and problems of present concern.

One such example of framing history with contemporary problems or issues can be seen in Rugg's treatment of American government in the pamphlet, *America's March Toward Democracy, Part I*. Rugg began the text by describing "the great strands of our political history," then followed that with a look at problems in political life today which he described as "threads through the political history." Among the problems, each illustrated by a cartoon, were the following: political parties, the history of voting, freedom of speech, public education, growth of the constitution, extension of government services, regulation of business, tariffs, methods of taxation, control of government by business, addition of territory, and world affairs. In each case the problem was briefly introduced by central, hard-hitting, and difficult focus question. For example: "What control does the government have over business? Is this old or new? Is the Government effective in controlling business for the benefit of the masses of the people?" (Rugg, Rugg, & Schweppe, 1923, p. 12).

Another example can be seen in Rugg's introduction to the modern world, *Changing Governments and Changing Cultures* (1933a). Much of the content is a narrative of European and world history from the Middle Ages to the modern era. However, Rugg frames the study of the past with a chapter on the present, and dramatic, world situation entitled, "Storm Centers of the World," in which he describes global areas of conflict illustrating that "the world is still in upheaval" (p. 5). The body of the text then traces political, social, and cultural developments over time with a focus on the struggle for democracy. The volume ends with a chapter titled, "World Conflict Versus World Organization," examining attempts at creating international cooperation and focusing on the League of Nations (Rugg, 1933a, p. 643).

Yet another example can be seen in Rugg's treatment of unemployment in the textbook, *An Introduction to Problems of American Culture* (Rugg, 1931b). In a chapter titled, "Machines, Men and Their Jobs," the focus is on the problem of unemployment, its causes and possible alternative solutions. At one juncture in the narrative Rugg poses the question, "Why should there be unemployment and starvation in the richest country in the world?" (p. 185). The chapter draws on a mix of data from the social sciences in examining this question and key policy alternatives.

Also worthy of note is the fact that the writing in both the pamphlets and the textbook series was appealing and down to earth, a major factor behind their success. For example, the narrative for one text began with an imaginary meeting of the Social Science Club of "George Washington Junior High School of Anystate, U.S.A.," in which members of the club discussed the problems and issues to be taken up in group study (Rugg, 1931b, pp. 3-10). The description is lively and engaging, and undoubtedly helped to spark the interest of many students in the remainder of the text.

The Rugg textbook series for the junior high school was titled *Man and His Changing Society.* Individual titles included: *An Introduction to American Civilization; Changing Civilizations in the Modern World; A History of American Civilization*; and *An Introduction to the Problems of American Culture.* The final volume of the first edition was published in January 1932. Revised editions appeared from 1936-1940.

RUGG'S SOCIAL RECONSTRUCTIONISM

By the early 1930s Rugg had established his credentials as a leading scholar in education. With the social studies program and publication of a number of highly regarded books including, *The Social Studies in the Elementary and Secondary School* (1923), *The Child Centered School* (Rugg & Shumaker, 1928), and *Culture and Education in America* (Rugg, 1931a), his activities during the great depression largely enhanced his reputation. During the early part of the decade, he came to be known, along with his colleague, George S. Counts, as one of the leading advocates of education for social reconstruction in the nation, and was a respected participant in debates over educational and social policy in the Social Frontier and other venues. Social reconstructionists believed that change could be directed and wanted schools, teachers, and the curriculum to play a strong role in the social transformation of American society, thus spearheading an effort to overcome social injustice and the evils of capitalism. In their vision, social studies teachers would play a special role in the vanguard of reform.

Rugg had been a long-term advocate of social reconstructionism through the schools, but influenced by the monthly Teachers College discussion group, and emboldened by the economic cataclysm of the depression, his rhetoric became more strident. During the 1920s Rugg's social thought was influenced in two main directions. He read social criticism, in which he felt the thrust of arguments for social engineering, and, at the same time, investigated the views of those who held that artists and writers should lead the way to social improvement. These strands matured in his thinking in the 1930s and stood behind his work on the textbook series and his books and articles calling for reform. Rugg's vision was of a better society, which he referred to variously as "the great society," "the great technology," and "the great new epoch." The reconstructed society was to be created through a combination of large-scale social and economic planning and a new educational program which would cultivate "integrated" and creative personalities, forming a critical mass of citizens who were oriented to transforming the present industrial system and its problems (Carbone, 1977). Achieving widespread popular consent for democratic social planning could only take place if the public were made more aware of existing social problems and potential reforms, thus the imperative to focus on social problems and issues in schools.

In *The Great Technology*, published in 1933, Rugg called for social engineering in the form of technological experts who would design, or "engineer," the economy in the public interest. Though he did not support all of its tenets, Rugg's thought was heavily influenced by the popular movement for technocracy during the early 1930s. As mentioned previously, the movement for technocracy, a variant on utopian socialism, promoted a vision of a society of shared abundance in which the industrial economy would be run by expert technicians and the suffering and class conflict associated with industrial capitalism would be overcome.

For Rugg, the economic problem was to design and operate a system of production and distribution which would produce the maximum amount of goods needed by the people and that would distribute them in such a way that each person would be given at least the highest minimum standard of living possible (Rugg, 1933b, p. 106). An additional share of abundance would be permitted to those who made excellent contributions through "greater creative ability and initiative," but this would be restricted to only "a low multiple of the minimum" (i.e., a low multiple would presumably be three, four, or five times the minimum).

Rugg's central concern continued to focus on his hope that social education could be used to help in the scientifically designed reconstruction of society for the general benefit of all. He called for a creative program of educational reconstruction facilitated by a "mammoth program of adult education" which would educate a minority to lead reform (Rugg, 1933b, p. 181). Rugg's "axioms" for the economic system postulated an economy of abundance, a shorter work week, redistributing income through progressive taxation, regulation of business and industry, and creation of consent for social reconstruction (Rugg, 1933b, pp. 171-182). He frequently described his vision as a "thousand year march" of democracy toward a "cooperative commonwealth" (Price, 1983, p. 1).

Many of Rugg's critics later cited press reports of his appearance at the 1934 Cleveland meeting of the Progressive Education Association which noted that Rugg had called for a campaign "to organize 14,000,000 persons into a 'pressure group' to force more radical changes in the economic system" (Rudd, Hicks, & Falk, 1941, p. 38). Despite such reported rhetoric, Rugg's social vision was never as radical as his critics portrayed, but placed him somewhere between New Deal liberalism and democratic socialism. Above all, his was a democratic vision (Rugg, 1940, pp. 16-19).

THE GATHERING STORM

Early criticism of the Rugg social studies materials foreshadowed what would transpire during the late 1930s and early 1940s. As mentioned above, Rugg's writings underwent a shift in the early 1930s with a more pointed advocacy of social reconstructionism and the goal of moving toward some form of "collectivism." It was, in part, these writings and subsequent media coverage of his speaking engagements which attracted the attention of self-appointed censors to Rugg's work. His success as an author, combined with his affiliation with unpopular causes, made him a target for criticism. In 1934, Rugg was listed as a "Communist" in Elizabeth Dilling's (1934) *The Red Network*. During 1935 Rugg spoke out against American Legion attempts to censor a classroom magazine, *Scholastic*, because of its perceived liberal bias. For the balance of the decade, in a series of major speeches, Rugg attacked patriotic societies, the Advertising Federation of America, the National Association of Manufacturers, the United States Chamber of Commerce, and the New Deal itself. His comments and outspoken views critical of the American Legion and other groups had the effect of making him the chief target of their attacks.

By 1939, against the backdrop of dictatorship and war, controversies over the Rugg textbooks spread like wildfire, and the American public was treated to a spectacle that received continuing national media coverage. The attacks were generated, early on, in the New York metropolitan area and represented an intense campaign orchestrated by relatively few people. The bulk of the attacks came from a combine of business writers and publicists, retired military of the American Legion, professional journalists, and a few loose cannons. The flames were fanned by extensive coverage in the Hearst press and the controversy spread. Attacks on the Rugg materials began as part of a blanket attack on American writers and texts, with Rugg gradually becoming the chief target.

Bertie C. Forbes, in his own magazine, *Forbes*, attacked the Rugg textbooks in an article titled "Treacherous Teachings" in which he charged Rugg with being against private enterprise and urged boards of education to "cast out" the Rugg books (Forbes, 1939). The Advertising Federation of America, led by Alfred T. Falk, attacked the books for carrying "anti-advertising propaganda." Merwin K. Hart, president of the New York State Economic Council, charged Rugg with "making a subtle sugar-coated effort to convert youth to Communism," and suggesting that capitalism "has been a failure and that socialism should be substituted in its place" (Myers, 1940, p. 17).

Controversies over the books in a number of cities and towns followed a typical pattern: a complaint, followed by the appointment of a committee to investigate, then debate and, frequently, public hearings. In a number of well-publicized cases, Rugg appeared in person to defend the textbook series. The outcome of the controversy varied from place to place. Binghamton, New York, and Englewood, New Jersey, had major controversies covered extensively by local and national media. In a number of cities and towns, including Binghamton, the books were removed. In Bradner, Ohio, the Superintendent ordered the books taken down to the furnace room and burned.

The next round of controversy was generated by two articles which appeared in widely read, nationally circulated magazines. The first of these was an article by Augustin G. Rudd, which was published in the

April 1940, issue of *Nation's Business*, and was titled, "Our 'Reconstructed' Educational System." Rudd posited that the "entire educational system" had been "reconstructed" with textbooks and courses teaching "that our economic and political institutions are decadent" (Rudd, 1940, p. 27). He blamed the widespread teaching of "social science," ... [instead of] ... "history, geography, and U. S. Government," and cited the Rugg textbooks as the major culprit. He argued that Rugg "subtly but surely implied a need for a state-planned economy and socialism" and aimed "to undermine the faith of children in the American way of life" (Rudd, 1940, p. 94).

The second article, by Orlen K. Armstrong, was titled, "Treason in the Textbooks," and appeared in the *American Legion Magazine*, September 1940, and was distributed to one million homes. The article contained a bitter denunciation of the writers and teachers of the "new history," and charged that Rugg sought to "cast doubt" upon the "patriotism" of the founding fathers and the constitution and "to condemn the American system" of private enterprise and inculcate "collectivism" (Armstrong, 1940, pp. 51, 70). Armstrong attacked fused courses like Rugg's and described them as "propaganda for a change in our political, economic, and social order" (Armstrong, 1940, p. 9).

Meanwhile, the entire controversy garnered increasing national attention. According to an article in *Time* magazine, by the end of the spring term in 1940, the Rugg textbooks had been banned from a half-dozen school systems. Critics objected to the Rugg texts, the article reported, "for picturing the U.S. as a land of unequal opportunity, and giving a class-conscious account of the framing of the U.S. Constitution" (*Time* 1940, pp. 64-65).

THE STORM UNLEASHED

The next major development in the Rugg story raised the stakes considerably as it involved the activities of the National Association of Manufacturers (NAM), a mainstream organization with considerable resources. On December 11, 1940, *The New York Times* reported that the NAM announced that it would initiate a survey of textbooks then in use in the schools to see if it could find evidence of subversive teaching. Ralph Robey, an assistant professor of banking at Columbia University, and a columnist for *Newsweek*, was hired by the NAM to prepare a series of abstracts of some 800 then currently used social studies textbooks to show the authors' attitudes toward government and business.

On Saturday, February 22, 1941, a headline at the top of the front page of *The New York Times* read: "UN-AMERICAN TONE SEEN IN TEXT-

BOOKS ON SOCIAL SCIENCES: Survey of 600 Used in Schools, Finds a Distorted Emphasis on Defects of Democracy, ONLY A FEW CALLED RED." The article reported that a "substantial portion" of the social science textbooks used in schools "tend to criticize our form of government and the system of private enterprise" (Fine, 1941, p. 1). The article cited the controversy over the Rugg textbooks and noted that several school systems had banned his books from the classroom (Fine, 1941, pp. 1, 6).

The story, including the reference to the Rugg controversy, appeared on the front page. The abstracts provided selected and provocative quotations from the texts, which raised questions about the functioning of government, the distribution of wealth and incidence of poverty, or the interplay of power and wealth. The quotations were provided without any sense of the remainder of each text, much of which would be found utterly innocuous.

Internal memoranda from the files of the NAM suggest that many in the organization's offices were rather squeamish about the entire enterprise, and feared that it could result in negative publicity for business and the NAM. As it turned out, these worries were well founded.[2] Protests, corrections, and replies to Dr. Robey's findings came quickly. Leaders of the National Council for the Social Studies (NCSS) made immediate contact with leaders of the NAM asking whether it "repudiates or endorses" Robey's statement (Hunt, 1941a). The NAM President, Walter D. Fuller, responded with a press release stating that Robey's criticisms were his "personal opinion only" (Fuller, 1941). Later, after a storm of stories and editorials in the press, the NAM attempted to further distance itself from the controversy and expressed regret that "distorted" impressions of the project had been given such wide currency (Hunt, 1941b, p. 328).

THE AFTERMATH

The defense against the attacks on the Rugg textbooks was mounted on several fronts. The Academic Freedom Committee of NCSS issued a statement supporting academic freedom, and later prepared "a packet of reading matter on freedom of teaching in the social studies area," which included a 66-page booklet on fending off attacks on textbooks (Curti, 1941). The Council of the American Historical Association asked Professor Arthur M. Schlesinger to draft a statement regarding controversial issues in textbooks. The statement, which was approved by the Council, gave strong support for the inclusion of controversial questions in "the historical account," and for encouraging a "spirit of inquiry" in young people (American Historical Association, 1941, p. 488).

Rugg himself was undoubtedly the chief advocate for the defense of social studies, and the Rugg textbooks, against the attackers. Numerous friends and colleagues rushed to his defense. One of the most active groups was the American Committee on Democracy and Intellectual Freedom organized in the late 1930s to address a range of intellectual freedom issues, and chaired by Franz Boaz at Columbia (ACDIF, 1941). Among other groups that furnished support were the Association of Textbook Publishers, and Rugg's associates on the journal *Frontiers of Democracy*. Even John Dewey came to Rugg's defense in an opinion editorial piece which appeared in *The New York Times* (Dewey, 1940). Like several groups and individuals, Dewey defended Rugg on the grounds of intellectual freedom even though he didn't always agree with Rugg's ideas or actions, and clearly did not think of Rugg as a major thinker (Dewey, 1944).

Rugg gave an able defense of his work, and attempted to meet every attack directly, appearing in person whenever possible. Rugg's confrontations with his accusers followed a familiar pattern. First, he would be accused of being a Communist, then he would be criticized over his plan for a socialistic society in The Great Technology. When pressed, critic after critic would admit that they had not read the books. Under siege on every side, Rugg wrote an autobiographical work to tell his side of the story. *That Men May Understand* was published in April 1941, and received generally favorable reviews (Rugg, 1941). *Publishers Weekly* endorsed the book and joined Rugg in attacking his critics, accusing Dilling, Forbes, and Hart of working on "the prejudices of the American people" and calling Rugg's book "a vigorous and adequate reply to his critics" (Publishers Weekly, 1941, p. 1533).

Discussion of the attacks continued in the professional literature. One article, written by a school superintendent, argued that many of the attacks were part of a deliberate effort to undermine "public confidence in the schools so that school appropriations may be reduced" (Dannelly, 1941, p. 32). Another author provided a larger historical context for the attacks and suggested that they were part of a larger "War on Social Studies" (Gould, 1941, pp. 83-91). The real animus of the critics, he wrote, "is against the whole modern conception of the social studies as a realistic approach to life" (Gould, 1941, p. 90). In opposition to the critics, he argued that young people have "the right to know what the world is all about and to learn what can be done about it" (Gould, 1941, p. 91).

As it turned out, February 22, 1941, the date of the Robey story ("UN-AMERICAN TONE SEEN IN TEXTBOOKS ON SOCIAL SCIENCES") in the *New York Times*, was a watershed in the war on social studies. Tension had been building while the movement for integrated social studies and a focus on issues and problems with a meliorist or reconstructionist purpose gathered steam. After the Robey article, however, the tide turned. By 1943 American Legion officers believed they had ousted the textbooks from approximately 1500 communities (Shumaker, 1943). By the middle of the decade, the Rugg textbook series and program had fallen from prominence and had virtually disappeared.

Though he never admitted it publicly or with colleagues, the loss of his textbook series and the leadership and prestige it had given him left Rugg deeply hurt (K. Alling, personal communication with the author, January 21, 2005; R. W. Evers, personal communication with author, June 14, 2003). Rugg continued to teach and write but focused on scholarly work and college level textbooks, giving up his efforts to revolutionize social studies in schools.

In 1951, though, he was at the center of another controversy. Sparked by his reputation as a "radical" and following a speaking engagement at Ohio State University, he became the subject of an in-depth FBI investigation focused on his supposedly socialistic comments in the speech and his many other activities over the years. Though the investigation continued until his death, Rugg was labeled "naive" and "misguided" but he was never added to the security index.[3] Despite the controversies and unfortunate fate which befell him, Rugg continued to maintain his beliefs, and continued to support education for social reconstruction, though his public profile was forever altered and subdued. On May 17, 1960, Rugg died of a heart attack at his home in Woodstock.

CONCLUSION

What can we learn from an account of Harold Rugg's life and work? His story is certainly full of drama, with a cast of heroes and villains and key turning points which capture, in microcosm, many of the basic ideological conflicts in American political and cultural life, as well as conflicting positions in American education and curriculum history.

Largely because of the controversies his work inspired, and because of his creativity in challenging the received wisdom of his age, Harold Rugg was undoubtedly one of the most influential social studies educators of the 20th century. His name is a touchstone to both advocates of issues-centered social studies and to those who support teaching for social justice. His social vision and conceptualization of the social studies field were both fresh and forward looking, built on the best works of the "frontier thinkers," the leading scholars of his time. His pamphlets and textbooks series were avant-garde, pedagogically innovative and far ahead of their time. His leadership as a social reconstructionist during the 1930s was equally innovative and courageous. He was a legendary warrior for social justice and for a modern approach to education and to life. His legacy is all the more powerful because of the criticism he endured during and after the textbook crisis. To many cultural fundamentalists and conservatives, he represents everything that was wrong with Progressive Education. To his supporters, he remains a larger-than-life figure, a tireless advocate, and a continuing source of inspiration.

A number of additional implications might be drawn from Rugg's life and the controversies he inspired. First, and perhaps most important, Rugg's example illustrates the importance, and the potential impact, of dreaming big and bold visions of reform, not only as a well-spring for inspiration, but as a source of ideas for practical action, praxis, with the aim of social improvement. Rugg had a worthy vision that was pedagogically advanced, and forward looking. It seriously questioned capitalism, its apparatus and influences. Moreover, Rugg's basic critique is largely still relevant in that a renewed questioning of capitalism and of the mainstream institutions in American life is still needed.

Second, though his textbooks and ideas were sure to inspire some criticism, Harold Rugg did not deserve his fate. Harold Rugg was a seminal thinker who fully deserved to receive the recognition and financial fortune that sometimes accompany a brilliant idea combined with hard work. The controversy that engulfed Rugg, and the defense offered by Rugg and those who rose to support him, suggests that some dreams are worth fighting for, even though the struggle may take its toll.

In the present era, it is especially important to keep alternative visions alive, to nurture deep dreams of justice and fair play, and to make sure that critics of a liberal or issues-centered social studies are met with a stout defense. The attacks on Rugg, and especially the sustained campaign carried on by the American Legion, present early examples of the power of interest group financing and organization. Recently, the revival of the teaching of traditional history, supported by similar forms of interest group financing, has had a significant influence on the direction of the social studies curriculum (Evans, 2004; Selden, 2004; Stehle, 1997).

Third, Rugg did make a few mistakes. Education for social justice can take many forms. There was some justification for the charge that Rugg presented more evidence in his textbooks and school materials on the side of the questions which he supported. So, it seems, in order to survive in schools, we must learn to include a balance of materials, sources, and interpretations, and challenge students to make up their own minds about the meaning of past and present institutions and societal dilemmas. Though this may not silence all critics, it is more easily defensible as part of the "American way," and as a clear example of John Dewey's method of intelligence applied to the social studies arena.

Given the interest among social studies professors in critical and social justice approaches to education, the continuing national support for standards, centralized curriculum making, and high-stakes testing, and the present climate of national and international crisis, it behooves us to be aware of, or be defeated by, the successes, the failures, and the mistakes—the "lessons"—of Harold Rugg.

APPENDIX

The second published edition of the *Social Science Pamphlets*, revised from 1923 through 1926, and influenced by the ongoing studies of the Rugg research team, included the following topics in this sequence:

Seventh Grade Pamphlets

Town and City Life in America
Resources, Industries, and Cities of America
Industries and Trade Which Bind Nations Together; Part I, The Great Industrial Nations
Industries and Trade Which Bind Nations Together; Part II, The Changing Agricultural Nations

Eighth Grade Pamphlets

The Westward Movement and the Growth of Transportation
The Mechanical Conquest of America
America's March Toward Democracy, Part I
America's March Toward Democracy, Part II

Ninth Grade Pamphlets

America and Her Immigrants
Problems of American Industry and Business
Problems of American Government
How Nations Live Together

NOTES

1. This manuscript is drawn from a book-length draft manuscript by R. W. Evans (in process), *This Happened in America: Harold Rugg and the Censure of Social Studies*, and from materials included in R. W. Evans (2004), *The Social Studies Wars: What Should We Teach the Children?* (New York: Teachers College Press). Portions of the chapter were previously published in somewhat different form in Evans (2006), "Social Studies vs. the United States of America: Harold Rugg and Teaching for Social Justice," in K. L. Riley (Ed.), *The Social Reconstructionists: People, Politics, Perspectives* (pp. 45-68, Greenwich, CT: Information Age).

2. See especially, C. E. Harrison, inter-office memo., to W. B. Weisenburger, July, 25, 1940; C. E. Harrison to H. W. Prentis, January, 10, 1941, and attached inter-office memo., C. E. Harrison to W. B. Weisenburger, January, 10, 1941; C. E. Harrison to H. W. Prentis, March, 19, 1941, all contained in Robey Textbook Survey folder, National Industrial Information Committee, Subject Files, box 847, series 111, National Association of Manufacturers Papers, Hagley Museum and Library, Wilmington, Delaware.

3. See especially, Campus Probe in Order, Columbus Dispatch, July, 23, 1951, Rugg folder, box 69, faculty files, Public Relations Office, Archives, Milbank Memorial Library, Teachers College, Columbia University; Ohio State Trustees Assail Rugg Speech, New York Times, September, 5, 1951, p. 29; Rugg FBI Memorandum. Office Memorandum, SAC, Cincinnati, to Director, FBI (J. Edgar Hoover), October, 1, 1951, Rugg FBI files, obtained from Federal Bureau of Investigation under Freedom of Information Act in 2003, Washington, DC, material unclassified, November 6, 2003; Murry R. Nelson and H. Wells Singleton, FBI surveillance of three progressive educators: Curricular aspects, Paper presented at the Society for the Study of Curriculum History, Annual Conference, 1977.

REFERENCES

ACDIF Press Release. (1941). A Committee of Ten Outstanding Social Scientists. Sunday, February 23, American Committee for Democracy and Intellectual Freedom, New York, Franz Boas Professional Papers, B61p, sub collection 2, box A-Bend, ACDIF folder, American Philosophical Society, Philadelphia.

American Historical Association. (1941). Freedom of Textbooks. *Social Education, 5*(7), 487-488.

Armstrong, O. K. (1940, September). Treason in the textbooks. *American Legion Magazine*, pp. 8-9, 51, 70-72.

Ayers, W., Hunt, J. A., & Quinn, T. (Eds.). (1998). *Teaching for social justice: A democracy and education reader.* New York: The New Press, Teachers College Press. Distributed by W. W. Norton.

Carbone, P. F., Jr. (1977). *The social and educational thought of Harold Rugg.* Durham, NC: Duke University Press.

Curti, M. (1941). Merle Curti to Wilbur Murra, 14 October 1941, file 1, box 2, series 7, Committee Records, Academic Freedom Correspondence, NCSS Archives, Milbank Memorial Library, Teachers College, Columbia University.

Dannelly, C. M. (1941). Facing a major threat. *The School Executive, 60*(10), 32.

Dewey, J. (1940, May 6). Investigating education. *The New York Times*, 16.

Dewey, J. (1944). John Dewey to Sidney Hook, 25 April 1944, Correspondence with Sidney Hook, John Dewey Collection, box 10, series 1, Dewey Papers, Dewey Center, University of Southern Illinois at Carbondale.

Dilling, E. (1934). *The red network: A who's who of radicalism for patriots*. Kenilworth, IL: Author.

Evans, R. W. (2004). *The social studies wars: What should we teach the children?* New York: Teachers College Press.

Fine, B. (1941, February 22). Un-American tone seen in textbooks on social sciences. *The New York Times*, (Late City Edition) 1, 6.

Forbes, B. C. (1939, August 15). Treacherous teachings. *Forbes*, p. 8.

Fuller, W. D. (1941). Walter D. Fuller telegram to Wilbur Murra, 24 February 1941, file 1, box 2, series 7, Committee Records, Academic Freedom Committee Correspondence, NCSS Archives, Milbank Memorial Library, Teachers College, Columbia University.

Gould, K. M. (1941, Autum). The war on social studies. *Common Ground*, 83-91.

Hunt, E. M. (1941a). Dr. Robey versus the NAM? *Social Education, 5*(4), 288-292.

Hunt, E. M. (1941b). The NAM restates its policy. *Social Education, 5*(5), 328.

Kay, G. A. (1969). *Harold Rugg: Social reconstructionist and educational statesman*. Unpublished doctoral dissertation, State University of New York, Buffalo.

Myers, A. F. (1940). The attacks on the Rugg books. *Frontiers of Democracy, 7*(55), 17-21.

Nelson, M. R. (1977). The dvelopment of the Rugg social studies materials. *Theory and Research in Social Education, 5*(1), 64-83.

Price, M. E. (1983, November 20). *A thousand year march: The historical vision of Harold Rugg*. Paper presented at the annual meeting of the National Council for the Social Studies, San Francisco.

Publishers' Weekly. (1941, April 12). Editorial: Rugg serves freedom of education. *Publishers Weekly, 139*, 1533.

Rudd, A. G. (1940, April). Our "reconstructed" educational system. *Nation's Business*, 27-28, 93-94.

Rudd, A. G., Hicks, H., & Falk, A. T. (Eds.). (1941). *Undermining our republic: Do you know what the children are being taught in our public schools? You'll be surprised*. New York: Guardians of American Education, Inc.

Rugg, H. O. (1921a). How shall we reconstruct the social studies curriculum? An open letter to Professor Henry Johnson commenting on committee procedure as illustrated by the Report of the Joint Committee on History and Education for Citizenship. *Historical Outlook, 7*(5),184-189.

Rugg, H. O. (1921b). On reconstructing the social studies: Comments on Mr. Schafer's letter. *Historical Outlook, 12*(7), 249-252.

Rugg, H. O. (Ed.). (1923). *Social studies in the elementary and secondary school*. Twenty Second Yearbook, National Society for the Study of Education, Part II. Bloomington, IL: Public School Publishing Co.

Rugg, H. O. (1931a). Culture and education in America. New York: Harcourt Brace.

Rugg, H. O. (1931b). *An introduction to problems of American culture*. Boston: Ginn.

Rugg, H. O. (1933a). *Changing governments and changing cultures*. Boston: Ginn.

Rugg, H. O. (1933b). *The great technology: Social chaos and the public mind*. New York: John Day.

Rugg, H. O. (1940). Confidential analysis of the current (1939-1940) attacks on the Rugg Social Science Series. Prepared by Harold Rugg in May-June 1940, Harold Rugg folder, box 58, William F. Russell Papers, Milbank Memorial Library, Teachers College, Columbia University.

Rugg, H. O. (1941). *That men may understand: An American in the long armistice*. New York: Doubleday, Doran.

Rugg, H. O., Rugg, E. U., & Schweppe, E. (1923). *The social science pamphlets*. New York: The Lincoln School of Teachers College.

Rugg, H. O., & Shumaker, A. (1928). *The child-centered school: An appraisal of the new education*. New York: World Book.

Selden, S. (2004, April). *The Neo-conservative assault on the undergraduate curriculum*. Paper presented at the annual meeting of the American Educational Research Association, San Diego, CA.

Shumaker, R. W. (1943). R. Worth Shumaker to John E. Thomas, August 4, 1943, Legion dead-letter files. Cited in Jones, O. E. (1959). Activities of the American Legion in textbook analysis and Criticism. Unpublished doctoral dissertation, University of Oklahoma, Norman, p. 82.

Stehle, V. (1997, June 30). Righting philanthropy. *The Nation*, 15-20.

Time Magazine. (1940, September 9). Book burnings. *Time*, 64-65.

Winters, E. A. (1967). Man and his changing society: The textbooks of Harold Rugg. *History of Education Quarterly*, 7(4), 509-510.

Winters, E. A. (1968). *Harold Rugg and education for social reconstruction*. Unpublished doctoral dissertation, University of Wisconsin, Madison.

CHAPTER 4

H. GORDON HULLFISH

Teacher, Reflective Thinker, Democratic Defender

Mary Lee Webeck, Susan Robertson, and Sherry L. Field

INTRODUCTION

In the year before his death, H. Gordon Hullfish, along with Philip G. Smith, published *Reflective Thinking: The Method of Education* (1961), a culmination of four decades of academic thought and work. In the preface, Hullfish outlined the purpose of the book, and in doing so, presented the philosophical views that guided his 40-year career as an influential teacher committed to social reform. As a professor, author, editor, and speaker, Hullfish always viewed himself as a teacher first. In his final book, he reiterated his belief that teachers belong at the center of reform movements, calling upon them to "move progressively" and stating that "it is the teacher who is, in the final analysis, the critical factor in advancing educational reconstruction" (Hullfish & Smith, 1961, p. ix). In the conclusion of *Reflective Thinking*, Hullfish summarized the educational philosophy that guided his career and life:

Addressing Social Issues in the Classroom and Beyond: The Pedagogical Efforts of Pioneers in the Field, 71–80
Copyright © 2007 by Information Age Publishing
All rights of reproduction in any form reserved.

71

The individual does not gain his freedom by first submitting himself to ideas others claim to be true. He gains it, when he does, by enlisting in the common effort to create social instruments that facilitate the sharing of a reflective approach to the problems all confront. It is this fact which provides the base for the professional growth of educators. It is this fact which creates the imperative that educators use what is known about the nature of thinking and learning to advance the thinking capacity of students and, in ways that are professionally proper, to advance respect for thought within the culture. It creates an imperative because it joins the best we know about learning with the best we know about man's relationship to man. (Hullfish & Smith, 1961, p. 265)

EARLY YEARS

H. Gordon Hullfish was born in 1894 and raised in Washington, DC by a mother who worked as a nurse to support three children. According to Arthur Wirth (1996), a former university student of Hullfish, Hullfish's boyhood home was located on the site of the present Supreme Court building and he spent his early years working both as a newspaper boy in Washington, DC and as a messenger at the U.S. Treasury.

As a young student, Hullfish was frequently in trouble at school. According to Wirth (1996), "The dull, restrictive quality of the traditional schools repelled him from the beginning. The content of studies and the sterile preoccupations of his teachers had a remoteness from live ideas and the texture of real life that made his school experience a graphic example of the waste in education that Dewey portrayed in *The Child and the Curriculum* and *The School and Society*" (p. 82).

Hullfish did not graduate from high school, but was able to attend the University of Illinois on the recommendation of a Washington lawyer who believed in his abilities. After earning an AB in journalism in 1921, Hullfish began his studies and his career at The Ohio State University, earning an MA and a PhD in educational philosophy in 1922 and 1924, respectively. While completing his graduate studies, Hullfish also became a teaching assistant at The Ohio State University in 1922 and remained at the university for four decades, serving as a professor of educational philosophy until his death in 1962. The university honored him with the Alumni Award for Distinguished Teaching for the academic year 1959-1960, an honor bestowed annually upon five faculty members for superior teaching. As a recipient of the award, Hullfish was also inducted into the university's Academy of Teaching, which provides leadership for efforts to continually improve teaching at The Ohio State University.

It was during his college years that Hullfish first encountered Dr. Boyd H. Bode, a professor of educational philosophy who would profoundly influence his beliefs and work for the remainder of his life. Bode taught first at the University of Illinois and later at The Ohio State University, mentoring Hullfish at each institution. He later welcomed Hullfish as a professional colleague at Ohio State, where the two taught together for more than two decades. According to Kridel, Bullough, and Shaker (1996): "For Bode, democracy was a 'way of life,' an expression of his faith in the common person's ability to make reasonable judgments when properly informed, to live intelligently, and to look beyond narrow self-interest in order to establish a wider community of interest for the good of all" (p. 56).

In Bode, "Hullfish found a teacher who made the class a place that was alive with ideas" (Wirth, 1996, p. 83). Hullfish's course with Bode during his junior year in college marked Hullfish's first formal study of philosophy, a field of study to which he committed his professional life. Bode's belief in democracy as a way of life and the role of education to develop democracy as an intellectual basis for the organization of life inspired Hullfish to realize new possibilities as an educator. Under the tutelage of Bode, Hullfish also developed a deep belief in American pragmatism, stating that it "denied the dualism of mind and body" (Hullfish, 1944, p. 7) that he believed was present in the behaviorism of psychology. Bode's ideas continued to influence Hullfish until the end of his life. In his final book, *Reflective Thinking*, Hullfish cited Bode, applying his definitions of meaning and thinking to the practice and promotion of reflective thinking.

In May 1944, Hullfish presented a paper at the Conference on Democracy and Education, held in honor of Dr. Bode upon his retirement from Ohio State. Describing his years working alongside Bode from 1921 through 1944, Hullfish stated: "Those who have known Professor Bode within this period of time—as colleagues, in the classroom, on the lecture platform, or through the written word—realize how extensive has been his influence in stimulating those whose task it is to teach to do so with a higher degree of reflection and with more faith in the ability of the average man to achieve the insight necessary to democratic living" (Hullfish, 1944, p. 3).

The second major influence in Hullfish's life was the work of John Dewey. Undoubtedly, Hullfish's mentor, Dr. Bode, was profoundly influenced by Dewey's pragmatism and his concept of democracy as a form of living that sought meaning in experience. Hullfish incorporated these ideas into his own teaching, asking his students to "develop a vision of the classroom that would be appropriate for the children of a free society" (Wirth, 1996, p. 84). With a Deweyan approach, he encouraged his students to create classrooms for a free and democratic people that would allow students to try out differing ideas and to learn to think independently. The evidence of Dewey's influence on Hullfish can be found throughout his many publications. For example, in *Reflective Thinking*, Dewey is cited 15 times. In *Education in an Age of Anxiety* (1953a), published during the era of the Red Scare, Hullfish quotes Dewey at length in arguing the need for democracy and freedom in education:

> If there is one conclusion to which human experience unmistakably points, it is that democratic ends demand democratic methods for their realization. Authoritarian methods now offer themselves to us in new guises. They come to us claiming to serve the ultimate ends of freedom and equity in a classless society. Or they recommend adoption of a totalitarian regime in order to fight totalitarianism. In whatever form they offer themselves, they owe their seductive power to their claim to serve ideal ends. Our first defense is to realize that democracy can be served only by the slow day to day adoption and contagious diffusion in every phase of our common life of methods that are identical with the ends to be reached and that recourse to monistic, wholesale, absolutist procedures is a betrayal of human freedom no matter in what guise it presents itself. (Hullfish, 1953a, p. 215)

PHILOSOPHICAL AND PEDAGOGICAL BELIEFS

The influences of Bode and Dewey were present in Hullfish's 1924 dissertation, *Aspects of Thorndike's Psychology in Their Relation to Education Theory and Practice*. His dissertation, which was later published as a book by Ohio State University Press in 1926, critiqued Thorndike's psychological concepts and theories as "an inappropriate model to follow for democratic education" that "ignores the role of meaning-seeking" (Wirth, 1996, p. 89). Following its publication, Hullfish publicly entered the debate between the conflicting educational theories of Edward Thorndike and John Dewey.

Dewey saw democracy as the guiding force in education and believed schools should be "transformed into communities built on action and freedom of thought" (Lagemann, 2000, p. 51). Dewey also emphasized the social aspect of schooling and argued that education should nurture new social capacities and skills. Thorndike, in contrast, became known as the "father of the measurement movement" following the publication of *An Introduction to the Theory of Mental and Social Measurements* in 1904 (Lagemann, 2000, pp. 56-57). Ignoring the social aspects of schooling which Dewey highlighted, Thorndike's psychological concepts instead emphasized inherited traits and characteristics that he believed determined one's ability to learn. According to Lagemann (2000), Thorndike's use of numerical measurements and his statistical approach to psychology "was narrowly behaviorist. Eliminating all considerations of consciousness, it reduced human actions to little more than responses to stimuli" (p. 62).

Hullfish's 1924 dissertation took a stance similar to Dewey's and laid the groundwork for his future work in educational theory. According to Wirth (1996), Hullfish argued: "The basic problem was Thorndike's insistence that all learning was analytic and ultimately is determined by elements in the environment; it leads teachers and students to the mechanistic assumption that the only learning that counts is learning that can be counted" (p. 89).

Throughout the changing educational climate and the culture wars of the following decades, Hullfish remained faithful to his earliest philosophical beliefs. He was, first and foremost, a teacher, and the democratic education of his university students remained his highest priority. Wirth (1996) recalled that Hullfish spent countless hours responding to his students' written work and mentoring future teachers, even perhaps at the expense of his own writing and publications. When asked by a colleague why he put so much time into these student-centered efforts, he replied simply, "I am a teacher" (Wirth, 1996, p. 87). Like his mentor Bode, Hullfish also believed being a university professor carried with it profound social obligations and a commitment to social reform.

Throughout the decades, Hullfish also championed the need for a philosophy of education. He strongly disagreed with Thorndike that there should be a separation of philosophy and psychology. Hullfish believed in the need for both studies, and when educational psychologists dismissed the need for philosophy, Hullfish argued that "a theory of the mind is indispensable to a theory of education" (Hullfish, 1944, p. 6). He joined the Philosophy of Education Society and served as its president from 1948-1949. In his 1944 address "Philosophy and Education in Interaction," to honor his mentor Dr. Bode, Hullfish described the need for philosophy in education:

> Philosophy is not charged with the mission of uncovering final things. Its work is humbler work. It has the mission of helping men think more deeply about the consequences of their daily acts in order that they may with greater wisdom choose those consequences which help all men extend the depth of their thinking. Philosophy, thus conceived, has the purpose of helping men tackle the problems which confront them with an increased ability to solve them reflectively. Its work, therefore, is never done. (p. 13)

THE 1930s, 1940s, AND 1950s

The 1930s Depression era proved to be a divisive period for the progressive education movement. The economic conditions of America led some in the progressive movement to favor a form of socialism, while others remained loyal to capitalism. The economic and political discussions of the decade overshadowed the progressive movement's original intent to eliminate the factory-model of schools and create a new, democratic system that met the needs of all students. During the politically divisive debates, Hullfish took the stance that teachers must remain free of indoctrination in order to focus on teaching the skills necessary for critical inquiry. Throughout this period, he remained faithful to the now-weakened progressive movement and retained membership in both the Progressive Education Association and the John Dewey Society.

As a member of the John Dewey Society, Hullfish published and spoke about the critical events of the 1940s and 1950s, including World War II, the atomic era, and the Red Scare. He viewed the Red Scare of the 1950s as a profound threat to democratic education and crusaded for freedom in education. In 1950, he published a chapter in the *Tenth Yearbook of the John Dewey Society: Democracy in the Administration of Higher Education*. The chapter, entitled "The Nature and Function of Democratic Administration," outlined Hullfish's "Principles of Democratic Administration": the principle of free intelligence, the principle of participation, the principle of individuality, and the principle of cooperation. Hullfish stated that in the function of democratic administration, these principles "are critical, in the sense that to neglect them is to neglect an opportunity to foster the democratic aspiration itself" (Hullfish, 1950, p. 53).

In 1953 he published *Keeping our Schools Free*, a public affairs pamphlet that addressed the suspicious climate of the era and its impact on educational institutions. Hullfish described the times as an era in which "the world is settling into two camps, two armed camps" (p. 6). The result of this phenomenon, according to Hullfish, was a breakdown in communication and a black-or-white approach to problem solving. Teachers became targets of scrutiny and censure, and "loyalty oaths" became a common condition of employment. The intent, argued Hullfish, was the restriction of teachers—a restriction of materials, ideas, teaching methods, and activities. As educators fell increasingly under investigation and became targets of congressional committees, Hullfish (1950) publicly laid out five "Basic Principles for the Protection of Teachers":

- No teacher or staff member should be suspended simply because he is subpoenaed by a committee;
- Each institution, within the limits of its faculty specialization, or in cooperation with its alumni and friends, should provide the individual with the opportunity to gain a fair view of his legal status when he is before a committee;

- No teacher or staff member should be summarily dismissed, or suspended, because of what he says before a committee or because of his refusal to say anything;
- In each institution, once a problem arises as a result of one of its faculty or staff members being called before a legislative committee, a committee of the faculty should conduct an investigation, if an investigation appears to be warranted; and
- Each institution, where legally possible, should reserve to itself the right to decide what manner of person it will employ, the conditions under which this will be done, and the conditions under which a severance of relations will take place.

In 1951, the College of Education at The Ohio State University also came under fire in the politically charged environment. The university's Board of Trustees interfered when the college invited Harold Rugg to give The Boyd Bode Lecture, calling the guest speaker "un-American." Rugg, a professor from Teachers College, Columbia University, and an outspoken social reconstructionist, had authored one of the most progressive social studies textbooks of the 1930s. The textbook series was being read by more than half of all American social studies students when it was condemned in 1938 by the American Legion, the Advertising Federation of America, the National Association of Manufacturers, and others as anticapitalist and promoting Marxism. When Rugg was invited to speak at Ohio State more than a decade later, the Board of Trustees called his textbook series "propaganda" and moved to screen all outside speakers. Hullfish and his fellow Executive Board Members of the John Dewey Society asked the *New York Times* to investigate, which resulted in the university's Board of Trustees retreating from its earlier position. The incident brought nationwide attention to the issue of academic freedom, with Hullfish playing a prominent role in the discussion.

In 1953, commissioned by the John Dewey Society, Hullfish edited *Educational Freedom in an Age of Anxiety* to further address the climate of fear and attacks on academic freedom in America. In this pivotal work, Hullfish described the "mounting anxiety" (1953a, p. 211) that was leading to the denial of freedom for teachers and schools. As in his earlier writings, Hullfish again addressed the banning of books and the loyalty oaths required of teachers, describing schools as becoming places that reflect the hysteria prevalent in society at that time. Hullfish argued that educational institutions must remain free if the society at large is to remain free. By restricting this freedom, Hullfish argued that schools would be stripped of the ability to prepare students to participate in a free world. In explaining the need for freedom and open inquiry in the classroom during this politically charged era, Hullfish stated:

> The classroom is not a place to push partisan or doctrinal ideas. But it is a place where ideas may be examined. There is a group of critics who don't like certain ideas that have given shape to recent developments in American life, ideas that bear upon the welfare of man in terms they reject. These ideas are variously called "new or fair dealish," "radical," "fascist," "socialistic," "leftist," "pinkish," and when some are intemperate in statement, "communistic." It is inevitable, if ideas are to appear in our classrooms at all, that these ideas shall be discussed by teachers and students, as it is inevitable that they will be discussed in books that students use. If we assume that a great many people will entertain honest differences on matters of basic social and economic concerns, then we must anticipate that these differences will be proper objects of study in the classrooms of this country. (Hullfish, 1953b, p. 4)

Sadly for Hullfish, the 1950s was also a period in which the prominence of the progressive education movement continued to decline. The political climate of the decade simply no longer supported progressive causes. While Hullfish served as president of the Progressive Education Association from 1951 to 1955, he was forced to disband the association in 1955 due to declining membership. In 1957, Hullfish also presided over the discontinuance of the journal *Progressive Education*. He did, however, remain a member of the advisory board of *Education Digest* until 1960.

In 1961, a year before his death, Hullfish coauthored *Reflective Thinking: The Method of Education*. The book presents the coauthors' philosophy of education and addresses the "paramount responsibility" of teachers to develop citizens who are able to think independently and reflectively. The book first addresses the problem of thinking as "the critical educational issue" and then analyzes the process of thought and presents types of intellectual activities that develop reflective thinking. The book also examines the tools of thinking and learning and presents "a theory of learning for teachers" (p. 169). The final section of the book provides suggestions for teachers, administrators, and supervisors for strengthening reflective thinking practices in the classroom and school community. It was this final section of the book, in which Hullfish provided thoughtful recommendations for educators, that his former student Arthur Wirth (1996) said "got to the heart of what he was about as a teacher" (p. 92).

Hullfish and Smith (1961) cited Dewey in describing reflective thinking as an "active, persistent, and careful consideration of any belief or supposed form of knowledge in the light of the grounds that support it and the further conclusions to which it tends" (p. 44). By adopting a reflective approach, Hullfish contended that the individual can better address the problems they confront and in doing so, gain his or her freedom. The preface of *Reflective Thinking* states that the book was written specifically to help classroom teachers and others who care about schools. The intent of the book was first to help teachers recognize that reflective thinking is a method of learning; second, to teach the techniques which make reflective thinking possible; and third, to promote the belief that the act of inquiry is necessary and precious for those who wish to attain freedom (p. vii). The intent, as presented by Hullfish, also clearly champions the cause of democratic education, an ideal to which he devoted his 40-year career.

HULLFISH'S LEGACY

Following his death in 1962, Hullfish's ideas continued to inspire the next generation of educational philosophers and social studies practitioners. In 1968, Maurice Hunt and Lawrence Metcalf cited Hullfish and Smith seven times in their highly respected and widely used work, *Teaching High School Social Studies*. The second section of the book, "Method and the Social Studies," draws frequently upon Hullfish and Smith's ideas as presented in *Reflective Thinking*. Most notably, Hunt and Metcalf emphasized problem solving and value conflict as aspects of reflective thinking. They discussed the need for teachers to recognize that individual differences exist within any classroom and that any problem confronted by a student "is always a personal affair" (Hullfish & Smith, 1961, p. 107). Hullfish and Smith's beliefs about the role of the teacher also influenced Hunt and Metcalf, as evidenced in the following excerpt: "A teacher of thinking will not accept every answer as right. Neither will he dismiss a wrong answer peremptorily, and thus fail to capitalize on its learning value. It is a teacher's treatment of an answer, whether it be right or wrong that determines whether a student engages in reflection" (Hunt & Metcalf, 1968, p. 70).

Hullfish's lifelong commitment to the teaching profession and his persistent dedication to the ideals of democratic education are likely his greatest personal and professional contributions to the field of education. Like his mentors Bode and Dewey, Hullfish dedicated himself to the belief that schools are the basis of democracy and social reform. At times when our society stood at a crossroads, Hullfish championed free schools and freedom for teachers as necessary to maintain a free society. He steadfastly maintained that the role of the teacher was not to indoctrinate or to protect the culture from change. Rather, the role of the teacher was to promote and develop acts of inquiry and reflective thinking to prepare individuals for a free world. Hullfish's profound belief in democracy, freedom, and the promise of human inquiry, can best be summarized in a passage from his final book:

The democratic culture is nurtured by the aspiration that all individuals shall have the opportunity to progress steadily toward increased measures of freedom. It must keep itself under constant scrutiny. It can never afford to become careless on this score; nor dare it become callous. Where men aspire to freedom they are obligated to create the conditions from which there may emerge a continuing stream of citizens who understand its meaning. Habit-ridden individuals will not do. Nor will fearful individuals. The case rests with individuals who have gained the ability to think—however awesome the problem—and who, equally, have gained the courage to deal with ideas—however strange they may seem. (Hullfish & Smith, 1961, p. 15)

REFERENCES

Hullfish, H. G. (1944). *Philosophy and education in interaction*. Conference on Democracy and Education. Columbus: Ohio State University.

Hullfish, H. G. (1950). The nature and function of democratic administration. In H. Benjamin (Ed.), *Democracy in the administration of higher education* (pp. 48-62). New York: Harper & Brothers.

Hullfish, H. G. (Ed). (1953a). *Educational freedom in an age of anxiety: Twelfth yearbook of the John Dewey Society*. New York: Harper & Brothers.

Hullfish, H. G. (1953b). *Keeping our schools free: Public affairs pamphlet No. 199*. New York: The Public Affairs Committee.

Hullfish, H. G., & Smith, P. G. (1961). *Reflective thinking: The method of education*. New York: Dodd, Mead.

Hunt, M. P., & Metcalf, L. E. (1968). *Teaching high school social studies* (2nd ed.). New York: Harper & Row.

Kridel, C., Bullough, R. V., Jr., & Shaker, P. (Eds.). (1996). *Teachers and mentors: Profiles of distinguished twentieth-century professors of education*. New York: Garland.

Lagemann, E. C. (2000). *An elusive science: The troubling history of educational research*. Chicago: The University of Chicago Press.

Oliver, D. W., & Shaver, J. P. (1966). *Teaching public issues in the high school*. Boston: Houghton Mifflin.

Wirth, A. (1996). H. Gordon Hullfish: Teaching from the fire inside. In C. Kridel, R. V. Bullough, Jr., & P. Shaker (Eds.), *Teachers and mentors: Profiles of distinguished twentieth-century professors of education* (pp. 81-94). New York: Garland.

CHAPTER 5

JESSE H. NEWLON AND EDUCATION FOR DEMOCRATIC CITIZENSHIP

Alan W. Garrett

INTRODUCTION

Jesse H. Newlon was a successful teacher, noted public school administrator, prominent Teachers College faculty member, and, especially during the 1930s, a clarion voice for a progressive education that would imbue students with the democratic values to address intelligently the nation's many social problems. Born in 1882, the eldest of eight children, Newlon's long-standing liberal views and progressive outlook likely were derived from his parents, who were involved members of their community (Stephens, 1967).

According to his lifelong friend and distant relative Walter G. Mead (1968), Newlon began his teaching career in New Albany, Indiana, before moving to Decatur, Illinois, where he served as teacher, coach, and principal. His success led him to a 1-year principalship in Lincoln, Nebraska, after which he assumed the superintendency there. Newlon left Lincoln to become superintendent of schools in Denver, Colorado, where he

Addressing Social Issues in the Classroom and Beyond: The Pedagogical Efforts
of Pioneers in the Field, 81–97
Copyright © 2007 by Information Age Publishing
All rights of reproduction in any form reserved.

achieved national prominence largely as a result of his well-known curriculum revision project. At Denver, he "blended administrative progressivism with clear pedagogical views on the pivotal role of the teacher in instructional and curricular decision making and the importance of having flexible, activity-centered schools that linked daily life to what students learned" (Cuban, 1984, p. 70). The visibility Newlon achieved at Denver led to his appointment as a Teachers College faculty member.

At Teachers College, Newlon gravitated to other liberal educators including John Childs, George S. Counts, L. Thomas Hopkins, Harold Rugg, and William Heard Kilpatrick and became closely allied with them throughout the 1930s. He was a prominent participant in the social reconstructionism movement (Beineke, 1998; Tyack, Lowe, & Hansot, 1984), which attracted a group of prominent and vocal educators during the 1930s. The severe and seemingly endless effects of the Great Depression led the social reconstructionists to believe "that the schools had to address ongoing social and economic problems by raising up a new generation critically attuned to the defects of the social system and prepared to do something about it" (Kliebard, 2004, p. 152).

Newlon was an original member of the Kilpatrick Discussion Group, an informal assemblage of Teachers College faculty members of varying educational outlooks that met regularly to consider topics in education of mutual interest founded in 1928 (Beineke, 1998). He was also an integral participant in the formation of the John Dewey Society, originally organized during the 1930s to explore ways in which schools might assist the nation in recovering from the Great Depression (Beineke, 1998; Tanner, 1991).

In 1933, Newlon contributed to the 1933 pamphlet "A Call to the Teachers of the Nation" that has been described as "the most radical educational document of this period" (Bowers, 1967, p. 464). "A Call" urged teachers to take a public stand and become active, especially through their classroom work and in their communities, in addressing the issues the nations faced during the Great Depression. Bowers described the document as written "in shrill language that often rivaled that used by the communists." The Progressive Education Association (PEA), original sponsor of the tract, disavowed it as a statement of the organization's positions or policies.

Ultimately, Newlon's participation with social reconstructionists, a group believed by many conservatives to offer dangerous, left-wing prescriptions for educational and social change, led to his investigation by the F.B.I. (Beineke, 1998). No government action beyond investigation appears to have occurred.

SCHOOLING IN A DEMOCRATIC SOCIETY

The perception clearly exhibited in the popular press of Jesse Newlon was that of an established public school leader turned radical mouthpiece for dangerous policies not in keeping with the American tradition is overtly simplistic and overlooks the consistency of his thought and his unwavering belief in the role schools should play in enhancing society and creating a better nation for all citizens of the United States (Garrett, 2005). In one of the earliest of documents written by him—and well before he reached national prominence—Newlon contended that "the responsibility of the nation is the responsibility of the schools," and "our system of education must lay the foundation for the future policy of the nation" (Newlon, 1917, p. 5). Eighteen years later, and at the peak of his career, he observed at a meeting of the National Education Association:

> The primary task of the school is to give the individual a realistic understanding of society, and its problems, to examine critically and to test by the democratic ideal the various proposals that are being brought forward for economic and social reconstruction. Education should be deliberately employed for the preservation and for the realization of democracy. (Newlon, 1935, July, p. 7)

The point is, the engagement of public school students and teachers in the study of social problems to seek democratic solutions for society's problems was a central theme of Newlon's work throughout his professional life.

Jesse Newlon occupied a unique position between the social reconstructionists and other liberal educators with whom he worked and often affiliated himself with at Teachers College. A successful and noted school administrator prior to beginning his career in higher education, he tempered his criticism of schooling as it existed in 1930s and 1940s America with the wisdom of practical experience. Writing to his long time friend Lloyd Crosgrave, a person who was vitally interested in education, politics, and U.S. society, Newlon (1927) observed, " ... there is no condition existing that would require a general assault from the outside or a revolution educationally.... In brief, I believe that our schools are much better ... than their critics think they are." Nonetheless, he recognized that there was ample opportunity for their improvement.

Newlon (1930, 1937a, 1939) asserted that the first responsibility of the school was the preparation of the individual for life in the modern United States (pp. 239, 593, and 84, respectively). Addressing the purpose of secondary education specifically, he wrote: "If the high school is to serve a useful function in American life, it must provide educational opportunities that will be better calculated to develop the potential powers of the individual, orient him toward modern life and give him opportunities and attitudes that will not only make him a social being, but will start him on the way to a life rich and meaningful to him" (Newlon, 1930, p. 239). Unlike the child centered educators of his era, Newlon viewed the focus on the individual not as an end in itself but as a critical first step in the preparation of students for citizenship and participation in a democratic society, for the "advancement of education and American life" were twin goals dependent on one another (Newlon, 1934b, p. 3). Ultimately, for him, educational policy was social policy. Although the obvious focus of schooling was the individual, the educated person began to change, and, hopefully, improve, society. According to his way of thinking, the school, in fact, was "a crucial element in national policy" (Newlon, 1939, p. 203). The school's articulated plan to change first individual students—and ultimately society in which they lived—was, according to Newlon, that which should constitute the curriculum.

At one and the same time, the Committee of the Progressive Education Association on Social and Economic Problems (1933), of which Newlon was a member, suggested that the curriculum "should provide for the development of the diverse abilities and gifts of the population" and, at the same time, "represent the highest possible integration of natural resources, cultural heritage, and technology in serving the general good and in fulfilling the democratic ideal" (p. 22). Such glowing generalities about curriculum are as common as they are ambiguous. They offer good feelings but little or no insight into what actually should transpire in classrooms. Newlon, for one, especially in his later work, ultimately addressed the need for specificity in curriculum discourse, and thus responded to a common criticism more conservative or practical-minded educators and citizens often made regarding progressive education. For example, speaking before the Society for Curriculum Study in February 1941, Newlon sounded more like a superintendent than a Teachers College leader of educational progressives:

> Now the truth is that we cannot learn without learning something. To understand our culture and its problems requires factual and conceptual knowledge and many perfectly definite understandings and appreciations. Knowledge contained in the printed page was never so important as in our complex reading of civilization. (1941a, p. 12)

Still, over the years, Newlon argued that a curriculum defined solely by subject matter was incomplete. More specifically, he asserted that given the roles schools played in society and the preparation of its members, no schooling that lacked a study of that society and its problems could be adequate or complete (Newlon, 1939, pp. 109-110).

ENRICHING THE CURRICULUM WITH THE
STUDY OF SOCIAL PROBLEMS

Newlon (1933a) criticized the Depression era curriculum as "too narrow, too little connected with the realities of American life" (p. 478). His solution—intended both to increase students' interest in school and to improve life for all citizens outside of schools—was to have students and teachers engage in a robust study of "the problems of American life" (Newlon, 1932, p. 24). He envisioned a thorough remaking of the curriculum at all levels and in all subjects. Speaking before the National Education Association's Department of Superintendence, Newlon (1936) articulated his vision more fully:

> The schools should aim definitely to give youth a realistic understanding of contemporary American culture in its historic form and world setting. To accomplish this purpose a thorough analysis of the great social trends of our times is essential for the purpose of isolating the critical economic, political, and social problems with which we must come to grips in the proximate future. This analysis should include also a study of the possibilities of life in the United States with the technological and natural resources at our disposal. The curriculum should in considerable measure be built around the problems and possibilities of American life. And at this point I want to insist that such a policy will involve every level of the school system and every subject matter area, not just the social studies, but science, mathematics, health and physical education, home economics, English, the arts and every other field. (pp. 7-8)

While he advocated a thorough and wide-ranging study of the problems of American life, Newlon (1932) was careful to distinguish between what he termed "critical" and "destructive" minds. "Critical minds" recognized problems and sought solutions based on thoughtful analysis of facts, leading to improved lives for all Americans. "Destructive minds," on the other hand, were ignorant of, or at least had little regard for, U.S. history and democratic traditions. They sought merely to tear down and impose their own will with little or no regard for the American cultural heritage. To Newlon, helping students develop critical minds through the thorough and intelligent study of social problems was necessary for the preservation of a democratic way of life.

While Newlon (1934a) urged the study of American problems in all areas of the curriculum, he was a realist and recognized that the social sciences and social studies would play a preeminent role in such a curriculum revision. He was well aware that existing textbooks were unsuitable for his desired purposes and that individual teachers lacked the time and resources to develop suitable curriculum materials independently. Recognizing such, he offered a possible solution to this problem:

> There is need for brief treatises on numerous subjects. I have in mind small books or monographs running from fifteen to forty thousand words, sometimes shorter brochures, each treating a single movement, process, trend, or problem authoritatively and interestingly.... The type of material which I am advocating would not supplant the longer more comprehensive treatise, but would supplement it and would stimulate American youth to think more deeply on the problems of our time by affording an abundance of factual and interpretative material that would supply data for thinking. (Newlon, 1933d, p. 74)

THE ROLE OF TEACHERS

Newlon realized that the study of contemporary social problems in schools would lead inevitably to questions regarding the proper role of the teacher. In that regard, Newlon (1939) argued that teachers should not remain neutral as they and their students studied the controversial issues he proposed, for, "The 'neutral' teacher or educational leader throws the weight of his influence on the side of opposition to change" (p. 220). Neutrality, he argued, indicated endorsement of the status quo.

Newlon went on to clarify that not all proposed change should become reality. Teachers themselves would have to engage in careful study and rigorous examination of factual data in order to determine their positions on issues addressed in classrooms. Newlon (1938) recognized that the widespread study of social problems and the role he envisioned for teachers inevitably would lead to "opposition from certain quarters, for the last thing that some interests desire is the application of intelligence to social problems" (p. 454), and thus it was imperative that they have strong rationales for their position(s) and pedagogical practices.

Newlon (1931b) called for teachers to lead a "less cloistered life" and to assume a more active and visible role in politics, community life, and the formulation of educational policies (p. 615). He argued that given teacher's specialized knowledge about and interest in schooling, they constituted a critical but historically overlooked group that should assume a more significant responsibility for setting the course for the education of the nation's youth. Without the leadership provided by teachers, he further argued, "the school will surely become a tool of reaction" (Newlon, 1939, p. 174). Such leadership, however, did not imply unilateral control. In the democratic society Newlon envisioned, all significant decisions, including educational ones, were to be made democratically and not ceded to specialists, elites, or special interest groups.

Jesse Newlon, obviously, had great respect for teachers, their abilities, and their potential. His many and varied oral and written statements attest to such as did his revolutionary curriculum revision project implemented in Denver during the 1920s. He also had high expectations for them:

> His work as a teacher ... should conform to the severest canons of his craft, for education is education and not mere conditioning or propaganda. Teaching must at all times conform to the democratic conception that the human mind must be intelligent to achieve freedom and must be free to achieve intelligence. To be efficient, teaching must employ all methods and techniques that have been validated by careful research and experimentation carried out in a frame of the most searching study of the problems, purposes, and processes of education for a free society. (Newlon, 1939, p. 171)

The expectations Newlon held for all teachers and the responsibilities with which he was prepared to entrust them called for "a thoroughgoing reconstruction" of their professional preparation, including a strong emphasis on scholarship and considerations of "social processes and problems," for, "teachers who do not think for themselves cannot teach others to think" (Newlon, 1934a, p. 15).

Newlon believed that no matter how competent the individual teacher, he or she alone was unlikely to have any significant impact on schools or the society they served. As a result, Newlon (1935), one-time president of the National Education Association (NEA), was an advocate for strong and active professional organizations for educators. In Newlon's mind, such groups faced a significant choice during the 1930s regarding their future direction: "They must decide whether their influence is to be used for the perpetuation of the economic status quo or as a genuine constructive force for building a more enlightened and humane society" (Newlon, 1935, p. 10). Newlon's preference for the latter was clear.

Newlon (1937b) believed that when developing and teaching their curriculum, teachers needed to seriously consider three major "limitations." First, they had to recognize "the maturity of the learner and develop curriculum and select instructional methods accordingly" (Newlon, 1937b, p. 274). Second, teachers had to realize that "the school is an educational institution and not an instrument of propaganda" (Newlon, 1937b, p. 275). He firmly believed that schools should be free of propaganda from all sources. Just as teachers were to seek to eliminate propaganda from outside agents, they were to refrain from disseminating propaganda of their own. Finally, "the wise teacher will always take into account the traditions, mores, the cultural situation, in the community in which he works" (Newlon, 1937b, p. 275). Jesse Newlon, Teachers College professor and liberal educator, admired by many people and despised by many others, always remained a realist and practical schoolman.

Despite these limitations, Newlon's expectations for teachers were significant and he believed that they should have great latitude in carrying out their jobs. His trust in teachers was not merely philosophical or theoretical but extended back to his work as a superintendent. He described the freedom he willingly provided his teachers in a report on the Denver curriculum revision project:

> We steadfastly refused to lay down a set of principles to guide committees in their work or to express our opinions as to what were the particular objectives to be attained in particular courses. On the other hand, we took the position that every committee should begin by making a survey of the writings, the experimentation, the practices, the controversies, and the unresolved problems in its field. (Newlon & Threlkeld, 1926, p. 234)

Concomitantly, during Newlon's NEA presidential address, he argued, that "teachers must stand firmly for the teaching of the truth, and the truth bears the imprint of no particular social, economic, or religious group" (Newlon, 1925, p. 10). His desire for the truth and lack of allegiance to established, powerful interests would be tested during the next decade, as he encouraged teachers to confront in their classrooms the nation's most significant social problem since the Civil War, the Great Depression.

EDUCATION FOR ECONOMIC RECONSTRUCTION

The effects of the Great Depression, which coincided with the most productive and prominent portion of Newlon's career, found expression in his concern for economic issues, which he recognized as intimately related to democracy. Newlon (1934a) held that "The ballot can mean little to the individual who is not only deprived of economic security but who can not even find steady employment" (p. 73). Thus, the future direction of the American economy became one of the primary topics Newlon believed students should address as a part of their studies.

The study of economic and other social problems was not a threat to liberty but a necessary step in the journey of making "the individual an intellectually free man" able to engage in democratic activities intelligently (1939, p. 102). Indeed, he believed that if students and teachers in schools were to address social problems, the topic of economic reconstruction—to lift the country from the Depression and, hopefully, prevent another such event in the future—could not be avoided.

For Newlon, the nation's economic problems and his concern about them predated the Depression. He expressed his early acceptance of "much of the Socialist program, but not the dogma," and observed "it is useless to debate whether we are to enter a collective society when we are already in one" (Newlon, 1928). Always the realist, he admitted the futility of voting in America for a Socialist and hoped during the 1928 election that the Democratic candidate, Alfred E. Smith, would garner a significant vote (Newlon, 1928). Despite his liberalism and desire for Smith to poll well, he, for unexplained reasons, voted for Herbert Hoover in the 1928 election (Newlon, 1933c).

In the midst of the Depression, Newlon (1933b) wrote to his friend Lloyd M. Crosgrave that he had pondered economic issues since around the turn of the century. Rampant poverty in a resource rich nation with the capabilities for significant agricultural and industrial production troubled Newlon (1931b, 1941a). To him, economic reform and equality, while important were not ends in themselves. Democracy itself could not reach its fullest potential "until economic security and justice are established" (Newlon, 1934a, p. 74). Newlon later developed this idea more fully:

> Equality may exist in political form, but where the disparities between individuals or classes are great, or long-continued, political institutions will become subservient to the class that wields the most power and enjoys the greatest prestige. It is for this reason that the glaring disparities in the economic conditions of the people that have developed even in this country in the last 50 years constitute so serious a threat to all our ideals and aspirations for the general welfare. (Newlon, 1939, p. 150)

Newlon (1935) believed that one avenue for reaching individual economic security, an essential prerequisite for equality and liberty, hence, democracy, was through the schools.

In Newlon's view (1933b), schools for too long had presented an incomplete portrayal of the United States—its history, present status, and future possibilities. He urged educators to provide students "the facts that will enable them to find solutions for their economic problems consistent with the ideals of their democratic tradition" (Newlon, 1935, p. 4), which, in turn, would "serve as the foundation of a thoroughly progressive political movement" (Newlon, 1935, p. 9). As the nation began to emerge from the Depression, Newlon (1940) recognized that economic reconstruction either by "a return to historic laissez faire or by sudden wholesale socialization" was unacceptable (p. 24). Instead, he advocated an enhanced role for the government in the regulation of private businesses, provision of social services, investment, and economic planning. Despite his admitted preferences for the future direction of the United States and its economy,

Newlon (1939) recognized that schools must not "become the tool of any political party or be employed to teach the blue prints of a new social order" (p. 224). Rather, he believed the ultimate decision must be left to the citizens in full possession of the knowledge required to make such a decision.

Newlon apparently believed that fully educated students who had studied the nation, its history, and its economy would, as adults and through democratic means, reach the same conclusions as he had concerning the economic future of the United States. Thus, schools did not need to advocate any particular vision of the future, for that was not their role in a democratic society. Nevertheless, Newlon was confident that the nation's ultimate direction was clear to the educated and informed mind.

That said, at times, Newlon's own rhetoric and that with which he associated his name became rather strident, especially considering the time and place he lived:

> In the collectivist society now emerging, the school should be regarded not as an agency for lifting gifted individuals out of the class into which they were born and elevating them into favored positions where they may exploit their less fortunate fellows, but rather as an agency for the abolition of all artificial social distinctions and organizing the energies of the nation for the promotion of the general welfare (Committee, 1933, p. 21).

Such language was certain to engender opposition, especially from those individuals or groups who believed they were entitled, for whatever reason, to favored positions and benefits. Newlon, in fact, was characterized in the popular press as a somewhat out of touch leftist who had little or no understanding of the world until the summer of 1940, when he made a speech critical of some of the educational practices that had been in place since the end of World War I ("Fallacies on War Laid to Teachers," 1940; "Newlon's Confession," 1940). In this speech made on July 10, 1940, to approximately 1,000 educators at Teachers College, Newlon addressed a number of "fallacies" he believed to be prevalent in the United States and its schools. He argued that isolationism and pacifism would not prevent future wars and that, at times, war was necessary for the preservation of democracy. He urged teachers to address the world situation honestly in their classrooms and to support war preparedness programs then being developed in response to the growing Nazi threat (Garrett, 2005). The viewpoint Newlon expressed in this speech was consistent with that which he had offered in *Education for Democracy in Our Time* (Newlon, 1939). Newlon consistently held that his educational and political positions had not changed in the summer of 1940, that he was a consistent advocate for democracy throughout this career and continued to remain one (Garrett, 2005).

THE THREAT OF ELITES AND SPECIAL INTERESTS

In 1941, Newlon applauded the fact that during the 1930s schools had become "socially more sensitive and meaningful" (Newlon, 1941a, p. 9), but at the same time, he was critical that they remained "lacking in social realism," because the understandings students "acquired have been so vague and general as to exert but little effect on their conduct as citizens" (1941a, p. 9). Newlon posited "that the people cannot have liberty and equality unless they are informed concerning social conditions and social problems ... " but he also recognized his plans would galvanize "[the] forces that would cripple education ... by the suppression of teaching designed to give youth knowledge of social conditions" (Newlon, 1935, p. 2). He termed such forces "the most dangerous influences in America today" (1935, p. 2). Speaking before the Department of Superintendence, Newlon (1936) addressed what he conceived as the motives of "the privileged classes that benefit most from" a capitalist economy: "These forces are beginning to oppose vigorously the study of critical economic problems in the schools and colleges. They fear to have the light of intelligence turned upon problems of capital and labor, or control, regulation, or public ownership of the instruments of production and distribution, for they fear that once the people are informed they may institute far reaching changes" (p. 2).

For too long, according to Newlon's (1932) view of the history of public education in the United States, such elite "forces" had manipulated educational and curricular policies in such ways as to use public schools as tools for social control. He did not consider his proposals for the meaningful study of contemporary social problems as revolutionary but merely a return to their historical roots in the "fight for the common people for political freedom and equality" (1935, p. 1).

AVOIDING INDOCTRINATION

Newlon recognized that the pressure on educators to remain neutral or to support the existing social order when dealing with controversial issues, often resulted in "an effective sort of self-censorship" (Newlon, 1937c, p. 301). He was also cognizant of the fact, and noted, that any attempt at neutrality in dealing with controversial issues merely resulted in support of the status quo. Yet, as previously mentioned, Newlon did not seek to replace what he considered support of one point of view, albeit at times subtle or tacit, with support for another one: "The policy which I am advocating is obviously not one of utilizing the school to propagandize youth to accept the blue prints of some new social order. Thus to use schools for propaganda would be to nullify completely the purposes of free inquiry, of teaching youth to do their own thinking with regard to these complex social problems" (1936, p. 8). In Newlon's complex, nuanced view, public schools would become forums for inquiry and discussion. Positions would be taken and supported, both by teachers and students, but, again, one form of indoctrination and social control would not be replaced by another.

Throughout Newlon's career, he envisioned schools as vital institutions to help provide youth the knowledge and skills necessary for citizenship in a democratic society. As such, all who entered their doors should engage in the disciplined inquiry of the problems facing that society before reaching their independent conclusions. Hopefully, students would continue the practices they learned in school throughout their lives. Speaking well before the beginning of the Great Depression, Newlon (1925) asserted that:

> The best service the schools can render is to foster the search for the truth, to teach boys and girls to think for themselves, inculcate in them the capacity for cooperation and self-control, and a high sense of personal civic duty and loyalty. Any program that is aimed at teaching youth what to think in controversial matters is a menace. There are already those among us who insist that youth shall be taught to hold particular views. Such a policy is inconsistent with the ideals of liberty and freedom on which our government was founded. Such a procedure is dangerous and the schools must stand consistently against it. (pp. 11-12)

Newlon's use of the word "inculcate" in relation to some of the characteristics required for life and decision-making in a democratic society demonstrates the value he placed on such a social organization. Democracy itself was not a negotiable issue in his mind, while the decisions made by individuals by democratic means were theirs alone to make. Thus, while Newlon did not advocate the indoctrination of students on individual issues or policies, he did contend, *vigorously,* that democracy must be supported: "... all education involves moulding of the individual, to modify his behavior in important respects. Merely to send the child to school where he is surrounded by a particular and planned environment is to influence his growth and development" (Newlon, 1939, p. 102). That "planned environment" had to be arranged in ways such that students, through free and open study of contemporary problems, gained experiences and habits that they later would transfer to adult life. Ultimately, Newlon's vision for schools in American society focused on the development of the informed, inquiring, freethinking, and critical individual. These traits were to be learned to a significant degree through the serious study of social and economic problems. In contrast with current (circa

2005) understandings of individualism, which often is viewed as an end in itself, Newlon's individual would find his or her highest fulfillment through cooperative involvement in the democratic process.

EDUCATION, DEMOCRACY, AND THE RISE OF FASCISM

The title of Jesse Newlon's most significant and comprehensive work, *Education for Democracy in Our Time*, is indicative of the importance he placed on the democratic form of government. Shortly before his death, he offered one of his most comprehensive descriptions of democracy:

> Democracy is a way of life. It is a value system that has implications for every aspect of life. Democracy is also a method by which members of a community study conditions, make decisions as to communal policies, whether locally, state or nationally, or in the realm of international affairs. Democracy is both ends and means. Democracy implies certain positive conditions, both as ends and means. Freedom of speech, of assembly, of association, are as essential to the functioning of democracy as method. As method, democracy is working for a society that will be characterized by more intellectual freedom than exists at the present time in any known society. Liberty, equality, fraternity are historic ideals of democracy but certain conditions are essential to their existence and fuller realization. These values are endangered in a society in which millions of individuals do not have economic security. Social caste and racial prejudices are antithetical to democracy. (Newlon, 1941b, p. 209)

Newlon (1935) thought the choice educators faced was clear, "Either the school will be employed as an instrument of enlightenment and social progress and thus democracy, or as an instrument of reaction" (p. 7).

In the years before Newlon's death in 1941, the need for such free people devoted to democracy became ever more obvious as the face of European fascism became clear even to the most isolationist Americans. As early as 1933, Newlon expressed a fear that his nation was moving in the direction of dictatorship. He later wrote, "If America is not to go the way of fascism, Americans must learn to deal more effectively with controversial issues in study and discussion" (1937b, p. 265). From Newlon's perspective, a great deal of responsibility for the future direction of the United States lay in the hands of its educators. Either they would create schools that lived and celebrated democracy, inculcating students in its values, or they would attempt to steer a noncontroversial course, hiding behind a thin veneer of asserted neutrality, leaving control of the nation to a small but powerful group of elites. The fact that Jesse Newlon had not prevailed in his vision for American schools, especially while the United

States faced the threat of imminent world war, troubled him during his final days. He believed that the exigencies of the coming war would "turn the schools back 50 years," returning "to fundamentals, rote teaching, and indoctrination," thus delaying, if not eliminating, the possibility for the robust democratic society he long had envisioned (Newlon cited in Hopkins, 1971, p. 26). Nonetheless, he remained committed to his vision of democratic schools in which students studied and debated a variety of national, state, and local problems.

CONCLUSION

Throughout his career, Newlon maintained a great deal of optimism. He continually expressed his confidence in students, educators, schools, his nation, and the democratic system. His career and thought also were marked by a great deal of pragmatism. Referring to a letter he had written some 30 years earlier, he reflected:

> Apparently, I then had a good deal of sympathy with the socialist point of view, but regarded the socialist party as Utopian, meaning impractical in many of its proposals. Well, I still think that is the trouble with the socialists of today. They are not only Utopian in their lack of political realism, but they have become what I call perfectionists. They are absolutists. As for myself, apparently I was something of a pluralist 30 years ago.... Well, I am a pluralist today. Incidentally, I am sure I do not need to tell you that I think Americans are the most fortunate people not only on the face of the earth but in all history. I have always believed this. Of course, this is not the same as saying that our country is absolutely perfect. (Newlon, 1941c)

Newlon demonstrated his pragmatism is his recognition of the necessity for traditional subject matter as well as the study of social problems. To him, both were necessary and neither was sufficient when constructing a curriculum.

Newlon's beliefs as expressed through his writing are perplexing at times. How could a man who abhorred indoctrination suggest, "The highly integrated character of our economy and the necessity for increased control of the instruments and processes of production and distribution by all the people in the interest of all people should be made clear" (1939, p. 216)? How could a man who celebrated democracy and civic life focus so much on the individual, contending that the primary purpose of schools was to "provide an environment which will allow the individual to realize his own potentialities" (1937a, p. 593)? The answers without much doubt exist in Newlon's unwavering faith in public education, the American people, and their democratic system. When given full information about controversial issues, he probably, but somewhat presumptively, believed that others would reach the same conclusions he had reached. If they did not, but had studied a problem and its potential solutions fully, Jesse Newlon likely would not have been demoralized. Decisions reached democratically by an intelligent, informed citizenry were his ultimate goal.

REFERENCES

Beineke, J. A. (1998). *And there were giants in the land: The life of William Heard Kilpatrick*. New York: Peter Lang.

Bowers, C. A. (1967). The ideology of progressive education. *History of Education Quarterly, 7*, 452-473.

The Committee of the Progressive Education Association on Social and Economic Problems. (1933). *A call to the teachers of the nation*. New York: The John Day Company.

Cuban, L. (1984). *How teachers taught: Constancy and change in American classrooms, 1890-1980*. New York: Longman.

Fallacies on war laid to teachers. (1940, July 11). *The New York Times*, p. 21.

Garrett, A. W. (2005). *One of the most sensible utterances that has come from anybody in a long time: Jesse H. Newlon's 'The teaching profession and the world crisis'*. Paper presented at the annual meeting of the Midwest History of Education Society Chicago, IL.

Hopkins, L. T. (1971). Jesse Newlon. Box 1, file folder 5, Jesse H. Newlon Collection, Special Collections and Archives, Penrose Library, University of Denver, Denver, CO.

Kliebard, H. M. (2004). *The struggle for the American curriculum: 1893-1958* (3rd ed.). New York: Routledge Falmer

Mead, W. G. (1968). Letter to Theodore R. Crane, July 22. Recollections of Newlon. Special Collections and Archives, Penrose Library, University of Denver, Denver, CO.

Newlon, J. H. (1917). *Training for national service*. Box 4, file folder 11, Jesse H. Newlon Collection, Special Collections and Archives, Penrose Library, University of Denver, Denver, CO.

Newlon, J. H. (1925). *The educational outlook at the end of the first quarter century*. Presidential address at the meeting of the National Education Association, Indianapolis, IN. Box 4, file folder 4, Jesse H. Newlon Collection, Special Collections and Archives, Penrose Library, University of Denver, Denver, CO.

Newlon, J. H. (1927). *Letter to Lloyd M. Crosgrave*. November 26. Box 2, file folder 7, Jesse H. Newlon Collection, Special Collections and Archives, Penrose Library, University of Denver, Denver, CO.

Newlon, J. H. (1928). *Letter to Lloyd M. Crosgrave*. November 5. Box 2, file folder 7, Jesse H. Newlon Collection, Special Collections and Archives, Penrose Library, University of Denver, Denver, CO.

Newlon, J. H. (1930). Two criticisms of the high school. *School Executives Magazine,* *49*, 238-239.

Newlon, J. H. (1931a). *Letter to Lloyd M. Crosgrave.* May 26. Box 2, file folder 7, Jesse H. Newlon Collection, Special Collections and Archives, Penrose Library, University of Denver, Denver, CO.

Newlon, J. H. (1931b). The status of the new school. *Teachers College Record, 32,* 608-618.

Newlon, J. H. (1932). Can the high school stimulate the intellectual interests of American youth? *Junior-Senior High School Clearing House,* 7(1), 21-25.

Newlon, J. H. (1933a). The administration of the curriculum. *Educational Method, 12,* 474-480.

Newlon, J. H. (1933b). *Letter to Lloyd M. Crosgrave.* November 16. Box 2, file folder 7, Jesse H. Newlon Collection, Special Collections and Archives, Penrose Library, University of Denver, Denver, CO.

Newlon, J. H. (1933c). *Letter to Walter G. Mead.* October 31. Box 2, file folder 18, Jesse H. Newlon Collection, Special Collections and Archives, Penrose Library, University of Denver, Denver, CO.

Newlon, J. H. (1933d). Need for new social-science materials. *The Clearing House,* *8*(2), 73-74.

Newlon, J. H. (1933e). Some implications of the indispensable school library. *Teachers College Record, 34,* 552-559.

Newlon, J. H. (1934a). *Educational administration as social policy.* New York: Charles Scribner's Sons.

Newlon, J. H. (1934b). *The role of leadership in the reconstruction of education.* Paper presented at the meeting of the Society for Curriculum Study, Cleveland, OH. Box 5, file folder 6, Jesse H. Newlon Collection, Special Collections and Archives, Penrose Library, University of Denver, Denver, CO.

Newlon, J. H. (1935). *The place of the educational profession in the national life.* Paper presented at the meeting of the National Education Association, Denver, CO. Box 5, file folder 7, Jesse H. Newlon Collection, Special Collections and Archives, Penrose Library, University of Denver, Denver, CO.

Newlon, J. H. (1936). *Shall the school curriculum seek to improve the type of society which maintains it?* Paper presented at the meeting of the Department of Superintendence, St. Louis, MO. Box 5, file folder 7, Jesse H. Newlon Collection, Special Collections and Archives, Penrose Library, University of Denver, Denver, CO.

Newlon, J. H. (1937a). Democracy and education in our time. *Progressive Education, 14*(8), 589-594.

Newlon, J. H. (1937b). Freedom and teaching. In W. H. Kilpatrick (Ed.), *The teacher and society. First yearbook of the John Dewey Society* (pp. 256-282). New York: D. Appleton-Century.

Newlon, J. H. (1937c). The teaching profession as a functional group in society. In W. H. Kilpatrick (Ed.), *The teacher and society. First yearbook of the John Dewey Society* (pp. 283-309). New York: D. Appleton-Century.

Newlon, J. H. (1938). Public support for a social studies program. *Teachers College Record, 39*(6), 453-458.

Newlon, J. H. (1939). *Education for democracy in our time.* New York: McGraw-Hill.

Newlon, J. H. (1940, October 7). Teachers and politics—1940. *Frontiers of Democracy, 7*, 22-24.

Newlon, J. H. (1941a). *The curriculum crisis in democracy.* Paper presented at the meeting of the Society for Curriculum Study, Atlantic City, NJ. Box 5, file folder 8, Jesse H. Newlon Collection, Special Collections and Archives, Penrose Library, University of Denver, Denver, CO.

Newlon, J. H. (1941b, April). Democracy or super-patriotism? *Frontiers of Democracy, 7*, 208-211.

Newlon, J. H. (1941c). *Letter to Lloyd M. Crosgrave.* April 30. Box 2, file folder 7, Jesse H. Newlon Collection, Special Collections and Archives, Penrose Library, University of Denver, Denver, CO.

Newlon, J. H., & Threlkeld, A. L. (1926). The Denver curriculum revision program. In H. Rugg (Ed.), *The foundations and technique of curriculum-construction. Part I of the twenty-sixth yearbook of the National Society for the Study of Education* (pp. 229-240). Bloomington, IL: Public School Publishing Company.

Newlon's confession. (1940, July 22). *Time,* p. 48.

Stephens, W. R. (1967). Jesse Newlon. *The Educational Forum, 32,* 71-80.

Tanner, D. (1991). *Crusade for democracy: Progressive education at the crossroads.* Albany: State University of New York Press.

Tyack, D., Lowe, R., & Hansot, E. (1984). *Public schools in hard times: The great depression and recent years.* Cambridge, MA: Harvard University Press.

CHAPTER 6

A REBELLIOUS JERSEY GIRL

Rachel Davis DuBois, Intercultural Education Pioneer

Chara Haeussler Bohan

Recognized as a pioneer by both her friends and adversaries, she [Rachel Davis DuBois] experienced both the glory and grief of all pioneers....

—Montalto, *History of the Intercultural Education Movement* (1982, p. ix)

INTRODUCTION

Rachel Davis DuBois possessed an unconventional outlook and rebellious spirit. As founder of the intercultural education movement, she held fervent convictions about honoring the contributions of ethnic minorities in the United States throughout her 101 years of life. Having lived throughout most of the twentieth century, she was a social educator whose interest in people of diverse ethnic and religious ancestry developed from her early work as a social studies teacher in southern New Jersey. In acting upon her deeply held belief in the valuable contributions of different ethnicities, she charted unexplored territory in American social education by

Addressing Social Issues in the Classroom and Beyond: The Pedagogical Efforts of Pioneers in the Field, 99–115
Copyright © 2007 by Information Age Publishing
All rights of reproduction in any form reserved.

establishing the intercultural education movement in the early 1930s. She promoted cultural understanding for teachers and students via their study of various ethnic groups, such as African Americans, Germans, Jews, Chinese, Italians, Japanese, and Irish. Indeed, DuBois promoted cultural awareness long before the current popularity of the multicultural education movement.

Rachel Davis DuBois' entire educational career was devoted to a concern for social issues. Honoring cultural contributions, fighting racism, discrimination, and prejudice through intercultural education were primary focal points of her movement. Nonetheless, Rachel Davis DuBois' pioneering work in intercultural education evoked intense reaction from detractors and defenders. Critics, who supported assimilation, attacked her work as divisive and un-American. Ultimately, they removed her from the very organization she helped establish. Furthermore, the controversial and liberal nature of the intercultural movement caused Rachel Davis DuBois to face investigation by Senator Joseph McCarthy. Her supporters, on the other hand, who believed ethnic differences ought to be celebrated, funded her projects, participated in her programs, and helped her write curriculum materials. For example, one of the most popular projects she helped to create was a 1930s award winning educational radio program titled, "Americans All—Immigrants All." This radio broadcast was sponsored by the U.S. Office of Education and was disseminated on more than one hundred CBS stations. DuBois' work, however, has been largely ignored as she remained outside mainstream educational thought throughout most of her career.

The intercultural education movement was established to provide curriculum development materials to elementary and secondary teachers throughout the nation who sought to teach about diverse ethnic groups in American life. DuBois developed several methods for promoting the intercultural education movement. These included the establishment of cultural assembly programs, intergroup organizations, group conversation methods, and publications on ethnic groups and teaching methods that fostered cultural understanding. Ultimately, DuBois' work led her to engage in international endeavors, as well. DuBois additionally furthered ethnic understanding by traveling around the world and assisting with refugee relocation negotiations and took part in pacifist activities, Quaker religious meetings, suffrage work, and the Civil Rights Movement. Considering the context of the times in which she worked, DuBois was a true pioneer—or viewed from a different perspective—DuBois was a rebellious and stubborn woman who passionately espoused her radical belief in the value of social education that celebrated cultural awareness.

BIOGRAPHICAL INFORMATION

Born on a farm in Woodstown, New Jersey, on January 25, 1892, Rachel Davis DuBois was the second of six children. Her father, Charles Howard Davis, and her mother, Bertha Priscilla Haines Davis, hailed from Quaker ancestors of English and Welsh origin. A devout member of the Society of Friends, DuBois' Quaker beliefs influenced her actions throughout her life, as she remained a pacifist through two world wars. Nothing in DuBois' upbringing, however, suggested that she was destined to become a pioneer in the world of social education. Family members had not attended college, nor did fellow students in her small south Jersey high school. Yet, Rachel's mother remarked that Rachel was different from her other children, and family folklore told of Rachel being brought up to the attic at birth so that she would become high-minded (DuBois, 1984).

Although she did not distinguish herself academically at Pilesgrove High School, DuBois was determined to attend college, and gained admission to Bucknell University in Leesburg, Pennsylvania. Because she came from a modest, rural farming family, she initially felt conspicuously out of place at Bucknell (Davis, 1999; DuBois 1984). She later claimed that her experience as a "misfit" provided her with empathy for people of minority group status in America. Gradually, she became involved in various activities at Bucknell, such as student government and drama. Rachel Davis graduated from Bucknell University in June 1914 with a degree in the natural sciences. One year later, she married fellow south Jersey native Nathan Steward DuBois.

Like many aspects of her existence, Rachel Davis DuBois' marriage was most definitely unconventional for the times. She had refused Nathan DuBois' earlier marriage proposals, as she was intent upon first earning a college degree. When the couple later married in 1915, she persisted in establishing what she referred to as a "50-50" marriage (DuBois, 1984). Such an agreement meant that if the couple did not have children, and a subsequent hysterectomy in 1935 ensured that she would remain child-less, she was equally free to pursue a career. Because not many professional options existed for women in science in the early 1900s, DuBois turned to teaching as an avenue of employment. In fact, she taught during her college years in order to help pay tuition.

DuBois' unwavering pursuit of a professional career in social education most certainly contributed to the ultimate dissolution of her marriage, as work increasingly took her away from her south Jersey home. Rachel Davis DuBois clearly chose to devote most of her energies to the promotion of social education that focused upon intercultural studies. In describing the circumstances that led to her 1942 divorce from Nathan DuBois, after more than a decade of living separately, she expressed a sense of relief that he had developed a relationship with their former housekeeper, Florence Willoughby. She recognized that Willoughby could more successfully meet her husband's needs than she could (DuBois, 1984).

Pursuit of graduate studies in the late 1920s and early 1930s at Teachers College, Columbia University, under the guidance of mentor Daniel Kulp II, was an initial factor that caused DuBois to leave south Jersey and her position as a social studies teacher at Woodbury High School (Davis, 1999; Montalto, 1982). Once she left her teaching position at Woodbury High School, her horizons became larger, but she basically never wavered from the purpose that she established in the assembly program (the latter of which is discussed below). She found a calling in teaching and celebrating the contributions of various ethnic groups.

At Teachers College, DuBois encountered many leaders in the field of progressive education, such as William Heard Kilpatrick and George S. Counts. In fact, George Counts' (1932) speech before the Progressive Education Association (PEA), *Dare the School Build a New Social Order?* was given while DuBois was a graduate student at Teachers College.

In the early 1930s, DuBois conceived the "Service Bureau for Human Relations" to help spread the Woodbury plan (which is discussed later in this chapter) to more schools. This organization had fits and starts, and eventually a man was selected to direct the organization, as DuBois was told that it would be difficult to obtain funding if a woman headed the group. In 1934, DuBois reconstituted her organization and founded the Service Bureau for Intercultural Education (Montalto, 1982). In the early 1930s, Counts served with F. C. Borgeson and Willard W. Beatty on the board of DuBois' intercultural education organization.

Eventually, because of financial difficulties, DuBois' intercultural education movement merged with the PEA's Commission on Intercultural Education (Davis, 2002; DuBois, 1984; Montalto, 1982). The relationship between the PEA and DuBois' intercultural education movement was short-lived, however. Questions about DuBois' administrative capabilities and philosophical differences over the direction of intercultural education emanating from the PEA's major source of funding, the General Education Board (GEB), led to a termination of the relationship between the PEA and DuBois' intercultural education organization (Davis, 2002; Montalto, 1982).

By 1940 William H. Kilpatrick served as Chairman of the Board of Directors of DuBois' reconstituted Service Bureau for Intercultural Education (SBIE), a position he likely came to regret. Kilpatrick found that he had to mediate a bitter conflict between DuBois, and Stewart Cole, a professor of religious education who had become the director of the Service Bureau. Cole questioned DuBois' pluralist approach to intercultural education and favored an emphasis on cultural unity due to his belief in the need for harmony during a time of impending war. In an attempt to resolve the dispute, the Service Bureau Board offered DuBois a temporary leave, told her to seek psychiatric advice, and sought her eventual resignation (Montalto, 1982). Initially, DuBois refused. Instead, she transferred relevant records to her home and rejected requests to return to the Service Bureau offices.

As the United States entered World War II in 1941, and an emphasis on national unity utterly pre-empted attention to ethnic differences, Kilpatrick and other leaders again requested that DuBois resign her position as director of the Service Bureau for Intercultural Education, the organization she had founded. After a protracted battle and a negative GEB evaluation of the Service Bureau's curriculum materials, DuBois resigned.

DuBois' departure from the Service Bureau for Intercultural Education facilitated the completion of her long-delayed doctorate in education (Davis, 1999, 2002; DuBois 1984). DuBois had been so busy with her work in intercultural education throughout the 1930s that she had neglected her own doctoral studies. With encouragement from Dr. Frederick Thrasher, she finally earned her PhD degree at New York University (NYU) in 1942. There are several reasons DuBois found it necessary to leave Teachers College (TC) and attend NYU to complete her doctoral work. First and foremost, her advisor at TC, Dr. Daniel Kulp II, had departed from the TC faculty. More importantly however, was the fact that her work was not accepted as scholarly by the Teachers College community. Finally, DuBois found a receptive and supportive educational environment at NYU, where she was able to complete her doctorate. Yet, educational accomplishments did not mean her work in intercultural education had ended. Indeed, her devotion to intercultural education was life long and had developed from a philosophy of pedagogy that began when she was a young social studies teacher in New Jersey.

PHILOSOPHY OF PEDAGOGY

Rachel Davis DuBois started teaching while a student at Bucknell University. Thus began her educational journey that lasted 8 decades. Despite numerous endeavors and accomplishments, she remained at heart a teacher. In her autobiography, written toward the end of her life, she remarked, "I have always thought of myself as a classroom teacher" (DuBois, 1984, p. 232). As stated earlier, in 1914, there were not many other career options available to women, but DuBois soon found that she enjoyed teaching. As a young, new teacher at Glassboro High School, DuBois was assigned the "leftovers" which included algebra, biology, and

American history. She found that she loved to perform history, and thus engaged her students in dramatic reenactments. Her pedagogical philosophy encouraged active learning, at a time when recitations and memorization were more standard methods (Bohan, 2005; Cremin, 1988).

DuBois also found that she extended her deeply held principles to her pedagogical philosophy, as well. When requested to sell war bonds, during World War I, her Quaker commitment to pacifism dictated against such an endeavor (Davis, 1999; DuBois, 1984). Her superintendent supported DuBois by explaining to her that she did not have to "yell it [her opposition to war] from the housetops" (DuBois, 1984, p. 26). Despite her political beliefs, DuBois remained well regarded. Clear evidence of this is the fact that she was asked to serve as the acting principal at Glassboro when the principal had to depart for military service.

DuBois' interest in political affairs increased after she attended the First International Conference of Friends in London in 1920. Sixteen hundred Friends attended this international gathering in order to explore topics such as race, peace, international relations, and community service. After talking with George Washington Carver at the conference, DuBois developed a concern for race relations in America. Prior to her conversation with Carver, DuBois had not contemplated the challenges African Americans faced in the United States. Because she had been raised in a rural community in South Jersey, she had not encountered or recognized the discriminatory treatment most African Americans confronted routinely. When she returned to the United States, she became involved with a "Fireside Club" that was a racially mixed group of people who met alternatively in homes owned by black and whites. These experiences later influenced DuBois' pedagogy, as she developed what she referred to as a group conversation method where people of different ethnicities came together and dialogued. Often group conversation methodology began with participants answering common questions about their own childhood experiences. DuBois developed this technique and elaborated on its process in her book *The Art of Group Conversation* (1963).

DuBois also became actively involved in pacifism when she joined the Women's International League for Peace and Freedom. This work brought her into contact with Jane Addams, founder of Hull House, and Janette Rankin, the first woman in Congress, who had voted against U.S. entry into World War One and World War Two. DuBois traveled to Europe with Jane Addams in the 1920s and lamented to Addams that she was concerned about being away from her husband for 3 months. DuBois and Addams noted, however, that a double standard existed for women, as no similar concern existed when a husband's work necessitated he be away from his wife for 3 months. Both DuBois and Addams were strong-willed women. Their common interests led them to become professional colleagues and friends. They were women who held renegade beliefs, but who also held leadership roles in American society. Ultimately, DuBois used her experience in Europe with Addams and her growing pacifist sentiments to write curriculum guides such as *War and Its Consequences* (DuBois, 1984). In Europe, at the International Conference on Women at the Hague, DuBois had the opportunity to meet Rankin. They did not become close friends, but held similar convictions about opposition to war. Rankin's pacifist beliefs supported DuBois' pacifism, and in the end influenced the curriculum materials that DuBois created.

In 1924, DuBois returned to full time teaching at Woodbury High School. At Woodbury, she was given responsibility for developing the assembly program, which came to be known as the Woodbury Assembly Project. This task was to have a life long impact on DuBois' pedagogy. She taught social studies, and selected a textbook developed by Harold Rugg rather than one given to her entitled *Americanizing Our Foreign Born*. DuBois selected Rugg's textbook instead of the one given to her by the school district because she believed that Rugg's textbook was better suited for her social studies classes, where intercultural education was a prominent theme. DuBois wanted to honor and celebrate different cultures in her classroom, not suppress different ethnicities to create uniform American citizens.

Although DuBois was white, she was one of the early members of the National Association for the Advancement of Colored People (NAACP), where she became friends with W.E.B. DuBois (an early and noted black activist who helped to found the NAACP in 1910) and acquainted with Langston Hughes (the noted author and poet).

Rachel Davis DuBois met W.E.B. DuBois at the annual convention of the NAACP held in Denver in 1925. They would often joke about their common last name, and he would tell people that they *might* be related.

W.E.B. DuBois (1903) is best remembered for his book *The Souls of Black Folk* and for his advocacy of the talented tenth which contrasted sharply with Booker T. Washington's accomodationist philosophy and support of manual training at Tuskegee Institute. W.E.B. DuBois signed a copy of his monumental book on black history *Black Reconstruction* (1935), for Rachel DuBois and, in doing so, wrote the words: "to the other Dr. DuBois" (DuBois, 1984, p. 70).

She developed a lifelong relationship with him during which he influenced her understanding of African Americans in society. She saw him most often when she served on the NAACP Board. In the 1940s, when she faced challenges over her intercultural education program at the Service Bureau, she visited W.E.B. DuBois for 1 week at his home in Atlanta. However, Rachel Davis DuBois may have overestimated her relationship with W.E.B. DuBois. W.E.B. DuBois' autobiography, published toward the end of his life in 1968, fails to mention Rachel Davis DuBois even in chapters dedicated to their common interests such as "Work for Peace." Rachel Davis DuBois likely placed greater value on their relationship because he gave her academic and political credibility. Nonetheless, Rachel Davis DuBois was profoundly interested in racial issues and pacifism and W.E.B. DuBois clearly influenced her thinking along these lines.

Rachel Davis DuBois' interest in race relations, coupled with the passage of the 1924 Exclusion Act directed against Asian Americans, and her teaching of social studies, led DuBois to develop the Woodbury Assembly program that celebrated and demonstrated the contributions of different ethnic groups in American life. Students participated in the programs through dramatization. Initially, DuBois believed the purpose of the assembly project was to help students develop "tolerant attitudes toward other races and nations" (DuBois, 1984, p. 54). Later, DuBois came to realize that people did not want to be tolerated, and she changed the word "tolerant" to "sympathetic." The assembly project featured groups that were loosely connected to holidays in American life. For example, an Italian program was held in October in connection with Columbus day, a German program was held in December in connection with Christmas, and an African American program was held in February in connection with Negro History Week. Today, German and Italians are not regarded as members of ethnic minorities, but in the 1920s they were recent immigrants who were viewed with suspicion by the white Anglo Saxon majority. Assimilation into the "American melting pot" was the common mantra.

DuBois' assembly program may not appear controversial, let alone progressive, to a modern audience, but in the early 1920s, many found her work objectionable. Indeed, members of the Woodbury Board of Education asked her to resign from teaching because of complaints from the local American Legion (Davis, 1999, 2002; DuBois, 1984). DuBois refused. Knowing that she was considered one of the best teachers in the school, she also believed that the New Jersey tenure law protected her. Teachers in other states were not as fortunate as DuBois, who was permitted to retain her position but without the customary salary increase.

As DuBois' assembly program expanded to other schools in south Jersey, she decided there was a need to evaluate the Woodbury Assembly program. As a result, she used the Neumann Attitude test in 1930 to measure its effects. She found a statistically significant difference in questions relating to international and interracial subjects for those who experienced the assembly program versus those who did not.

INFLUENCES ON RACHEL DAVIS DUBOIS

Unfortunately, DuBois did not only experience gender discrimination early in her academic career. She also witnessed racial discrimination, first-hand. She sought to share a New York City apartment with Dr. Harriet Rice, an African American graduate of Wellesley College, Boston Conservatory of Music, and who later earned a medical degree. When DuBois spoke to the Dean of Women at Teachers College of their difficulty in locating an apartment, the Dean explained that DuBois could pass (as white) but not her friend. DuBois surprised the Women's Dean when she explained that she *was* white. Because DuBois possessed a dark complexion she would, on occasion, be mistaken as having African American ancestry. The experience of discrimination most certainly influenced DuBois' outlook, led her to befriend several prominent African American leaders, and caused her to become an activist for civil rights. In addition to W.E.B. DuBois, she counted A. Philip Randolph (who was the President of the Brotherhood of Sleeping Car Porters, which was the first African American labor union to sign a collective bargaining agreement with a U.S. corporation, the Pullman Company) among her associates. DuBois came to work with A. Philip Randolph in the 1960s when she became involved in the Civil Rights struggle.

DuBois was also influenced by several prominent American Jews, including Reconstructionists Mordecai Kaplan, Rabbi James Weinstein, and Rabbi Milton Steinberg. DuBois also developed a relationship with the American Jewish Committee (AJC) which agreed in 1935 to financially support DuBois' intercultural education work. Funding was initiated during the depths of the Great Depression, but seeds of conflict were sewn in DuBois' relationship with the AJC. Controversy over how Jews were to be viewed existed within the American Jewish community itself. Kaplan, who was the director of the Teachers Institute and Professor of Homiletics at the Jewish Theological Seminary of America (Montalto, 1982), helped to found the Reconstructionists, who called for Jewish participation in modern life, but who also emphasized for young Jews the importance of Jewish history, culture and traditions. DuBois' relationship with the Reconstructionists served to strain her relationship with some members of the AJC, who supported cultural assimilation, and believed Jews were not to be viewed as a separate ethnic group, but instead should be considered as a religious classification, like Baptists, or Quakers. DuBois, however, was committed to a multicultural approach in teaching and learning about American Jews, just as she celebrated the contributions of many different groups in American life. She believed in cultivating "the soil of cultural diversity" whereas many AJC members favored a unified culture approach (Mantalto, 1982, p. 229).

DuBois was inspired by several academicians, but she considered Louis Adamic one of the greatest influences upon her thinking and her work in intercultural education. In 1934, Adamic had written an article on immigrants titled, "Thirty Million New Americans" in which he explored ethnic alienation and called for the creation of an educational organization that taught about the contributions of the newer immigrants. DuBois believed her intercultural education organization served the very purpose Adamic described in his article. In fact, she asked teachers enrolled in her inservice courses what they were doing to instill pride in minority culture groups, and if and how they were helping students to share their heritage with others. Adamic, who was only vaguely aware of DuBois' Service Bureau for Intercultural Education when he published his article, later welcomed DuBois' work when he became better acquainted with the Service Bureau. DuBois cited Adamic's work routinely in articles and speeches that she gave about intercultural education.

Finally, Rachel Davis DuBois was profoundly influenced by Martin Luther King, Jr. and the Civil Rights Movement. After being forced to resign from the Service Bureau for Intercultural Education in 1941, DuBois formed a new organization, initially called the Intercultural Education Workshop, and later renamed the Workshop for Cultural Democracy (Davis, 1999; Lambert, 1993; Montalto, 1982). The Workshop focused on the group conversation method as a means of bringing people of different backgrounds together in dialogue. She believed group conversation was a means of easing tensions between groups and in schools. DuBois' work in-group conversation led to an invitation in 1964 from Martin Luther King, Jr. to come to Atlanta and join the staff of his Southern Christian Leadership Conference for 6 months to establish a Dialogue Department officially called "Operation Dialogue" (DuBois, 1984, p. 219). Rachel Davis DuBois' role in Martin Luther King's Civil Rights Movement led her to establish a permanent facility for group conversation methods in Atlanta. DuBois recalled an early trip to Atlanta to facilitate the establishment of a Dialogue Department in which she was driven around the town by a white "bigot" who talked about Dr. King's mistress and who used the "N" word (DuBois, 1984, p. 227).

Martin Luther King, Jr. greatly appreciated her efforts, and noted as much. Sadly, DuBois received a letter from Dr. King one day after his assassination, which had been dictated a week prior, in which he thanked DuBois for her part in the struggle for racial justice.

DuBois' work in Atlanta ultimately led to the permanent establishment of the Atlanta Dialogue Center. DuBois' involvement with the Civil Rights Movement also led to an ongoing professional relationship with Corretta Scott King who wrote the forward of DuBois' autobiography. King believed that Rachel Davis DuBois' work was critical to furthering the cause of Civil Rights in the United States, and she believed DuBois helped to promote her late husband's legacy.

ASPIRATIONS AND ACCOMPLISHMENTS

DuBois held high aspirations, remained radical in perspective, and somewhat outside the mainstream educational establishment. A prolific author, she first began writing articles about her work in intercultural education for such journals as *The Crisis, The English Journal, Friends Intelligencer, Progressive Education,* and *Childhood Education.* She also wrote curriculum guides for teachers and eventually authored more than a dozen books. She considered her 1943 work, *Get Together Americans,* her first publication (DuBois, 1984), but in reality she had written and edited many works about intercultural education throughout the 1930s. Among some of the many books she wrote, coauthored or edited between 1935 and 1971 were: *The Germans in American Life* (1972, 1936) and *The Jews in American Life* (1935) both edited with Emma Schweppe, *Build Together Americans: Adventures in Intercultural Education* (1945), *Neighbors in Action* (1950), *The Art of Group Conversation* with Mew-Soong Li (1963), and *Reducing Social Tension and Conflict* with Mew-Soong Li (1971). Her final work was an autobiography, *All This and Something More: Pioneering Intercultural Education* (1984) with Corann Okorodudu, which she completed at the age of 92.

DuBois' success can be attributed to an ability not to dwell on failures, and perseverance in the face of adversity. DuBois initially struggled in her career after being forced to resign from the Service Bureau for Intercultural Education in 1941, as the United States entered World War II and cultural unity in defense of democracy became policy. However, she regrouped, with the support of loyal colleagues, including Eduard Lindeman, New York University professor of sociology; Leonard Covello, Principal of Benjamin Franklin High School in East Harlem and former member of the Service Bureau's advisory board; W.E.B. DuBois; and Reconstructionists Mordecai Kaplan, Rabbi Milton Steinberg and Rabbi James Weinstein. During this period she created the Workshop for Cultural Democracy, an organization dedicated to promoting intercultural education, similar to the Service Bureau for Intercultural Education.

In the summer of 1945, she co-directed with the noted anthropologist Margaret Mead, the Wellesley Institute on Community Affairs, a summer program dedicated to teaching group conversation methods. As tensions increased in New York City schools, which led to gang warfare, DuBois' organization helped to ease tensions by working at the community level. DuBois described the New York City project in *Neighbors in Action* (1950).

DuBois' success with the Workshop for Cultural Democracy ultimately led to post war work in Germany in 1950. For DuBois, her trip to Europe held tremendous import as she worked with the U.S. State Department under the Marshall Plan among twelve million people expelled from countries that had been occupied by the Soviet Union (DuBois, 1984). As a result of the Potsdam Agreement, persons of German ancestry living in Eastern Europe were forced to relocate to Germany, even if their ancestors had lived in Eastern Europe for hundreds of years. According to DuBois, this situation created tremendous problems in intercultural relations. Despite her own language barrier, DuBois succeeded in bridging intercultural relations, with the assistance of interpreters, through the demonstration and implementation of the group conversation method.

DuBois achieved many academic goals, especially considering the early time period (1900s) in which she began her studies and work. Few women then attended college, and even fewer earned doctoral degrees (Gordon, 1990; Hamilton, 2004; Lucas, 1994; Solomon, 1985). She taught courses at several universities; and in the 1930s she likely taught the first courses in intercultural education. Throughout her career, she taught courses at Boston University, New York University, Wellesley College, Teachers College, Columbia University, and the New School to preservice and inservice teachers. She also earned several honorary degrees toward the end of her life in recognition of her achievements. For example, Rowan University (formerly Glassboro State College), and her alma matter, Bucknell University, bestowed honorary degrees on her, and the Reconstructionist Rabbinical College of Philadelphia gave DuBois an award for her interfaith work (DuBois, 1984).

Toward the end of her life, DuBois' work became more oriented toward religious faith, as she became involved in Quaker dialogue and interfaith organizations. In the late 1950s and 1960s, she traveled to more than 400 Quaker homes throughout the United States and Europe. Her involvement with the Southern Christian Leadership Conference and the Civil Rights Movement also led her to work with interfaith groups, which was sponsored by various denominational churches throughout the United States. In fact, Rachel Davis DuBois participation in the Civil Rights Movement, especially the Southern Christian Leadership Conference, helped her become more religious in outlook. And as she became more involved in civil rights work and more deeply religious, DuBois came to believe that Whites in Birmingham, Alabama needed to ask for forgiveness from Blacks.

Interestingly, DuBois' religious convictions led her to experiment with alternative realities, clairvoyants, and Ouija boards. These activities fell outside the mainstream educational establishment, but DuBois remained open-minded about educational methods, rebellious in spirit, and steadfast in her convictions.

FRUSTRATIONS AND BARRIERS

Like many pioneer women, Rachel Davis DuBois encountered frustrations and barriers. Despite such, she was convinced of the correctness of her philosophy which celebrated ethnic differences, and countered the popularity of ethnic assimilation (Lambert, 1993). Even when forced to resign from the organizations she helped to create, such as the Service Bureau for Intercultural Education, she did not alter her fundamental beliefs. During World War II, assimilationists dominated educational thought, but DuBois remained steadfast in her commitment to honoring individual ethnic identity. Her work was often conducted outside the mainstream educational establishment, and was viewed by many educational leaders as lacking scientific credibility (Davis, 1999).

Evaluations of DuBois' intercultural education organization, such as those conducted by the General Education Board (GEB) and the American Jewish Committee (AJC), were at times critical of her policies and procedures. The GEB was a major philanthropic agency founded by John D. Rockefeller, and was a major source of funding behind the Progressive Education Association (Mantalto, 1982). The separate study of different ethnic groups did not appeal to the GEB and numerous other groups, all of which believed her work encouraged, "unwarranted cultivation of group pride" and posed a threat to national unity (Mantalto, 1982, p. 137). GEB opposition led to the dissolution of the relationship between DuBois' intercultural education organization and the PEA. The AJC decided in the late 1930s that in order to continue to financially support DuBois' Service Bureau for Intercultural Education, reorganization and a shift in philosophical orientation was warranted. Frank Trager, as administrative officer of the Survey Committee, was given the task of leading the transformation. Trager, a philosopher from Johns Hopkins and a former Labor Secretary of the Socialist Party, believed that DuBois was "too set in her ways" and lacked "intellectual acumen" (Mantalto, 1982, p. 221). Critical evaluations and concerns over DuBois' leadership and intellect led to funding problems, as well.

The radical nature of DuBois' work and her association with activists such as W.E.B. DuBois led to her investigation by Senator Joseph McCarthy in the 1950s. She appeared before the Senate Sub-Committee on Government Operations in 1953, and the entire experience was unnerving for DuBois. In fact, she found it necessary to consult a lawyer to prepare for her defense. She also contacted James Weshler, editor of the *New York*

Post, to learn about his own experience as a subject of McCarthy's investigation. While DuBois was rattled by her confrontation with Senator McCarthy, she did not allow fright to prevent her from asking Senator McCarthy, "What protection do I and other citizens who have been put in a position like this have against the harmful effects of sessions like this on our work and our professions?" (DuBois, 1984, p. 164). Senator McCarthy did not provide a response.

As mentioned earlier, DuBois also faced gender discrimination. Because she was a female in a male dominated society, her professional authority and credibility were sometimes challenged. DuBois' organizational skills apparently were weak, and she was informed that a female should not head the intercultural education organization because a woman would have more difficulty obtaining funding.

Despite a prolific career, her intercultural education work was neglected in the 1940s in volumes on democratic human relations and intercultural attitudes edited by prominent Teachers College professors such as William Van Til, Hilda Taba, and William Heard Kilpatrick (Davis, 1999). In addition to criticism that DuBois' work lacked scientific credibility, intercultural education was also derided for attention to "foods and festivals" as is typical of the current "holiday" curriculum frequently practiced in elementary social studies classrooms. Although DuBois' work may have been discounted by her contemporaries in academia, the influence of the holiday curriculum in social education has been long lasting. Currently, *The National Standards for History includes* holidays, such as, Martin Luther King's birthday, Presidents' Day, Memorial Day, the Fourth of July, Labor Day, Veterans Day, and Thanksgiving in the K-4 curricula. However, a significant difference exists between the current emphasis on holidays, and DuBois' work. Current celebrations commemorate "democratic values and principles," to help students understand the influence of ideas rather than to appreciate different cultural contributions as DuBois desired (Nash & Crabtree, 1996, p. 33).

In practice, the "holiday curriculum" has several weaknesses. It has been criticized for promoting superficial understanding of cultural heritage, rather than fostering in-depth thinking and problem solving skills. Furthermore, such a curriculum is viewed as stereotypic and sterile in content (Chapin & Messick, 1999; Seefeldt, 2005). Because the holiday curriculum typically promotes commonly celebrated American holidays, national identity and pride is fostered, but such a nation-centered curriculum frequently does not promote comprehensive understanding of other cultures and holidays that are celebrated in various parts of the world, as DuBois supported.

CONTRIBUTIONS TO EDUCATION

Sadly, DuBois' name and her intercultural education movement have "languished in obscurity" (Davis, 1999, p. 180) even though her contributions served as a foundation and precursor to the current multicultural education and ethnic studies movements.

Indeed, DuBois' pioneering work in social education and her concern for social justice merit increased recognition. She possessed a determined and rebellious spirit that catapulted her forward in pursuit of helping students and teachers recognize the contributions of various ethnic, racial, and religious groups, such as Germans, Jews, and African Americans. As a Quaker, she remained committed to pacifism through two world wars, and throughout her life demonstrated deep concern for race relations in the United States. She authored many books and articles that promoted ethnic understanding, group conversation methods, community action, and educational curriculum methods. She also developed the popular radio program, "Americans All—Immigrants All."

Even today DuBois would have her detractors. Arthur Schlesinger, Jr. (1992) believes that there are healthy consequences in celebrating difference and recognizing ethnicity, however, he cautions that the "cult of ethnicity" poses a danger of "fragmentation, resegregation, and tribalization" in American society (pp. 16-18). In his work *The Disuniting of America* (1992) he also argues that "hearing nice things about one's own ethnic past" will not solve the problem of low self-esteem that many students face (p. 101). Diane Ravitch (2000; Ravitch & Vinovskis, 1995) and William Bennett et al. (1999) are also champions of cultural unity, and warn against the dangers of ethnocentrism. Indeed, Bennett notes that attention to women, minorities, and cultures are healthy developments for schools, but warns that multiculturalism should not, "keep us from teaching students about the common inheritance that binds Americans together" (1999, p. 243).

James Banks, however, adopts an approach that celebrates cultural pluralism and ethnicity similar to DuBois' approach, especially in *Teaching Strategies for Ethnic Studies* (1991) where he discusses concepts and strategies for studying Native Americans, African Americans, European Americans, and Asian Americans. He, however, advocates deep understanding that pushes learning beyond "foods and festivals" and transforms curriculum and multicultural understanding. For example, Banks' dimensions of multicultural education include content integration, knowledge construction, prejudice reduction, equity pedagogy, and empowering school and social structures (Banks, 1997, p. 69). Certainly, DuBois sought similar goals, but often her complex work was simplified in school assembly programs.

CONCLUSIONS

Rachel Davis DuBois died in 1993 at the age of 101 years old. She lived a long life, dedicated to celebrating cultural pluralism. She worked to improve social education and fought for social justice, especially with respect to race relations. Her strategy for incorporating holiday celebrations may have been implemented in a manner that was watered down by teachers, but her ideas were fundamentally sophisticated and progressive for their time. Furthermore, DuBois sought practical solutions to real problems that could be implemented in real schools. Assembly programs, holiday curricula, group dialogue, and conflict resolution are lasting legacies of DuBois' intercultural education work and because of that and more, her pioneering efforts and accomplishments deserve to be remembered.

REFERENCES

Adamic, L. (1934, November). Thirty million new Americans. *Harpers Monthly Magazine, CLXIX*, 684-694.

Banks, J. A. (1997). *Educating citizens in a multicultural society.* New York: Teachers College Press.

Banks, J. A. (1991). *Teaching strategies for ethnic studies* (5th ed.). Boston, MA: Allyn & Bacon.

Bennett, W. J., Finn, C. E., & Cribb, J. T. E., Jr. (1999). *The educated child.* New York: The Free Press.

Bohan, C. H. (2005). Digging trenches: Nationalism and the first national report on the elementary history curriculum. *Theory and Research in Social Education, 33*(2), 266-291.

Chapin, J., & Messick, R. (1999). *Elementary social studies.* New York: Longman.

Cremin, L. A. (1988). *American education: The metropolitan experience 1876-1980.* New York: Harper & Row.

Counts, G. S. (1932). *Dare the school build a new social order?* Carbondale & Evansville: Southern Illinois University Press.

Davis, O. L., Jr. (2002). Rachel Davis DuBois. In M. S. Crocco & O. L. Davis, Jr. (Eds.), *A legacy recovered: Women working in the social studies—Bulletin 100* (pp. 51-52). Washington, DC: National Council for the Social Studies.

Davis, O. L. Jr. (1999). Rachel Davis DuBois: Intercultural education pioneer. In M. S. Crocco & O. L. Davis, Jr. (Eds.), *Bending the future to their will: Civic women, social education, and democracy* (pp. 169-184). New York: Rowman and Littlefield.

DuBois, R. D. (1943). *Get together Americans: Friendly approaches to racial and cultural conflicts through the neighborhood-home festival.* New York: Harper & Brothers.

DuBois, R. D. (1950). *Neighbors in action: A manual for local leaders in intergroup relations.* New York: Harper & Brothers.

DuBois, R. D., with Okorodudu, C. (1984). *All this and something more: Pioneering in intercultural education*. Bryn Mawr, PA: Dorrance & Co.

DuBois, R. D., & Li, M. S. (1963). *The art of group conversation: A new breakthrough in social communication*. New York: Association Press.

DuBois, W. E. B. (1968). *The autobiography of W. E. B. DuBois: A soliloquy on viewing my life from the last decade of its first century*. New York: International Publishers.

DuBois, W. E. B. (1903). *The souls of black folk*. New York: Bantam Books.

Gordon, L. D. (1990). *Gender and higher education in the progressive era*. New Haven, CT: Yale University Press.

Hamilton, A. (2004). *A vision for girls: Gender, education and the Bryn Mawr School*. Baltimore, MD: Johns Hopkins University Press.

Lambert, B. (1993, April 2). Rachel Davis DuBois, 101, educator who promoted value of diversity. *The New York Times*, p. B7.

Lucas, C. (1994). *American higher education: A history*. New York: Griffin.

Montalto, N. (1982). *A history of the intercultural education movement, 1924-1941*. New York: Garland.

Nash, G., & Crabtree, C. (1996). *National standards for history*. Los Angeles, CA: National Center for History in Schools.

Ravitch, D. (2000). *Left back: A century of battles over school reform*. New York: Touchstone.

Ravitch, D., & Vinovskis, M. A. (Eds.). (1995). *Learning from the past: What history teaches us about school reform*. Baltimore, MD: Johns Hopkins University Press.

Schlesinger, A. M., Jr. (1992). *The disuniting of America: Reflections on a multicultural society*. New York: W. W. Norton.

Seefeldt, C. (2005). *Social studies for the preschool/primary child*. Upper Saddle River, NJ: Pearson.

Solomon, B. (1985). *In the company of educated women*. New Haven, CT: Yale University Press.

CHAPTER 7

"TAKE A WALK AROUND YOURSELF"

Diversity and Equity in the Work of Alice Miel

Mindy Spearman

INTRODUCTION

As a new principal in a small Michigan elementary school in 1937, Alice Miel found herself supervising a teacher who was "very set in her ways" (Harbage, 1977). To inspire the teacher to broaden her horizons, Miel centered her faculty meetings around the motto: take a walk around yourself. "There are things you might see if you look," she told her teachers during these meetings (Harbage, 1977). To Miel, the phrase "take a walk around yourself" meant several things. First, that one should reflect inwardly before superficially judging human differences. Second, that educators should "branch out" and teach children about other people and various social problems, such as homelessness, the lack of medical

Addressing Social Issues in the Classroom and Beyond: The Pedagogical Efforts of Pioneers in the Field, 117–134
Copyright © 2007 by Information Age Publishing
All rights of reproduction in any form reserved.   117

care, and hunger (Miel & Brogan, 1957). The maxim, "take a walk around yourself," was emblematic of Miel's life and work.

As a leading twentieth-century educational scholar, Alice Miel sought to encourage democratic practices in school curriculum, instruction, and administration. Her long career as an educator included roles as a public school teacher, principal, curriculum coordinator, university professor, action researcher, and citizen activist. As an advocate for social change, Miel frequently wrote about the importance of including social issues in the curriculum. She was principally interested in issues of equity and diversity, especially as she approached the end of her career (Yeager, 1999, p. 220).

Speaking of Miel's interest in diversity, Louise Berman, a noted professor in the field of curriculum and instruction who recently retired after a long and distinguished career at the University of Maryland, College Park, observed that

> [Alice] was very interested in diversity issues and would always be very sensitive to people's feelings. I co-taught several courses with her in New York, and she worked a lot on the basis of feeling. She was very careful and sensitive to how students would take different comments. I think that she was very sensitive to the types of backgrounds her students came from, different lands, rich and poor, etc. (L. Berman, personal communication with author, February 2006)

Miel also addressed and supported the concept of global cooperation in regard to such concerns as human rights issues, urban reform, peace education, and the democratic socialization of youth.

Miel insisted that democratic social learning be the primary goal of public education. Especially important to her conception of democratic education was helping children "extend their life-space." Commenting on what she meant by this, she wrote: "We must help learners extend their life-space by bringing new persons into it. Face-to-face or, if necessary, vicarious contacts can help students become aware of persons different from themselves in race, religion, socioeconomic status, language, or nationality" (Miel, 1996). She considered such expansion intrinsic to a successful democracy.

Miel also believed that it was important to eliminate "tight life-space boundaries" early in a person's life (Miel, 1992), and thus "targeted" the upper elementary grades (pre-adolescents between the ages of 8 and 14) in this regard (Miel & Brogan, 1957). During the pre-adolescent period of human growth, youngsters begin to form tight bonds with other humans, particularly in close same-sex friendships. Miel felt that "this is the time when, developmentally, it is possible to see the world through the eyes of another, a best friend" (1957, p. 59). Through empathy gained from burgeoning best friend relationships, Miel thought youth would be able to develop a lifelong base for democratic social learning.

INFLUENCES ON MIEL'S THINKING AND PEDAGOGICAL EFFORTS

German psychologist Kurt Lewin first coined the term "life-space" (*psychologischer Lebensraum*), conceptualizing it as a web of interpersonal and intrapersonal relationships unique to the perception of the individual. In particular, Miel was struck by Lewin's idea that heterogeneity could have a positive effect on group dynamics (Miel, 1946, p. 89). More specifically, Miel interpreted Lewin's ideas as "diversity within unity," searching for "conditions which will allow different individuals to live in unity while exercising their rights to uniqueness" (Ambrose & Miel, 1958, p. 7). In an ideal democracy, she believed "we are alike together and we are different together" (Miel & Brogan, 1957, p. 6). She also believed that unity need not "come at the price of diversity" (Miel, 1970, p. 84).

Miel applied Lewin's ideas to schools by urging educators to help children remove "the blanket of conformity" (Miel & Kiester, 1967a, p. 46)—that is, a rigid adherence to following the system and cast out "miscreants." She was very much concerned that young students often failed to stand up for their personal feelings when encountering social situations. This homogeneity, she feared, had in part been created by the school system itself. Miel recommended that educators be "creative" and "resourceful" in combating this problem (Psaltis & Miel, 1964). For example, she asked teachers to seat students in ways that would encourage diversity, and to mix up classroom seating arrangements frequently. Furthermore, Miel suggested that through roundtable discussions about controversial subjects students could better see multiple sides of issues and foster a tolerance for different opinions. She also urged administrators to pay foreign students, like substitute teachers, to come and sit with children during the class day (Psaltis & Miel, 1964). Importantly, she advised educators to teach more than simple tolerance (Miel & Kiester, 1967b). In doing so, Miel asked that teachers help students respect human differences (Miel, 1991).

THE SHORTCHANGED CHILDREN OF SUBURBIA

To help address issues of human diversity in schools, Miel directed the Study of Schools in Changing Communities research team. From 1958 to 1962, Teacher's College (Columbia University) researchers gathered data from a suburban school system in New York. To preserve anonymity, the seaside suburb was given the pseudonym "New Village" By way of teacher, parent, and student interviews, the project examined if and how suburban homogeneity affected the young learners of New Village:

> How well is suburbia—the home of vast numbers of Americans and increasingly the trend-setter for the entire population—preparing the young people of today for such a future? Lacking first hand contact, how do suburban children learn about human difference, and what do they think about it? How can they acquire respect for persons whom their middle-class society brands less acceptable than themselves? And what can adults—parents, school administrators, classroom teachers, community organizations—do to groom the coming generation for a proper role in a middle class society? (Miel & Kiester, 1967a, p. 11)

A 1964 *Educational Leadership* article entitled "Are Children in the Suburbs Different?" discussed results from one portion of the 4-year study—a questionnaire given to New Village sixth-graders. Co-written by Miel and Betty Psaltis, an assistant professor at San Francisco State College, the researchers noted that the data suggested a "striking uniformity" in children's responses to questions about human differences (Psaltis & Miel, 1964, p. 437). Three years later, the American Jewish Committee funded the publication of *The Shortchanged Children of Suburbia: What Schools Don't Teach About Human Differences and What Can Be Done About It*. Coauthored by Miel and Edwin Kiester, Jr., this book detailed the study in its entirety, including children's responses to researcher questions, teacher interviews and general impressions.

The Shortchanged Children of Suburbia garnered a great deal of publicity, including evening news broadcasts in the New York City area (Yeager, 1995) and a lengthy article in *The New York Times* (Miel & Kiester, 1967b). Miel recalled favorable reactions to the study, including feedback from parents around the country who reflected upon the conformity issues raised by the publication (Yeager, 1995). *The New York Times* also printed several letters to the editor in support of the study. One reader wrote: "The article by Alice Miel with Edwin Kiester Jr. gave scholarly support to a situation which I have observed during my teaching experience at an elementary school in a New Haven suburb" (Menon, 1967). A New York City schoolteacher wrote: "It makes a point that a segregated education is by its very nature an inferior education because it does not acquaint children with the diversity of American life" (Albro, 1967). In recognition for their efforts in *The Shortchanged Children of Suburbia*, Miel and Kiester were awarded the 1968 National Education Association's Human Rights Award (Yeager, 2002, p. 76).

In *Shortchanged*, Miel and Kiester divided their discussion into four major areas. "From Many Lands" discussed cultural diversity, including ethnic prejudice against immigrants and "foreigners." In "Black and White," Miel and Kiester addressed instances of racial bias exhibited by New Village children. The chapter "Protestant, Catholic, Jew" discussed the ways in which children exhibited confusion about diversity of religion, such as misunderstanding different holiday celebrations and lacking an awareness of non-Judeo-Christian religious traditions. Finally, "Rich and Poor" covered economic materialism and poverty. Miel targeted these four areas—"different nations, races, religions and economic backgrounds" (Miel & Kiester, 1967a, p. 8)—not only in *The Shortchanged Children of Suburbia*, but throughout her life and work.

FROM MANY LANDS: CULTURAL AND ETHNIC DIVERSITY

Today's young people must know how to work with persons from other cultures in improving the world we share. (Miel, 1986, p. 323)

Miel's mother, Ane Marie Jensen, emigrated from Denmark in 1902 at the age of 18. Jensen was hired to work for Lucas M. Miel on his farm in rural Michigan. She cooked, cleaned, and cared for Miel's terminally ill wife and his three children. When her employer's wife died in 1903, Jensen immediately returned to Denmark. However, heartfelt letters from Miel and the children "lured [Jensen] back to marry her former employer" (Miel, 1992). Alice Marie Miel was born soon after, on February 21, 1906.

By 1911, most of her mother's family had moved to Michigan from Denmark. Miel's family frequently held large get-togethers with their Danish relatives. "I always knew there was a world outside my own country," Miel recalled (Miel 1992, p. 458). This early exposure to a foreign culture sensitized Miel to issues of ethnic and cultural diversity. Indeed, Miel acknowledged the extent that her mother's heritage influenced her educational thought:

I grew up proud of my Danish-born mother. As her eight brothers and sisters and finally her aging mother and father followed her to America, I became immersed in a second culture. This experience no doubt influenced me in my later educational writing, where the thread running through is the importance of teaching for understanding and cooperation among persons not only in one's own country but throughout the world. (Quoted in "Contemporary Authors On-line," 2005)

Frequent opportunities for travel also played a role in shaping Miel's ideas about the importance of cultural diversity. Her first trip abroad was to Europe in 1935, with a group of schoolteacher friends. Miel visited seven different countries, including her mother's hometown of Jutland in Denmark. Miel believed that "travel is enlightening and broadening even when one can be only a tourist in a country" (Miel, 1992, p. 461). She personally traveled around the world twice during her life (Harbage, 1977). However, Miel thought that actually living or working in another country offered even deeper opportunities for understanding. Among the countries where she spent significant time were Japan, Afghanistan, Uganda, and Tanzania.

Louise Berman, who met Miel when she (Berman) was in her early twenties and remained friends with her throughout her adult life, notes that

> Alice was quite a hostess to everyone, particularly her students. She had students from many lands, and was always interested in their lives. Her co-op in New York City was furnished with artifacts she had collected from her international travels and she would entertain students four times a year in her home. She had a particular fondness for foreign students, especially ones from Africa, and would ask them about their lives and interests. (L. Berman personal communication with the author, February 2006)

Miel was particularly inspired by her work in Puerto Rico. "It was a different culture, a different language," Miel recalled of her first visit there in the early 1940s (Harbage, 1977). She traveled to Puerto Rico under the direction of Gordon Mackensie, then chair of Teacher's College Department of Curriculum and Teaching, as part of a curriculum survey team of faculty and graduate students. While in Puerto Rico, they trekked to isolated rural schools, meeting with students and staff: "It was just fascinating to get into those rural schools way up in the mountains that you couldn't get to except by walking two or three hours" (Harbage, 1977). In Puerto Rico, as in other countries to which she journeyed, Miel reflected upon the importance of "gained persons in my life-space through travel abroad" (Miel, 1992, p. 462).

When she researched New Village schools for The Shortchanged Children of Suburbia project, Miel found that "there was almost no evidence of ethnic prejudice" (Miel & Kiester 1967a, p. 37). The majority of interviewed parents responded that they favored curricula that explored people of differing national origins. Indeed, Miel noted that ethnic diversity was the only area where parents rejected suburban conformity (Miel & Kiester 1967a, p. 36). Much like Miel's own childhood experience, "one reason for these positive attitudes may have been that such contacts usually involved members of the family—a grand-parent or other relative who had been born abroad" (Miel & Kiester 1967a, p. 37). The only concern raised by the study concerning ethnic origins was that, perhaps, educators over-relied on textbooks and facts; not every teacher was "able to bridge the gap between 'paper' understanding and truly deep understanding of other people" (Miel & Kiester, 1967a, p. 42). Miel suggested that teachers could help improve understanding by striving for geographical balance when covering different nationalities. Rather than focusing on just Europe and North America, schoolchildren should study Asia, Africa, Latin America and Australia as well (Miel & Kiester, 1967a, p. 66). Miel also lobbied for curriculum that recognized differences in nationality among nonwhite races, such as black Americans, for example, who came from the West Indies, Puerto Rico and South America (Miel & Kiester 1967a, p. 67). Finally, Miel urged educators to be cognizant of unspoken platitudes of American superiority: "Stress the fundamental truth that America and its culture are not the measure of all others—that we look as strange to other peoples as they do to us" (Miel & Kiester, 1967a, p. 67).

Miel continued to write and theorize about global understanding throughout her career. As chair and co-chair of the Association for Supervision and Curriculum Development's (ASCD) Commission on International Cooperation (1966-1971), she was heavily involved with the 1970 ASCD world conference in Asilomar, California (Yeager, 1995). During the conference, Miel asked that educators convene under the theme "Unity with Diversity" as a world community (Miel, 1970). She hoped that international meetings like the Asilomar conference could help educators conduct multinational research, solve educational problems and better plan intercultural curriculum. Intercultural curriculum, Miel believed, had two major goals: "One aspect of it is helping children discover how much like other people we are, what we have in common with them, how similar are our wants and needs. The other is helping children understand why differences in cultures have arisen and helping them to value those differences as a means of enriching the lives of us all" (Miel, 1944, p. 16).

BLACK AND WHITE: RACIAL DIVERSITY

The issue of race is the one where improved teaching is most urgently needed. Children must be taught to recognize that the white society surrounding them is very different from the rest of the globe, where the majority is non-white. (Miel & Kiester, 1967b, p. SM50)

The small town where Miel was raised was homogeneously white. Of the 800 inhabitants in Stanton, Michigan, there was but one black family, who lived on a farm outside of town (Miel, 1992, p. 463). During her work as a teacher (1924-1936), principal (1936-1939) and curriculum coordinator (1939-1942) in the Michigan school system, Miel had an ever-increasing opportunity to work with parents and students of different races. Then, when she took a position at Columbia University's Teachers College (TC) in 1942, Miel lived in a cooperative on West 123rd Street that was located in a racially diverse neighborhood of New York City (Berman, 1996, p. 1976). Through this setting, and through her close work with minority students and faculty at the university, Miel became part of an open and inviting diverse community.

Elizabeth Yeager, Miel's primary biographer, conducted extensive interviews with Miel in 1994. During her talks with Yeager, Miel revealed a particularly poignant experience that impacted her thoughts about race relations. Miel recalled stopping at a cafe with a group of Teacher College students near New York City: "We went in, and they refused to serve us because we had one black person with us. So we all walked out in a body, and we got back to the bus and were going to find another place, but this person (the black student) just disappeared, didn't stay with us any longer. I felt so hurt, so angry ... it stayed with me for a long time (quoted in Yeager, 1995, p. 95).

At this time, Teacher's College was one of the few universities to accept black students (Berman, 1989, p. 100). Because of this open-door policy, Miel herself frequently enrolled black students in her courses (Yeager, 1995).

Miel's concern for racial equity was manifest in *The Shortchanged Children of Suburbia*. Many of the interview questions targeted racial issues. In one case, primary students were shown a photograph of a black boy and white boy walking arm and arm down a street. "Which boy would you choose to play with and why?" the interviewers asked. Of the 235 children interviewed, 187 chose the white child. When asked to explain their choice, most of the children exhibited anxiety and looked uneasy. Many tried to avoid the topic of race, calling the white boy "the little one" or the "better-dressed one"—even though the two children were dressed identically (Miel & Kiester, 1967a, p. 17). In a similar act of avoidance, most New Village teachers shied away from discussions about race. Many teachers spoke about race only during Social Studies—usually in a History unit about the Civil War or George Washington Carver. In one case, a teacher admitted to anxiety when discussing slavery:

> I recently had an Abraham Lincoln story, and I shuddered when we came to the slaves, one teacher recalled. I have a colored boy in my class, and he felt very uneasy, I know, when I started to read it. I purposely omitted the word 'Negro.' I just slipped by and said 'slavery,' and I didn't show them pictures

of that particular thing; I just turned the page and hoped no one would ask. (Miel & Kiester, 1967a, p. 16)

The problem with suburban schools such as New Village, Miel thought, was "what the schools don't teach" (Miel & Kiester, 1967a, p. 52). Some of the interviewees' spouted platitudes such as minorities were "entitled to their rights" and that racial slurs were "not nice" (Miel & Kiester, 1967a, p. 15). Yet, their willingness to offer such culturally approved statements did not necessarily mean that they honored those feelings in their hearts. By avoiding the topic of race in school, students exhibited only a surface tolerance instead of a "mutual understanding and appreciation" (Miel, 1944, p. 16). Speaking of the study, Miel commented that: "Like their elders, many children talked a tolerance they did not feel—a state of affairs that cannot have been conducive to good mental health. It had been impressed on them that it was improper to make anti-Negro remarks, but no one had taken the complementary step of inspiring them with real respect for Negroes as human beings" (Miel & Kiester, 1967a, p. 56).

Miel suggested that teachers introduce new subject matter that addressed the topic of race. In doing so, she encouraged the teaching of a curriculum that brought potentially difficult social issues to the forefront, such as riots, voting-rights litigation, school desegregation, and labor unions (Miel & Kiester, 1967a, p. 62).

Although she never returned to research on suburban children after completing the Study of Schools in Changing Communities research, Miel's commitment to racial equity continued throughout her career. For example, she called educators to practice global cooperation by relating to all peoples in her 1991 article "Education and Democracy in a New World." Later, in 1996, Miel asked that society take "'a new post-O. J.' look at race relations" (Miel 1996).[1]

As a political activist, she became an advocate for affirmative action policies and social spending for minority programs. As a researcher, she mentored many graduate students and young faculty at Teacher's College (Columbia University), many of whom were influenced by her work as an activist. In recent years, specifically since Yeager's scholarly attention to Miel's life and work, educational historians have begun acknowledging the importance of Miel's efforts to bring racial issues into the classroom during the Progressive Era.

RICH AND POOR: SOCIOECONOMIC DIVERSITY

We must now educate for more concern over the growing gap between the extremely rich and the very poor. (Miel, 1996)

In 1936, during the height of the Depression, Miel became principal of the Patrick Donovan School on Wall Street in Ann Arbor, Michigan. During this period, Miel saw schools suffering from severe budget cuts that resulted in a loss of teachers and materials (Koopman, 1961). Since the school was so small, she became a "teaching principal"—not only providing administrative support but also substitute teaching, spending time with children in classrooms, and accompanying them on field trips (Harbage, 1977). Through this formative experience she worked closely with students from poverty-stricken homes, most of whom "did not have the normal advantages" (Reade & Wineberg, 1992, p. 106). Located in a particularly impoverished section of the fifth ward, families near the tiny school struggled to find clothing and shelter. Miel thus became aware of the "increasing distance between the standards of living of the affluent and the poor" (Lewis & Miel, 1972, p. v).

Miel felt that witnessing socioeconomic struggles during this time instilled in her "important democratic building blocks" that influenced her educational thought (Miel, 1991, p. 269). At this time, she was particularly inspired by Franklin Roosevelt's "galvanizing phrases" about freedom—including freedom from fear and freedom from want (Miel, 1991, p. 269).

From Miel's perspective, the school environment often exacerbated the gap between the rich and the poor. She acknowledged that children from different socioeconomic environments had different needs that schools were failing to reach (Ambrose & Miel, 1958). In particular, children from lower social classes were negatively affected: "The dissatisfaction with the middle-class culture of the school on the part of children in the lower social classes has long been decried" (Psaltis & Miel, 1964, p. 440). She referred specifically to the wide gulf between the middle-class values taught at school and the real life experiences of the bulk of the children in attendance. Miel believed that curriculum which targeted economic differences would help children gain insight into their own values and better understand the values of others. Miel considered the data gathered on children's perceptions of economic differences the most appalling result of "The Shortchanged Children of Suburbia" study.

The children of New Village knew almost nothing about persons less well off than themselves. Moreover, their attitude toward the less fortunate was almost insufferably patronizing—a response that was not surprising in view of the great emphasis placed on material wealth in New Village, as in most suburbs (Miel & Kiester, 1967a).

When shown a photograph of poor white children, New Village children made inferences like "The white girls are not Americans, because they don't look like Americans. They must be refugees" (Miel & Kiester, 1967a, p. 28). Miel found that when teachers discussed poverty in their classrooms, it was in an international context only, thus failing to address issues of economic equality in their own society (Miel & Kiester 1967a, p. 27). Interestingly, it had never occurred to some of the New Village teachers to discuss impoverished Americans. For example, one participating teacher commented, "Goodness, they really don't know much about poor white children, do they? They don't see many, I guess" (Miel & Kiester 1967b).

Miel suggested that teachers introduce studies of poverty into the school curriculum, including the "human condition generally" (Miel & Kiester, 1967a, p. 63). First, she argued, the curriculum should include the study of basic economic concepts—wants and needs, resources, choice, occupations, etc. Second, children should learn about government institutions designed to promote economic welfare, both at the national and international level, for example, Social Security, Medicare, public housing, the United Nations, UNESCO and the Peace Corps (Miel & Kiester, 1967b, p. 63). Finally, students should learn about historic aspects of poverty (e.g., the Great Depression and sweatshops). In order to address these topics, Miel suggested using "literature, films, photographs and magazine articles" as well as hands-on field trips (Miel & Kiester 1967a, p. 63).

Yet, Miel realized, that in order to educate students, teachers themselves had to possess an understanding of economic inequality in the United States. Miel recommended that school faculty study Warner and Lunt's *The Social Life of a Modern Community* in order to gain an understanding of the different socioeconomic classes that constitute American society (Miel, 1946). Such a book study, she believed, might help teachers shed some of their "middle class mores" and learn how better to interact with parents and children of every class (Miel, 1946, p. 97). If that happened, she believed that educators would more likely be able to write curriculum that demonstrates "That all persons do not share equally in material things, under the American system, but that all, nonetheless, are full and equal members of democracy, and that the work of some is no less worthy for being less highly rewarded than that of others" (Miel & Kiester, 1967a, p. 62).

PROTESTANT, CATHOLIC, JEW: RELIGIOUS DIVERSITY

Teach comparative religion, even at early ages ... help students understand the common elements of various faiths, as well as the kinds and sources of differences between them. (Miel & Kiester, 1967b)

Miel grew up in a community without significant religious diversity. Her family, friends, and most of her neighbors were Protestant. Of her early life in Stanton, Michigan, Miel remembered that: "There was only one Jewish family, but I did not discover that they were Jewish until it was mentioned casually, without malice, long after I had gone away to college. The Catholic Church was too small to have a resident priest and we rather looked down on its members because their religion seemed somewhat strange" (Miel, 1992, p. 463).

Upon encountering people of differing faiths in later years, Miel became interested in promoting religious equity. When invited to direct the "Study of Schools in Changing Communities" sponsored by the American Jewish Committee, Miel accepted.

Researchers found that New Village children knew more about religious diversity than any of the other human differences included in the "Shortchanged Children of Suburbia" study. Furthermore, the children rarely exhibited religious bias; in fact, more often they expressed a curiosity about the belief systems of others:

> At Christmas, one teacher reported, a child asked in class, "Is it possible for a Jew to believe in Christmas?" On Ash Wednesday another teacher was asked why she had an "ink spot" on her forehead. During Lent, a Protestant child wanted to know why Catholics gave up something as a sacrifice. When it was explained, she said she wished she were Catholic so she could give up something, too. (Miel & Kiester 1967a, p. 32)

However, it was generally only on the occasion when a student brought up the subject by chance that teachers actually addressed the subject of religion in the classroom (Miel & Kiester, 1967a). Miel was aware that part of the avoidance may have stemmed from a controversy brewing in the New Village system over whether Christmas or Hanukkah should be studied in the schools (Miel & Kiester, 1967a). Be that as it may, Miel reasoned, and commented, that teachers could teach about religious differences without proselytizing: "A reasonable working rule is that religious indoctrination and devotional exercises—even non-sectarian ones—do not belong in the public school, but that objective study about religion, as an important part of human life, culture, and history, has a place there. Similar criteria would seem to apply to holiday activities" (Miel & Kiester, 1967a, p 64).

Miel recommended that school boards, communities, and parents come together to make decisions about how to include religion in the curriculum. Once a district had clear-cut policies that upheld the Bill of Rights, Miel suggested involving religious leaders in the curriculum by sponsoring field trips and providing factual information (Miel & Kiester, 1967a). She also stressed that: "Religion does not correspond to race or appearance. For instance, show photographs of a Chinese Protestant, a blond Jew, or a Negro Catholic" (Miel & Kiester, 1967a, p. 65).

Importantly, Miel did not limit her call for religious equity to Judeo-Christian faiths only. More specifically, she urged teachers to consider the following: "As children grow in understanding, go beyond Protestantism, Catholicism and Judaism to include Islam, Hinduism, Buddhism, Confucianism" (Miel & Kiester, 1967a, p. 65). Additionally, she believed it important to discuss religious tenants like polytheism, animism and ancestor worship. She also suggested that teachers include secular philosophies like agnosticism, humanism and atheism (Miel & Kiester, 1967a). This, Miel thought, could help address children's natural curiosity, promote religious understanding, and clear up much of the confusion that children have about how their own personal value systems connect to those of others.

Understandably, "the American Jewish Committee was pleased with the final product" of the study conducted by Miel (Yeager, 1995, p. 299).

THE WORLD COUNCIL FOR CURRICULUM AND INSTRUCTION (WCCI)

Miel was extremely committed to spreading ideas about democratic social learning internationally. As an active member of the Association for Supervision and Curriculum Development (ASCD), she organized a special ad hoc committee on international relations and served as its Chair and Co-Chair. The committee's efforts culminated in the Asilomar, California, World Conference on Education, March 5-14, 1970. Speaking of the events leading up to the conference, Louise Berman made the following observation:

> After I got my doctorate, I went to work for ASCD [the Association of Supervision and Curriculum Development]. I got many letters from people all over asking what ASCD was doing for international education. I decided that I would get together all the people who wrote letters and would have them meet with Alice. When I arrived at that meeting, which she was chairing, they were talking about having a world conference with two representatives from every nation. It was very much not USA based; they wanted it to be a true world conference. When I walked out of that meeting, I thought, "Well, these folks are really pipe-dreaming!" But Alice made it happen. She was a very remarkable person. We had the Asilomar conference and it had the kind of representation that they wanted. (L. Berman personal communication with the author, February 2006)

More than 350 participants from 60 different nations attended the conference (Harbage, 1977), whose purpose was "to initiate the development of a worldwide community of educators who would view their fields in cross-national ways" (Berman 1970, p. vi). Although the focus of the conference was not specifically social issues, some of the papers presented targeted ideas such as social environments, worldwide problems, and cooperative education.

The 1970 Asilomar conference gave birth to the World Wide Council for Curriculum and Instruction (WCCI), of which Miel is recognized as one of its cofounders. More specifically, she helped draft the organization's constitution, which included a powerful commitment to diversity: "to provide professional, ideological, and moral support in order to free people from prejudices and strengthen them to find ways and means to solve the problems they face" (Yeager, 1995, p. 322). With Betty Reardon, a longtime peace educator based at Teachers College, Columbia University, she served as Executive Secretary for the first 10 years of WCCI (1970-1980). Referring to her involvement during the first few years of WCCI, Miel said: "an organization needs to get on its feet with the managerial things" (Harbage, 1977). Consequently, she organized membership lists, sent out mailings and set-up several international committees (Harbage, 1977). She also helped to orchestrate WCCI's first two triennial conferences—one in England and one in Turkey.

In 1974, the WCCI broke away from its parent organization, the Association for Supervision and Curriculum Development, and became a nongovernmental organization (NGO) affiliated with the United Nations. Miel served as a lifetime member of the WCCI executive board (Berman, 1998). She attended every international conference throughout the 1970s and 1980s and remained an active participant in the organization during her lifetime (Berman, 1989). Miel's contributions to the organization are commemorated each conference year with the "Alice Miel Memorial Lecture" and a special scholarship fund set up through the WCCI.

A MENTOR, A COLLEAGUE, A FRIEND

Even though Alice Miel was revered by her students and others, she was not only approachable but kindhearted and welcoming to friends and strangers alike. O. L. Davis Jr., a noted curriculum specialist and longtime professor of curriculum and instruction at the University of Texas, Austin, relates this story about his initial contact with "Dr. Miel":

> I first met Alice at the Spring 1958 Curriculum Research Conference in Chicago. Dave Turney, my Peabody classmate, and I asked to take her to lunch the first day of the meeting … and she accepted our invitation. I couldn't believe it! Alice Miel, whose books we had read and whose students thought

that she sat near, if not at, the right hand of God, had agreed to have lunch with these two almost-strangers, Dave who had come to Peabody from Washington state and I who had come to Peabody after 3 years active duty in the navy. So what do you do when you have lunch with "Dr. Miel?" Why you talk with her about what you have been doing and want to do, she insisted, and we did. The lunch extended effortlessly into 2 hours and, by that time, "Dr. Miel" had become "Alice" and we never called her anything but by this name for all the years that we knew her. Oh yes, I remember that she told me that she liked my dissertation findings. A lunch can't get much better than that. (O. L. Davis, personal communication with the author, January, 2006)

As Davis recalls, Miel could also be all business. Here Davis speaks about an important lesson that he and other young members of the ASCD-sponsored Professors of Curriculum Group learned from her:

Alice continued to participate in the Professors of Curriculum group [that met at ASCD for many years] long after her retirement from TC. One year, she listened to several of the younger members talk about what some of the senior curriculum workers "thought" during some unspecified period of time. I noticed that Alice was becoming more than a bit irritated as this discussion proceeded. When the moderator invited questions or comments, Alice asked if she might address the group. I wish that someone had tape-recorded her remarks; we are left only with our memories. As I recall, Alice noted that she "thought" throughout her life and career and, furthermore, she wanted everyone to know that her "thoughts" had not remained the same over the course of her life. Simply, she had changed her "thoughts" as a result of her thinking. She never betrayed anger although she seemed a bit flinty that afternoon as she requested her younger colleagues [as well as others] to search for changes in scholars' and practitioners' thinking over time—changes that likely exist—and never to assume that her or another's position on an issue at one particular time represented her or their position at another time. At that occasion, all of us present surely must have understood Alice's insistence that her career or, even, dimensions of her career (e.g., her consultancies, her research, her writings) not be characterized as some generalized "thought" or "action." Rather, she knew—and wanted the rest of us to know—that her thinking and acting and writing always were affected by her encounters with new people, new articles and books, new conversations, new ideas, new.... At least some of us heard Alice that afternoon. Her response has influenced us in a number of ways, from our choice of verb tenses as we have portrayed individuals' ideas and as we insist that our students seek to understand reasonable differences, even nuances of meanings, in the work and writings of other practitioners and scholars. What an afternoon! (O. L. Davis, personal communication with the author, January, 2006)

CONCLUSION: TAKE A WALK AROUND YOURSELF

Miel was proud of her efforts to diversify curriculum. She felt that, at the time, she was a "lone voice" advocating for the inclusion of human differences within insipid suburban curricula (Yeager, 1995, p. 299).

Louise Berman, who met Miel when she (Berman) was in her twenties and was lifelong friends with her, recalls Miel's final speech:

> Her final talk—I think when she was 90—was for Kappa Delta Pi. She was a distinguished Laureate with Kappa Delta Pi and that year was the year they brought Alice in. She was very feeble at that time ... I don't think I realized how feeble she was ... but she still spoke. As I recall, it had to do with having a world-mindedness, which she called "cosmopolitanism." The speech was sort of a summary of some of the things that I've heard her talk about over the years. (L. Berman personal communication with the author, February, 2006)

Miel's *New York Times* obituary praised her as a pioneer in the curriculum field: "Her concern was that too many children were growing up without a clue to their country's social and racial diversity. It was a conclusion that most of her peers had yet to reach" (Saxon, 1998).

Miel was convinced that teachers had a responsibility to educate students about human differences—both for the benefit of democracy and for their own personal well being; that is, children should be brought "into contact, both directly and indirectly, with people from racial, cultural, and ethnic groups other than their own so they may grow to identify themselves with mankind" (Miel, 1958, p. 91). By providing educators with practical advice as to how to teach about equity and diversity, her ideas helped teachers accomplish such a goal at the classroom level.

Au: Did not find Miel, 1958 in the reference list. NOTE: this reference will be deleted if not furnished with the index.

Miel's contributions to educational thought are manifold. She wrote about cooperative supervision, democratic leadership, international collaboration, creative teaching, and social learning. Yet it is her work with human differences that emerges as particularly illuminating. Miel's maxim, "take a walk around yourself," necessitates abandonment of the "me-first" attitude that tends to permeate society (Miel, 1996). Her ideas for incorporating diversity into school curriculum broaden the life-spaces of both teachers and students. It is important that Miel's suggestions for including social issues in the curriculum continue to enrich classroom practice today.

NOTE

1. Miel, of course, was referring to the great amount of tension that arose between many whites and blacks as a result of the arrest and court trial of O. J. Simpson, a famous former football star in the National Football League, who was accused, but subsequently found not guilty, of killing his estranged young white wife and a white man she was with.

REFERENCES

Albro, S. (1967, April 30). Another side (Letter to the Editor). *The New York Times*, p. 233.

Ambrose, E., & Miel A. (1958). *Children's social learning*. Washington, DC: Association for Supervision and Curriculum Development.

Berman, L. (1970). Introduction. In A. Miel & L. Berman (Eds.), *In the minds of men: Educating the young people of the world* (pp. vi-vii). Washington, DC: Association for Supervision and Curriculum Development.

Berman, L. (1989, Winter). Alice Miel: Leader in democracy's ways. *Childhood Education*, pp. 98-102.

Berman, L. (1996). Alice Miel: Exemplar of democracy made real. In C. Kridel, R. V. Bullough, & P. Shaker (Eds.), *Teacher and mentors: Profiles of distinguished twentieth-century professors of education* (pp. 173-183). New York: Garland.

Berman, L. (1998). Alice Miel: 1906-1998. Retrieved August 27, 2005 from http://www2.alliant.edu/gsoe/wcci/miel.htm

Harbage, Mary (1977). Interview (of Alice Miel) by Mary Harbage, November 1977. Archives of the Association for Childhood Education International (ACEI), Collection # 87-190, Hornbake Library, The University of Maryland.

Lewis, A., & Miel, A. (1972). *Supervision for improved instruction: New challenges, new responses*. Belmont, CA: Wadsworth.

Koopman, G. R. (1961). *Curriculum development*. New York: The Center for Applied Research in Education.

Miel, A. (1944). Living in a modern world. In G. Mackenzie (Ed.), *Toward a new curriculum: Yearbook of the Department of Supervision and Curriculum Development and National Education Association* (pp. 11-21). Washington, DC: National Education Association.

Miel, A. (1946). *Changing the curriculum: A social process*. New York: D. Appleton-Century.

Miel, A. (1970). Toward a world community of educators: Unity with diversity. In A. Miel & L. Berman (Eds.), *In the minds of men: Educating the young people of the world* (pp. 83-88). Washington, DC: Association for Supervision and Curriculum Development.

Miel, A. (1986, Spring). Teaching for a democracy. *The Educational Forum, 50,* 319-323.

Miel, A. (1991). Education and democracy in a new world. In D. L. Burleson (Ed.), *Reflections: Personal essays by 33 distinguished educators* (pp. 268-278). Bloomington, IN: Phi Delta Kappa Educational Foundation.

Miel, A. (1992, Summer). Roaming through a life-space. *The Educational Forum, 56*, 457-463.

Miel, A. (1996, Summer). Curriculum that matters: Visions of what ought to be. *The Educational Forum, 60*, 340-342.

Miel, Alice Marie (2005, March 25). *Contemporary authors online*. The Gale Group.

Miel, A., & Brogan, P. (1957). *More than social studies: A view of social learning in the elementary school*. Englewood Cliffs, NJ: Prentice-Hall.

Miel, A., & Kiester, E., Jr. (1967a). *The shortchanged children of suburbia: What schools don't teach about human differences and what can be done about it*. New York: Institute of Human Relations Press, The American Jewish Committee.

Miel, A., & Kiester E. (1967b, April 16). The shortchanged children. *The New York Times*, p. SM50.

Menon, M. (1967, May 7). The children have their say (Letter to the Editor). *The New York Times*, p. 265.

Psaltis, B., & Miel, A. (1964). Are children in the suburbs different? *Educational Leadership, 21*, 436-440.

Reade, M., & Wineberg, S. (1992). *Historic buildings in Ann Arbor, Michigan*. Ann Arbor, MI: Ann Arbor Historic District Commission.

Saxon, W. (1998, February 15). Alice Miel, 91, expert on role of wider world in curriculum. *The New York Times*, p. 44.

Yeager, E. (1995). *Alice Miel's contributions to the curriculum field*. Unpublished doctoral dissertation, The University of Texas at Austin.

Yeager, E. (1999). "Alice Miel: Progressive advocate of democratic social learning for children. In M. Crocco & O. L. Davis, Jr. (Eds.), *Bending the future to their will: Civic women, social education and democracy* (pp. 207-233). Lanham, MD: Rowman and Littlefield.

Yeager, E. (2002). Alice Miel. In M. Crocco & O. L. Davis, Jr. (Eds.), *Building a legacy: Women in social education 1784-1984* (pp. 75-76). Silver Spring, MD: National Council for the Social Studies.

CHAPTER 8

ALAN F. GRIFFIN

Role Model for the Reflective Study of Modern Problems

William R. Fernekes

INTRODUCTION

During the period 1931-1945, the world was plunged into a catastrophic series of conflicts that culminated in the most destructive war known in human history: World War II. With the end of World War II and the emergence of the Cold War, the global struggle between allies of the United States and the Soviet Union engendered numerous conflicts that heavily influenced the daily conduct of civic affairs. As a result, educational leaders in the United States were faced with a daunting question: how should public education respond to the ideological challenges posed by the rise of fascism, communism, and totalitarianism, while providing a meaningful critique of democratic life? Of those who seriously engaged this question prior to the mid-1960s, few were more eloquent or influential in his contributions to the study of social issues in democratic life than Alan F. Griffin, professor of education in the field of social studies at the Ohio

Addressing Social Issues in the Classroom and Beyond: The Pedagogical Efforts of Pioneers in the Field, 135–158
Copyright © 2007 by Information Age Publishing
All rights of reproduction in any form reserved.

135

State University. In this chapter, Griffin's life and major works are examined to illustrate his considerable influence on the study of social issues during his lifetime and later through the works of other scholars, including Lawrence Metcalf and Shirley Engle.

TRAINING, FORMATIVE INFLUENCES, AND EARLY PUBLICATIONS

Alan Griffin was a native Ohioan, born in 1907, in Barnesville, Ohio. He was the third son born to William and Georgia Griffin, and it was Alan Griffin's destiny to face hardships in his early years which substantially influenced his later outlook on life. When only 8 years old, his mother died of Huntingtons disease, while his brother John, who was also afflicted with this disease, was left an invalid for life. Following his mother's death, Griffin's father made arrangements with his sister Flora to have both Alan and his brother John live with her in Mansfield Ohio, while his father relocated to West Virginia to make a fresh start. Griffin's lifelong skepticism, particularly regarding organized religion, was to some degree shaped by the loss of his mother, while his deep concern and affection for his own family were another consequence of this traumatic period in his early life (Farley, 1978, p. 30).

Following his move to Mansfield, Griffin attended elementary and junior high and simultaneously held a job at the local dairy, one of a series of jobs that helped Griffin develop empathy for the working class, which later translated into a lifelong interest in economic issues and helped Griffin relate to a broad cross-section of the population. Such experiences may have contributed to his becoming committed to the study of social problems (Farley, 1978, p. 36). Another important event which had a critical influence on Griffin's worldview was the growth of anti-German feeling and intolerance toward anyone who questioned the United States war effort during World War I. Book burnings, attempted lynchings of local residents of German background and other acts of intimidation were interpreted by Griffin as examples of fear and ignorance, acts that he decried, and which no doubt were extremely significant in shaping his strong commitment to academic freedom and his opposition to censorship and McCarthyism during the post World War II period (Farley, 1978, p. 39).

During his high school years, Griffin became involved in a variety of academic and co-curricular activities, including debate and forensics, drama, football, and the yearbook. His class annual (yearbook) description provides a capsule summary of how his peers viewed Alan "Mutt" Griffin: "A synonym for athletics, debate, oratory, genius, unexcelled class work, social activities—in fact for anything in the school curriculum, including the writing of a play" (quoted in Farley, 1978, p. 44).

Not only was Griffin well liked by his peers, but he assumed leadership roles, including serving as captain of the football team. At the same time, Griffin's penchant for displaying simultaneously a deep and almost obsessive interest in some topics while demonstrating reluctance to explore areas that did not stimulate him began to emerge before his graduation from high school. As John Robert Farley (1978) notes:

> This was his tendency—to be a brilliant, but reluctant (some would say lazy) student in the conventional sense. More than most students, Griffin seemed to have had a low tolerance for those things that did not interest him. On the other hand, in those areas which he found stimulating, he displayed an enthusiasm and energy which stood in marked contrast to his lethargic approach to routine activities. (p. 44)

Following high school graduation, Griffin enrolled at Case Western Reserve University in 1925, where he remained only 2 years, transferring to the University of Illinois in 1928. Economic difficulties forced Griffin to return to Mansfield in 1928, where he worked in the Empire Steel Foundry. Soon however, Griffin's intellectual interests led him to seek a position as a teacher in the Mansfield public schools. Despite having completed only 2 years of his university education, Griffin secured a position at John Simpson Junior High school, where he began teaching French and Latin in September 1929, continuing there until 1936. Griffin's wide-ranging intellectual interests led him to not only teach languages, but to serve as advisor to the school newspaper, coach the dramatics and debate team, and become active in Democratic party politics. During his public school teaching tenure, he served on the executive committee for Richland County and ran twice for the state legislature, both times unsuccessfully. Now a married man and a father, he also worked as a radio announcer in Mansfield (1927-1930), and as a reporter for the *Mansfield News Journal* (1930-1932), while pursuing his Bachelor of Science degree at the Ohio State University, which he received in 1936. From that point on, Griffin was a member of the Ohio State University staff until his death in 1964. He received his doctoral degree in 1942 from Ohio State, advancing from the position of department assistant in 1946 to the rank of full professor in 1949.

As a student of Boyd Bode, Griffin was heavily influenced by Bode's work in the Progressive Education movement, and by extension, the ideas of John Dewey. Robert Jewett, who first met Alan Griffin in 1935, and later became his doctoral advisee and a colleague at Ohio State, made it clear that Boyd Bode's work had a very substantial influence on Griffin's intellectual development:

> I know that Griffin took all of his [Bode's] courses and seminars, and they became intimate friends too. And I'm sure that Bode's knowledge and interest in John Dewey's form of thinking was largely transferred to Alan Griffin. I would say that he [Bode] was Griffin's major influence in becoming, I would almost say, a follower of Dewey. (R. Jewett, personal communication with author, July 30, 2005)

A strong believer in the active engagement of citizens in civic life, Griffin's work challenged teachers of history and the social sciences to emphasize reflective thought as the primary approach to social studies instruction. In doing so, Griffin endorsed a fundamental premise of progressive education, specifically the application of a critical, socially engaged intelligence to the problems of daily life in a democracy where each citizen collaborated in seeking solutions focusing on the common good.

Griffin also shared Dewey's and Bode's skepticism regarding the positivist emphasis found in much of the educational inquiry during the pre-World War II period. In his 1927 work *Modern Educational Theories*, Bode had argued against the "reduction of curricular decision-making to mathematical and engineering formulas which ignored the ethical basis of educational decisions" (Fernekes, 1985, p. 99). Like Bode, Griffin viewed ethical and moral issues as central in both the content of the curriculum, and in the process of inquiry about human experience.

Simultaneous with the ongoing debates between advocates and critics of progressive educational thought, the emergence of totalitarian regimes in Europe and Asia during the post-World War I period and the worldwide economic crisis of the late 1920s and 1930s challenged educational theorists to reconsider how best to educate citizens in a democratic society. Even before completing his doctoral dissertation in 1942, Alan Griffin had thought deeply about this problem, and published a book directed at a young adult audience, *Freedom American Style* (1940). His rationale for authoring the book is clearly stated in the work's preface:

> The idea of freedom is so much a part of our American tradition that we have come to take it for granted. Now, the impact of a world crisis is shocking us into an awareness that we need to take a fresh look at the tenets of our national faith—to explain it all over again to ourselves and to those around us who seem not to understand what is at stake. Young people especially, whether in school and college or not, need and want to know why we Americans believe in liberty. For the future belongs to them, and they will have to live in it, with or without freedom. (Griffin, 1940, p. iii)

This paragraph contains the seeds of Griffin's mature thinking on the appropriate role of social studies instruction and the social studies teacher in a democracy, ones that he would fully develop in his doctoral dissertation 2 years hence. First, there is an assumption that it is not only appropriate, but obligatory to reexamine the core values and ideas of democratic life. Second, in order to do so, individuals who live in a democratic society need to actively engage in such a reexamination not simply receive beliefs or ideas from leaders without challenging or questioning them. Griffin elaborates on this crucial component later in the work's preface: "Patriotism under a dictatorship is an easy matter requiring nothing more than blind unquestioning obedience. Patriotism in a democracy makes more difficult demands, requiring us to think things through, to understand the meanings of freedom, and to make our own decisions within the frame of our beliefs" (Griffin, 1940, p. iii). Third, the individual in a democracy needs to reflect on his/her own beliefs and values in light of lived experience; in other words, he or she must "build their own framework of beliefs, all the while trueing it up with the facts of their experience" (Griffin, 1940, p. iii).

In contrast to those educators and others who would advocate the inculcation of values within formal schooling from the early grades through the end of secondary education, Griffin argued for the development and consistent use of reflective thought, which he contended was the only way to determine the truth of a proposition or subject. Reflective thought by definition required systematic and continuous inquiry so that beliefs and other forms of knowledge were challenged and examined in light of evidence. Beginning with the existence of doubt or perplexity, the inquirer would then engage in a search for evidence (facts, for example) to reduce doubt to the degree that action could then occur (McAnich, 2004, p. 63). In this respect, Griffin's work draws heavily upon Dewey's definition of reflection from his seminal work *How We Think* (1910/1997), where Dewey defined reflective thought as "Active, persistent, and careful consideration of any belief or supposed form of knowledge in the light of the grounds that support it and the further conclusions to which it tends" (Dewey, 1997, p. 16).

Later in *Freedom American Style*, Griffin delineates and expounds on two additional core elements of his educational philosophy, both of which were closely aligned with the progressive education movement. According to Griffin, any conception of democratic life must be founded on these two premises because they "lie back of a democratic faith in the ability of human intelligence to develop more freedom for all men" (Griffin, 1940, p. 27). These ideas are (1) that freedom to choose is possible and (2) that man is capable of indefinite improvement (Griffin, 1940, pp. 27, 29). The fact of making choices in a democracy was critical for Griffin because making a choice requires the simultaneous exercise of liberty and restraint, or as he puts it, "We are forced to choose which of several possible freedoms we care most about" (Griffin, 1940, p. 32). Griffin's belief that humans can continually improve based upon the application of a reflective process indicates that Griffin rejected a pessimistic, Hobbesian view of human nature. Indeed, for Griffin, a person's nature was not fixed because he or she could consciously act to improve society so long as he or she recognized that in a democracy such efforts at improvement were inevitably a social activity affecting the quality of life for other members of the society. In this sense, Griffin saw daily life in a democracy as a continuous social experiment, one which obligated all citizens to engage in thinking. He claimed that "No one really lives in a democracy unless he takes part in the common living of his society—and no one can do that without thinking" (Griffin, 1940, p. 56), and that "Democracy cannot survive unless men can and will use thinking to direct their acts" (Griffin, 1940, p. 56). Contrasting democracy with totalitarian societies (e.g., Nazi Germany, Mussolini's Italy, and Stalin's Soviet Union), Griffin summarizes their differences concisely in the following statement, again highlighting the critical role of reflection in a democracy:

> Democracy holds that all beliefs are to be examined critically in the light of evidence whenever any doubt of their soundness arises. Communism in Russia, Nazism in Germany and Fascism in Italy have this one thing in common; they are all opposed to thinking and conferenc[ing] as the methods by which their people may reach more satisfactory beliefs. (Griffin, 1940, p. 54)

The final chapter of *Freedom American Style* is entitled "Worth Fighting For" and is essentially a summary of his core beliefs about how to sustain the democratic way of life in light of the increasingly dangerous threats posed to it by totalitarian societies such as Nazi Germany, Fascist Italy and the Soviet Union. Interestingly, Griffin argues that Americans have often been more prone to social criticism of their own institutions while taking for granted the freedoms they have enjoyed. Given the urgent threats from totalitarian regimes, he contends that Americans (in this case, his young adult audience), must recognize that there are internal threats to democracy, specifically from individuals who model the same types of thinking evident in totalitarian societies. These self-proclaimed "super patriots," as he calls them, "are certain that they know the one right answer to our nation's problems, and that they have no need of any help from the rest of us in thinking through important questions" (Griffin, 1940, p. 180). Griffin argues that such people will "set up a pattern in which they, instead of joining with the rest of us in the solution of problems, will tell us the answers and force us to accept their leadership" (Griffin, 1940, p. 180), and in the process model the same patterns of behavior displayed in societies run by dictators—blind obedience, restricted choices and intellectual stagnation. Only through the active defense of democracy, which requires the direct involvement of citizens as reflective thinkers about social issues, can democracy remain a vital way of life and serve as an environment where the systematic improvement of the human condition is possible.

GRIFFIN'S DOCTORAL DISSERTATION

Without question, Griffin's 1942 doctoral dissertation "A Philosophical Approach to the Subject Matter Preparation of Teachers of History" stands out as his most important contribution to social studies education, and to the examination of social issues in the school curriculum. His dissertation's influence on the theory and implementation of reflective teaching was first discussed by Lawrence Metcalf in his 1963 chapter on "Research on Teaching Social Studies" in the *Handbook of Research on Teaching*. Metcalf claimed then that Griffin "stands almost alone in his attempt to elaborate in practical and theoretical terms what reflective theory means for teaching history and for the subject-matter preparation of high school history teachers" (Metcalf, 1963, p. 934). Almost two decades later, Shirley Engle, former Dean of the School of Education at Indiana University and a leading theorist in social studies education, stated that Griffin's dissertation "may well be the most clearly thought out statement ever written of the necessary goals of the social studies in a democracy as those relate to the learning process, to the content and to the teaching methods employed in social studies instruction" (Engle, 1982, p. 45). So impressed with Griffin's work, in the early 1990s the National Council for the Social Studies published Griffin's dissertation with a preface by his former doctoral student Peter Martorella: "We see in Griffin a unique social studies educator whose singular work almost a half-century later remains the most important translation of Dewey's ideas and the ideals of democracy in the teaching of social studies (Martorella, 1990). Furthermore, other scholars of social studies education and issues-centered curricula have referenced it in works such as the *Handbook on Teaching Social Issues* (Evans & Saxe, 1999) and works on social studies teacher education (McAninch, 2004 is one example), while major sessions at national social studies conferences have been devoted to examining Griffin's legacy (Martorella, 1990).

Griffin's dissertation was clearly shaped by the historical conditions of the late 1930s and early 1940s. It contained central ideas about the role of reflective thought and its relationship to the survival of democracy, as well as the critical need for active engagement of citizens in making well-informed choices about social issues. But the dissertation also addresses the fundamental issues of rationale faced by classroom teachers of history and the social sciences, and provides them with a theoretical framework for using reflective teaching as the central method for constructing and evaluating truth claims in a democratic society.

By the time Griffin completed his dissertation in 1942, he had taught for 6 years in the Ohio State College of Education, teaching both undergraduate and graduate students in the social studies education program, which was a testing ground for the type of reflective pedagogy delineated in his dissertation. Robert Jewett makes clear that there was no distinction between Griffin the theorist and Griffin the teacher, since his advocacy of reflective thought as the principal method for social studies in a democracy was what he practiced on a daily basis in his own classroom:

> His [Griffin's] method of teaching was usually to start out with a lecture on a particular topic or phase of a topic, but it would soon develop into a dialogue with the class members. He would flow back and forth between lecture and discussion, and he was very skillful at drawing out students, and then pursuing their particular topics. I would say the class was informal, and rich in illustrations, for example. I would say that in a 50 minute period, it was likely to have about 10 minutes of lecture and the rest of the dialogue would grow out of that. And his students always felt free to give opinions and to ask questions, both at the under-graduate and graduate level. (R. Jewett, personal communication with author, July 30, 2005)

Griffin argued that history as a school subject had no inherent value as content for the development of democracy, unless its study was mediated by the use of reflective thought processes that were modeled by classroom teachers and taught to students. Believing that conceptual learning could only be done effectively through the use of reflective method, Griffin claimed that efforts to simplify the core ideas of history and social sciences and then present them to students in the belief that such information would promote democratic behaviors and ideals were not productive (Engle, 1982, p. 47). Griffin's theoretical position was grounded in the identification, elaboration, and challenging of student beliefs about social experience, which would promote doubt and perplexity as the first step toward the creation of knowledge, and eventually the development of grounded truth claims. As Engle (1982) observed, Griffin believed that "reflection is possible only if one identifies or is caused to identify his beliefs about the matter," and "[it] ... progresses as one raises—or has raised for him—doubts about his beliefs" (p. 51). The substantiation or repudiation of these beliefs based upon the search for information then occurs, concluding in either "better grounded or dependable beliefs with a higher degree of certainty" (Engle, 1982, p. 51).

For Griffin, there was little value in the contention made by historians such as Allan Nevins and others that more history instruction would lead to an improved understanding of democracy by young adults. Rather, Griffin believed that for democracy to survive it was essential that opportunities to promote perplexity and doubt be placed at the center of educational method. And indeed, Griffin believed that using teaching opportunities for this purpose was the first step in constructing meaningful knowledge. Eugene Gilliom, professor emeritus of social studies education at Ohio State who studied with Griffin during the late 1950s and early 1960s, offered a compelling portrait of Griffin's commitment to stimulating reflection in the classroom:

> He would come in with a contradiction or a problem that he anticipated was embedded in the minds of the students, or he created a disjunction or a problem in the minds of the students and challenged the students to work through the problem with his serving in a Socratic role, probing and questioning and urging people to clarify their thinking, looking for the logic involved and dealing with the illogic that people were functioning with. It was almost a gadfly approach to teaching. He did not come in with a lot of answers that he provided people and that he expected they would parrot back to him. He came in with questions, rather, that he felt would stir their thinking and their imagination, the ultimate goal being the quality of their thinking to be improved. (E. Gilliom, personal communication with author, July 28, 2005)

Griffin was very clear in placing the development of reflective capacities in students as central to the mission of the public schools: "In the long run, the development of the student's capacity for independent reflection is the school's special contribution to the democratic way of life" (Griffin, 1942, p. 60). Since democracies rely on knowledge rather than "hallowed belief," reflection is an essential societal value and one which opposes the suppression of knowledge, or the placement of barriers to free inquiry. Griffin's position in this regard was clear: "What is needed in the present world, if democracy as a way of life is to have a fighting chance for survival, is a reliance upon reflection, not as a method, but as the method for determining the truth of any proposition about any subject whatever" (Griffin, 1942, p. 61).

Consequently, Griffin believed that a fundamental role of formal education is the challenging of unquestioned beliefs engendered in young children during their early lives, through the development of the child's reflective capacities. In this regard, the selection of content should focus on information that would promote a "so what?" response from the student, or one that forces the student to reflect on the significance and meaning of the information for action. Content which was amenable to the creation of hypotheses to test truth claims, he believed, was much preferable to that which simply promoted the uncritical acceptance of what Griffin called "patterns-of-action." An example of "patterns-of-action" content is the inclusion of the process of completing a job application in a unit on unemployment. In contrast, content which promotes reflection would serve as data in the testing of hypotheses about behavior and/or beliefs. Rather than learning only how to complete a job application, the teacher could have students construct hypotheses about the relative strength of the local labor market, examine job opportunities available in their community, apply for jobs they identified, gather data on how those opportunities relate to indicators of economic well-being, and test their hypotheses in light of new evidence. This type of content, according to Griffin, is more important since it promotes conceptual learning and is compatible with reflective method.

Griffin was aware of the critical need to examine what Hunt and Metcalf later labeled the "closed areas" of American culture in their highly regarded social studies methods textbook, *Teaching High School Social Studies*, first published in 1955, and revised and reissued in 1968. Since both Maurice Hunt and Lawrence Metcalf were doctoral students of Griffin at Ohio State, the linkages between their work and Griffin's are particularly significant. Griffin stated in 1942 that there were specific areas of American culture where "the method of reflection is not freely permitted to operate," noting two as quite prominent: economics (specifically the study of class conflict) and religion. He also cited race, nationalism, and sex customs as facing opposition to reflective inquiry, although he viewed them as becoming progressively more open over time (Griffin, 1942, pp. 63-64). Hunt and Metcalf (1955/1968) subsequently defined closed areas in 1955 in the following way:

> Certain areas of conflicting belief and behavior are largely closed to thought. In these areas, people usually react to problems blindly and emotionally. Closed areas are saturated with prejudices and taboos. Inconsistency or mutual contradiction in beliefs and values rule behavior in any closed areas. There is usually a reluctance to examine certain ideas because it is believed that they are "impractical," theoretical, or in violation of common sense.
>
> … Those areas of belief which are most important to individuals are likely to be those in which rational thoughts are least valued. In our culture, irrational responses commonly occur in such areas as power and the law; religion and morality; race and minority-group relations; social class; sex, courtship and marriage; nationalism and patriotism; and economics. (pp. 26-27)

Griffin's influence is clear not only in the identification of problems (closed areas) that resist open and reflective inquiry, but in the recognition that there exists a dearth of rational inquiry into those problems. The two major "closed areas" (religion and economics) cited by Hunt and Metcalf were also noted by Griffin some 13 years earlier. Referring to the study of religion, Griffin (1942) said that "In most areas we readily accept reflection as the method for determining truth; but in selected areas, of which religion is one, we underwrite both the method of revelation and the method of intelligence as it was invoked by Jesus and earlier Jewish prophets" (p. 68). Regarding economics, Griffin (1942) was equally forceful: "In the area of economics, the need is clearly for a critical examination of our business system not only in terms of the democratic ideal, but also in the light of the principles under which the system is alleged to operate, and in the light of the needs of our people and of the world" (p. 69).

Hunt and Metcalf (1955/1968) built upon another critical element in Griffin's dissertation when they discussed the contradictions between American ideals and the examination of social problems:

> Our closed areas exist as sources of totalitarian belief and practice in a cul-
> ture that strains in two directions, democratic and authoritarian. The term
> totalitarian is appropriate here because the behavior of the American peo-
> ple with respect to closed areas is akin to behavior of leaders of totalitarian
> states. Each closed area has a set of sanctioned (albeit often irrational and
> inconsistent) beliefs that everyone is expected to follow, and which we try to
> inculcate in the minds of the young through propaganda; no one is taught
> to rely upon independent thinking for his answers, but on tradition, the
> church or political leaders. (p. 28)

In 1942, Griffin had stated that for students to understand American culture and the American tradition, the school had to embrace as its central purpose "the task of helping young people toward an understanding of their own way of life and a conscious choice between democracy and authoritarianism as guiding principles" (p. 72) To do this (for example, in regard to the study of economics and class conflict), the school "has no business to indoctrinate a loyalty to any competing system of economic organization; the task of the democratic school is to make the student intelligent about his culture, rather than to win his adherence to predetermined courses of action" (Griffin, 1942, p. 70). Whereas Griffin was writing his dissertation without knowing the outcome of the Fascist-Allied struggle in World War II, Hunt and Metcalf's book was written during the height of the Cold War, when the threats of totalitarianism posed by fascism no longer existed. Despite the importance of maintaining a national commitment to countering Soviet authoritarianism, the chilling effects of the post-World War "red scare" in the United States had done little to encourage social studies teachers to investigate controversial issues and social problems. In fact, the effect was just the opposite—the inducement of fear in those teachers who wished to examine such issues.

Given Hunt and Metcalf's comprehensive concern with the pervasiveness of "closed areas" and the lack of systematic reflection in the social studies classroom to address them, one can only conclude that the clarity of Griffin's vision about the centrality of reflection as the central method of instruction in the public schools was not widely understood by the time the first edition of the Hunt and Metcalf text appeared.

Griffin recognized that all societies, both authoritarian and democratic, "place upon teachers the obligation of modifying the beliefs, habits, attitudes and values of students" (Griffin, 1942, p. 89). That said, he argued that the role of the teacher in an authoritarian system was to inculcate preferred values and beliefs, place those values and beliefs outside of critique, and restrict access to knowledge that could challenge the basis of preferred values and beliefs. In a democracy, Griffin contended that the teacher's role was to help the student develop knowledge, but in a manner that relied on reflective thought. He stated "democracy places its final reliance for securing commitment to common goals upon common knowledge, and upon the development in each individual of the capacity for generating knowledge out of his experience" (Griffin, 1942, p. 105). This capacity for generating knowledge "out of his experience" owes a clear debt to Dewey's conception of education as continuous reconstruction, or as Dewey defined it, as "that reconstruction or reorganization of experience which adds to the meaning of experience, and which increases the ability to direct the course of subsequent experience" (Dewey, 1944, p. 76). Thus, for Griffin, the role of the teacher in a democracy can be summarized in this way: it is a person who places all beliefs under scrutiny as "proper subjects for examination by the method upon which democracy places its basic reliance" (Griffin, 1942, p. 108), which includes the testing of beliefs to determine their capacity to "explain and to organize human experience" (Griffin, 1942, p. 108). One would do this by questioning a belief and rephrasing the statement of belief as a hypothesis, which must then prove its "adequacy to explain and to order such relevant facts as may be adduced to test it" (Griffin, 1942, pp. 108-109).

For Griffin, no meaningful reflection could take place without the serious and persistent examination of student beliefs and values. He defined subject matter as "any belief or purported knowledge which enters into the process of reflective thinking" (Griffin, 1942, p. 135). What students brought into the classroom needed to be considered of prime importance when instructing them, not just because these ideas had emerged from prior experiences and would necessarily influence the student's perspective on formal curricular content, but because "the beliefs that have in fact developed within a student as the result of extra-school experiences must necessarily be involved as subject-matter in any learning experience the school may set up" (Griffin, 1942, p. 137). For Griffin, the experiences of a young person were a core component of school subject matter because they constituted formulations (in language) of student truth claims, and thus became fertile topics for investigation using the reflective method. He summarized his position as follows:

> We have seen that to make reflective thinking central in the teaching of history will at once compel us to modify our conception of "subject-matter" so as to admit into that category any formulation in language to which the pupil attributes truth, as well as all material, from whatever source, which is utilized in testing the adequacy of a student's belief, and thus takes its place, for that student, among what may be called "the facts of the case." (Griffin, 1942, pp. 138-139)

Once students had been invited to examine their own beliefs, attitudes, and values, Griffin claimed that the time was ripe for students to seriously investigate social issues (or, as Griffin called them, "modern problems"). Through engaging students in the examination of their own positions on such "problems," teachers committed to reflective inquiry would avoid the trap entered by many teachers who "presented" contemporary social problems to students but never had the student take ownership of the problem, because they had neglected to have students seriously examine their own perspectives on such problems using a reflective method. The reflective method for Griffin builds upon Dewey's conception that "something is believed in (or disbelieved in), not on its own direct account, but through something else which stands as witness, evidence, proof, voucher, warrant; that is, as *ground of belief*" (Dewey, 1997, p. 8, italics in original). The teacher must therefore provoke in students "a state of perplexity or doubt," and then engage them in "a search for facts which will reduce doubt (or induce belief, which is the same thing) in a degree sufficient to allow action to go forward" (Griffin, 1942, p. 171). To do this, the teacher should utilize the following sources, which provide the raw material for engaging students in reflective thought:

1. Statements of student beliefs;
2. The teacher's knowledge of American history, or of the community in which the school exists;
3. The teacher's recollection of his/her own adolescent beliefs;
4. The teacher's observation of groups of students in school settings;
5. Writing by the student that reveals the open and free expression of beliefs, attitudes and values; and

6.   The subject matter content of history which the teacher knows, and whatever else the teacher knows from defined subject fields (Griffin, 1942, pp. 176-178).

None of the foregoing sources would have any value in Griffin's view if the teacher did not provide what he referred to as "occasions for reflection." The latter meant that an atmosphere conducive to questioning and criticism needed to be developed, and most important, that a conflict was posed that could be examined by the development of hypotheses that might explain the conflict and move the search for grounded truth claims forward. Once such hypotheses were prepared and critiqued, then those hypotheses would be tested by calling into action "all relevant facts, historical or drawn from current situations, that anyone in the group knows or can dig up" (Griffin, 1942, p. 184). Reiterating the core significance of a broad conception of subject matter for the testing of hypotheses, Griffin argued that the teacher must use "any subject-matter that happens to be accessible, out of the experience of the students or the teacher, out of the materials of the course or from any other source as it may be encountered. The only test for subject matter will be the test of relevance to a belief under examination" (Griffin, 1942, pp. 189-190).

Accordingly, if teachers of history and the social sciences actively employed reflective inquiry as their central method of instruction, Griffin argued that three major benefits would accrue that could sustain an active, participatory democracy:

1.   Teachers who welcomed and took seriously opinions, convictions and hypotheses of students would encourage students to actively participate in the reflective examination of problems in society;

2.   The critical investigation of here-to-fore unexamined beliefs, attitudes and values which have often been held hostage to tradition would inspire students to question the sources of knowledge upon which social cohesion rests, and thus encourage students to question and reformulate their beliefs, which Griffin claimed was a central tenet of democratic life; and

3.   Regular use of the reflective method would invite students to "conceptualize reflection itself," and thus depend upon that process as a basis for determining truth in a democracy' (Griffin, 1942, p. 191). Just as reflection is democracy's method for reaching judgments, so walling off of preferred values is the method of authoritarianism for protecting specific beliefs from examination (Griffin, 1942, p. 191).

Such a commitment to democratic life would then necessarily require that students examine conflicting beliefs, particularly those which represent inconsistencies between espoused democratic values and actual patterns of social experience. Griffin (1942) stated clearly that "students should be brought to see conflicts among their beliefs as exemplifying familiar controversial issues" (p. 193), and that the choice of subject matter from "those areas which are most sharply controversial within our culture should be deliberately preferred over equally evidential but relatively less highly charged subject-matter" (p. 194). Without question, this statement by Griffin represents a very clear commitment to issues-centered instruction, while serving as a strong foundation for the more detailed rationale for issues-centered social studies later elaborated in Hunt and Metcalf (1955/1968).

GRIFFIN'S LATER WORK

Although Alan Griffin's dissertation is his most influential work on issues-centered curricula and social studies education, he did not publish widely in social studies journals and other major curriculum publications prior to his untimely death in 1964. That said, he was a major consultant on the social studies for the *World Book Encyclopedia*, and coauthored a variety of pamphlets for the Junior Town Meeting League dealing with processes for promoting active democratic participation—the study of controversial issues, the improvement of classroom discussion, and youth discussion on television. He also was heavily involved as a consultant to the Education Ministry of India, and served as a visiting professor at Ohio Wesleyan University and the University of Denver.

Although he published little during a career that spanned close to three decades in university-level teaching, Griffin spent considerable efforts outside of the classroom to support the various principles that he deemed essential for the survival of democratic life. In the early 1950s, a conservative professor in the College of Education at Ohio State who was a supporter of then U. S. Senator Joseph McCarthy attacked colleagues at Ohio State, by claiming that he had lists of faculty whose loyalty to the United States was questionable. The chilling effect these claims had on the College of Education did not go unnoticed by Alan Griffin and Griffin's colleague H. Gordon Hullfish, another student of Boyd Bode. As Robert Jewett recalls:

Hullfish was one of the leaders on campus fighting McCarthyism and Alan [Griffin] through that became a leader too, both organizationally and individually. Alan was very outspoken on McCarthy and McCarthyism and its influence on thinking, teaching, and learning. He was, I would say, in the university as a whole—which had about 20,000 students at that time—he was in the upper 10% of the faculty who articulated their opposition to McCarthyism. (R. Jewett, personal communication with author, July 30, 2005)

Consistent with a commitment to racial equality that he articulated in his 1942 dissertation, Griffin (with the support of Hullfish) led the fight to integrate Phi Delta Kappan, the national education honorary society, which in the early 1950s continued to exclude women and African-Americans from its membership. As Robert Jewett notes, "The chapter here [at Ohio State] led the fight, and was thrown out for a while, against an all-white rule for membership. He [Griffin] was very, very active in that, at the national level as well as local. That went on for two or three years. By the way, the two leaders in that were Hullfish and Griffin." (R. Jewett, personal communication with author, July 30, 2005)

When he did make the time to write, Griffin's publications from the early 1950s display a strong issues-centered emphasis, in both cases reinforcing his commitment to academic freedom by focusing on the importance of maintaining academic freedom and promoting reflective practice as bulwarks of democracy. In a 1952 article in *Educational Leadership* entitled "The Teacher as Citizen," Griffin reiterated his commitment to reflective inquiry as the central method of education, but in a provocative manner—by asking not whether teachers had rights as citizens, but whether any or all citizens were qualified to be teachers. Written during the height of the Cold War, Griffin's piece challenged teachers to engage students in actual reflection, and argued that "no one [should] be certified to teach who had not demonstrated a thorough understanding of the reflective process and a commitment to its encouragement which transcended any private loyalty" (Griffin, 1952, p. 8). Apparently written in response to the challenges brought against teachers in the United States who were labeled "attitude-cultivators" by critics of the public schools, Griffin's article is a strong defense of a broadly-defined academic freedom, but one which is grounded in the preparation of reflective practitioners who recognize the dangers of indoctrination—and, most significantly, model reflective thought in their own practices and in their classroom instruction. As Griffin (1952) aptly stated in his essay, the alternative to having thoughtful, reflective practitioners in classrooms would be having increased pressures from "various competing groups to staff our schools only with 'their side' or with 'neutrals.' Practically, this will mean employing only 'neutrals' or people willing to act like 'neutrals' regarding all-important questions—that is to say, ciphers or worms" (p. 8) In Griffin's view, a reflective practitioner was one who saw no reason to keep his or her views secret from the students; rather, "neither he [the teacher] nor they [the students] should attach any special importance to an idea simply because the teacher happens to hold it" (Griffin 1952, p. 9). This candid and concise restatement of Griffin's commitment to reflective practice was a bold and important challenge to educators, inviting them to examine their own beliefs about how they taught, and confirming his commitment to the open, rational examination of social issues in a democracy.

One year later, Griffin contributed a chapter to the volume *Educational Freedom in an Age of Anxiety*, edited by his Ohio State colleague H. Gordon Hullfish. In a chapter entitled "Community Pressures and Education," Griffin discussed the tensions between schools and communities in the post-World War II era, placing considerable emphasis on the importance of maintaining a strong commitment to the open, reflective examination of issues in classrooms. Similar in tone to his 1952 *Educational Leadership* article, this 1953 work reflects Griffin's concern that clashes between interest-based groups in communities and the public schools could lead to the erosion of academic freedom, and ultimately to the weakening of democratic institutions. Building his argument on the apparent loss of social cohesion resulting from the massive changes in American society during the postwar period (suburbanization, tensions of the Cold War, development of the mass consumer society) and the concurrent emergence of less cohesive, more fragmented sets of "interest-communities," Griffin contends that schools face a daunting challenge to meet the demands of those "interest-communities" which attempt to impose their own priorities on teachers and students. Instead of being primarily concerned about the welfare of the particular students being taught, the latter's "direct orientation is toward the purposes, broad or narrow, of the particular interest-community to which the individual gives his allegiance" (Griffin, 1953, p. 156). Noting the danger to democratic life inherent in this approach, Griffin plainly argued as follows: "If the American public school ever comes to be seen by its many publics as a place maintained by the national and state governments for the purpose of converting the young into effective instruments for national and state ends, we shall have reached the end of the road so far as any change for genuine education is concerned" (Griffin, 1953, p. 159). Later in the chapter Griffin criticized the contention by some interest groups that schools should focus on avoiding controversy and thus limit the role of the teacher so he or she would never face public criticism. His critique was founded on his commitment to reflective thought and is couched in a powerful restatement of the central ideas set out in his dissertation but written in a way that was aimed at reaching a much broader readership:

Leaving out of account the fact that today's children must somehow learn to reconcile the many divergent interests and purposes represented by strong groups in our society, and confining ourselves solely to the single matter of developing in each child the ability to think for himself, it seems perfectly clear that the teacher will again and again find it necessary to challenge or bring into question ideas, lines of argument, or even concepts which are taken for granted as obvious both by an individual child and by the adults from whom he absorbed them. (Griffin, 1953, p. 163)

Reiterating a central theme from his 1952 *Educational Leadership* article, Griffin also called upon teachers to educate the public about how true reflection operates, and its central role in a democratic society. Noting the rising tide of concern about attacks on academic freedom, Griffin asserted that much was at stake unless teachers communicate the importance of the reflective process to parents and other community members: "Sooner or later, either parents must come to understand why the unexamined opinions of children must be called into question and made the basis for an inquiry into relevant factual materials, or they will simply refuse to sanction the process" (Griffin, 1953, pp. 165-166).

Calling upon teachers to seize the opportunities to educate parents in their own communities, Griffin concluded by noting that such efforts may have the effect of leading to "appropriate changes in public attitudes and expectations" (Griffin, 1953, p. 166); in essence, he challenged teachers to function as democratic change agents by inviting local residents to reflectively examine their own beliefs.

GRIFFIN'S LEGACY

Griffin's most prominent legacy was through his teaching and direction of graduate students, a number of whom became leaders in the social studies field, among them being Maurice P. Hunt, Lawrence E. Metcalf, Peter Martorella, James Barth, and M. Eugene Gilliom—all of whom made important and lasting contributions to the field through publications, research and teaching. Griffin was recognized by students at Ohio State as a very dedicated, extremely knowledgeable and reflective pedagogue. In this regard, Robert Jewett recently commented that "He [Griffin] was very easy to approach and he was interested in people, and that's one reason he placed his teaching above all his other professional activities." (R. Jewett, personal communication with author, July 30, 2005) This view of Griffin was seconded by Eugene Gilliom, who was a graduate student of both Robert Jewett and Alan Griffin, more than 20 years after Jewett first met Griffin in the 1930s:

I thought he certainly was a friendly type, with a sense of humor and a type of healthy sarcasm that was omnipresent. He pursued interests he had with a passion. He loved to play and I can still see him sitting in the faculty club at lunch virtually every day when I was a graduate student playing chess with his colleagues, and he did that with a passion. And he was serious about the business of education and was passionate about it. (E. Gilliom, personal communication with author, July 28, 2005)

Students who were mentored by Griffin during their doctoral programs, and particularly those who experienced Griffin as both advisor and teacher were quick to note his profound influence on their intellectual development and professional practice. Gillom observed that:

Without question, [Lawrence] Metcalf ... Larry until the day he died, said that the major influence on his thinking and on his life intellectually and as a teacher was Alan Griffin. He never wavered on that and I talked many times with Metcalf about that. There was a point in the early 1960s after teaching a year or two at SFS, that Metcalf and the University of Illinois offered me a job to go to Illinois and work with Larry Metcalf, and part of the reason for that I'm sure was that Larry Metcalf knew I had been a student of Alan Griffin. (E. Gilliom, personal communication with author, July 28, 2005)

Similarly, Peter Martorella, one of Griffin's last doctoral students, was deeply influenced by Griffin: "Perhaps more than any other professional, Griffin influenced my views on teaching, scholarship and intellectual standards, the nature of subject matter, and the nature of the relationship between the social sciences and history to the social studies curriculum (Martorella, 1990).

As an advisor of graduate students, Griffin promoted intellectual inquiry and freedom of thought. His approach was remarkably consistent from the beginning of his career to the end, as described by Robert Jewett:

He [Griffin] never pushed an idea or a concept or a title for a dissertation on the candidate—he liked it to come from the candidate. It would mushroom out of their conversations and would be something that Griffin would be interested in, but he gave great freedom to the individual candidate to make the selection. With Griffin's vast knowledge of the field, he was capable of helping the candidate once the candidate made his selection. Really, the initiative came from the candidate. (R. Jewett, personal communication with author, July 30, 2005)

Although Eugene Gilliom's doctoral advisor was Robert Jewett, Griffin essentially functioned as a co-advisor in his doctoral program during the late 1950s and early 1960s. His recollections show the direct influence first of Griffin on Jewett, and then both Jewett and Griffin on Gilliom's development:

> Alan [Griffin] was one of my doctoral advisors, but my major advisor was Bob Jewett. Griffin and Jewett worked pretty much hand in glove, that is each of them took a nondirective approach to advising. They were both there and ready to advise when one needed help, but they were supportive of one's finding one's own way. That was consistent throughout. Partly as a result of that, those of us who came through the doctoral program at that time became self-sufficient as professionals. (E. Gilliom, personal communication with author, July 28, 2005)

As noted earlier in this essay, Griffin's influence on Hunt and Metcalf's seminal work *Teaching High School Social Studies* was massive. In addition to advocating the study of "closed areas" as a core purpose of social studies education, Griffin's contribution to their thinking and work extended to concerns about efforts by pressure groups to limit inquiry into traditional values, which Griffin had challenged in both his dissertation and in his early 1950s articles on academic freedom. Echoing Griffin's concerns, in 1955 Hunt and Metcalf stated that "The attempts by McCarthyism or [John] Birchism to label subversive any criticism of traditional values illustrate the kind of temporary setback that has as its only consequence a fostering of greater degrees of moral uncertainty, confusion, and cynicism" (Hunt & Metcalf, 1955/1968, p. 41). Regarding the study and teaching of history, Hunt and Metcalf built substantially on Griffin's dissertation by outlining the development and use of "springboards" for reflective inquiry, which, if done systematically, "makes the school subject of history an accessory in the building of social theory" (Hunt & Metcalf, 1955/1968, p. 154). And in one of their most significant contributions, a chapter entitled "Techniques for Stimulating Reflection" in their *Teaching High School Social Studies*, Hunt and Metcalf once again build upon Griffin's dissertation by claiming that "Teachers must familiarize themselves with present knowledge, understandings, and beliefs of students.... [Continuing, they assert that] ... students beliefs are raw materials—starting points—for reflective learning" (Hunt & Metcalf, 1955/1968, p. 168). Subsequently, they outline the criteria for the selection of issues to study in a history course, which are only a slight elaboration of the key principles elucidated by Griffin in 1942:

1. Beliefs should be capable of being related to important social issues;

2. Priority should be given to sharply controversial issues;

3. Beliefs selected should be held by a large portion of the students, meaning that the beliefs should be strongly held; and

4. The belief should be one that can lead to fruitful study, meaning the teacher has the knowledge to handle the issue and factual data can be brought to bear for its examination (Hunt & Metcalf, 1955/1968, p. 170).

While not Griffin's student, Shirley Engle was a major figure in the social studies field from the 1940s to the 1990s, serving for many years as professor of social studies education at Indiana University. Engle and Anna Ochoa's *Education for Democratic Citizenship: Decision-Making in the Social Studies* (1988) articulated a comprehensive rationale that placed issues-centered study at the center of social studies education, offering a sharp contrast to the history-centric, discipline-centered works of the 1980s by authors such as Diane Ravitch, Chester Finn, and the Bradley Commission on History in the Schools. Griffin's substantial influence on Engle and Ochoa is clear in three areas: (1) their emphasis on cultivating citizens who "have the facility to make intelligent political judgments related to controversial issues in our society" (Engle & Ochoa, 1988, p. 5); (2) their strong focus on the reflective study of issues as essential for the preservation of democracy, particularly when they contend that it is a prime responsibility of social studies education to help children and youth "acquire the knowledge and intellectual skills needed to keep the discussion open to enable the young citizen to participate in the process of improving the society" (Engle & Ochoa, p. 8); and (3) their commitment to the critical examination of unexamined truth claims, which often are developed in the home and during the early years of schooling to socialize the young child as a participant in their culture, and which can be addressed by "counter-socializing" youth during the middle and high school grades to develop the critical skepticism, problem-solving skills, and the capacity for reflective decision-making. This approach is strongly reminiscent of Griffin's argument that democracy's survival depends upon a citizenry who relies on knowledge, not unexamined beliefs, for the development of the common good.

In 1963, only 1 year before Griffin's premature death at the age of 57, Lawrence Metcalf, former doctoral student of Griffin and professor of social studies education at the University of Illinois, wrote a review of research in the field of social studies education in which he painted a bleak picture of the field, highlighting Griffin's dissertation as one of the few well argued and comprehensive theoretical statements on reflective teaching in the social studies (Metcalf, 1963). Bafflingly, in a comprehensive review of the research on social studies curriculum published in 2001, Griffin's dissertation and his influence on major figures in the field such as Hunt and Metcalf, Barth and Martorella is nowhere to be found (Vinson & Ross, 2001).

Similarly, Linda Levtsik and Keith Barton (2001) make no mention of Griffin in their admirable chapter-length review of research on the study and teaching of history in the schools, despite the fact that it contains an entire section on how history's place in the curriculum can contribute to democratic citizenship—a statement that appears quite compatible with the rationale that Griffin articulated in his 1942 dissertation. Although the authors recognize that this rationale for the study of history has deep roots in the field, going so far as to state that it is their own preferred rationale—"one characterized by an engaged and active citizenry, dense and diverse networks of associational life, public discourse and action centered on the common good, and a conscious, sustained effort to expand the range of voices that make up the debate" (Levtsik & Barton, 2001, p. 125)—they make no connection at all with Griffin's pioneering efforts along this very line. Indeed, they cite neither Griffin's 1942 dissertation, nor his 1963 *Social Education* article on curriculum revision in the social studies, an essay which is remarkably consistent with the 1942 work in its emphasis on reflective study of the disciplines (history, economics, others) *and* the central place of social problems in the pre-collegiate social studies curriculum (Griffin, 1963).

Despite the recent publication of a fine analysis of Griffin's work and its implications for social studies teacher education (McAninch, 2004), the central role of Alan Griffin's work as a theorist of reflective practice and as an advocate of issues-centered curricula remains largely unexamined in contemporary educational literature. This is extremely unfortunate, because many of the students who experienced Alan Griffin directly are no longer active in the social studies field, thus limiting Griffin's influence even more. Eugene Gilliom put it well as he reflected on Griffin's place in the history of the social studies field:

> When those of us who experienced Alan directly and personally are finally gone, then the legacy I suspect will diminish as time goes by. Partly because, we don't have a rich written legacy to draw upon. For those of us who experienced him, and who were here at the time, it certainly was an education, a life-shaping experience. (E. Gilliom, personal communication with author, July 28, 2005)

Griffin's powerful ideas, modeling of reflective practice, clear and compelling prose, and courage to oppose those who would limit academic freedom and thus erode democracy are qualities that should not be forgotten, and from which every social studies educator can benefit. At its finest, Alan Griffin's work represents a classic statement of how reflective thought can serve as the central foundation for democratic citizenship, while strengthening our commitment to the progressive improvement of the common good.

AUTHOR'S NOTE

The author thanks the following individuals for their invaluable contributions during the research for this essay: Tamar Chute, Associate University Archivist at The Ohio State University Archives, for providing documentary sources, and Drs. Robert Jewett and Eugene Gilliom, both retired professors of social studies education at The Ohio State University, who participated in telephone interviews regarding their work with Alan Griffin.

REFERENCES

Dewey, J. (1997). *How we think*. New York: Dover. (Original work published 1910)

Dewey, J. (1944). *Democracy and education*. New York: The Free Press. (Original work published 1916)

Engle, S. H. (1982, Fall). Allan Griffin, 1907-1964. *Journal of Thought, 17*, 45-54.

Engle, S. H., & Ochoa, A. S. (1988). *Education for democratic citizenship: Decision making in the social studies*. New York: Teachers College Press.

Evans, R., & Saxe, D. (1999). *Handbook on teaching social issues*. Washington, DC: National Council for the Social Studies.

Farley, J. R. (1978). *The life and thought of Alan Griffin*. Unpublished doctoral dissertation, The Ohio State University.

Fernekes, W. R. (1985). *Critical curriculum inquiry and the teaching of American history in U.S. secondary schools*. Unpublished doctoral dissertation, Rutgers-The State University, New Brunswick.

Fernekes, W. R. (1996). Theory and practice of issues-centered education. In R. W. Evans & D. W. Saxe (Eds.), *Handbook on teaching social issues* (pp. 339-346). Washington, DC: National Council for the Social Studies.

Griffin, A. F. (1940). *Freedom American style*. New York: Henry Holt.

Griffin, A. F. (1942). *A philosophical approach to the subject matter preparation of teachers of history*. Unpublished doctoral dissertation, Ohio State University, Columbus.

Griffin, A. F. (1952, October). The teacher as citizen. *Educational Leadership, X*(1), 4-9.

Griffin, A. F. (1953). Community pressures and education. In H. G. Hullfish (Ed.), Educational freedom in an age of anxiety (pp. 149-166). New York: Harper and Brothers.

Griffin, A. F. (1963, October). Revising the social studies. Social Education, 27(6), 534.

Hunt, M., & Metcalf, L. (1968). *Teaching high school social studies* (rev. ed.). New York: Harper and Row. (Original work published 1955)

John Dewey Project on Progressive Education. A brief overview of progressive education. Retrieved May 29, 2005 from John Dewey Project on Progressive Education, University of Vermont College of Education and Social Services: http://www.uvm.edu/~dewey/articles/proged.html.

Levtsik, L. S., & Barton, K. C. (2001). Committing acts of history: Mediated action, humanistic education, and participatory democracy. In W. B. Stanley (Ed.), *Social studies research for the 21st century* (pp. 119-148). Greenwich CT: Information Age.

Martorella, P. (1990). *The Legacy of Alan Griffin*. Presentation at the College and University Faculty Assembly of the National Council for the Social Studies, Annual Meeting, Anaheim CA.

McAninch, A. C. (2004). Reflection in social studies teacher education: Revisiting the work of Alan F. Griffin. In S. Adler (Ed.), *Critical issues in social studies teacher education* (pp. 59-74). Greenwich CT: Information Age.

Metcalf, L. (1963). Research on teaching the social studies. In N. L. Gage (Ed.), *Handbook of research on teaching* (pp. 929-965). Chicago: Rand McNally.

Vinson, K. D., & Ross, E. W. (2001). In search of the social studies curriculum: Standardization, diversity, and a conflict of appearances. In W. B. Stanley (Ed.), *Social studies research for the 21st century* (pp. 39-72). Greenwich CT: Information Age.

CHAPTER 9

SHIRLEY H. ENGLE

A Persistent Voice for
Issues-Centered Education

Mark A. Previte

INTRODUCTION

How can the impact of an individual be measured? Lawrence Cremin
(1964), the noted educational historian, once attempted to describe the
difficulty inherent in judging this phenomenon: For example, to what
extent were William Heard Kilpatrick's 35,000 graduate students actually
influenced by Dewey? Or conversely, to what extent should Dewey be held
responsible for the "project method," which Kilpatrick formulated and
preached for four decades as the pedagogical extension of Dewey's philosophy? What was Dewey's responsibility for pointedly clarifying his differences with Kilpatrick? And in the absence of such clarification—Dewey
was a gentle man—was Dewey responsible for whatever distortion of his
thought Kilpatrick might have introduced? Now, if the same questions are
raised with a host of other disciples once, twice, and trice removed, the
difficulties of assessing Dewey's significance become enormous. The prob-

Addressing Social Issues in the Classroom and Beyond: The Pedagogical Efforts
of Pioneers in the Field, 159–185
Copyright © 2007 by Information Age Publishing
All rights of reproduction in any form reserved.

lem cannot be solved merely by recourse to what Dewey actually said (though this may often clear the air), for a man's influence frequently exceeds his intentions, and sometimes in quite unexpected directions (Cremin, 1964, p. 238).

To those who knew him well, Shirley H. Engle was a genuinely pleasant individual who was passionate about his philosophy of social studies. Gerald Marker, a former graduate student of Engle's, remarked that Engle was the kind of person who would fervently disagree with you when debating any issue but after all was said and done he would welcome you into his house with open arms (G. Marker, personal communication with the author, November 21, 1991). During the summer of 1991, I called to ask if I could come to Louisiana to interview him. I was ready to reserve a hotel room and rental car but he would not hear of it. Shirley informed me in emphatic terms that I would stay at his house and partake of his hospitality. And so, for 3 days in August 1991, I experienced the many facets of the Engle personality while staying at his home in Slidell, Louisiana, interviewing and conducting research for my dissertation on his educational career. His passion for life and social studies knew no boundary as I found out. At 84 years of age, Engle's voice resonated with pride and melancholy as he articulated the triumphs and tragedies of the reflective/issues centered movement, the successes of his presidency of the National Council for the Social Studies (NCSS), and the contributions of his former graduate students and colleagues from around the nation. During the final years of this life, whether it was observing his oratorical style during his final two NCSS conferences in 1991 and 1992, or through our letters and telephone conversations, his enthusiasm and tenacity never waned.

He spoke fervently for his causes but this should not be perceived as self-promotion for he viewed himself as an educator and not a politician. Gerald Marker remarked that Shirley "had so many things to say that he wanted to say in addition to what he wanted to speak about. People would come out of his sessions very enthusiastic" (G. Marker, personal communication with the author, November 21, 1991). Even if this were the case, Engle's multiple roles as teacher, writer, and leader should place him, along with his predecessors, at the heart of the reflective/issues centered legacy (Evans, 1989a,b; Gross, 1989; Massialas, 1989; Shaver, 1989).

PHILOSOPHY

The philosophical foundation of the Reflective Inquiry tradition, one of three competing traditions (the others being citizenship transmission and social science) (Barr, Barth, & Shermis, 1977), possesses a strong genealogy shaped by the writings of Progressive educators (Dewey, 1916, 1933;

Engle, 1960; Griffin, 1942; Hunt & Metcalf, 1955; Oliver & Shaver, 1966; Rugg, 1923). The span of Engle's career demonstrated a determined persistence to the supposition that a reflective thinking, issues-centered curriculum should be the dominant tradition in social education. Engle's philosophy of citizenship education with the focus on integration of decision making and countersocialization ("the process of expanding the individual's ability to be a rational, thoughtful, and independent citizen of a democracy") (Engle & Ochoa, 1988, p. 29) presented a significant counterweight to his philosophical opponents who called for increased study of factual content in the individual disciplines. His fundamental principles remained resolute throughout his life and continue to gather support through the issues-centered education movement (Evans, 2004; Evans & Saxe, 1996).

Shirley H. Engle was born on April 16, 1907, on a farm near Bloomingdale, located in the southwestern part of Indiana near the Illinois border. Education was a common denominator on both sides of the family. His mother completed her college degree and his two uncles received their education at the Quaker Academy located in Bloomingdale. From his father, Washington J. Engle, whom he described as a liberal, the young Engle gained an appreciation of reading and discussing current social issues and public affairs. It was in this environment that Engle acquired the values of independent thinking, social justice, and tolerance of others (Engle, n.d.). In 1920, Engle graduated from a country school near his new home in Urbana, Illinois. It was in high school that the young Engle continued his desire to consume all that he could about the social studies and in 1924 he graduated and was "cited for leadership and service to Urbana High School" (Engle, n.d., p. 1).

In 1928, Engle received his Bachelor of Science degree from the University of Illinois. That year he accepted a position as teacher of social studies at Bement Township High School, Bement, IL. Here he would spend 8 years teaching world history, American history, civics, and economics. According to Engle's autobiographical statement, Bement afforded him a great deal of practical experience in the teaching of social studies: "I was fortunate in that I began my teaching experience in a community that believed in and was willing to support good schools, with a faculty group who were congenial, cooperative, wholesome and unusually well trained people, and with a superintendent, Mr. H. E. Slusser, who was not only able but understanding and loyal as well. I have always felt since that I could say I know the feel of a good school" (Engle, n.d., p. 2).

Upon completion of his first year of teaching, Engle decided to continue his studies at Illinois concentrating in history. Over the next five summer sessions, Engle devoted his time to taking courses in American History. Besides a graduate seminar, he signed up for two courses focusing on the early history of the United States. It was also at this point that Engle was first introduced to the works of John Dewey and the problems approach to social studies. In a telephone conversation, Engle identified a professor by the name of Mr. Cameron as having played a major role in influencing his philosophy for the class constantly discussed Dewey's work *Democracy and Education* (S. H. Engle, personal communication with the author, February 17, 1991).

In 1933, Engle received his MS in education from the University of Illinois. He would now move on and assume the position of economics instructor in the Bement Township High School Adult Evening School for the next 2 years. The experiences accumulated during his time at Bement would lay one more building block in the foundation that would become the basis of his supporting and advocating the Deweyan notion of a problems curriculum: "This was one of the most interesting and challenging experiences of my life and I have harbored ever since the desire to again engage in adult evening school work. Out of this experience has come my firm belief that many of the problems we face in America today would dissolve in the face of an adequate program of adult education freeing as it were the secondary schools as at present constituted for a more direct and appropriate attack on the problems of youth" (Engle, n.d., p. 1).

The summer of 1936 was a turning point in the development of the Engle philosophy. Engle was preparing to attend a seminar by the distinguished American historian Frederick L. Paxson, a professor from the University of California at Berkeley, and one of the foremost scholars and experts on the history of the American West. Engle was impressed when Paxson began to lecture about his "problems"; not his personal problems but problems inherent in the study of history. Paxson's notion of problems contradicted the Deweyan notion of "felt problems" or problems that are directly experienced. As Engle noted in a letter to me:

> Was Custer really there?... What really happened at Fallen Timbers ...? When did this really happen and or did it happen some other time and is this exactly what happened or did somebody just tell a good story?... And it went on and on. He came back the third day and talked about his problems. He came back the fourth day and talked about his problems. They were real problems.... We got so carried away and picked up on this process that we almost would tear out of the room to go to the library to help him solve his dammed problems. It was just a wonderful experience.... He encouraged people to ask questions and there was some exchange but he didn't lecture. (Shirley Engle, personal communication, July 6, 1989).

Engle had become impressed with this essentialist notion of focusing on the teacher's problems. He would reevaluate the influence of Dewey,

especially concerning the kinds of problems that were selected for classroom discussion:

> John Dewey fathered most of us who believe that social problems are the
> focal point of all instruction in the social studies.... I happen to think that
> Dewey trivialized the problems approach by over-emphasizing the immedi-
> ate, here and now problems of children and underestimated the capacity of
> youth to deal with more distant and global problems. I see no sign that mid-
> dle school kids are not about as capable as adults, or even congressmen [sic],
> to deal with our larger social problems such as the environmental crisis or
> [issues that arose during the] revolutionary war days. (Personal communica-
> tion with Shirley Engle, July 6, 1989)

Engle found this conflict over the type of problems to be discussed in
the classroom to be quite perplexing for later on he had come to define
and criticize college teaching as strict lecturing. A portion of his writings during his retirement years would focus on the dual role of the professor as scholar and teacher. As scholars, they work in the hypothetical
mode; as teachers, they shift into the expository mode. He would remi-
nisce about the effect that social science professors had on future teacher
candidates:

> As scholars they hold truth in great tenuousness; they are not all of one
> mind; their disciplines are hotbeds of controversy; they are forever correct-
> ing one another's errors. But once they have laid aside their research eye-
> shades and donned the teaching robes, they become authorities whose
> mission is considered to be the transmission of their superior knowledge to
> students. Teachers, and this includes many college professors, find it either
> too arduous a task, or possibly inappropriate, to share with students the
> problems and questions in the field. [In fact], teachers are poorly prepared
> by their own education to confront the controversy and uncertainty that is
> the real bone and sinew of scholarship. They are poorly prepared to help
> students learn the skills of social criticism that are so important to democ-
> racy. (Engle, 1986, p. 21)

Another turning point came when Engle decided to pursue his doctoral degree at the University of Illinois. From 1928 to 1942, Engle had
been teaching in Bement, West Chicago and La Grange, Illinois. He spent
his summers taking classes in order to earn credits for his doctorate in
economics with a minor in history but his financial shortcomings prevented the completion of his degree. It was at this time that a recruiter
from the University of Illinois offered him the opportunity of a lifetime.
Engle could receive a full scholarship to Illinois if he resigned his teaching position and moved. His situation at La Grange had been in decline

for sometime, due to student apathy toward academic achievement, so he accepted the offer and moved to Champaign.

While at Illinois, Engle was immersed in the works of John Dewey. The first course he took was entitled "Democracy and Education" named after Dewey's 1916 publication. As the course progressed, he recognized how his pedagogical efforts dovetailed nicely with Dewey's philosophy.

Another course, "Education in School and Society," team-taught by William O. Stanley, Archibald Anderson, Edwin Reeder, and Harold Hand, nurtured Engle's philosophical development (S. H. Engle, personal communication with the author, November 20, 1993). The four professors, in Engle's words, "presented an atypical situation." The course comprised 12 doctoral students who discussed and debated the merits of the social foundations philosophy and composed papers on controversial issues in which every student had to defend a thesis. Debating such significant educational issues with such colleagues created an environment that Engle enjoyed immensely. According to Engle, this seminar was:

> The high point of my education.... The sessions were 3 hours in length and then [we] adjourned to a foundation across the street where the debate lasted until midnight. They were the most exciting discussions I have ever experienced. [The] faculty took turns with students in presenting papers. Among those were Mannheim, Durkheim, Pareto, Spencer, Mead, Linton, and Myrdahl [sic]. My life was never the same there after [sic]. (S. H. Engle, personal communication with the author, November 20, 1993)

The conjoining of the Deweyan and Paxsonian paradigms of problems laid the foundation for Engle's (1947) writing of *Factors in the Teaching of Our Persistent Modern Problems*. Therein, Engle (1947) argued that problems in the classroom should not be studied for the sake of memorization:

> A social problem exists when people, knowing the full implications of a particular or alternative course of action, disagree as to whether it should be followed. The disagreement is in the purposes or goals which different people think to be desirable. The idea of differing goals as the crux of the social problem pushes us back inevitably to the values that people hold and to their consequent beliefs about facts as the real object of study in the problems course. (p. 167)

One distinguishing characteristic that separated the Engle approach from other approaches in addressing social issues was the inclusion of a values component. Engle hypothesized that students would become attracted to social studies if individual values and beliefs were examined under the beacon of the reflective process espoused by Dewey. Ideally, by examining their beliefs and values, students would construct generalizations to explain various phenomena. Consequently, this would lead in part to a further examination as to the validity of the students' generalizations:

> There are three rubrics under which a belief may be examined and evaluated. First, a belief may be examined as to its historical origin or as to the reasons that it exists. Second, we may ask whether or not a belief is consistent with facts. Third, we may ask whether or not the belief is in agreement with other possibly higher-order beliefs held by the same individual or by the same group of individuals. (Engle, 1947, p. 169)

What now becomes apparent is the formation of the Engle philosophy of social studies as it relates to centering on the concept of decision making. Students were to not only focus on dilemmas that possessed some relevant concerns but to continue to discuss the possible solutions and their consequences. This process, which would open up an active, constructive notion of citizenship education, would continue to be honed over the next 13 years (from 1947 to 1960) culminating in his seminal article "Decision Making: The Heart of the Social Studies Instruction" (Engle, 1960).

Succinctly stated, students should be able to identify a problem, state a hypothesis, identify value assumptions, identify alternatives and consequences, and justify the decision. This was to be incorporated within an issues-centered approach. These issues or felt problems can be student and/or teacher generated. The issues must possess relevance and meaning for the discussants and the society in which they live or else the only by-products will be metal gymnastics and student apathy.

Even though empirical studies and an inflexible school culture demonstrated that the reflective teaching philosophy could not overcome the expository mode of instruction as the dominant mode (Cuban, 1991; Leming, 1989; Mehlinger, 1981), Engle continued to advocate an open classroom environment that would afford students the comfort to voice their position, concerns, and queries that would lead to better decision making. To promote active, critical citizenship, all ideas, verified by facts, were welcomed with open arms in the Engle classroom.

In response to the New Social Studies movement (Haas, 1977) and its core belief of studying the individual disciplines, Engle merged his emphasis of the problems approach with the decision making process as the structure around which social studies education should be organized. If schools are to prepare its students to become intellectual citizens and take their rightful place in the community, Engle believed, then the curriculum must be organized around the study of a number of social problems selected and solved by the student. Inherent in the decision making process were two key viewpoints. More specifically, they involved the following: (a) the decision as to what a set of descriptive data means, how these data may be summarized or generalized, and what principles they suggest; and (b) decision making at the level of policy determination, which requires a synthesis of facts, principles, and values usually not found on one side of any question (Engle, 1960, p. 301).

Engle advanced the notion that students were not empty vessels waiting to be filled with facts and data for the sole purpose of amassing information. Engle argued that memorization and regurgitation, the bane of social studies teaching, should be replaced with a pro-activist social studies program that challenged students to confront problems and issues by gathering data, making conclusions, and analyzing alternatives and consequences that would solve the problem. Facts, he also argued, should be used only if they were relevant to the problem.

Where are these facts located? Engle postulated that teachers had become too dependent on the classroom textbook for information and interpretation of events. Therefore, social studies teaching had become a mélange of facts and data to be regurgitated during exams. Believing that textbooks did not offer the type of information that large quantities of supplementary materials would be able to offer the student, Engle asserted that teachers should branch out and utilize different types of sources such as primary documents, newspapers, magazine articles, oral histories and audio-visuals. Different perspectives and points of view, Engle asserted, would encourage student thinking. Furthermore, Engle addressed the "ground-covering fetish" that is all too familiar among many social studies teachers (Engle, 1960, p. 302). Engle noted that as the school year came to a close, teachers often scrambled to reach the end of the textbook out of fear that the public would complain that the students were not learning the basic factual content in their courses. Engle stated that such arguments were based on the false assumption that mere remembering and understanding were all there was to knowing. He also asserted that the general public believed "the equally false notion that one must be well drilled in the facts before he can begin to think" (Engle, 1960, p. 302).

Many individuals and groups contributed to the accumulation of data used in making decisions and solving problems but Engle desired to address his attention to social scientists. Social scientists, he believed, fulfilled a necessary service by providing data that would be the grist for social science investigation. This would include "all of the scholarly, investigative work of historians, political scientists, economists, anthropologists, psychologists, and sociologists, together with such parts of the work of biologists and geographers as they relate primarily to human behavior. Closely related fields include philosophy, literature, linguistics, logistics, and statistics" (Engle, 1960, p. 302).

Committed to the problems approach, the study of values, and the integration of concepts and themes from various disciplines, decision-making would add another building block to the Engle definition of the social studies. He stipulated that the social sciences were concerned with research, and the role of the social scientist was not to teach students history, geography, economics and the like, but to conduct investigations to provide information and conclusions in an attempt to explain human behavior. On the other hand, the social studies "are centrally concerned with the education of citizens" (Engle, 1960, p. 302).

Engle and Anna Ochoa, professor of social studies education at Indiana University, greatly elaborated on the Engle model in their 1988 publication *Education for Democratic Citizenship: Decision Making in the Social Studies*. As a high school teacher in Michigan during the 1960s, Ochoa developed an issues-centered philosophy without any knowledge of Engle's viewpoint. Her first meeting with Engle occurred in 1966 at a meeting of the Michigan Council for the Social Studies. Ochoa remembers standing in the back of a room listening to Engle speak and thinking to herself "this man believes the same things I do" (interview with Anna Ochoa-Becker by the author, November 22, 1997). From Engle's point of view, this partnership would combine the efforts of two individuals with a strong connection to the philosophy of Harold Rugg. Engle was a passionate admirer of the Rugg brothers and their contributions to the social studies during the 1930s. (The students in his final seminar at Indiana University in 1977 presented him with a parchment honoring him as the President of the Rugg brothers fan club that brought tears to his eyes [R. H. Pahl, personal communication, September 9, 1991].) Ochoa's role as co-editor would solidify this social studies lineage through the Rugg family tree: from Rugg to his advisee B. O. Smith, from Smith to his advisee Engle (Smith was Engle's thesis advisor), from Engle to Byron Massialas (Engle's thesis advisee), and finally to Anna, who worked with Massialas for 5 years at Florida State (personal communication by the author with Shirley Engle, August 20-23, 1991).

Anyone visiting Shirley at his home in Slidell, Louisiana, would feel a genuine warmth and hospitality. Anna Ochoa, Engle's coauthor of "Education for Democratic Citizenship" was no exception. Ochoa made the trek to Slidell on several occasions to discuss the planning and specific content of the book. She found these sessions with Engle quite demanding as they were centered around their philosophical tenets vis-a-vis an issues-centered form of social studies.

During a break in one of their writing sessions, Shirley went outside and spotted his dog, Joe, chasing and finally capturing a squirrel. Searching for Engle, Ochoa was astonished as she observed Shirley standing over Joe and giving him a lecture about the immorality of his actions.

Ochoa said that Joe actually looked quite chagrined about the poor decision he had made as Shirley admonished his behavior. Turning to Ochoa, Engle commented that animals have a moral sense and that Joe had learned his lesson (Personal communication with Anna Ochoa by the author, November 23, 1991).

The writing of *Education for Democratic Citizenship* resulted in great conflict over style and substance, and it was obvious to Ochoa that her writing style did not coincide with the Engle vision. Her first draft of the chapter entitled "Socialization and Countersocialization of Youth in a Democracy" delineated the research on how students are politically socialized. Ultimately, she received a phone call from Engle asking for less description and more passion. Many years later she was still able to remember, verbatim, most of the last three sentences that she wrote for that chapter: "In the context of democratic education, students are not bundles of stimulus and response connections, nor are they mindless robots. Democracy as a political system is distinguished by the high value it places on each individual. Democratic education must do no less" (Engle & Ochoa, 1988, p. 48).

As for the aforementioned elaboration, Engle and Ochoa's book (*Education for Democratic Citizenship*) was divided into two sections: the rationale for democratic citizenship and the components of the curriculum. More of the Engle model became apparent through the discussion of topics such as the intellectual dimensions of decision making, democratic values, decision making at the elementary level, humanistic studies, intellectual skills, reflective decision making with regard to public actions and public policy, resolution of social problems, and the tentativeness of information and testing truth claims.

The rationale for this curriculum was based on commitment to the democratic ideal focusing on democratic principles such as respect for the individual, "the right to be knowledgeable and to participate with others in making the decisions that concern them and all of society" (Engle & Ochoa, 1988, pp. 23-24). The authors thought this was essential in light of the fact that "democracy" is such a relative term that any group, conservative or liberal, patriotic or revolutionary, can fashion their own definition of it by wrapping it around their own political agenda. Engle and Ochoa charted a definite progressive course by crystallizing their understanding of democracy as spelled out in the works of Broudy (1949), Myrdal (1944), Niebuhr (1971), Murray (1964) and Johann (1965).

Engle and Ochoa believed that the diversity of culture in the United States permits both the dominant and minority voices to debate the definition of democracy and how best to make it work. Engle and Ochoa proposed that teachers move their students in a direction where they can become aware of the rights granted to each of the nation's citizens, cherish the diversity of its citizenry, and maintain democratic values through an open discussion of significant issues. In other words, they argued, and believed, the dominant voice should not be permitted to establish permanent control.

The central focus of *Education for Democratic Citizenship* highlights the twin cornerstones of socialization and countersocialization. Socialization necessitates that students be inculcated with the existing customs, traditions, rules, and practices of the general society and subcultures to which they belong. Part of the United States educational prescription is to preserve the existing order. Students, it is believed by many, should possess a basic understanding and appreciation of the culture, heritage, and ethnic background (Engle & Ochoa, 1988, p. 30). In this regard, Engle and Ochoa argue that the elementary grades should use socialization as the primary philosophical foundation due to the student's undeveloped reflective skills.

It must be noted that the one problem that persisted throughout Engle's career that continued to amaze and embitter him was his observance of social studies teachers, especially secondary teachers, whose main pedagogical approach was an over-reliance on textbooks and teacher dominated monologues. Consequently, Engle created the counterpart to socialization, countersocialization. Engle was greatly distressed that students were memorizing facts and principles devoid of any analysis, synthesis, and evaluation. A constituent component of education, as he understood it, had to be one that underscored independent thinking and responsible social criticism. Decision making and problem solving skills, he argued, are essential if there is to be any hope at all in preparing students to tackle real life situations, which, ideally, would ultimately lead to active debate and promising social action.

Engle and Ochoa argued that socialization is a necessary function to socialize young children into their own society by teaching them the values, mores, and rules of their specific culture. Equally important, they argued, was countersocialization, for it permits student examination of society through different colored lenses. The question remains: when should the process of countersocialization begin? Engle and Ochoa (1988) acknowledged that this process "can begin at the elementary level" (p. 31). The authors did not support this with any documented empirical research but they did refer to "the increasing maturity and intellectual capability of students" as justification to begin the countersocialization process (Engle & Ochoa, 1988, p. 32). They suggested that it is always in the hands of the teacher to determine the readiness of the students and the willingness of their families and community to support such an approach, which is radically different to the typical approach (Engle & Ochoa, 1988, p. 7). Essentially, Engle and Ochoa were attempting to move teachers toward a more open curriculum where teachers, for example, would feel comfortable discussing controversial topics with their students—such as discussing the pros and cons of saying the Pledge of Allegiance with a group of fifth grade students (Kavett, 1976). The authors suggested that no better opportunity exists than to help students generate arguments and defend them with evidence. If students are to become participatory citizens and good problem solvers, it is of greater importance to focus on helping people make intelligent and responsible decisions for themselves than it is to tell them what to think (Engle & Ochoa, 1988, p. 7). Ochoa was asked by Engle to rewrite certain passages with a more passionate style that would "plead the case" for an open classroom environment that would afford students the comfort to voice their position, concerns, and queries that would lead to better decision making (personal communication with Anna Ochoa by the author, November 23, 1991).

To promote active, critical citizenship, all ideas, verified by facts, are to be welcomed with open arms in the Engle-like classroom. This model— one predicated on the need for a democratic education with its focus on an open curriculum and a blurring of the lines separating the disciplines—still flies in the face of what has become traditional social studies teaching. In regard to this situation, a former Engle graduate student has expressed the following concerns: "[Engle's] model requires a person to be so knowledgeable and so well read, with such broad perspective and such depth of understanding that I'm not sure how many people reach that level. It's like the last level of Kohlberg. It's out there someplace, but there are few people you can point to who can reach that (J. Dick, personal communication with the author November 23, 1991).

The classroom was always Engle's first love, whether it was teaching U. S. History, World History, Civics or Economics in public high schools in Indiana and Illinois or teaching curriculum and instruction courses at Indiana University. Whether in a high school or a college classroom, teaching was highly significant to Engle for this was where the nuts and bolts of the educational process happened.

As previously mentioned, in his classes, Engle created open classroom environments that provided students with the comfort to voice their positions, concerns, and queries, all with the aim of assisting them to become better decision makers. At one and the same, he insisted that the comments and questions debated be relevant and meaningful to the discussion otherwise the result was little more than mental gymnastics with student apathy as the primary by-product.

Tellingly, if there was one significant memory that Engle's students retained over the years, it was the open-ended atmosphere and the constant questioning Engle used to probe their positions. One of Engle's former high school students was so enamored by this teaching philosophy that he concluded, "Mr. Engle was the best teacher he ever had including grade school, high school and the university" (Engle, n.d., p. 7).

Even after three decades of teaching at different levels, Engle's preparation for class remained constant. Leaving strict instructions with his secretary that there would be no student visits, phone calls, and distractions, Engle would barricade himself in his office for an hour or more to prepare for class. Once in the classroom, Engle would pepper his students with questions and hypotheses forcing them to defend their specific curriculum and instructional positions. He could become quite dramatic in his presentation to the point that he would get up and approach somebody and lay on hands and talk directly into the student's face in order to make the point (C. Benjamin Cox, personal communication with the author July 29, 1994). In fact, his experiences in rural, suburban, and urban settings afforded him the opportunity to hone his teaching skills in different settings and prepare him for his position of assistant professor at Indiana University in 1945.

He championed a teaching philosophy that motivated students to question values and beliefs on issues that mattered most to them. He believed that teachers must empower their students by exposing them to the issues of the day and their connections to citizenship behavior. In other words, he believed that school life should be viewed as a subsystem of life in the real world.

On a different but related note, Engle's support of teacher and student rights was unparalleled. His position on academic freedom staunchly defended the rights of educators to teach issues deemed crucial to the survival of democracy and citizenship education. Engle's voice constructively criticized the philosophy and the evidence presented by those who wished to continue expository teaching.

In Engle's mind, his promotions were based on his teaching for this was the primary reason why he was hired at Indiana in 1945. At the time there was no pressure to publish—or perish. One of the shining moments of his professional teaching career occurred in May of 1959, during the celebration of Indiana University's 139th Founder's Day when he received the Frederic Bachman Lieber Award for Distinguished Teaching. In presenting the award, President Herman B. Wells remarked, "if the undergraduate is the lifeblood of the University the great teacher is the heart which pumps and moves the blood" (Malenshek, 1959, p. 7).

CURRICULUM

The first half of Engle's life was clearly influenced by the Great Depression and the New Deal, and his political and educational attitudes were shaped by the forces of the Progressive philosophy.

During the Great Depression, the nation was faced with enormous problems and with the ascendancy of Franklin Roosevelt's New Deal, the government would now be responsible for solving the nation's woes. Educators were not immune to these problems. Unemployment, bankruptcy, hopelessness were part and parcel of the daily fabric of school life. Engle's work at Bement Township High School from 1928 to 1936 provided him with a daily reminder of the difficult times faced by his students. Indeed, in his work as coordinator of the Bement Adult Evening School, educational philosophy and pedagogical concerns were not the only issues facing Engle. Farmers, factory workers, coal miners, and steel workers were just a small number of the many groups of citizens who faced a seemingly endless stream of problems that directly affected their families and jobs. Teachers were no different. Many social studies teachers during this time period faced the dilemma of continuing to teach in a rural school or moving to an urban school district where the salary, benefits, and educational conditions were more favorable. And this is exactly the dilemma Engle faced.

In 1936, Engle moved to take a similar social studies position at West Chicago Community High School in Chicago, Illinois. Engle would now be teaching in a suburban school district where salaries would be higher and opportunities to develop progressive educational ideas would be encouraged. Engle immediately took advantage of this opportunity by expanding his repertoire of teaching and curriculum experiences. One of these experiences included the construction of an American history course "without the doubtful benefit of a textbook" (Engle, n.d., p. 2). He explained his motivations this way: "I had often contemplated the possibility of infusing new life and meaning into the American history course by breaking away from the logical and chronological sequence of material and organizing a course instead from a psychological approach around the great and significant problems of American life to which a knowledge of history may contribute understanding" (Engle, n.d., p. 2).

During his years at West Chicago, Engle regarded the value of active participation in professional and community organizations as highly significant, and, in fact, he was quite active. More specifically, he served as the chairman of the West Chicago Faculty Council from 1939 to 1940. During that same period he served as chairman of the Reorganization Committee of the Du Page Valley Division of the Illinois Education Association, which "carried through to completion the reorganization of the division of broadening the basis of participation of teachers in the work of the division" (Engle, n.d., p. 2). He was also "elected to the Executive Committee of the Du Page Valley Division of the Illinois Education Association and ... served as a delegate to the State Convention of the Association in Springfield."

Engle envisioned the social studies curriculum as a bicycle wheel with the important issues of the day as the hub and the spokes symbolized the integrated social sciences along with the humanities, the hard sciences, and other disciplines. He believed that the social studies could not afford to take an elitist position by isolating itself from the other disciplines. Nor could it continue to spin off different curricular trends and fads that would move social studies from its point of origin. Engle continually emphasized that education must be a reflection of society, and he believed if teachers bought into this belief as well, they would be more likely to paint their classrooms with a holistic brush, and be compelled to participate in an active, ongoing process of curriculum development.

While Engle's approach constituted a synergy of the ideas and needs of practitioners, they never quite became part of mainstream thinking because the open-ended curriculum model was viewed by many as quite unstructured. This may explain why at times Engle was faced with the dilemma of compromising his Progressive philosophy in order to achieve mainstream recognition. Two cases during the 1960s point this out.

In the mid-1960s, Indiana University organized its own curriculum center for the purpose of developing curriculum materials for a required government course since none of the other New Social Studies projects and centers were developing political science materials for junior and senior high students.

The mission of the center was to improve social studies education in elementary and secondary schools. The High School Curriculum Center in Government would now be earmarked as one project being run by the new development center. The remainder of the life of the project, renamed "American Political Behavior" (Mehlinger & Patrick, 1972), a two-semester course to take the place of civics and government courses, would be left in the capable hands of Howard Mehlinger, a noted social studies educator and fellow faculty member of Engle's, and John Patrick, a graduate student of Engle's and research assistant to the project. Engle had hoped that the center would undertake the one objective that had eluded him up to this point: that of developing curriculum materials espousing his particular brand of social studies. Engle would be left alone to support the social studies while the Mehlinger/Patrick duo defended the social science camp. Engle's workload that year prevented him from spending time on the project and building the curriculum according to his vision, and thus it was left to Mehlinger and Patrick to complete the project from a social science perspective. Mainstream recognition pressured Engle into compromising his philosophy of an integrated, issues approach to a single discipline approach that included inquiry and decision making.

Why would Engle support a project that was anathema to his philosophy of social studies? First, this was an ideal opportunity for Engle to get in on the ground floor of the new social studies movement. Second, Ginn and Company, a reputable book company, was putting its reputation behind the effort. Improved sales would produce national recognition not only for him but for the curriculum center as well. Third, regardless of the political science orientation of the project, Engle's reflective concepts of learning and teaching would be embedded in the final product. Lastly, Engle was quite consumed with his other responsibilities—so much so that he placed the direction of the project in the hands of its director, Howard Mehlinger (author phone interview with the H. D. Mehlinger, February 10, 2006).

Indeed, over the course of the next few years, Engle's participation in the center noticeably declined due to an increase in his responsibility in the areas of teaching, leadership in the National Council for the Social Studies, writing and consulting, and the strain began to show. Over and above that there were other issues he was dealing with. Speaking of such, he wrote:

> The nervous energy required to compensate for an inadequate office space is beginning to wear me out. My teaching is not as good as it can be because there is no quiet and uninterrupted time in which to prepare. I can't think of a better way to waste the resources of the University than to undermine the productivity of a senior professor by such poor working conditions. (Engle, 1970, p. 13)

During their meetings and casual conversations, Mehlinger sensed disappointment in Engle's voice and demeanor about the project's philosophical direction (personal communication Mehlinger, February 10, 2006). Engle also came to believe that the Wesley definition of the social studies had become so entrenched in the field that teachers continued to control the classroom through lecture, knowledge transmission and dependence on a single source (Wesley, 1937, P. 4). Fifteen years later, Engle would look back at the new social studies movement with mixed feelings. Engle, though, was also convinced that the new social studies had brought something new to the curricular table, even if they were remiss in certain ways:

> The new social studies did not treat adequately the needs of citizens to deal in an integrated way with problems that cut across the boundaries of sepa-

rate disciplines, nor the needs of citizens to deal skillfully with problems of valuing, nor the needs of citizens to develop skill at social criticism. At the point we left them, the new social studies introduced intellectual integrity and rigor and excitement to the study of subjects where mindlessness and apathy had prevailed before. In this respect, they promised to provide an important ingredient of democratic citizenship education. The pity is that they were not encouraged to succeed and develop further. (Engle, 1986, p. 22)

Mehlinger's relationship with Engle would continue into the 1970s as colleagues at Indiana University. Mehlinger described Engle as a close personal friend but he also noted that the two of them fought constantly about the past, present, and future condition of social studies. In fact, Mehlinger was quite impressed with Shirley's belief that colleagues should never kowtow to his declarations. Continuing, Mehlinger commented, "Everyone is a fan of Shirley Engle, but few are his disciples" (author phone interview with Howard Mehlinger, February 10, 2006).

Ultimately, Engle's imprint on curriculum was mixed at best. Local and state projects such as The Hillsborough County Social Studies Workshop (1948), The Indiana Experiments (1963), The Oregon Lectures (1965), and Project Necessities (1968-1970) were decidedly marked by the Engle vision focusing on student habits and attitudes, enlarging student's horizons and the selection of relevant problems to students' lives, through the utilization of sequential learning, interrelated units, democratic teaching, pupil planning, critical thinking, and controversial issues. Conversely, the National Council for the Social Studies Scope and Sequence Task Force (1983-1986), charged with the responsibility of selecting a K-12 social studies scope and sequence from six submitted models, rejected the Engle and Ochoa model. The Social Studies Curriculum Planning Resources Guide (1990) and The NCSS Curriculum Standards for Social Studies (1994) chose to follow the social studies disciplines returning to the philosophy of Edgar Wesley and avoiding three significant Engle components: the study of controversial issues, intellectual processes, and citizen participation (Ochoa-Becker, 2001).

As stated previously, one of the greatest disappointments of Engle's career was the unwillingness of social studies educators to embrace his educational philosophy on a practical level. The specter of Edgar Wesley haunted Engle throughout his career; in fact, this was, in his mind, the preeminent reason why the curriculum and instructional philosophy of the Progressive wing were met with resistance. Wesley was considered to be part of the old guard establishment. While he was forward looking in certain ways (e.g., as President of the National Council for the Social Studies in 1934, he was instrumental in establishing an independent NCSS annual meeting, the noted NCSS publication *Social Education*, and a permanent headquarters for NCSS) (Wronski, 1982), his definition of the social studies was highly traditional: "the social studies are the social sciences simplified for pedagogical purposes "—which became the baseline for the "traditional disciplinary approach" to social studies education (Dougan, 1988-89, p. 21). Disconcerted, Engle (1979) voiced his concerns to the man who had been the power broker in social studies education for the last five decades:

> I have always thought that you and I were of very different beliefs with respect to the desirable nature of the social studies.... I persist in the belief that the social sciences, taken alone, whether simplified for purposes of pedagogy or not, are inadequate and even inappropriate content for the social studies.... I persist in the view that the social studies should be a much broader and, in some ways, a very different enterprise than the mere exposition of disciplines simplified or not. In my thinking, the focus of the social studies should be on perfecting the process of problem solving and decision making, always in view of the values at stake, and ultimately in the broad social context in which a citizen, in real life, is required to operate. Social sciences may be instruments in this process, not the sole ones at that, and are never treated as ends merely to be learned, as your definition seems to imply. (Engle, 1979, n. p.)

Engle clearly recognized that the Wesley definition had attained a great deal of influence in the social studies arena whereas the reflective, issues centered definition did not attain much acceptance at all:

> [I]t is clear to me that your definition rather than any other that I have been associated with has carried the day in the field of practice. Rather than pointing a way to something supposedly better, your definition describes a reality and it does so today with even greater accuracy than it did in the 30s when shades of Rugg and Dewey were shaking the bushes. People of my persuasion were never of much force in social studies practice. We are little heeded today. In fact, we are in retreat before the "back to basics" movement. Allan [sic] Griffin's worthy student, Larry Metcalf, is in deep despair at the sorry state of the social studies. The bright young men from Harvard: Oliver, Shaver, and Newman [sic] are nearly forgotten and have more or less given up the ship. My impression is that what we were asking was too risky for the profession to implement. (Engle, 1979, n.p.)

Ultimately, Engle hesitantly spoke to the presumed shift to Wesley's definition of the social studies:

> It is a little hard for me to believe that the author [Wesley] of *The Social Studies*, which everyone in our field knows by heart, and which has ruled social studies practice all these years, and still rules it today, now embraces my position. But whether it is so or not, I can think of nothing more rewarding

to me than the opportunity to talk this matter over with you. (Engle, personal communication with E. Wesley, February 15, 1979)

Cognizant of the fact that Engle was preparing to make a trip to California in early 1979 to visit family, James S. Barth, professor of social studies at Purdue University, extended an invitation to Engle to visit Edgar Wesley at his home in Carmel, California. Barth proposed that the two men should meet to work out their differences over the definition of the social studies. Unfortunately, Engle did not receive Wesley's invitation until after he returned from his California trip. Thus, the conversation never took place. But it might have been just as well. After more than 50 years of debating the definition and purpose of the social studies without any movement toward rapprochement, Engle may have possessed justifiable suspicions of Wesley's motives. Throughout his involvement with NCSS, Engle viewed himself as the rural kid from the Midwest fighting against the NCSS old guard establishment headed by Wesley and his cronies on issues such as the definition of the social studies and the power structure of the organization (J. S. Barth, personal communication with the author, November 23, 1991).

Abandoning his beliefs because they embraced an unpopular position was unacceptable to Engle. But the constant campaigning to secure advocacy for the movement did take its toll. In 1990, Gross recounted the uphill battle that he and Engle encountered:

A host of social studies personnel actually reject the concept of a problem-centered, issue-resolving, skill-oriented course of studies that should exist and be experienced under the title of the social studies. Others only accept the idea in its name, but do not follow it in practice. Some of us [Gross, Engle] have struggled for over 50 years to properly shape the social studies. Near the end of our careers we find it difficult to retain our spirit and optimism when we examine certain current curricular trends that threaten to move school programs back to the 1890s. (Gross, personal communication with author, August 16, 1990)

Another reason for Engle's disappointment can be directly tied to his roots at the University of Illinois. Engle was a prisoner of his educational background, which was philosophical rather than a "materials development tradition" (author interview with G. Marker, November 21, 1991). As a result, Engle could not translate his ideas into curriculum materials for the classroom. Engle provided examples and vignettes in his publications to provide some direction to his audience but he also believed that developing curricular materials would seize from teachers the power to decide what materials were classroom appropriate.

Mehlinger had stated that the closest anyone came to emulating the ideas of Engle was Don Oliver and James Shaver's work on the Harvard Pubic Issues project in the mid 1960s. Shaver regarded Engle as one of the seminal minds in social studies. As he read more of Engle's works during the 1960s, Shaver concluded that he could have been one of Engle's doctoral students (Shaver, letter to the author, August 30, 1990). Toward the end of his professional career, Engle used Shaver as a sounding board as Engle wrestled with his continuing search for the definition of the social studies, citizenship education, and the role of conformity and activism in the schools. While the two former presidents of the National Council for the Social Studies shared their common concerns, Engle was in the midst of developing an outline for a book that would tackle these and other questions that perplexed these two advocates of an issues-centered approach to social studies. But this would be an opportunity missed; with a heavy heart, Shaver, in the midst of a mid-career crisis, informed Engle that his depleted energy level would prevent him from participating in a project that was near and dear to his heart. Thus, the book Engle wanted Shaver to collaborate on, *Education for Democratic Citizenship: Decision Making in the Social Studies*, would be coauthored by Anna Ochoa, Engle's former colleague at Indiana University.

During the last decade of the twentieth century, Engle's influence on social studies curriculum and instruction has gathered some momentum. While Leming and Nelson's citation analysis of the 1991 *Handbook of Research on Social Studies Teaching and Learning* indicated a virtual disappearance of Engle from the literature (though it must be noted that *Democratic Citizenship* placed third in the "most frequently cited source" category, Leming and Nelson, 1995), conversely, his works were cited 35 times in the *Handbook on Teaching Social Issues* (Evans & Saxe, 1996). The latter is not surprising as this was Engle's area of expertise and many of the contributing authors were former graduate students and colleagues of Engle, as well as supporters of issues-centered education.

POLITICAL LEADERSHIP

Throughout his career, Engle attempted to establish a stronger network among social studies educators through his political leadership in national and state organizations. His organizational efforts to resurrect a moribund Indiana Council for the Social Studies in the late 1940s were partially successful due, in part, to his relentless pursuit to increase the membership rolls. His recollections of the presidency appeared in the beginning to be one of hopelessness and detachment:

The attendance at the 1947 meeting at Bloomington was a little better than the 1946 meeting. The mistake had been made of meeting in a very large hall. There were so few present the meeting appeared almost surrealistic. At this meeting, I was elected president. I think my election came from desperation. The possibility was that a new face could turn the thing around. What I remember most about serving as president was the immense loneliness of being president of an organization that hardly existed. I received almost no mail. We had no money. I remember writing letters in longhand to almost any name and address I could come by to implore teachers to join the council. (Holt, 1989, p. 13)

That said, he generated enthusiasm by using his public school experience to demonstrate how such an organization can benefit the classroom teacher.

His contributions as a member of the National Council for the Social Studies (NCSS) assisted in the shaping of that organization's policy toward curricular and instructional practices. Furthermore, his writings on citizenship education, decision making, and an integrative, open curriculum were instrumental in sustaining the voice of the issues-centered wing within NCSS.

His involvement in NCSS was largely motivated by the principle of citizenship participation. If successful change was to occur within the scope of social studies education, Engle believed that a working relationship between universities and public schools was imperative.

In 1957, Engle joined NCSS' Subcommittee of the Committee on Relations of State and Local Councils which laid the plans for organizing a "House of Delegates" whose purpose was to enlist mass participation to bridge the gap between university and public educators (Vaneria, 1957). This plan was finally adopted by NCSS in November 1956 and implemented by an amendment to the NCSS Constitution (National Council for the Social Studies, 1957).

In 1968 and 1969, Engle served NCSS in the positions of president-elect and president, respectively. Engle used his influence to generate more decision-making positions for classroom teachers for he believed that such individuals were the soul of NCSS. Breaking with tradition, Engle became the first president to take a leave of absence from Indiana University to devote his full time to the presidency. One of his first actions was to address needed changes in the running of the organization based on the assumption that the national organization represented and served all social studies educators. Election reforms were moved ahead to insure representation of classroom teachers at all grade levels on the NCSS Board of Directors. In a letter to then Executive Director Fran Haley, Engle second-guessed this decision when he said that some may feel that in our zealousness to be democratic, we have lowered the competence and influence of the Directors (Engle, 1985, n. p.).

As past-president of NCSS, Engle did not permit himself to be reduced to the role of figurehead. He maintained his steady attendance regimen at the yearly NCSS conventions in order to speak out on issues that greatly mattered to the organization. As an officer of NCSS, Engle demonstrated a great deal of attention to the plight of the classroom teacher by conceiving future meetings that were relevant to the needs of those who attended. An "impromptu speakout" was held for anyone who wanted to criticize the shortcomings of the 1968 conference, to create solutions to improve the conference and to discuss problems within the NCSS organization. The list of complaints included a lack of relevance to the conference theme, repetitious sessions from year to year, irrelevant theoretical sessions, poor public relations efforts and favoritism shown to theorists over practitioners (personal communication in a letter from S. Engle to M. Arnoff, February 13, 1969). Transforming a plodding educational edifice into an organization that was willing to take a stand for its beliefs were key to moving NCSS closer to a unified field. Engle played an active role in constructively criticizing the organization when it began to move in directions not commensurate with the true purposes of social studies. As some of his ideas were integrated into NCSS doctrine, he bequeathed to future generations a system of beliefs and a set of accomplishments garnered through his persistent efforts.

GRADUATE STUDENTS

It has been argued by some that the most lasting contribution of Shirley Engle was his graduate students. During the period from 1955-1975, the Engle torch was passed along to succeeding generations of college educators and public school teachers who assimilated what they considered to be the most influential thinking of Progressive education. Their influence appeared nationwide on the pages of educational publications and in the classrooms of the nation's schools and universities. Their interpretations of the Engle philosophy ran the gamut from the philosophical to the practical.

Engle's role as doctoral advisor was most visible as intellectual or theoretical career mentor. Dougan's (1984) description of the Indiana lineage of educators indicated that "the underlying philosophical base appears to be closely tied to Engle's commitment to reflective inquiry" (p. 201).

As stated previously, Engle's current influence in the field depends upon which publication one happens to be reading. This appears to be true with his graduate students as well. Carole Hahn, Beverly Armento, and Ronald VanSickle, considered second-generation descendants of Engle, were the only Indiana alumni that appeared in the "most cited handbook authors" in the 1991 *Handbook of Research on Social Studies Teaching and Learning* (Leming & Nelson, 1995). Armento, along with Lee Ehman, a first generation descendant, were included in the "most frequently cited research sources" category from the handbook. As for *The Handbook on Teaching Social Issues*, works by Byron Massialas, C. Benjamin Cox, Lee Ehman, Robert Elsemere (first generation) and Carole Hahn and Beverly Armento (second generation members) were cited. Hahn, Massialas, and Wilma Longstreet, another member of the first generation group, authored articles for the handbook.

EPILOGUE

The reflective flame that burned so brightly at Indiana University under the careful watch of Shirley Engle has lost some of its luminescence over time. Former students have retired and others have drifted off into different areas. Toward the end of his life Engle rejected the notion that his career greatly affected social studies education at all. In 1989, Engle reminded this author that no matter how logical an educational philosophy may sound, the litmus test of that philosophy should be based on hard data:

> I am afraid you give me too much credit [for the philosophical underpinnings of the reflective tradition]. It is a little frightening to me to have such an important topic hang so much on my opinion, supported as it is by so little hard data. The Indiana Study went a short way toward establishing a relationship between exposure to problem solving and citizen behavior but the study did not afford anything like conclusive evidence. But neither do the expositor-memoritor people support their claim with really hard evidence. Short answer paper and pencil tests of facts remembered have practically no validity for predicting the behavior of citizens. Both sides are talking through their hats. We have logic on our side but little else. (S. H. Engle, personal correspondance with author, July 6, 1989)

Gerald Marker, an Indiana colleague and former graduate student of Engle's, concurred that the future for social studies education is a somber one (Nelson, 1994). Conversely, the building of a firm theoretical foundation for the issues-centered approach by Engle and his followers has led to practical applications that were a major stumbling block in the past to the acceptance of such by classroom practitioners (Broadhurst, 1992; Chilcoat & Ligon, 2000; Harwood, 1999; Hess, 2005; Koeppen, 2003;

Ochoa-Becker, Morton, Autry, Johnstad, & Merrill, 2001; Previte, 2002; Rossi & Pace, 1998).

Shirley Engle died on April 7, 1994 at his home in Slidell, Louisiana, at the age of 86. He had dedicated his career to a philosophy that intertwined education and life. His gentleness and kindness, in conjunction with an ardent articulation of a social studies paradigm, stirred a new legion of university professors and public school teachers of educators who are carrying his message far beyond the confines of Indiana. Indeed, the reinvigorated NCSS Issues-Centered Education Special Interest Group, almost 100 members strong (including Byron Massialas, a former doctoral student of Shirley's, and Anna Ochoa-Becker, a former Indiana University colleague of Shirley's), illustrated that these two groups could possibly bridge the gulf between their cultures to continue the tradition of this approach. This is a beginning but it will be a complex process to bring change to an institution that is preserved by the status quo.

The life and career of Shirley H. Engle promoted a legacy dedicated to the goals of citizenship education and decision making as the heart of social studies. The dedication demonstrated by Engle and his supporters will not end the debate over the direction of social studies education. But, as Engle noted four decades ago, "the great debate over education continues undiminished. This continuing debate is a healthy sign" (Engle, 1959, p. 82).

REFERENCES

Barr, R. D., Barth, J. L., & Shermis, S. S. (1977). *Defining the social studies. Bulletin 51*. Arlington, VA: National Council for the Social Studies.

Broadhurst, A. R. (1992). Foreign policy issues: A high school application for the Engle and Ochoa reflective teaching model. *Social Studies, 83*(3), 104-108.

Broudy, H. S. (1949). *Building a philosophy of education*. Upper Saddle River, NJ: Prentice Hall.

Broudy, H. S. (1981). *Truth and credibility: The citizen's dilemma*. New York: Longmans.

Chilcoat, G. W., & Ligon, J. A. (2000). Issues-centered instruction in elementary classrooms. *Theory and Research in Social Education, 28*(2), 220-272.

Cremin, L. A. (1964). *The transformation of the school: Progressivism in American education, 1876-1957*. New York: Vintage Books.

Cuban, L. (1991). History of teaching in social studies. In J. P. Shaver (Ed.) *Handbook of research on social studies teaching and learning* (pp. 197-209). New York: Macmillian.

Dewey, J. (1916). *Democracy and education*. New York: Macmillian Press.

Dewey, J. (1933). *How we think*. Lexington, MA: D. C. Heath.

Dougan, A. M. (1984). *Mentoring in the social studies: World War II to the present time*. Unpublished doctoral dissertation, University of Indiana, Bloomington.

Engle, S. H. (n. d.). *Autobiographical statement*. Palo Alto, CA: Hoover Institution on War, Revolution and Peace, Stanford University.

Engle, S. H. (1947). Factors in the teaching of our persistent modern problems. *Social Education, 9*(4), 167-169.

Engle, S. H. (1959). The role of education in free government: The American way of life in the Republic of the United States. *Bulletin of the Indiana Department of Public Instruction, No. 230* (pp. 79-85). Indianapolis: Indiana Department of Public Instruction.

Engle, S. H. (1960). Decision making: The heart of social studies instruction. *Social Education, 51*(7), 301-304, 306.

Engle, S. H. (1970). *Faculty Annual Report: 1969-1970*. School of Education, Indiana University.

Engle, S. H. (1979). Personal communication with E. Wesley. February 15. Palo Alto, CA: Hoover Institution on War, Revolution and Peace, Standford University.

Engle, S. H. (1985). Personal communication with Frances Haley. November 5. Palo Alto, CA: Hoover Institution on War, Revolution and Peace, Stanford University.

Engle, S. H.. (1986). Late night thoughts about the new social studies. *Social Education, 50*(8), 20-22.

Engle, S. H., & Ochoa, A. (1988). *Education for democratic citizenship: Decision making in the social studies*. New York: Teachers College Press.

Evans, R. W. (1989a). The future of issue-centered education. *The Social Studies, 80*(5), 176-177.

Evans, R. W. (1989b). How should we direct present efforts to promote the issue-centered vision? *The Social Studies, 80*(5),197-198.

Evans, R. W. (2004). *The social studies wars: What should we teach the children?* New York: Teachers College Press.

Evans, R. W., & Saxe, D. W. (1996). *Handbook on teaching social issues. Bulletin 92*. Washington, DC: National Council for the Social Studies.

Gross, R. E. (1989). Reasons for the limited acceptance of the problems approach. *The Social Studies, 80*(5), 185-186.

Griffin, A. F. (1942). *A philosophical approach to the subject-matter preparation of teachers of history*. Unpublished doctoral dissertation, The Ohio State University, Columbus.

Haas, J. D. (1977). *The era of the new social studies*. Boulder, CO: ERIC Clearinghouse for Social Studies/Social Science Education and Social Science Education Consortium, Inc.

Harwood, A. M. (1999). *Developing pre-service teachers' knowledge of issues through service learning*. Paper presented at the Annual College and University Assembly for the National Council for the Social Studies, Orlando, FL.

Hess, D. E. (2005). How do teachers' political views influence teaching about controversial issues? *Social Education, 69*(1), 47-49.

Holt, E. R. (1989). *ICSS at 50, remembering for renewal, 50th anniversary commemorative edition*. Bloomington: Indiana Council for the Social Studies.

Hunt, M. P., & Metcalf, L. E. (1955). *Teaching high school social studies*. New York: Harper & Row.

Johann, R. O. (1965). Authority and responsibility. In J. C. Murray (Ed.), *Freedom and man* (pp. 141-151). New York: Kenedy and Sons.

Kavett, H. (1976). How do we stand with the pledge of allegiance today? *Social Education, 40*(3),135-140.

Koeppen, K. E. (2003). Issues-centered social studies: Promoting active citizenship in the classroom. *Social Studies and the Young Learner, 15*(4),15-17.

Leming, J. S. (1989). The two cultures of social education. *Social Education, 53*(6), 404-408.

Leming, J. S., & Nelson, M. (1995). A citation analysis of the handbook of research on social studies teaching and learning. *Theory and Research in Social Education, 23*(2),169-182.

Malenshek, J. (1959). Shirley Engle named distinguished teacher; Gets Lieber Award at I.U.'s birthday celebration. *The Indiana Daily Student*, p. 7.

Massialas, B. G. (1989). The inevitability of issue-centered discourse in the classroom. *The Social Studies, 80*(5), 173-175.

Mehlinger, H. D. (1981). Social studies: Some gulfs and priorities. In H. D. Mehlinger & O. L. Davis (Eds.), *The social studies: Eightieth yearbook of the National Society for the Study of Education* (pp. 244-269). Chicago: The University of Chicago Press.

Mehlinger, H. D., & Patrick, J. J. (1972). American political behavior. In S. H. Engle, H. D. Mehlinger, & J. J. Patrick (Eds.) *Report of the high school curriculum center in government.* (Final report). Washington, DC: U. S. Department of Health, Education, and Welfare, Office of Education, text-fiche, ERIC Document ED 092 439.

Murray, J. C. (1964). *Challenges to democracy: A tenth anniversary symposium of the fund for the republic.* New York: Praeger.

Myrdal , G. (1944). *An American dilemma.* New York: Harper & Brothers.

National Council for the Social Studies. (1957). *Minutes for the first meeting of the house of delegates.* Document delivered at the 35th annual meeting of the National Council for the Social Studies, Pittsburgh, PA. 2. New York: Special Collections of the Milbank Library at Teachers College, Columbia University, Teachers College.

National Council for the Social Studies. (1994). *Curriculum standards for social studies.* Washington, DC: Author.

Nelson, M. (Ed.) (1994). *The future of the social studies.* Boulder, CO: Social Science Education Consortium.

Niebuhr, R. (1971). Democracy's distinction and danger. *Center Magazine, 4*, 1-4.

Ochoa-Becker, A. S. (2001). A critique of the NCSS curriculum standards. *Social Education, 65*(3), 165-168.

Ochoa-Becker, A. S., Morton, M. L., Autry, M. M., Johnstad, S., & Merrill, D. (2001). A search for decision making in three elementary classrooms. *Theory and Research in Social Education, 29*(2), 261-289.

Oliver, D. W., & Shaver, J. P. (1966). *Teaching public issues in the high school.* Boston, MA: Houghton Mifflin.

Previte, M. A. (2002). Seeing the whole board: An exercise in presidential decision making. *The Review: Journal of the Ohio Council for the Social Studies, 38*(1), 13-20.

Rossi, J. A., & Pace, C. M. (1998). Issues-centered instruction with low achieving high school students: The dilemmas of two teachers. *Theory and Research in Social Education, 26*(3), 380-409.

Rugg, H. O. (1923). Do the social studies prepare pupils adequately for life activities? In G. M. Whipple (Ed.), *Twenty-second yearbook of the National Society for the Study of Education, Part II* (pp. vii-27). Bloomington, IL: Public School Publishing Company.

Shaver, J. P. (1989). Lessons from the past: The future of an issue-centered social studies curriculum. *The Social Studies, 80*(5), 192-196.

Vanaria, L. M. (1957). *The National Council for the Social Studies: A voluntary organization for professional service.* Unpublished doctoral dissertation, Columbia University, New York.

Wesley, E. B. (1937). *Teaching the social studies: Theory and practice.* Boston, MA: D. C. Heath.

Wronski, S. P. (1982). Edgar Bruce Wesley (1891-1980): His contributions to the past, present, and future of the social studies. *Journal of Thought, 17*(3), 56.

CHAPTER 10

MAURICE P. HUNT

Activist Teacher, Scholar, Collaborator

Sherry L. Field, Mary Lee Webeck, and Susan Robertson

INTRODUCTION

A simple, five-sentence obituary published in *The Fresno Bee* on April 10, 1979, did little to highlight the significant and far-reaching career of Maurice Phillip Hunt, activist teacher, scholar, and collaborator. Yet in conducting research about Hunt's life and scholarship for this chapter, we found many reasons for which he is—and should continue to be—remembered. As a coauthor with professional colleagues Lawrence Metcalf in social studies education and Morris Bigge in educational psychology, Maurice Hunt's powerful ideas on teaching secondary social studies, promoting values inquiry, and the psychological and social foundations of education were promoted. Hunt's advocacy for deep and critical thinking about solving real problems in United States society and recognition of the key role that teachers play in that endeavor was seeded during his graduate study and grew through his scholarly publications.

Addressing Social Issues in the Classroom and Beyond: The Pedagogical Efforts of Pioneers in the Field, 187–200
Copyright © 2007 by Information Age Publishing
All rights of reproduction in any form reserved.

Maurice P. Hunt began his career in higher education in 1951 at Fresno State University (Fresno, California) in the midst of a social and intellectual climate that would become a movement known as the New Social Studies. He and future writing partner in the social studies, Lawrence Metcalf, had been fellow doctoral students at The Ohio State University and while there, worked with Boyd Bode and H. Gordon Hullfish, two decided influences upon both Hunt's and Metcalf's scholarship, stances toward active learning in the secondary school classrooms, and research agendas. In the field of social studies, Hunt and Metcalf are best known for their scholarship in secondary social studies methods. They coauthored two editions of *Teaching High School Social Studies* (1955/1968), both of which continue to be influential in contemporary social studies educational thought.

EARLY INFLUENCES

Primarily through Hunt's writing and that of his colleagues, one is able to glean important insights into Maurice Hunt's life. In his *Foundations of Education: Social and Cultural Perspectives* (1975) textbook, Hunt revealed to his readers the "evolution of the author's present viewpoint—reared a Christian idealist; as a late teenager converted to a stubborn Comtist positivism; as a university student veered sharply toward a Deweyan scientific-humanism; as an adult, developed a major commitment to a liberal-democratic mode of human relations and a relativistic world view reflecting the convergence of the Peirce-James-Dewey philosophical tradition and a Lewinian cognitive-field psychology, upon which is superimposed a certain warmth toward existentialism" (Hunt, 1975, p. ix). For the students who would be studying this Foundations text, Hunt wanted to explain the lens through which he wrote the book and, further, provide them glimpses into his early life. This description provides a mirror by which to interpret the thinking of Maurice Hunt, the teacher and humanist.

Hunt's rural upbringing and subsequent schooling experiences, along with his rugged individualism and stanch sense of independence, powerfully shaped his views about education, teaching, and curriculum. Toward the end of the Foundations textbook, Hunt (1975) revealed even more information about his childhood and early school years:

> The present author was privileged to have had his first eight grades of schooling in a traditional, one-room red brick schoolhouse, located in a strictly rural setting (the nearest farm-house was almost half a mile distant). Students in all eight grades sat in the same room, each at a desk wide

enough for two students—a situation which made it possible for students to study together by pairs when the teacher gave permission. We had a different teacher each year, each one inexperienced in teaching, with only a high school diploma and one summer of normal school training as preparation. Only one of the eight teachers knew much about subject matter.

The teaching materials were county-adopted textbooks, poorly written and often factually inaccurate. The curriculum included reading, writing, arithmetic, geography, civics, and history, with the addition in the eighth grade of health education. There was the traditional daily flag salute and group recitation of the Lord's Prayer. All we can remember learning from the formal curriculum was a slight increment in reading and arithmetic, which we had learned primarily from our parents, and a smattering of largely irrelevant geography—mostly promptly forgotten.

But the amount of life-related learning was tremendous. The younger children learned about sex from the seventh and eighth graders. We learned a considerable amount of biology: a nearby stream provided frogs and many creepy crawly things to slip into the teacher's desk. Birds, small animals, and vegetation were abundant. We played and fought together, loved and hated one another. We talked incessantly about all manner of subjects. The teachers shared in much of our play. Teachers could not hide their humanness: when one of my nineteen-year-old teachers took up with a twenty-three-year-old eighth grade boy everyone knew about it and took it quite in stride.

So we learned a great deal about people and nature and their interdependence. We had abundant opportunity to test ourselves in our games, our fighting, our making up, and our loving. Above all, we learned to function as a community, in which participatory democracy developed naturally. Our education was humanistic in the best sense of the term. The erroneous textbooks were too incidental to damage us. The canned problems in arithmetic did not make robots of us nor did the teachers' flash card drills, because every day was devoted to problem solving for humanistic ends. (p. 554)

From Hunt's description of his early schooling experiences, we can clearly see his frankness and understanding of human nature. We also catch glimpses of his notions of what classroom discussion might be, and what the subjects about which students should discuss could be. A certainty of the natural way in which students should interact with one another and teachers should interact with their students' glimmers through in this narrative.

ACTIVIST TEACHER

Maurice Hunt taught education and economics classes at Fresno State University for 28 years, from 1951 until his death in 1979. His ideas about reflective teaching were heavily influenced by the philosophy and educational thought of John Dewey and his mentor at The Ohio State University, H. Gordon Hullfish. As for the influence of Hullfish on their book, Hunt and Metcalf (1955/1968) duly noted that "the imprint of H. Gordon Hullfish's thinking will ... be visible, particularly in the ... interpretation of moral conflicts in representing choice between competing goods" (acknowledgments page).

Considering the time period (the early 1950s) when Hunt was a young assistant professor, he was an unusual teacher. Poised as the period was in the midst of the Cold War and the beginning of the Civil Rights Movement, Hunt's classes typically included much discussion and attention to cases and to the value-laden dilemmas which Hunt routinely used to promote reflective thinking and impassioned dialogue among his students. Class sessions always included attention to the larger social and historical milieu, and they presented a space for students to dialogue and debate in ways they had never had an opportunity to do before. Stanley Shermis, one of Hunt's former students and a noted social studies educator himself, described his mentor's teaching in this way:

> In 1955 there was little about Maurice Hunt that any of us—his advisees and students—could have identified with greatness. In that year I took my first course with him; it was also the year of publication of his and Lawrence Metcalf's *Teaching High School Social Studies*. At that time we saw him simply as a shy, unassertive man whose teaching consisted largely of asking questions. He began the class—a required methods course—by asking us our reactions to the problem of a well-to-do man who had installed a mistress in his townhouse but was still loyal to his own family. A fellow student, Ed, told me once or twice that this was the damndest methods course he had ever seen. Others were bewildered. But a number of us were intensely stimulated. Indeed, the words "stimulate" and "provocative" were, for Maury, words of high praise. I should, he urged, take a course from Bigge because he was "stimulating." And so I did. And Maury was right. Between Hunt and Bigge I was ruined; never thereafter could I tolerate the cant, cliché's and banalities that passed then—and now—for much scholarship in education. (Quoted in Bigge & Hunt, 1980, p. xiii)

Exhorting in his scholarship the role of education and, consequently, the role of teachers in a democratic society, Hunt often expressed key concerns as the need for preservice teachers to learn about the "national culture in its international setting" and "certain educational problems ... linked to broad national and international problems." Soberingly, he drew many of his ideas from "scholarly interpretations of a number of critical national social issues which—unless resolved in a rational manner—[he believed] could lead to the destruction of a viable human culture and conceivably even to the end of life on earth" (Hunt, 1975, p. vii). Additionally, Hunt urged his students to consider the imminent possibility that schools "could play a decisive role in keeping democracy as it now exists alive in an advanced industrial culture" (p. viii). Moreover, he opined "teachers should all be social philosophers and in the final analysis be even more concerned with broad long-ranging goals of education than with specific course objectives" (Hunt, 1975, p. 3).

Hunt taught his students about three roles which teachers had played in the past "and which may remain viable for a long time in the future" (Hunt, 1975, p. 93). These included: (1) Teacher as conservator of culture; (2) Teacher as a democratic leader in amending the culture; and (3) Teacher as a cultural architect. Hunt believed that teachers should consider both positive and negative aspects of a "reconstructionist" position. He believed that reconstructionism called for "personal and social reconstruction [of education] in a literal sense" (Hunt, 1975, p. 102), and he drew upon the work of George Counts, Harold Rugg, and Theodore Brameld to teach the philosophy to his own students.

Just as Hunt had highly-developed notions of what education should be and the roles that teachers should play in schools, so too did he sense the importance of an innovative curriculum. More specifically, he promoted nonadherence to the status quo, and was especially strong in his advocacy for cultural studies by all students in social studies. In this regard, he said: "Until democracy is solidly enough established in the United States so that some form of fascism will not continue to be an ever-present threat, it would seem logical that cultural studies could best be pursued through reading and field-laboratory programs…" (Hunt, 1975, p. 552). Hunt also recognized and asserted "the public school curriculum has been overloaded with courses which in no way serve the fundamental purposes of public education as the Founding Fathers envisioned them, and that those courses which should serve these purposes have no useful long-range impact on a majority of pupils who take them" (Hunt, 1975, pp. 552-553).

Hunt always created personalized curricula for the classes that he taught at Fresno State University; and for some of these courses, the curricula consisted, at least in some part, of the textbooks he had authored or coauthored. Telling examples of Hunt's thoughts about curriculum are located in such curricular efforts. For example, in his Foundations textbook, Hunt shared his "author's commitment to candor" and noted that his writing would "be as honest as the author can make it" and it was "bound to be controversial—as probably all textbooks should be" (Hunt, 1975, p. ix). True to this warning about his candor, Hunt suggested that what was most needed to improve education was to "improve the quality of teaching in subjects that lend themselves most readily to cultural study.… We need a crash program, particularly in the literary and social studies areas, to revamp both the content of the curriculum and the effectiveness of instruction" (Hunt, 1975, p. 553).

Byron Massialas, a noted social studies educator and researcher, has commented on the unique way that Hunt drew a significant distinction about appropriate content for secondary social studies learners. More specifically, he noted that with Metcalf, Hunt analyzed:

> Content based on the scholarly disciplines of the social sciences and reflective content [content based on issues or problems that are of the utmost importance to individual students and their communities]: "the content of reflection—in contrast to the content of history, political science, geography, and so on—includes every relevant aspect of the mental and physical environment in which a given act of thought occurs, everything a thinker brings to bear on a problem." In *How We Think,* John Dewey (1933) reasoned that an act of thought begins when an individual experiences a felt need. He or she then moves on to explore alternative solutions to the difficulty, projecting and testing implications and logical consequences. During the process of thinking, the individual draws upon relevant resources, including previous personal experiences as well as information contained in the traditional social sciences. In this process, "content assumes an emergent character. From the standpoint of a learner, it comes into existence as it is needed; it does not have a life independent of its own." (Quoted in Massialas, 1996 p. 46; Hunt & Metcalf, 1955/1968, pp. 214-215)

Choosing to serve his students at Fresno State University for his entire career, Hunt also portrayed a commitment to his local community. He served the larger scholarly community through his writing and quiet leadership outside of the classroom as well. During his tenure at Fresno State, Hunt was elected President of the Far Western Philosophy of Education Society in 1962. At that time, the Society was at its incipient stage. The Society held its 50th anniversary meeting in 2003. A quick overview of the program of the 51st annual meeting of the Society revealed paper presentations with titles that surely would have interested Hunt immensely: "An Aesthetic Evaluation of Teaching," "The Media's Miseducation of Young People," "Turning it On: Affect in the Classroom," "Liberty and Liberal Education: A Philosophical Analysis," "Diversity and the Socratic Method," and "Moral Expertise in Plato's Laches."

SCHOLAR AND COLLABORATOR

As a scholar and a collaborator, Maurice Hunt was a major contributor to the field of education. With his coauthor, Lawrence Metcalf, he championed the field of social studies. For example, Cox and Massialas (1967) opened their book, *Social Studies in the United States: A Critical Approach*, with a tribute to the prescience of Hunt and Metcalf in predicting the future of social studies:

> It is increasingly clear that there are changes afoot in social studies. Not the least of these was heralded ... by Hunt and Metcalf's *Teaching High School Social Studies*. Perhaps more than any other single publication, this text in social studies education clearly predicted future trends in the field. Hunt and Metcalf asserted in 1955 that social education in a democracy demands a "much greater emphasis on developing higher thought processes, with all that this implies for reflective examination of critical social issues." They predicted that the social studies curriculum would "eventually rely heavily on data supplied by social scientists, particularly in the fields of sociology, anthropology, psychology, and psychiatry." The demand, they hypothesized, was for a more systematic means of social judgement in a democracy; the curriculum trend would necessarily be toward a wider spectrum of social knowledge, emphasizing the disciplines of social analysis. (p. 1)

Democracy as a component in American education was a consistently strong theme throughout the academic and curricular writing of Maurice Hunt. He defined democracy simply as "a method by which people relate and by which they make group decisions. [It is] a method, or process, rather than a set of institutional structures" (Hunt, 1975, p. 7). With his colleague at Fresno State University, M. Bigge, Hunt considered the nature of a democratic group when they noted,

> A democratic group is self-governing. But it must provide for situations where disagreement occurs. Ideally, democratic decisions are by consensus ... reached through discussion and compromise. Then, by common consent, action is taken. However, if it is time for action and consensus is not yet possible, a democratic group votes. Each person has an equal vote, and a majority vote wins. So, votes are taken to facilitate action, not to enforce views or opinions.... If a democratic society is to survive over time, a majority of its members must learn to make reflective decisions where socially important questions are involved. A democratic society assumes competence on the part of its members; any different assumption would lead to distrust and rejection of the principle of equal participation. *If democracy is to survive, its members must take steps to insure the principle of reflection is employed as widely as possible in making choices of group concern* (italics added). (Bigge & Hunt, 1980, p. 512)

Throughout his academic life, Hunt believed deeply that democracy could best be promoted through relevant cultural study. His preferred pedagogical methods toward this end were those of discussion, problem solving, and reflection. One of the most intriguing ways in which reflective teaching was promoted was with the introduction of what Hunt and

Metcalf called "closed areas" of a culture—or, certain areas of conflicting belief and behavior ... [in which people] usually react to problems blindly and emotionally" (Hunt & Metcalf, 1955/1968, p. 26). Contemporary scholars Evans and Brodkey (1996) observed that "Hunt and Metcalf (1955/1968) proposed a curriculum that would inquire into the problematic areas of culture, focusing in particular on 'closed areas' of culture as appropriate in a given community. They proposed that 'problems, units, projects, blocks of work—call them what you will—should focus on a problematic area of culture,' and suggested that such an approach 'does not require major disruption of present curriculum patterns. It does require that teachers conceive social-studies courses more broadly" (p. 255).

If a teacher were to address controversial, or closed issues, use of a Problem Solving Model was recommended. The Hunt and Metcalf Problem Solving Model (Hunt & Metcalf, 1955/1968) continues to be widely used by contemporary social studies educators such as Nelson and Michaelis (1980, p. 151) and authors in Evans and Saxe, *Handbook on Teaching Social Studies, NCSS Bulletin 93* (1996), who will be discussed later in this chapter. This Problem Solving Model, developed by Hunt and Metcalf for their first edition of *Teaching High School Social Studies* (1955), was an important centerpiece of the second edition in 1968.

While Nelson and Michaelis (1980) readily acknowledged the influence of Dewey in the development of what is currently known as inquiry-based instruction ("[his] description of thinking has been modified and variously labeled as the scientific method, reflective thinking, problem solving, and inquiry ... " (p. 93)), their textbook featured Hunt and Metcalf's (1955/1968) Reflective Thought Model, as one of a few "models currently used in the social studies" (Nelson & Michaelis, 1980, p. 93). (Among others that were noted were Nelson's Model of Inquiry, Fenton's Mode of Inquiry, and Cassidy and Kurfman's Decision-Making Process.)

As Nelson and Michaelis (1980) noted, the Hunt and Metcalf Reflective Thought Model was forthright and open to a multitude of queries. Steps in the model included (parenthetical illustrations are provided by Nelson and Michaelis) the following:

1.   Recognizing and defining a problem (a sensed discrepancy in data or beliefs, for example, Why is juvenile delinquency increasing?).
2.   Formulating hypotheses (for example, due to increased use of automobiles, growth of permissiveness, and so forth).
3.   Elaborating logical implications of hypotheses (for example, deducing testable propositions, such as, If increased use of automobiles is a factor, then we will find more auto users among delinquents).

4. Testing of hypotheses (for example, collecting data on an adequate sample).

5. Drawing of a conclusion (for example, stating whether or not the hypothesis is supported by the evidence) (Nelson & Michaelis, 1980, p. 93).

The Problem Solving Model likely found its way into the social studies classrooms across the nation of those teachers who were interested in powerfully opening dialogue and classroom discussion for their students. It, in fact, proved to be a practical tool to help clarify values about controversial topics. Commenting on the Hunt and Metcalf Model, Oliver and Shaver (1966) observed "These authors suggest that conflict between two values may be resolved by referring to a more basic third value upon which there is agreement" (Oliver & Shaver, 1966, p. 34).

Bringing values and moral conflict to the forefront of social studies education also gained Maurice Hunt and Lawrence Metcalf attention during the decade of the 1970s. According to them, "social studies teachers must focus on 'questions of policy at the level of moral conflict' if they want moral education to be something more than indoctrination in the right virtues" (Hunt & Metcalf, 1955, p. 90 as cited in Lange, 1975, p. 279). Hunt and Metcalf draw a sharp distinction between methods of instruction, which do and do not emphasize the importance of choice in the face of two conflicting goods. It is the former approach to instruction in values, which represents the crux of moral education. The following description develops that observation:

> If the difficult decisions of life involved only choices between good and evil, where would be the problem? Who would deliberately choose evil? Unfortunately, moral choice is not this simple. It never involves merely distinguishing between right and wrong. For a person making a choice, moral decision requires distinguishing between two or more good things. It is when at least two desired courses of action come into conflict that moral choice becomes necessary. (Lange, 1975, p. 279)

It is noteworthy that Hunt and Metcalf provided for teachers an outline of the teaching procedures for dealing with both conceptual and empirical aspects of valuation. Its components included the following:

I. What is the nature of the object, event, or policy to be evaluated? This question plainly poses a task in concept analysis. If the students are trying to evaluate the welfare state, they should define the object as precisely and clearly as possible.

A. How is the welfare state to be defined intensionally and extensionally? By what criteria is it to be defined intensionally?

B. If students disagree over criteria, and therefore in their definition of welfare state, how is this disagreement to be treated? Must they agree? Can they agree to disagree? Are there criteria by which the welfare state ought to be defined? On what basis can we select among different sets of criteria?

II. The Consequences Problem.

A. What consequences can be expected or anticipated from the policy in question? Is it true, as some have claimed, that the growth of the welfare state destroys individual incentive? How does one get evidence for answering this kind of question?

B. If students disagree in their projection of consequences, how is this difference to be treated? Can evidence produce agreement? What is the difference between a disagreement over criteria and a disagreement over evidence?

III. Appraisal of Consequences.

A. Are the projected consequences desirable or not?

B. By what criteria are the consequences to be appraised? How do different criteria affect one's appraisal of consequences?

IV. Justification of criteria.

A. Can criteria for appraising consequences be justified? How?

B. If students disagree on criteria, and therefore in their appraisal of consequences, how can this difference be treated? What relationship ought to exist between one's criteria and one's basic philosophy of life?

C. Are students consistent in their use of criticism? (Hunt & Metcalf, 1955/1968, p. 134).

Hunt and Metcalf believed that teachers should help their students with the "problem of justification" outlined above, suggesting that if decisions and policies could not be justified via definitions, then moral paralysis would occur. Likewise, the question of a teacher sharing personal positions on topics with students was an important one, and one that was deliberated by Banks (1973), who believed that a teacher cannot and should not be asked to assume a neutral position when discussing such explosive topics as racism, legalized abortion, artificial contraceptives, and women's liberation. More specifically, Banks argues that "To demand that a teacher be neutral on such issues is, as Hunt and Metcalf (1955/ 1968) cogently argue, 'to deny him the freedom and right to voice his opinion openly in a public forum' (p. 120). They suggest that the teacher should express opinions at an appropriate time but after the students have had ample time to arrive at their own positions and ... deal with social issues honestly and openly" (Banks, 1973, p. 333).

Massialas, Sprague, and Hurst (1975, pp.14-15) also brought the work of Hunt and Metcalf to the forefront of their book, *Social Issues Through Inquiry*. More specifically, in their introductory chapter, "Why Teach Social Issues?", Massialas et al. (1975) turned to Hunt and Metcalf's ideas about studying interpersonal and intrapersonal social conflicts and the need to pay special attention to the closed areas in our culture: power and the law, nationalism and patriotism, religion and morality, economics and business, race and minority-group relations, social class and customs, and sex, courtship, and marriage.

Jack Fraenkel, another social studies luminary, also highlighted Hunt and Metcalf's work in his book, *Helping Students Think and Value: Strategies for Teaching the Social Studies* (1980, p. 246), by noting the pedagogical significance of the study and discussion of controversial issues. Fraenkel also borrowed an ethical dilemma from Hunt and Metcalf regarding a secretary whose employer had provided good working conditions and benefits, but when she realized that he had not been honest about tax reporting she wondered what to do. Fraenkel (1980) mused, "How can we help students deal with this kind of values conflict? As Hunt and Metcalf suggest, to be told that one should always value both honesty and kindness doesn't help much when the two conflict" (p. 246). Again in the same chapter, Fraenkel (1980) drew upon the work of Hunt and Metcalf in a vignette that continues to be relevant today: the intervention of the United States in the affairs of other nations (p. 256). Finally, Fraenkel posited several questions that Hunt and Metcalf suggested for secondary social studies teachers following an audio or video recording (p. 338). Questioning, defining, and differentiating strategies used by Fraenkel for these teaching vignettes and strategies were all attributed to Hunt and Metcalf.

A LASTING PRESENCE

A scholar's longevity and lasting influence can be partially measured by a continued presence in contemporary academic literature, which could be considered especially true if the academic literature is devoted to one of the scholar's key areas of interest. In 1996, NCSS Bulletin 93 was devoted to teaching social issues. Within the pages of the large *Handbook on Teaching Social Issues*, edited by Evans and Saxe, are 44 chapters, many of which build either directly or indirectly, on Hunt and Metcalf's secondary social studies education scholarship, some 40 and 50 years after their first and second editions of *Teaching High School Social Studies* were published, respectively. Nine citations were found for Hunt and Metcalf in the volume. In the *Handbook's* introductory chapter, Evans, Newmann, and Saxe (1996) call attention to 14 luminaries in the field of social studies who promoted practice "centered around the teaching of social issues" (p. 5). Hunt and Metcalf were 2 among the 14 specified, which also included Dewey, Rugg, Griffin, Oliver, Shaver, Massialas, Cox, Newmann, Gross, Muessig, Engle, and Ochoa. In the same book, Nancy Fichtman Dana (1996) names 22 "leaders in the field," advising "preservice teachers who are exploring issues-centered instruction" to read works by them (p. 302). Maurice P. Hunt is among the 22. In their chapter in the *Handbook*, Ligon and Chilcoat (1996) highlight the work of Hunt and Metcalf in their introductory section when they ask, "To what extent do students today experience what Hunt and Metcalf called 'intrapersonal conflict' and are 'uncertain as to what to believe or value'?" (p. 220). Evans (1996) points out that, along with models developed by Oliver and Shaver, those of Hunt and Metcalf are important for teachers to consult for ideas about how to apply issues-centered approaches (p. 155). In yet another chapter in the *Handbook*, Evans and Brodkey (1996) include a table, "Hunt and Metcalf's Problematic Areas of Culture," that highlights such issues as power and the law; economics; nationalism, patriotism, and foreign affairs; social class; religion and morality; race and minority-group relations; and sex, courtship, and marriage (p. 256).

CONCLUSION

We find it fitting to conclude this chapter with two powerful tributes from Byron Massialis and Stanley Shermis. Massialis's accolade was written about 15 years after the death of his colleague Maurice Hunt; Shermis's tribute was written just days after the death of his mentor and teacher. Both speak to the enduring nature of the scholarship of Maurice P. Hunt and both remind us to read, and reread, his work in light of contemporary issues.

Massialis (1996) wrote the following:

> In 1955, Hunt and Metcalf proposed that schools develop curricula based on a catalog of "cultural inconsistencies," namely, deeply seated beliefs held by groups in a society that are different from each other, especially in the "closed areas" of subjects that are considered taboo in the classroom.... Educators thought this an unrealistic proposal. Today, more than forty years later, their proposal makes more sense than ever. (p. 44)

In his tribute, Stanley Shermis (1980) wrote, in part, the following:

Years later, after I had begun my own career, Maury's teaching and his published ideas began to fall into place. I saw that the emphasis on "provoca-
tiveness" was quite intelligible: One needed to be provoked into sensing a
problem—for with-out this the rest of Dewey's complete act of thought
would never take place. This simple notion has yet to find a place in education. Eventually, after I had consulted his works, not dozens but literally
hundreds of times, I recognized that Hunt had attempted to capture the
relationships among democracy, learning theory, problem-solving, social
studies, and culture. It then became clear to me that, to use an uncongenial
Aristotelian term, Maury had penetrated to the very essence of things.
(Shermis, quoted in Bigge & Hunt, 1980, pp. xiii-xiv)

REFERENCES

Banks, J. A., with Clegg, Jr., A. A. (1973). *Teaching strategies for the social studies:
Inquiry, valuing, and decision-making*. Reading, MA: Addison-Wesley.

Bigge, M. L., & Hunt, M. P. (1980). *Psychological foundations of education: An introduction to human motivation, development, and learning* (3rd ed.). New York:
Harper & Row, Publishers.

Cox, C. B., & Massialas, B. G. (1967). *Social studies in the United States: A critical
approach*. New York: Harcourt, Brace.

Dana, N. F. (1996). An issues-centered teacher education. In R. W. Evans & D. W.
Saxe (Eds.), *Handbook on teaching social issues: NCSS Bulletin 93* (pp. 299-305).
Washington, DC: National Council for the Social Studies.

Evans, R. W. (1996). A critical approach to teaching unites states history. In R. W.
Evans and D. W. Saxe (Eds.) *Handbook on teaching social issues* (pp. 152-160).
Washington, DC: National Council for the Social Studies.

Evans, R. W., & Brodkey, J. (1996). An issues-centered curriculum for high school
social studies. In R. W. Evans & D. W. Saxe (Eds.), *Handbook on teaching social
issues: NCSS Bulletin 93* (pp. 254-264). Washington, DC: National Council for
the Social Studies.

Evans, R. W., Newmann, F. M., & Saxe, D. W. (1996). Defining issues-centered
education. In R. W. Evans & D. W. Saxe (Eds.), *Handbook on teaching social
issues: NCSS Bulletin 93* (pp. 2-5). Washington, DC: National Council for the
Social Studies.

Evans, R. W., & Saxe, D. W. (Eds.). (1996). *Handbook on teaching social issues: NCSS
Bulletin 93*. Washington, DC: National Council for the Social Studies.

Fraenkel, J. R. (1980). *Helping students think and value: Strategies for teaching the
social studies* (2nd ed.). Englewood Cliffs, NJ: Prentice-Hall.

Hunt, M. P. (1975). *Foundations of education: Social and cultural perspectives*. New
York: Holt, Rinehart, and Winston.

Hunt, M. P., & Metcalf, L. E. (1968). *Teaching high school social studies* (2nd. ed.).
New York: Harper and Row. (Original work published 1955)

Lange, D. (1975, October). Moral education and the social studies. *Theory into Practice, 14*(4), 279-285.

Ligon, J. R., & Chilcoat, G. W. (1996). Teaching issues-centered anthropology, sociology, and psychology. In R. W. Evans & D. W. Saxe (Eds.), *Handbook on teaching social issues: NCSS Bulletin 93* (pp. 220-227). Washington, DC: National Council for the Social Studies.

Massialas, B. G. (1996). Criteria for issues-centered content selection. In R. W. Evans & D. W. Saxe (Eds.), *Handbook on teaching social issues: NCSS Bulletin 93* (pp. 44-50). Washington, DC: National Council for the Social Studies.

Massialas, B. G., Sprague, N. F., & Hurst, J. B. (1975). *Social issues through inquiry: Coping in an age of crises.* Englewood Cliffs, NJ: Prentice-Hall.

Nelson, J. L., & Michaelis, J. U. (1980). *Secondary social studies: Instruction, curriculum, evaluation.* Englewood Cliffs, NJ: Prentice-Hall.

Oliver, D. P., & Shaver, J. P. (1966). *Teaching public issues in the high school.* Boston, MA: Houghton Mifflin.

CHAPTER 11

IMAGINING THE FUTURE

Theodore Brameld on the Frontiers of Multi-cultural Education

Karen L. Riley

INTRODUCTION

The term "multiculturalism" is of fairly recent vintage and is a term fraught with misunderstanding and politics. Mid-twentieth century educationists would not have recognized "multiculturalism" as an all-purpose term that today means anything from diversity of race to diversity of opinion. The term multicultural embraces ethnic groups, cultural groups, gender groups, and explores issues on every front including issues of sexual orientation and the physically disabled. Instead, at the half-century mark, education jargon contained words such as "inter-generational," "inter-cultural" (Giles, Pitkin, & Ingram, 1946, p. 39), "human relations," "human interaction," or even "multi-racial" (Daniel, 1950, p. 388), the meanings of which today fall under that all-purpose rubric of what educators call multiculturalism. And while current educators point to individuals such as James Banks, Gloria Ladsen-Billings, or Geneva Gay, as scolars

Addressing Social Issues in the Classroom and Beyond: The Pedagogical Efforts of Pioneers in the Field, 201–220
Copyright © 2007 by Information Age Publishing
All rights of reproduction in any form reserved.

who have contributed greatly to the literature base on multiculturalism and its related programs and their spinoffs, such as "sensitivity training," their efforts have been made easier owing to the work of others more than half a century before. In fact, the roots of multiculturalism were planted, in part, in the heady days of Progressive Era activism—and in particular, within the philosophy of Social Reconstructionism.

Under the umbrella term of Progressivism, one finds early 20th century progressives in nearly every sector of public life—political progressives, social progressives, and educational progressives. As Link (1959) succinctly states, "[a]ctually, of course, from the 1890s on there were many 'progressive' movements on many levels seeking sometimes contradictory objectives" (p. 836). Whatever the arena, reform was the overarching goal of progressive thinkers, including progressive educators (Chambliss, 1963). The excesses of capitalism, which included the alienation of workers, labor strife, ostentatious wealth and inflated securities, in the 1920s, thundered to a halt following the stock market crash of 1929. Within this historical context, some educationists sought reform of what they believed to be a political and economic system run amuck and one that perpetuated social inequality, an inequality that philosophers such as Maxine Greene argue has been perpetuated despite American educators' optimism (Franklin, 1984, p. 319). These educators pushed an agenda of social reconstruction, a philosophy of education whose purpose for schooling was to identify problems and alleviate them by teaching students through scientific method how to identify and solve social ills.

Social Reconstruction as a branch of Progressivism suited activist-minded educators who dedicated themselves to righting the wrongs of America's capitalist experiment. Social Reconstruction educators whose proclivity toward politics was matched by their zeal for social reform included George S. Counts, Harold O. Rugg, and Theodore Brameld, who coined the theme "education as power" (Wheeler, 1967, p. 11), and who was described by Ozmon (1966) as "the most outstanding Reconstructionist in American Education at the present time (p. 186). While all three may have believed in social equality with a certain working-to-make-the-world-a-better-place world-view, it was Brameld, the utopian's utopian, whose work pushed the boundaries of human interaction and paved the way for researchers to carry forward the struggle to understand the nature of culture in all of its dimensions. That said, Brameld would likely have rejected the label "utopian," claiming that "[t]he term 'utopian' has usually connoted a starry-eyed, castle-in-the-air idealism—an attitude quite out of tune with our more typical concern for 'know-how,' for techniques and processes, for practical ways of doing things congenial to the habits of a present-centered culture" (Brameld, 1952,

p. 435). Nonetheless, it is upon his shoulders that today's multicultural researchers and writers stand.

BACKGROUND

In the recent movie *The Emperor's Club*, Mr. Hundert reminds his class "a man's character is his fate." This simple saying when applied to the life and work of Ted Brameld reveals an individual whose course was set in childhood and whose path remained true to its origins and beginnings. Of the many factors that help to shape the intellectual character of the individual, family and place are perhaps the most important. For Brameld (1904-1987), the second son of an English father and German-American mother, the idyllic landscape and small town intimacy of agrarian Wisconsin provided him with a sense of connectedness. He felt especially connected to his father's English-village roots (Stone, 2003, p. 3). He came to know his English grandfather, an Anglican vicar for more than 40 years, largely through family stories (Stone, 2003, p. 3). As an adult, Bramweld's interpretation of Social Reconstruction contained what one might call a religious tone. (See, e.g., Brameld's *Toward a Reconstructed Philosophy of Education*, 1956, pp. 170-171.) Moreover, his lifelong struggle for social and economic equality often took on a certain evangelical zeal; his letters to the editor of this or that paper (he began writing to newspapers in high school) often reflected his passionate stance on the topic of inequality. His mother's Lutheran upbringing complemented the religious understandings of his father's Anglican world-view, especially in the areas of cooperation and noncompetitive social and economic endeavors.

Brameld's birthplace, Neillsville, Wisconsin, mirrored other small towns and villages that dotted the Wisconsin landscape, a state settled by scores of Scandinavians and Germans. In the bosom of what one might refer to as "old world culture," Brameld came to understand the economics of cooperation and what he would later call in one of his major writings, "the group mind as end and means" (Brameld, 1956, pp. 102-103). In short, Wisconsin farmers understood the concept of dairy cooperatives where labor, resources, and "know how" were shared by all and interdependence transcended competition. According to Stone (2003), by 1905, the year after Brameld's birth, Clark County (Neillsville was the county seat) counted 28 creameries, 30 cheese factories and 24,457 cows, although earlier the primary industry of the area had been timber. While dairying accounted for a generous portion of the county's prosperity in the early part of the 20th century, other necessary economic enterprises also contributed such as a milling company (flour), a sawmill, a wagon manufacturer, a foundry and a machine shop, to name but a few (Stone,

2003, pp. 14-15). In the environment of America's midwest, group consensus took precedence over individual expression, a notion that in theory is ironically and fundamentally anti-American. Brameld's later "social consensus theory" may have been developed and nurtured by his village and small town roots, within the social and religious context of Protestant America as largely defined by northern Europeans and their social and economic world view of cooperation.

Other factors that influenced Brameld's early life and helped to shape his character included his close relationship with his mother and the provincial nature of rural Wisconsin. According to Midori Kiso, Brameld's third wife, the philosopher fondly recalled on occasion that his self-confidence, bordering on a certain know-it-all attitude, could be attributed to his upbringing. With characteristic German pride and the weight of British heritage, Brameld's childhood charted his course toward adult self-assurance, or as some would later charge, cockiness. For her part, Minnie Brameld (Ted's mother) doted on young Ted. Occasionally, she invited the "neighbor ladies" over for a chat at which times she proudly showed off her youngest child (Ted), a handsome boy with blond curls. Kiso believes that Brameld's penchant for attracting attention was formed early in childhood as a result of his mother's somewhat excessive pride in her youngest offspring and also due to the fact that, as Brameld once admitted, he was a "mama's boy" (M. Kiso, Interview Questionnaire, 2005). Whatever the truth, Brameld's critics and sometimes supporters throughout his lifetime accused him of being somewhat arrogant. In fact, T. V. Smith, Brameld's graduate advisor at the University of Chicago, criticized him for being conceited, or as Brameld recalled in an oral history interview, of having "a well-developed façade of intellectual sophistication that was coming across as egotism" (Stone, 2003, p. 71). His know-it-all attitude nearly landed him in the exit row of the doctoral program at Chicago. Despite this incident, Smith and Brameld, according to Brameld's biographer, Frank Stone, remained on good terms throughout their lifetimes.

While Brameld's family, especially his mother, contributed much in terms of shaping the philosopher's self image, one must also examine, as previously mentioned, place, as well as time and environmental factors. All of these of course, are major influences that shape and sharpen an individual's self perception and conscience. Understandably, then, Ted Brameld the philosopher must be understood within the context of the following: his German/English heritage, German patterns of settlement in the United States, and geo-ethnic surroundings. Although half British, Brameld was most influenced by his maternal (German) side. After growing to young adulthood in a state largely populated by Germans, Brameld would later recall these formative days in Wisconsin as limiting and provincial (M. Kiso, Interview Questionnaire, 2005; Stone, 2003). In explaining the "German mind" and influence in Wisconsin, Dorpalen (1942), who investigated the German element during the American Civil War, concluded that Germans as a people are susceptible to what he calls environmental pressure. For example, Germans "accepted, and adopted, conditions as [they] found them. While zealous German Mennonites in Pennsylvania clamored against the 'vicious' institution of slavery, Germans in the Carolinas and Georgia found nothing objectionable in the use of slavery" (pp. 55-56). In other words, Germans as a group or distinct people were impressionable, and suffered to some degree from what this writer (Riley) calls the "chameleon syndrome."

Material gains, particularly the acquisition of land, motivated Germans politically and socially to a far greater degree than a sense of moral righteousness. As Hanley (1991) states, "[c]onvinced that the United States held a divinely appointed commission to usher in Christ's millennial Kingdom on Earth, [Protestant] ministers supposedly sanctioned the nation's material and political development as integral to spiritual advancement" (p. 203). Thus, the German quest for material riches, especially land, was perfectly consistent with their religious understandings, at least those who were Protestant. Another scholar of Germans in America (Stange, 1970), claims that Lutheran Germans in the Wisconsin Synod were "particularly conscious of their German heritage" (p. 354). Hence, the intellectual, religious, and philosophical impulses that shaped the thinking patterns of Germans, Swedes, Norwegians, and Finns, who were farmers, merchants, villagers, and town folk in upper midwest Wisconsin, included a belief in northern European superiority (Dorpalen, 1942) and an almost divine right to America's promise and progress vis-à-vis the westward expansion.

However, not all Germans resonated to orthodox religion or were shaped by purely religious ideas. In fact, a groundswell of German immigration occurred in 1848, just two generations before Brameld's birth in 1904. These Germans were "educated, articulate, and steeped in German rationalism and romantic nationalism … " and they "found in American liberty new opportunity to combine antireligious sentiment with an unbending political faith in democracy, equality, and social justice" (Hanley, 1991, p. 217). German transcendentalists captured the imagination of hard-working Americans of European stock with their unvarnished faith in political progress, which meant within the confines of the American landscape, equality, freedom, and social justice. Thus, caught between the notions of acquisition as a measure of Protestant spirituality (German Lutheranism) and notions of equality and social justice as constructs in a universal and secular belief system, German nationals in the United States and their children between the 1850s and 1900, as an educated, self-assured elite, believed in two distinct, often opposing, streams of thought: their god-given right to material riches and the quest for freedom, equality, and social justice.

While Stone (2003) believes that Brameld's intellectual development and attraction to global, inter-cultural, and intergroup education was largely a result of his breaking free from the narrow confines of rural Wisconsin to worldly places such as Chicago and New York, where he came into contact with men who would challenge his pre-existing ideas, this writer (Riley) believes something quite different. One should not forget the words of individuals like T. V. Smith (Brameld's advisor at Chicago) who accused him of being conceited and a know-it-all. Perhaps what Smith saw, but did not at the time understand, were Brameld's cultural underpinnings at work. This writer believes that one cannot subordinate generational, cultural, and familial knowledge to that of more recent vintage. In other words, Brameld's innate character and childhood understandings were only modified by his later adult experiences and intellectual journey, rather than remolded. Hence, German impulses toward social justice and a belief in European superiority seem to reflect what some might say were Brameld's later intellectual interests on the one hand and his personality on the other.

Upon completion of his compulsory studies, Brameld moved, in a figurative sense, from small-town, rural America, to what some might call an even smaller—in the philosophical sense—sphere of influence. His first encounter with higher education was as a student at Ripon College. After what Stone (2003) referred to as a "shaky start," Ripon College enrolled its first students in 1851. While Stone's (2003) intellectual biography of Brameld illuminates key individuals at Ripon who likely influenced the up-and-coming philosopher, a study conducted 4 years after Brameld's graduation from college offers much in terms of beliefs and attitudes held by Ripon seniors who were Brameld's contemporaries. The researchers in this study surveyed seniors at seven midwestern colleges and presented a number (25 propositions) of social and political concepts and problems (Dudycha, 1932, p. 775). Respondents (n = 305) were asked to rank order these propositions. The results of this survey are important as they reveal attitudes held by contemporaries of Brameld and therefore suggest that what influenced them may likewise have influenced him. The first three rankings included the following: a belief that the home is a necessary social institution, the institution of marriage is necessary to society, and the church is necessary to society (Dudycha, 1932, p. 777). These findings are consistent with the conservative nature of small town, largely homogenous, populations with strong religious underpinnings. However, traditional Ripon College was also established within the shadows of 19th century experiments in communitarian social arrangements. The confluence of traditional "American" values and utopianism—historian Arthur Bestor (1953) draws a distinction between utopians and communitarians—made for an interesting pair of intellectual streams of thought.

While Ripon was established as a liberal college but shortly turned to a religious rescuer (the Congregational Church) for its continued existence, it had as one of its original Directors a man by the name of Warren Chase, who Stone (2003) describes as a Ceresco visionary. Ceresco, a communitarian community, or what Bestor (1953) describes as a "Paten Office Model," subscribed to a secular doctrine of social reform that called for its members to model for others the kind of life that upholds ideals of social justice, harmony, brotherhood, and the like (p. 506). This model in theory (Guarneri, 1996, p. 463) could be duplicated again and again, thereby establishing scores of model communities throughout the land. Guarneri (1996) suggests that the history of communitarianism as a movement rather than an ideal has never been explored, but that in fact it was a movement connected by shared ideals of cooperation and the free exchange of ideas to name a few. This is an important point because Wisconsin is nearly the geographic center of the communitarian movement in the United States. But what does this have to do with Brameld? For one, the town of Ripon was founded in 1844 by members of the Wisconsin Phalanx, a communitarian order that established the town in an area that members called the Creseco Valley. Within 6 or 7 years of the town's founding, the Congregational Church assumed custodial status of the fledgling college, albeit under the early direction of Warren Chase, a communitarian. And two, the ideas of Ripon's founders are essential in understanding the intellectual climate that Brameld encountered as an impressionable college student. While numerous writers on Brameld's work argue that the origins of his ideas are purely Marxist—Brameld wrote *A Philosophic Approach to Communism* (see Sabine, 1935, in Descriptive Notes, p. 405)—his biographer (Stone, 2003) and this author believe that what is more likely is that Brameld absorbed ideas on topics such as social justice and the equal distribution of wealth from the rich communitarian environment of Ripon in particular, and Wisconsin, and the Middle West in general.

One cannot fail to notice similarities between Brameld's philosophy of social reconstruction and the tenets of communitarianism. In Brameld's (1956) *Toward a Reconstructed Philosophy of Education,* the philosopher envisions a new order based upon six principles. While all six easily reflect a socialist program, the sixth principle seems to be drawn directly from earlier communitarian impulses. It reads as follows: "human beings, regardless of race, religion, nationality, sex, age, or economic status, would share equally in all rights and all obligations related to the economic, political, scientific, esthetic, and educational phases of man's future" (p. 170). It is instructive to compare Brameld's ideas of social, economic, and political justice to the writings of the French social philosopher Charles Fourier whose ideas formed the basis for Fourieristic experiments like the Wisconsin Phalanx. Fourier, in condemning the existing social, economic, and political order of early 19th century France, railed against "the waste, the absurdity, the injustice, the inequity, of the present forms of society; the accumulation of money in the hands of the few; the competition between workmen; the suffering and degradation of the laboring classes" (Pedrick as cited in Stone, 2003, p. 36). While Fourierism as a whole was unpalatable to most Americans—Fourier's complex philosophy included a hierarchical and controversial theory on erotic relationships within Phalanxes, which surprisingly show up in Brameld's later work—his ideas on small communal, cooperative, and interdependent social groups excited scores of individuals from Western New York to South Dakota (Guarneri, 1982). This intellectual environment would not have been missed by someone with Brameld's curiosity and penchant for "standing out."

BRAMELD AS EDUCATIONAL PHILOSOPHER

At a meeting in Deland, Florida, of the Society for Educational Reconstruction, Robert Nash, one of Brameld's former doctoral students, recalled that in a speech at the University of Vermont in 2001, he asked Brameld's third wife, Midori Kiso, if "Ted" had died a spiritual person. Kiso answered in the following way:

> Robert, Ted was always looking for something more in his life. He never stopped growing. He often tried to meditate, and he was strongly attracted to Zen Buddhism. But he died a proud humanist to the core. I hope that you are not disappointed. (Nash, 2001, n.p.)

If one could characterize the influences on an individual's thinking and, in turn, how that individual influenced others in their thinking as resembling a child's kaleidoscope, then the picture of isolated bits of color and texture refracted as dozens of uniformed images might be helpful in understanding the seemingly disparate bits and pieces of Brameld's life that come together to form a somewhat clear image of the man and philosopher. Brameld's struggle to find spirituality at the end of his life after decades of dedication to a humanist tradition speak to his instinct as a philosopher and/or his desire to know what he may have deemed as unknowable. What then, prevented Brameld from truly embracing the spiritual realm? And more important, what does the question have to do with a historiographical approach to Brameld's life and work?

For one, Brameld's struggle with the existence of a spirit or spiritual world is and was a counterweight to his abiding faith in the power of human beings to define themselves, their culture, and to transform their world. In fact, he dedicated his entire academic life to refining ways and means for individuals and groups to realize their fullest potentials. And two, this struggle helps us to understand the durability of early patterns of learning. For example, the communitarian principles he likely absorbed as a student at Ripon College in Wisconsin blended and supported the pragmatic vision of John Dewey that he learned about as a graduate student (Burns, 1960, p. 60). Both Kiso (personal communication with author, 2005) and Nash (2001) believe that Dewey was perhaps the single greatest intellectual influence on Brameld. In fact, Nash's remarks that follow provide us with an insight into Brameld as a philosopher and some of the forces that drew him into the field of education, while establishing the source of his pivotal work as stemming from the American philosopher John Dewey.

> Brameld chose to become a faculty member in the field of education, rather than in academic philosophy, because, like John Dewey, he felt that philosophy needed to be more than an abstract, isolated field of study; done well it needed to be directly applied to the analysis and resolution of pressing social problems. Therefore, Brameld decided to cast his lot with the educationists, because in his words, they were "closer to the firing line of the human condition … dealing with such issues as severe economic dislocation, world wars, virulent nationalism, and racial and class exploitation.… " He went on to teach at three large, urban universities, finally ending his long career at Boston University, where Dave Conrad and I studied with him. He often said to me that he never ever regretted his early choice to spend his entire career teaching in schools of education. (Nash, 2001, n.p.)

As a doctoral student of Brameld's, Nash has a unique advantage when it comes to understanding the philosopher's work. Nash and a handful of other doctoral students cofounded the Society for Social Reconstruction in 1969, perhaps as a tribute to a mentor who influenced them and scores of others to play the educator/activist role that Brameld himself had modeled over the years. According to Nash, "[m]ost of Brameld's students went on to become frequent publishers, speakers, and activists of one kind or another, due largely to the example he set" (Nash, 2001, n. p.).

And what of Brameld's ideas? What did he teach to his students that they could take out into their classrooms and in turn use to influence others? Brameld's central construct can be found in the official statement of purpose of the Society for Educational Reconstruction: "The Proper Purpose of Education at All Levels Is Political Transformation, and Its End Product Is Cooperative Power, Global Order, Self-Transformation, and

Social Democracy" (Nash, 2001, n. p.). As a prolific writer, Brameld used his gift as a thinker and writer to excoriate those who would hold hostage the futures of young Americans within a system of schooling that only served the status quo. He protested against oppressive forces such as nationalism, absolutism, unbridled social interest, and inequality at all levels. In his *Patterns of Educational Philosophy*, Brameld (1971) illuminates for us what he believes is the heart of the matter:

> Frustrated as human beings have so often been by life-denying customs, by ignorance and superstitions, by cleavages in loyalty and other values, they have never approached anywhere near full command of their own energy, creative intelligence, and strength. They have been ruled over far more frequently than they have ruled. They have been starved, hoodwinked, exploited, cajoled, intimidated, frightened far more often than they have been decently fed, well informed, respected, encouraged, and aroused. With all the weaknesses that remain for human beings to conquer, the next development in human evolution will be the mature social development of humanity itself. This is the foremost task of education throughout the world today. (pp. 36-37)

And what a task for education and educators! Brameld envisioned a tall order for educational systems of all stripes at home and abroad.

One is reminded of Taba's (1963) warning that "education is a social institution which is intimately bound with the culture in which it functions" (p. 172), hence, since the advent of the Enlightenment, one cannot separate school systems from the aims and goals of their respective political systems. In other words, it would not be in any government's self interest to educate its youth for the purpose of fostering a revolution. Hence, as powerful and seductive as Brameld's ideas were in bringing about a new social order, they would find little support or allure from the power brokers and their supporters who actually determine educational purpose. Moreover, Brameld as a macro-visionary viewed the political, economic, and social evils at home (the United States) not as an isolated case, but as part of a global problem that called for global solutions, one of which was subordination to a global political structure and set of international laws. Even in today's market place of global ideas, Brameld's philosophical positions of some three or four decades ago seem ultra-revolutionary, despite the fact that his focus on philosophical questions on education were largely in the mainstream (e.g., "What is the purpose of education?" and "What are the most effective methods of teaching?" (Brameld, cited in Price, 1955, p. 622). In synthesizing his ideas regarding the philosophy of education, he ended with this final thought on the matter: "To learn these lessons would mean, in other words, that our public schools at last subscribed to a philosophy of education at once appropriate to our present age and directed toward the *future* of democracy" (italics in the original) (Brameld, 1950b, p. 240). The point is, Brameld's earlier intellectual curiosity with Lenin's theory and philosophy (the subject of his dissertation) was just that, curiosity. He appears not to have strayed far from his own cultural underpinnings and American Midwestern values.

That Brameld embraced the problem of social reconstruction as a global one spoke to his belief that "the world's" problems of social, political, and economic inequality are by-products of the post-Renaissance world, which he viewed as ushering in an era of unbridled individualism (Brameld, 1950a, p. 319). Of course, "the world" Brameld referred to in 1950 was largely the western world. Brameld saw individualism as the culprit in keeping humans from coming together in creative ways to solve a myriad of problems. In his article, "Conceptualizing Human Relations," Brameld (1950a) explained that just as knowledge is compartmentalized in the adult world—psychologists, sociologists, political scientists, economists, etc.—thus effectively limiting "competency" to narrow spheres, so is knowledge compartmentalized in schools or divided up into separate subjects (p. 319). These divisions are what Brameld viewed as barriers to deeper understandings about the nature of man and his universe. He went on to claim that "[t]he rise of capitalism as an acquisitive economy encouraged the belief and practice that the individual is the 'be-all' and 'end-all' of life—that success is a virtue to be measured by his capacity to compete with and win out over other individuals" (p. 319). In contrast, what Brameld attempted to do early to midway in his career was to establish a set of principles or a conceptual structure for understanding human relations.

Unlike the multiculturalists of today who seek to understand the complexities of this or that particular group and explain to the larger audience the nuances that exist in whatever exclusive case is under consideration (the African-American experience, the Hispanic experience, etc.), Brameld sought the universal. He wanted to know that which was common to all groups. While his life's work never yielded the hoped-for set of universal principles, he nevertheless continued throughout his life to attempt such a discovery.

Brameld's desire to know the intricacies of culture opened the door to new intellectual challenges. He was naturally drawn to anthropology and its methodology of participant/observer through extended interaction. As a result of his extensive cultural studies, Brameld was credited with coining the term "anthropotherapy" or a kind of cultural therapy designed to raise cultural awareness (Spindler & Spindler, 1989, p. 41). Moreover, his work in Japan and Puerto Rico demonstrate how he attempted to reconcile the field of anthropology with the field of educational philosophy

(Clayton, 1961, p. 26). Brameld's field work in Puerto Rico generated a number of scholarly works in which he sought to show how "the concepts of 'explicit and implicit culture' can help to explain the consistencies and inconsistencies of a culture with its political and religious values, and how these values and value conflicts are reflected in educational experience" (Brameld & Sullivan, 1961, p. 71). He used interviews and questionnaires from a small spectrum (n = 36) of ordinary citizens to national leaders in determining the role of education in Puerto Rico in shaping social development (Adams & Adams, 1968, p. 247).

Nobuo (Ken) Shimahara, a Brameld protégé, recalled in a telephone interview (February, 2006) with this writer that as an educational anthropologist, Brameld was interested in how cultural groups formed their opinions. And thus, for example, in 1962, Brameld and Shimahara went to Japan to study the Burakumin, a sub-cultural Japanese group. According to Shimahara (personal communication with the author, March 18, 2006), philosopher Sidney Hook was originally chosen for the study, but in the end, it was Brameld who went to Japan. Shimahara and Brameld interacted with group members every day as part of their study, although gaining the trust of the Burakumin villagers was not easy. The Burakumin had decided among themselves that both Brameld and Shimahara were United States spies and therefore, in the beginning, refused to cooperate. The first order of business then was to gain the villagers' trust.

Shimahara (personal communication with the author, March 18, 2006), recalled a "telling" story about Brameld's personality style while working in this small Japanese village. It seemed that the village was divided into a pro-Communist group whose opponents were conservative. As outsiders—Brameld, a Caucasian from the United States, and Shimahara, a native-born Japanese, but not Burakumin—worked to gain the trust of village leaders. As one might imagine, pro-Communist village leaders and those representing conservative leadership greatly distrusted each other. Therefore, Brameld and his assistant had to "win over" both groups in order to obtain the information they needed. For participant/observers, the goal is to live and interact on a daily basis with one's target population; thereby creating a seamless context for one's extended study. However, their plan nearly failed when Brameld unintentionally offended the procommunist leader (it became known that he had visited one of the village's conservative leaders). This situation led to a heated exchange between Brameld and the Burakumin procommunist leader, with neither backing down. Shimahara (personal communication with the author, March 18, 2006) urged Brameld to apologize, pointing out that he needed to be aware of proprieties in this part of the world, although one might reasonably ask if Brameld as an educational anthropologist should not have already known this. Brameld "dug his heels in" and insisted that he had done nothing wrong and would not apologize. For his part, Shimahara humorously recounted how he somehow had to make peace with the Burakumin leader in order to continue the study. What to do? Shimahara decided to extend an olive branch (with two bottles of wine attached). He slung the two bottles around his neck, hopped on a motor scooter and headed for the home of the procommunist village leader in the pouring rain. Shimahara laughingly recalled how he approached the man's front door and was invited in. He offered the wine and apologies, assuring this village leader that Brameld's interaction with the conservative village leader should not be viewed as endorsement of the latter's position and that Brameld equally valued his relationship with him (the procommunist leader) (Shimahara, personal communication with the author March 18, 2006). This seemed to satisfy the man's sensitivities and their (Brameld's and Shimahara's) work went forward.

Brameld's year-long study in Japan formed, in part, the three core constructs of his version of educational anthropology—cultural order, cultural process, and cultural goals (Shimahara, personal communication with the author March 18, 2006). Brameld's interest in anthropology should be viewed as a natural outgrowth of his early career interest in identifying barriers to communication between groups in general and then finding common avenues that could encourage dialogue and partnership, especially between what he termed "experts in education and experts in culture" (Brameld, 1955, p. 67). However, Brameld's faith in the power of intergroup education—attacking group tensions through educational methods and means (Hager, 1950, p. 279)—involved more than a simple belief in placing individuals together for the sake of working out problems. The key to group problem solving success relied on the qualities of those within the groups and not on the phenomenon of the group experience itself, although he concluded that where individuals of various races and cultures freely associated, tensions and confusion dissolves (Bristow, 1948, p. 224). Taba (1953) viewed the field of Intergroup Education as one that at first lacked substance, was 'unlettered' and unscientific, but eventually developed research concepts, experimented with and tested new ideas, and developed action programs that included evaluation plans. It is the latter "form" of Intergroup Education that attracted Brameld, who educated a generation of doctoral students to study in-depth the nuances of culture and group dynamics.

In his anthropological text entitled, *Cultural Foundations of Education*, Brameld (1973) sought to explore both enculturative and acculturative processes. One of the methods that he used with students was a sort of "cultural immersion" approach whereby students stayed in homes and visited cultural institutions during study trips (Quintana & Sexton, 1961, p. 101).

Brameld's work in the field of educational anthropology also meant participation in international conferences, such as the "Conference on 'Education for Mankind'," held in Chicago in 1968. At this meeting, participants discussed such topics as violence, the preservation of minority cultures, and understanding. Brameld joined educators, social scientists, and official representatives of sovereign states, in discussing how diversity could be preserved in light of inter-cultural tensions (Brameld, 1971, p. 76).

Brameld's work in the field of Inter-cultural relations remains perhaps his most striking legacy and one that exemplifies his contribution to social reconstruction. He also remained steadfast in his belief in the superiority of the scientific method to resolve problems of human relations. As for the concept of human relations, he described it in this way:

> [a] field of knowledge and action constructed for the purpose of coping with areas of misunderstanding, tension, prejudice, hatred, conflict. Throughout the world, human beings are suffering from their inability, thus far, to associate together in such ways as to produce individual and social harmony, appreciation of one another, group cooperation, and the pervasive feeling of well-being that stems from sound, healthful interpersonal and intercultural relations. (Brameld, 1950a, p. 316)

Brameld's use of medical metaphors (e.g., "however stubborn chronic human strains and hostilities may be, they are potentially curable") underscored his faith in science to find a "cure" for what ails all social groups and his belief that "the scientific method *must* be applied to human relations if human beings are not to destroy themselves" (italics in the original) (Brameld, 1950a, pp. 316, 317, respectively). Brameld viewed any barrier that kept people apart as detrimental to what he called, to borrow from Plato, "the good life," be it racial restrictions, class warfare, or nationalism (Brameld, 1950a, p. 327). Added to his list of dangerous barriers were negative attitudes toward sex, which he viewed as immoral. Brameld (1950a) believed that "rich sexual expression" is not only good, but that "efforts to place women in a subordinate position, to deny them equal opportunity, are totally indefensible" (p. 327). His interest in erotic expression was likely connected to the cultural knowledge he absorbed from his college days at Ripon in Wisconsin and the influence of Fourier Phalanxes such as the Wisconsin phalanx, although Kiso, Stone, and former student and colleague Shimahara (personal ommunication with author, February, 2006), believe that this interest stemmed from Brameld's desire to "out grow" his childhood patterns of enculturation.

Nash (one of Brameld's doctoral students) explained in a telephone conversation (January 5, 2006) with this writer that Brameld was highly interested in Eros and erotic expression. He believed that artificial barriers to sexual expression such as marriage laws mandating monogamy were detrimental to reaching the highest levels of self-expression. Nash also suggested that Brameld perhaps wrestled with his views on erotic expression because his intellectual veneer was buttressed by a strong conservative upbringing, one which probably would have prevented him from giving full rein to his intellectual curiosity on this topic. Shimahara (personal communication with the author, March 18, 2006) described Brameld's interest in Eros as one which stemmed from the philosopher's belief in sexual liberation—which he believed contributed to one's self realization. In fact, Brameld believed that inhibition stifled creativity. When asked by this writer (Riley) if he (Shimahara) believed that Brameld's interest in erotic expression was purely intellectual, or, an attempt to "whitewash" or justify his private pursuits in the name of scholarship, Shimahara (personal communication with the author, March 18, 2006) answered that it was likely both. In any event, this dimension of Brameld's work is perhaps the most obscure owing to most American's distaste for overt sexual discourse or out-of-the-mainstream-sexual practice and one that at first glance seems to have little to do with pressing problems of social, political, or economic inequality. While Brameld is perhaps best known for his work on the Floodwood project (Hartmann, 1946, p. 86), and later inter-cultural work in Japan and Puerto Rico, the aim of this chapter is to furnish the reader with a composite of Theodore Brameld through an examination of what influenced him as an individual and intellectual vis-à-vis his interest in and teaching about key social issues.

BRAMELD AS AN INDIVIDUAL

Brameld's professional and intellectual life, along with the forces that shaped his early learning patterns, is only part of his story. The personal dimension of an individual is often the most telling about his or her fundamental character. As with most people, Brameld was a complex individual. On the one hand, he enjoyed the loyalty of a tightly knit group of doctoral students who founded a conference in his honor (Nash, Lecture, 2001; M. Kiso, personal communication with author, 2006; K. Shimahara, personal communication with author, March 18, 2006). He was responsible, in part, for the career success of dozens of former students, including Nubuo (Ken) Shimahara, formerly of Japan and now Professor Emeritus from Rutgers University, who described his former mentor as a compassionate and caring man (K. Shimahara, personal communication with author, March 18, 2006). In fact, he and Brameld formed such a close relationship that at times their disagreements ended in a yelling match, although Shimahara quickly stated "we were partners," referring to their close working relationship. As a teacher, Brameld took a "hands off" position. When doctoral students wanted him to lecture, and Shimahara recalls that he was a "wonderful lecturer," Brameld would simply tell them that the best way to learn was active learning and that they should seek out what they wanted to know on their own. Shimahara believes that this method of teaching was one that he, Brameld, learned from his former professor, T. V. Smith, while at Chicago. But Shimahara was quick to point out that Brameld cared deeply about his doctoral students and that on more than one occasion eased the pain of graduate student life by extending personal loans. (K. Shimahara, personal communication with author, March 18, 2006)

On the other hand, the fact that he was married three times raises questions about his approach to American cultural values such as commitment and fidelity. Brameld's first marriage to college sweetheart Georgene ended in a bitter divorce (Stone, 2003; M. Kiso, personal communication with author, 2006). While Brameld may have perceived his relationship with his first wife as one that simply unraveled after the birth of their two daughters and his trying first years as a professor, Georgene likely felt betrayed as Brameld met his second wife Ona while still married to her. Whatever the cause, it ended and remained a bitter event in both of their lives, although third wife, Midori Kiso, recalls spending pleasant holidays with Ted and his daughters from his first marriage, a daughter from his second marriage, and his second wife, Ona (M. Kiso, personal communication with author, 2006). And one should not forget the times. The height of his career fell neatly in the middle of the 1960s, a time of protests, an emerging "free love" culture, and the provocative feminist movement that urged women to explore their sexuality.

Brameld's professional life was as uneven as his romantic life. While his army of loyal students could be counted on for support and admiration, some of his colleagues were quite another thing. Kiso (M. Kiso, personal communication with author, 2006) recalled that at NYU, Brameld became involved in a heated disagreement with George Axtell, a colleague, over the establishment of new graduate courses. In fact, Shimahara (personal communication with author, March 18, 2006) remarked, "they hated each other." Their disagreement must have been extremely serious as Brameld left NYU and it took some 20 years and the intervention of their mutual colleague, Maxine Greene, to persuade them, at a conference, to finally shake hands stating that "it's about time to forget the old animosities" (M. Kiso, personal communication, 2006).

Almost from the beginning of his career, Brameld encountered opposition. His dissertation, an exploration of communism, brought out any number of public enemies bent on heckling his speeches. During one such public address, he had to stop speaking owing to protesters who supported Senator Joseph McCarthy (M. Kiso, personal communication, 2006).

Additionally, during his time at Boston University, Brameld's graduate students engaged in discussions involving two controversial topics: (1) Can education remain neutral?; and, (2) Should the philosophy of communism be taught in schools, and if so, at what level? Never one to avoid controversy, Brameld required his graduate students to read articles written by some of his strongest critics, such as George Kneller and Sidney Hook, who Brameld considered a McCarthy apologist (Shimahara, personal communication with the author, March 18, 2006). In these works, he was labeled a utopian freak, dogmatic, doctrinaire, and even totalitarian (M. Kiso, personal communication, 2006).

CONCLUSION

What can be said about the measure of the man, Theodore Brameld? How should we understand him? How do we reconcile his personal and private life with his professional and intellectual life? For one, his intellectual side was shaped in large part as he emerged on the historical stage in 1904, in the particular geographic location of Neillsville, Wisconsin. The environmental factors that helped to shape Brameld as a person included an English/German ethnic background, an excessively prideful and adoring mother, deep Protestant roots, and a certain "relaxed" or intimate way of life that one experiences growing up in a small town or village.

The milieu of turn-of-the-century (20th) America, complete with its burgeoning cities filled with immigrant populations all seeking the American dream and most being denied even the most basic of needs—along with labor unrest, war, unbridled capitalism—enveloped by the safety of rural and small-town village life was the social, political, and economic environment in which Theodore Brameld grew from infant to manhood.

Early on Brameld discovered that he enjoyed commanding the attention of others. Throughout his lifetime, family, friends, critics, and supporters, alike, described him as both conceited and somewhat arrogant, which they may have mistaken for a certain German predisposition toward self-assurance. Whatever the case, Brameld has never been described in existing literature as hesitant or unsure. The human mind and spirit are not formed or shaped in a vacuum. Brameld was a product of his time, an age of exuberance and excess countered by reform and a call for social regeneration.

His education at Ripon College continued to infuse him with a certain world view born of German and English values, along with a certain midwestern "commonsenseness" way of knowing that he took with him to the

University of Chicago where he completed a PhD. As the Progressive Era brought forth an abundance of reformers and ideas, Brameld settled into his professional life as a teacher of teachers. His interest in culture, human interaction, and intergroup relations formed the core of his research interests throughout his career. His productive professional life intersected with an often frenetic personal life, complete with several divorces, bitter feelings, and then later joyful new relationships. Brameld's forays into erotic expression almost seem to come from nowhere, yet one must not overlook the sexual revolution of his time, when the word "sex" was spoken and not whispered, when females chose partners instead of being chosen, and when one chose divorce over languishing in an unfulfilling relationship. While Brameld's private life is not well known, his activism in the form of a seemingly constant barrage of "Letters to the Editor" is legendary among the rank and file of educational philosophers. His contributions to the fields of educational philosophy and educational anthropology remain unparalleled.

Among those who knew Brameld best describe a man who was passionate about schools teaching students to solve social problems. He believed that the scientific method was not only the best way, but also the only way to accomplish that goal. Brameld worked throughout his lifetime to discern the nuances of culture and human interaction. He believed that it was possible to discover a set of universal principles upon which all people could agree and which would supply the infrastructure for global cooperation and harmony. While current multiculturalists have traveled down paths that focus on differences in people and groups, Brameld's work stands as foundation stones for current multicultural efforts, albeit his vision focused on universal qualities as avenues for change. Brameld's keen mind generated some 13 books and more than 150 articles, book reviews and translations, many of which serve as classics on the subject of social reconstruction, while his text entitled *Patterns of Philosophy* remains one of the clearest treatments on educational theories of American educational practice.

In his professional life, he served on the faculties of The University of Minnesota, New York University, City University of New York, University of Hawaii, Adelphi College, and Long Island University. He retired as Professor Emeritus from Boston University. While Brameld's intellectual interest and academic work in the areas of human interaction and intercultural knowledge serve as a faint pulse for today's exploration of multiculturalism, the politics of the former energized philosophers such as Brameld, and challenged them to find answers to pressing social problems so that men might live in equal abundance and in harmony with one another.

Perhaps in the end, what can be said about Ted Brameld is that, like many of us, he spent his adult lifetime being professionally fruitful while at the same time trying to shed the cultural baggage most bring from home, all the while constantly trying to unlearn rigid lessons from childhood and attempting to unleash the innate feelings we feel are important to us as individuals.

REFERENCES

Adams, D., & Adams, J. (1968). Educational and social development. *Review of Educational Research, 38*(3), 243-263.

Bestor, A. (1953). *Educational wastelands: The retreat from learning in our public schools.* Chicago: University of Illinois Press.

Brameld, T. (1950a). Conceptualizing human relations. *Journal of Educational Sociology, 23*(6), 315-328.

Brameld, T. (1950b). *Ends and means in education: A midcentury appraisal.* Westport, CT: Greenwood Press.

Brameld, T. (1952). Letters to the editor. *Journal of Educational Sociology, 25*(7), 434-436.

Brameld, T. (1955). Culture and education. *The Journal of Higher Education, 26*(2), 59-68, 111.

Brameld, T. (1956). *Toward a reconstructed philosophy of education.* New York: Dryden Press.

Brameld, T. (1971). *Patterns of educational philosophy.* New York: Hart, Rinehart and Winston.

Brameld, T. (1973). *Cultural foundations of education.* Greenwood, CT: Greenwood Press.

Brameld, T., & Sullivan, E. B. (1961, February). Anthropology and education. *Review of Educational Research, The Social and Philosophical Framework of Education, 31*(1), 70-79.

Bristow, W. H. (1948). Curriculum: Foundations. *Review of Educational Research, 18*(3), 221-230.

Burns, H. W. (1960). Pragmatism and the science of behavior. *Philosophy of Science, 27*(1), 58-74.

Chambliss, J. J. (1963). The view of progress in Lawrence Cremins' The transformation of the school. *History of Education Quarterly, 3*(1), 43-52.

Clayton, A. S. (1961). Philosophy of education. *Review of Educational Research, 31*(1), 20-37.

Daniel, W. G. (1950). The responsibility of education for the preparation of children and youth to live in a multi-racial society. *The Journal of Negro Education, 19*(3), 388-398.

Descriptive notes. (1935). *The Philosophical Review, 44*(4), 402-412.

Dorpalen, A. (1942, June). The German element and the issues of the Civil War. *The Mississippi Valley Historical Review, 29*(1), 55-76.

Dudycha, G. J. (1932, March). The social beliefs of college. *The American Journal of Sociology, 37*(5), 775-780.

Franklin, B. M. (1984). Educational ideas and school practice to Kieran Egan and Maxine Greene. *Curriculum Inquiry, 14*(3), 319-326.

Giles, H. H., Pitkin, V. E., & Ingram, T. (1946). Problems of intercultural education. *Review of Educational Research, 16*(1), 39-45.

Guarneri, C. J. (1982, October). Importing Fourierism to America. *Journal of the History of Ideas, 43*(4), 581-594.

Guarneri, C. J. (1996, Autumn). Reconstructing the antebellum communitarian movement: Oneida and Fourierism. *Journal of the Early Republic, 16*(3), 463-488.

Hager, D. J. (1950). Some observations on the relationship between social science and intergroup education. *Journal of Educational Sociology, 23*(5), 278-390.

Hanley, M. Y. (1991). The new infidelity: Northern protestant clergymen and the critique of progress, 1840-1855. *Religion and American Culture, 1*(2), 203-226.

Hartmann, G. W. (1946). Interrelations of education and democracy. *Review of Educational Research, 16*(1), 81-93.

Link, A. S. (1959). What happened to the progressive movement in the 1920s? *The American Historical Review,* LXIV, No. 4.

Nash, R. (2001). Unpublished Lecture, University of Vermont.

Ozmon, H. A., Jr. (1966). If philosophers served on textbook committees. *The Elementary School Journal, 66*(4), 182-188.

Price, K. (1955). Is a philosophy of education necessary? *The Journal of Philosophy, 52*(22), 622-633.

Quintana, B., & Sexton, P. (1961). Sociology, anthropology, and schools of education: A progress report. *Journal of Educational Sociology 35*(3), 97-103.

Spindler, G., & Spindler, L. (1989). Instrumental competence, self-efficacy, linguistic minorities, and cultural therapy: A preliminary attempt at integration. *Anthropology & Education Quarterly, 20*(1), 36-50.

Stange, D. C. (1970). Al Smith and the Republican Party at prayer: The Lutheran vote, 1928. *The Review of Politics, 32*(3), 347-364.

Stone, F. A. (2003). *Theodore Brameld's educational reconstruction: An intellectual biography.* San Francisco: Caddo Gap Press.

Taba, H. (1953). Research: Oriented programs in intergroup education in schools and colleges. *Review of Educational Research, 23*(4), 362-371.

Taba, H. (1963). Cultural orientation in comparative education. *Comparative Education Review, 6*(3), 171-176.

Wheeler, J. E. (1967). Philosophy of education. *Review of Educational Research, 37*(1), 5-20.

CHAPTER 12

EDUCATING FOR LIFE IN A DEMOCRACY

The Life and Work of Richard E. Gross

Paul Robinson and Murry Nelson

INTRODUCTION

Richard E. Gross was a nationally prominent social studies educator whose career spanned the second half of the 20th century. Born in Chicago in 1921, he earned his bachelor's and master's degrees from the University of Wisconsin at Madison and his doctorate in education from Stanford University in 1951. After a 4-year teaching stint at Florida State University, he returned to Stanford as a faculty member in 1955 and spent the rest of his career there, retiring in 1990. Gross is probably best remembered for the large number of graduate students he mentored at Stanford. These doctoral and masters' students, ultimately spread across the United States and around the world, positioning themselves in universities, state departments of education, and schools, where they helped shape the development of history and social studies curriculum and

Addressing Social Issues in the Classroom and Beyond: The Pedagogical Efforts of Pioneers in the Field, 221–234
Copyright © 2007 by Information Age Publishing
All rights of reproduction in any form reserved.

instruction, frequently in significant ways. As he observed in his annual newsletter to his former students, prior to the National Council for the Social Studies annual meeting in Portland in 1979, "This year I am pleased to note 31 of us on the program! I am sure no other university can match that number. It is personally and professionally rewarding to myself to find such a strong representation." A decade later, as Gross contemplated retirement in emeritus status and the conclusion of 35 years at Stanford, he wrote to his former students, "After just over 100 doctoral students and about 1500 masters students, it seems very important to maintain the program with its outstanding record of graduates." Not a vain man, he nevertheless took pride in his students and in being referred to as "Mr. Social Studies."

In this chapter we set ourselves the task, not of arguing for Gross' pioneer status, but of demonstrating his influence on the practice of social studies, with particular attention focusing on social issues as a key component of the social studies curriculum.

INFLUENCES

Gross' thinking and his career were shaped by a number of political and social influences which converged in the middle decades of the 20th century. But his personal biography had great impact as well.[1] One early, major impact was initiated by his undergraduate advisor at the University of Wisconsin, Merle Curti, who, ironically, as a future President of the American Historical Association (1954), encouraged him to switch from his original major in history to a broader focus, American Studies, encompassing the disciplines of history, sociology, political science, and economics—what might be called a liberal arts major today. Gross accepted Curti's advice and subsequently, throughout his career, championed a broad field emphasis on social studies, rather than a narrower disciplinary perspective on a single content area.

Gross' father encouraged him in a different direction, toward following him into business, but he died while Gross was still in college, and the young student found that he wasn't particularly interested in business pursuits. Several cousins, who were already teachers, warned him of the economic pitfalls in becoming a teacher, but the childhood influences of his grandparents' storytelling, his interest in foreign countries, and his lifelong love of reading, coupled with lessons on the relatedness of social knowledge he discovered in his new American studies major,[2] directed his attention toward teaching.[3] Although the American studies program did not provide for teacher certification, he managed to squeeze all his teacher training coursework into his senior year at Madison.

A significant professional influence on Gross was his methods instructor at the university, Burr Phillips. Years later, Gross recognized that many of his own instructional practices in teaching methods courses derived from Phillips' example. Furthermore, he acknowledged that it was Phillips' gentle pressure (i.e., not a requirement but a strong recommendation) on his methods students to join the National Council for the Social Studies (NCSS) and to take part in local council meetings that initiated his own career-long involvement with that professional organization, culminating in his election as president of NCSS in 1966. That professorial nudging toward organizational involvement became a part of his own methods and graduate course practice at Stanford University, as a generation of preservice and doctoral students could attest.

Initially, Gross found that he could not find a teaching job as the Depression lingered, but when the Second World War broke out jobs did become available. Since he found his draft status to be 4-F, he entered teaching rather than the military. He was offered a social studies position at Central High School in Madison, and he "loved it." At the same time he followed a career advancement path practiced by many teachers, pursuing a Master's degree (a joint program in education and history) at Madison, by taking courses in the summer and evenings. However, his Master's advisor, Edward Krug, a well-known historian of education, called him into his office one day and told Gross that he really should become a college professor. At first hesitant, the young social studies teacher let the proposal slide for a year or two. Krug then informed him that he was resigning from the University of Wisconsin to take a position at Stanford University (where he had received his doctorate) and invited Gross to join him and fill an assistantship accompanying the position he had been offered. Gross made what he called an "idealistic decision"; that is, that he could make more of an impact in social studies education as a professor than as a school teacher. Considering that Stanford, along with the University of Minnesota (where Edgar Wesley, a professor of education and history who had the leading social studies methods book, was located) and Teachers College, Columbia University, were the top places in the country for such an education, and with the encouragement of his wife, Jane, he resigned his teaching position and prepared to head west for the first time in his life. Unfortunately, just after he had resigned, he learned that Krug, his personal connection, who had left for Stanford the year before, had been rehired by Wisconsin as a full professor with a big increase in salary. Having cut himself adrift from Wisconsin, and not knowing a soul at Stanford, Gross and his wife contemplated their future. They decided to make a go of it at Stanford. He was later to claim that it was the "best thing I ever did."

At Stanford, Gross encountered a group of professors with national reputations who helped him establish himself in the field of social studies. I. James Quillen (his *Education for Social Competence*, 1948, coauthored with Lavone A. Hanna, was an important resource for Gross in thinking about social issues instruction) became his advisor, and he worked with Paul Hanna, of elementary social studies renown, as well.

Gross completed his dissertation at Stanford in the spring of 1951 but found that he faced a limited job market. In fact, nothing came through that spring or summer. Then all at once, in the first week of August, three possibilities arose: San Francisco State College offered him a full-time job supervising student teachers; the University of Minnesota called to see if he would be interested in a position there; and Paul Hanna told him he had received a call from Florida State University—they needed someone in social studies—and had put forward his name: "I think you're the best person we have to recommend." Gross decided to take the job at San Francisco State College, because he and Jane had grown fond of the West Coast and the Bay Area. Quillen and another professor at Stanford, Harry Porter, told him, "Don't do it!" They argued that there are two different leagues in the world of teacher education, "an unfortunate fact of life," and that a state college was not in the same league as a state university. Gross recalled that such an argument got him thinking, "I wanted to have a good career." He had experienced the Midwest and its winters, so Minnesota was out, and, reversing his decision on San Francisco State College, he followed his mentors' advice and took the Florida State position, "as a part of [his] total growth."

Florida State at that time had a dean in the college of education who wanted to compete with the University of Florida by appointing subject matter specialists rather than Gainesville's generalists. So Gross was one of a handful of young, bright, ambitious content-area professors brought into Tallahassee in the fall of 1951. But Gross knew that he and Jane wanted to return to Stanford eventually, and he committed himself to developing enough scholarly writing ("I'm going to write myself out of here!") so that when an opening arose, he would be able to seek it. Four years later Quillen became dean of the School of Education at Stanford, and a position in social studies education opened up. By that time Gross had established a record of publication sufficient so that when Quillen invited him back to take his former position, Gross could accept. Over the next 35 years Gross became a fixture on the faculty at Stanford, receiving offers to leave, but never interested in doing so.

Gross had been shaped by his 8 years of school teaching, 4 years in Madison and 4 years at Menlo School and College (a fortunate income replacement for the Krug assistantship he missed out on when he moved to the Stanford area), and by the professors he encountered at Madison and Stanford. Now it was time for Gross to exert his own influence. How-ever, that influence was to be wielded in a nation still recovering from the aftershocks of global war and the new threat of Communist aggrandize-ment. Educators were trying to figure out how to educate young people for the role of citizen in a democracy beset by international threat and internal tensions. In educational circles, the vicious attacks in the 1940s on Harold Rugg's approach to social studies curriculum and instruction—a promotion of students employing critical thinking and problem solving approaches to deal with real-world problems—suggested great caution would have to be exercised to find a viable pedagogy for the times. Appar-ently without a systematic approach in mind, but with a keen sensitivity to the needs of young people and the aims of a democratic society in the midst of the Twentieth Century's second Red Scare, Gross felt his way toward a progressive pedagogy of problem solving and dealing with social issues.

PHILOSOPHY OF EDUCATION

From the time that Gross first entered the teaching profession he grounded his teaching in certain pedagogical beliefs. First was a Dewe-yean notion that the curriculum should be shaped with an understanding of one's students, both as a whole and individually. Second was the dynamic nature of curriculum, that is, the curriculum should be con-stantly reexamined to meet the needs of students and society. In this sense Gross appeared to emulate Harold Rugg and other social reconstruction-ists. Gross seemed to be quite enamored of Rugg's 1921 piece, "How Shall We Reconstruct the Social Studies Curriculum?" which had been written in response to the *1916 Report on the Social Studies of the NEA Study on the Reorganization of Secondary Education.* Gross seemed to have been strongly influenced by such pedagogical theories by his professors and his times. Gross's professors would have been very much aware of Rugg's thinking as well as the difficulties with the Rugg Social Studies Curriculum. Those, taken together, would have been instrumental in Gross strongly espousing teacher freedom in the selection of content and in the right of teachers to speak their minds. That notion, however, would have been tempered by Gross' concern to not unduly influence one's students, but rather to assist them in forming their own opinions based on evidence and purposeful objectives. Thus, one important aspect of Gross's philosophy involved stu-dents thinking critically and responding to real problems and issues. These notions were a reflection of his progressive education views that were both child-centered and social reconstructionist. Social reconstruc-tionists felt that the schooling and the curriculum should be dynamic and designed to constantly strive to improve society. Gross actually tilted toward the latter of the philosophical schools, but he was not an activist, per se, in his interpretation. He did believe that students should be actively engaged in a variety of dispositions in the classroom and out, but it would be a stretch to call him a social activist.

Active engagement, to Gross, involved projects, including students writing letters to the editor, doing community service, conducting community surveys and examining how different news media might report on the same event or topic. In one of his first published articles ("Teaching Controversial Issues Can Be Fun"), which appeared in 1948 in *Social Education*, he illustrated a number of these descriptive tenets. Gross, who by this time was in California pursuing his doctorate at Stanford and teaching at the Menlo School and College in Menlo Park, CA, describes a teaching incident from his experiences at Madison (WI) Central High School, where he taught before moving west. In order to get his students more involved with the events of the day, he proposed to the students that they work on examining the platforms of the major two presidential candidates of 1944, Franklin Roosevelt and Thomas Dewey. Gross's students were predominately for Roosevelt so he ended up providing a great deal more assistance to his small number of Dewey supporters. The students researched the issues and the presidential stands, presented those to the class and then there was the usual class election. He, too, participated in the class voting, but his ballot was left in his desk drawer until the counting. Because of his enormous support for the Dewey camp, the students were in universal agreement that he was a Republican. The students were quite shocked to find that he had voted for Roosevelt and this made the students consider more than outward appearances when making decisions. Gross was pleased that they had come to this conclusion "themselves."

The message from these experiences was reiterated in Gross' NCSS Presidential Address in 1967. "Within the sanctuary of your classrooms, reveal to them the worthwhile virtues of full investigation and analysis and of suspended judgment..." (Previte & Sheehan, 2002, p. 284). He then went on to note that, "Boys and girls should have recurring opportunities to learn that they are not free citizens just because they live in a free country, but that they and their country will maintain liberty only so long as they live and act as free men and women" (2002, p. 286).

During Gross's doctoral work, he took history courses along with education courses and was quite interested in the history of education. For many years during his professorship at Stanford he taught a history of education class and became quite enamored of certain philosophers of education who seemed to espouse views consonant with his own. One such view was that of John Amos Comenius, a Moravian Bishop who was a proponent of what Gross referred to as "the realistic movement" in education in the seventeenth century. Comenius advocated education for all, and not rote learning but, rather, perceived experience as the key to learning and thus was in favor of students learning by doing. He also noted that each learner was unique and education should "bend" to the child. These ideas are obviously reminiscent of John Dewey, but, as Gross said, with admiration, Comenius was far ahead of his time.

Gross also was quite taken with Johann Herbart, who was so influential in the basic philosophy that formed the science of education. Herbart's five steps in education were the basic forerunner of the scientific method, and the early American Herbartians formed a Society that became the National Society for the Scientific Study of Education (NSSSE). This eventually evolved into the National Society for the Study of Education (NSSE). Gross felt that Herbart's methods demanded a great deal of teacher action as the teacher would need to design and lead lessons that involved student direction, thus putting a great burden on the teacher for the student's learning. He felt that Dewey's balance of child and teacher was better, but he admired Herbart and his ideas.

Thus, Gross was a strong Deweyean with a scientific base grounded in Herbart but with the active learning inspired by Comenius. He felt that learning should take place in and out of the classroom and advocated a variety of experiences for his students to gain knowledge and insight. He also felt that students should be active, engaged citizens, but his definition was more toward community service than what might be seen as activism today.

ASPIRATIONS

As a professional teacher educator and scholar, Gross often found his aspirations coalescing with his personal and family hopes. In his role as teacher educator, Gross wanted to highlight the importance of controversial issues in teaching. He emphasized to his students both the risks of and the need for introducing the study of controversial issues in the classroom. He drew from his own experiences and incorporated those into his own professional writing on this topic. His NCSS How To Do It pamphlet, "How to Handle Controversial Issues," was published by NCSS in 1952 and revised three times, with Gross always trying to make the information more contemporary and relevant without departing from the important basic message.

The concern with controversial issues was part of a larger view that Gross professed, that of teaching social studies generally around an issue-oriented format. He hoped that eventually textbooks would highlight social issues within a basic curricular framework, which he almost always viewed as best presented historically. Gross wanted to see social studies curriculum as dynamic, but felt that dynamism was best expressed in some version of what the 1916 Committee on Social Studies had called Problems of Democracy (POD). Gross espoused what the Committee had suggested—that is, that the POD course should be the "capstone" to the social studies curriculum—and he hoped that some dynamic version of this course would become re-entrenched in the curriculum.

His notion of the curriculum was also the topic of professional aspirations; he hoped that a national social studies framework would be promulgated. In that hope was embedded the desire to see a continued examination of the nature of social studies in the United States with a concomitant body then appointed to create a national framework. In the 1970s he was able to craft such a status report, at least in a minimal manner, but the impact was disappointing.[4]

Another aspiration that melded professional and personal ambitions was Gross's interest in and experience with internationalism. From his youth onward, Gross had read and been captivated by world history and geography and he always greatly desired the opportunity to experience life in other cultures. Ultimately, he traveled throughout the world and taught in a number of countries including England, Wales, and Australia on extended assignments. Most of those journeys yielded professional publications and made him want to travel all the more. One of the highlights of his travel after he retired was the trip that he and his wife, Jane, took on the ancient Silk Road from Turkey through Iran, Turkmenistan, Uzbekistan, Kazakhstan, Kyrgystan and across China to Xian. It was a taxing trip but one that fulfilled a long-held desire by Gross.

From the time that he joined NCSS in the 1940s Gross aspired to be an officer in that organization and have some impact on the state of social studies in the United States. He met that goal in several ways. For example, Gross was active in the California Council of the Social Studies, was one of the founders of the Florida Council of the Social Studies, and was elected to the Board of Directors of the National Council of the Social Studies in the mid 1960s. In 1967-1968 he served as the President of NCSS, reaching yet another professional goal.

Gross did not have much of a research agenda (as he readily admitted), but he did have great desires to write and publish extensively. He had always liked to write and aspired to be read and his publication record was extensive.

A final professional aspiration (and a source of personal pride) was that his doctoral students would make an impact on the field of social studies and reflect well on Stanford and him, as well as be recognized in their own right for their contributions. This, too, was achieved and will be discussed more fully below as part of his legacy.

FRUSTRATIONS AND BARRIERS FACED

Gross acknowledged that for social studies instruction focused on social issues to move forward, it would require the support of the school administration to protect teachers against conservative reaction. Reflecting on his own school teaching days, he cautioned against the individual teacher promoting student engagement with contentious social issues without adequate backing.

Gross was frequently concerned with what he saw as the messiness of the social studies field. Becoming "very concerned with how the social studies was going" following the spurt of national curriculum initiatives flowing from the 1960s, he directed a status survey of the field and found the results "pretty devastating." By the mid-1970s, he believed, education had "reached the apex, thank God, of the anarchical curriculum," and was moving back toward a more carefully articulated structure. He advocated the need for national commissions or other formal bodies coming to a consensus on the nature and extent of the curriculum. Moreover, in conducting a survey of social studies methods instructors and their practices (in preparation for organizing and writing a methods textbook), he discovered to his dismay that he could gain no clear direction from the results. "What is being done in the social studies methods courses reflects the tremendous over extension and variation that beset our field" (personal letter from R. Gross to P. Robinson, October 4, 1982). He seemed to be torn between his own "catholic interest in a great variety of things," and his affinity for the correspondingly broad curricular area of the social studies field on the one hand and a fear that it lacked focus and structure on the other.

Even though Gross' position as a tenured professor at one of the leading universities gave him a great deal of security, he worried intermittently about the status of the field of social studies at Stanford. He fretted about the organizational perspectives of new deans, the hiring of new faculty, and the adequacy of support for social studies teacher education at Stanford. It was, for example, an unhappy shock to him when Paul Hanna had a change of heart late in his academic career and refocused on international education while instructing the Stanford faculty to do away with elementary social studies. Upon his retirement from Stanford, he was equally saddened when his position in social studies education was not retained as he had developed it. Respected historian of education Larry Cuban took over the Secondary Teacher Education Program's (STEP) social studies interns, but there were no longer new admissions in social studies education. After Cuban subsequently retired, the emphasis of the new opening, reflective of the times, was on preparing history teachers, and the faculty member hired to do so was interested in the specific discipline of history, not the broad field of social studies. Gross was deeply disturbed by this and feared for the continued existence of social studies education nationally, not just at Stanford. He remained troubled over this trend up until his death.

ADDRESSING SOCIAL ISSUES IN HIS WORK

Gross would probably have been the first to say that writing about controversial issues was an area he had fallen into largely by happenstance. In the course of his doctoral program he had written a paper for Professor Quillen on controversial issues. Having been encouraged by Quillen that it was publishable, he revised it and saw it published in *The Social Studies* ("Controversial Issues and Educational Freedom," May 1951). That article led to further involvement in the topic and eventually to the authorship of the NCSS How To Do It pamphlet, *How to Handle Controversial Issues*. When reminded that he had already evinced an interest in controversial issues in almost the first thing he had ever written for publication, "Teaching Controversial Issues Can Be Fun," for *Social Education* in 1948, Gross recalled that he had "got burned as a high school teacher," and so had a continuing interest in the topic. This contretemps involved a parental complaint about him being a Communist because he was teaching about the Soviet Union.

As mentioned earlier, Gross conceived of the opportunities schools could afford students to develop as citizens more in the realm of community service than in the area of political activism. If we think of a typology of controversial issues along the lines Diana Hess (2005) has laid out (1) private/personal decisions; (2) public policy issues; and (3) legal or constitutional issues, Gross' emphasis was to be found in the private/personal category, along with some connection to public policy issues. He cautioned teachers to find out if there was anything taboo in the local situation before taking on a social issue, and to reserve one's own opinion until students had developed their own view through study and reasoning.

Furthermore, Gross understood that a focus on social issues rarely, if ever, could function alone as an approach to social studies education. Even in *Educating Citizens for Democracy*, arguably his most prominent work, he acknowledged as one of his guidelines "the problems approach," is "*not the only appropriate method nor always the best form of organization for all teachers and all classes*" (Italics in the original) (Gross & Zeleny, 1958, p. 360). "While proponents of the problems approach," he continued, "speak loudly in its favor, more studies are needed to prove its efficacy" (Gross & Zeleny, 1958, p. 360). Nevertheless, he was adamant in proclaiming, again in his NCSS Presidential Address, that, "A frank problem-centered social studies program, I believe, offers the best hope of producing youth who will strive on their own to keep America becoming America" (Gross, 1968, p. 225).

MAJOR CONTRIBUTIONS REGARDING
TEACHING ABOUT SOCIAL ISSUES

Although it seems clear that Gross was not a social activist and did not consider himself one, he did much in his work to promote attention to social issues in social studies teaching and to provide guidelines for instruction in this area. Three of his most prominent publications, the NCSS bulletin, *Problem-centered Social Studies Instruction: Approaches to Reflective Teaching*, which he co-edited with Ray Muessig, the NCSS How To Do It booklet, *How to Handle Controversial Issues,* and the chapter on a problems approach in *Educating Citizens for Democracy,* introduced a generation of social studies teachers to the whys and hows of teaching about social issues. In addition, several of his briefer articles took up particular aspects of the topic, e.g., "Controversial Issues and Educational Freedom" (1951), "Teaching Controversial Issues Can Be Fun" (1948), and "World History and Issues-centered Instruction" (1996).

Gross had determined that his idea of educating young people for life in a democracy—meshing students' needs and the aims of society through the social studies curriculum—would most readily occur not through large-scale curriculum revision, but rather through the preparation of teachers: "*The point of attack must be the individual instructor*" (italics in the original) (Gross & Zelany, 1955, p. 9). This resulted in his devotion to teaching his own methods classes, to directing summer teacher workshops, and to developing a methods textbook that could spread his perspectives nationally. Even though Gross was personally self-effacing, he knew that he was in some important respects providing pioneering leadership. In a 1977 letter to one of the authors (Paul Robinson, personal communication, October 7) he noted that his 1955 textbook, *Educating Citizens for Democracy,* was out of print, but that while the book was "not normally recognized as being the first of the so-called new Social Studies volumes, it actually was, and some day may be, recognized as somewhat of a landmark."[5]

LEGACY

In the last analysis, Gross's legacy to the advancement of social issues within education is not a spectacular one. He created no model of his own, contrary to Chilcoat and Ligon's claim (2004). He didn't break new ground in scholarship. Rather, his contributions lay in the persistence of his vision and the durability of his vocation. For more than 40 years he proclaimed his message from one of the most prominent pulpits in professional education, a professorship at Stanford University. Gross noted that he did little real research, but his interest in status studies of social studies over time allowed the field to be viewed as both dynamic and having consistent, basic values.

As mentioned earlier, Gross became enthralled as a doctoral student at Stanford in the 1940s with the state of the social studies field, and with studies that had been done at both the state and national level describing the circumstances and contours of the field. From this interest emerged Gross's dissertation, a status study of social studies in California. In his 1967 NCSS Presidential Address Gross called for the creation of a National Commission for the Social Studies, calling it "our best hope" (Gross, 2002, p. 294). Gross continued to espouse such a Commission and pursued additional status studies of the field. He was successful in getting NCSS to support another small, national status study of social studies in the early 1970s. This, ultimately, was a factor in the decision to create the 1983 National Commission on the Social Studies.

As a veteran social studies scholar who knew the territory as few others did, Dick Gross broadcast—through his popular and scholarly writing, his teaching and direction of workshops and institutes, and his leadership within the profession—a straightforward message that the study of controversial issues by means of a problem solving approach was a necessary—and achievable—focus for social studies teaching and learning. He recognized both the potential dangers of this type of teaching and its much greater benefits and sought to explicate those for all social studies teachers. His multitude of students and readers are extending that legacy to this day.

Gross's former graduate students often pursued work in social issues as a result of their work with him. Many of them coauthored books or articles with him that focused on social issues. These former doctoral students included Dwight Allen (later Dean of Education at the University of Massachusetts-Amherst); Ray Muessig (Professor of Education at Ohio State University); Jack Fraenkel (Professor of Education and Director of Research at San Francisco State University); June Chapin (Professor of Education at the College of Notre Dame in California); Ron Evans (Professor of Social Studies Education at San Diego State University, and the co-editor of *Handbook on Teaching Social Issues. NCSS Bulletin 93);* and his former doctoral colleague, Jack Searles (Professor of Education at Penn State University), and among others. They have continued the legacy of "Mr. Social Studies."

NOTES

1. Much of the following biographical information comes from an oral history interview with Richard Gross, conducted by George Mehaffy, November 5, 1976.

2. Gross called it an "epiphany," that history by itself could never explain the total social scene, and that it had to be enriched by understandings and processes from other fields.

3. He did take one exploratory course in law, which confirmed his interest in becoming a teacher rather than a lawyer.

4. As some may remember, there was a National Commission on the Social Studies finally appointed in the mid-1980s, but their report, "Charting a Course for the Social Studies," was also not well-received and never had any impact.

5. Leslie Zeleny of the then Colorado State College at Greeley had originally conceived of this book project and had asked Gross to write the chapter on American history. Zeleny found that Gross had so many ideas for the volume that he asked him to co-edit it and agreed to have Gross listed as the first author. Gross eventually came to feel that the title he had picked for the book, *Educating Citizens for Democracy,* was a mistake, that it didn't "say anything," and didn't reveal that it was a methods textbook.

REFERENCES

Chilcoat, G. W., & Ligon, J. A. (2004). Issues-centered instruction in the social studies classroom: The Richard E. Gross problem-solving approach model. *Social Studies Review, 44*(1), 40-46.

Evans, R. W., & Saxe, D. W. (Eds.). (1996). *Handbook on teaching social issues. NCSS Bulletin 93.* Washington, DC: National Council for the Social Studies.

Gross, R. E. (1948). Teaching controversial issues can be fun. *Social Education, 12*(6), 259-260.

Gross, R. E. (1951). Controversial issues and educational freedom. *The Social Studies, 42*(5), 195-198.

Gross, R. E. (1964). *How to handle controversial issues.* How to do it series No. 14. Washington, DC: National Council for the Social Studies.

Gross, R. E. (1968). This I have learned. *Social Education, 32*(3), 223-228.

Gross, R. E. (1977). Personal Letter to Paul Robinson, October 7.

Gross, R. E. (2002). This I have learned. In M. Previte & J. Sheehan (Eds.) *The NCSS Presidential Addresses 1936-1969,* (pp. 281-294). Silver Springs, MD

National Council for the Social Studies and ERIC Clearinghouse for Social Studies/Social Science Education.

Gross, R. E. & Muessig, R. H. (Eds.). (1971). *Problem-centered social studies instruction: Approaches to reflective teaching.* Curriculum series, No. 14. Washington, DC: National Council for the Social Studies.

Gross, R. E. & Zeleny, L. D. (1955). *Educating citizens for democracy: Curriculum and instruction in secondary school social studies.* New York: Oxford University Press.

Hess, D. (2005, June 7). *Presentation for Methods Professors at the University of Florida.*

Mehaffy, G. (1976, November). Interview with Richard E. Gross. Cassette Recording.

National Education association. (1916). *The social studies in secondary education: Report of the committee on the social studies, Bulletin No. 28.* Washington, DC: Bureau of Education.

Previte, M. A., & Sheehan, J. J. (Eds.). (2002). *The NCSS presidential addresses, 1936-1969--Perspectives on the social studies.* Silver Spring, MD: National Council for the Social Studies and the ERIC Clearinghouse for Social Studies/Social Science Education.

Quillen, I. J., & Hanna, L. A. (1948). *Education for social competence.* Chicago: Scott, Foresman.

Rugg, H. (1921, May). How shall we reconstruct the social studies curriculum? *The Historical Outlook,* pp. 184-189.

CHAPTER 13

LAWRENCE E. METCALF

In the Right Place at the Right Time

Jeff Passe

INTRODUCTION

The work of Lawrence E. Metcalf sits squarely on the trajectory from the philosophy of John Dewey to the "new social studies" of the 1960s. As will be delineated herein, not only was Metcalf a product of his times, but he was also a leader among the generation of post-World War II social studies scholars. Because of his commitment to reflective theory and liberal values, he became a spokesperson for issues-centered social studies during a period of anti-Communist fervor and conservative educational thinking.

PHILOSOPHICAL FOUNDATIONS

Metcalf's most significant ideas evolved from the prewar philosophical foundations of John Dewey and Boyd H. Bode, as well as the social studies theories of his mentor, Alan Griffin. He was also influenced by such

Addressing Social Issues in the Classroom and Beyond: The Pedagogical Efforts of Pioneers in the Field, 235–251
Copyright © 2007 by Information Age Publishing
All rights of reproduction in any form reserved.   235

contemporaries as H. Gordon Hullfish, Ernest E. Bayles, and, of course, his longtime coauthor, Maurice P. Hunt. He and Hunt were students of Griffin at the Ohio State University in the 1940s.[1]

When Metcalf became a professor in 1947, the field of social studies scholarship was in its infancy, with only a handful of institutions offering doctorates in social studies education. What set Metcalf on his path to leadership among the social educators of his time? The answer lies outside of social studies, in the then nascent field of cognitive psychology, from which Jerome Bruner emerged.

It is not that Bruner had a direct impact on Metcalf's original thinking. After all, Bruner's pioneering works, *A Study of Thinking* (1956) and *The Process of Education* (1960) were published after Hunt and Metcalf's (1955) classic *Teaching High School Social Studies*. Rather, it was Bruner's influence on the field of education that brought legitimacy to the Hunt and Metcalf (1955) text because academic thought had been transformed to the extent that education professors would have been looking for texts that correlated with Bruner's contention that children are interested, at their own levels, in theoretical ideas. Bruner's ideas lent legitimacy to Hunt and Metcalf's model of issues-centered social studies, a model in which students are encouraged to explore the complex, often abstract, nature of personal and societal problems. Metcalf and Hunt, were, so to speak, "in the right place at the right time." And as a result, *Teaching High School Social Studies* became the most popular methods text of its time.

After 1960, Metcalf's writing consistently referred to Bruner and other cognitive psychologists (e.g., Festinger's concept of cognitive dissonance) to support his contentions. There was, one must note, a degree of bemusement in Metcalf's tone when he was able to attribute the theory behind his argument to psychologists. The former had a certain cachet as it were, unlike more standard educational writing that was often dismissed by critics outside the field. By citing psychologists other than Dewey, Metcalf gained a measure of *gravitas*.

METCALF AND DEWEY

As previously mentioned, John Dewey was a key figure in Metcalf's thinking. It was Dewey who laid the foundation for most of Metcalf's most important contributions. In Metcalf's (1988) tribute to Dewey, he acknowledged his debt, citing Dewey's positions on the relation of theory to practice, the role of schools in developing thinkers, subject matter knowledge, and democracy. In that same review, Metcalf noted Dewey's concerns over the schools' separation of the student's experiences from the world of subject matter. Lamentation over this separation was a constant theme in Metcalf's career.

Because several contemporary critics tended to discredit Dewey's thinking at the time, scholars in education suffered from guilt by association and, as a result, they were less likely to be received positively by those who were skeptical or suspicious of Deweyan thought. Metcalf was often frustrated by such criticism because he believed that it was based on an inaccurate understanding, if not outright distortion, of Dewey's ideas. Foremost among those misperceptions was the belief that Dewey opposed teaching the "organized body of knowledge found in academic disciplines" (Metcalf, 1988, p. 51). Metcalf, in fact, made a point of noting and arguing that Dewey favored such a goal (p. 51).

Dewey, though, did not help matters by writing in a style that was not only difficult to read, but was also somewhat complex and subject to multiple interpretations. When Dewey revised some of his early thinking, as is the wont of any scholar, additional confusion ensued. As a result, scholarly debate over what Dewey really meant served as a distraction for any educational commentator, and was a significant bane of Metcalf. That said, Metcalf (1988) lauded Dewey's "open-mindedness," wherein he "never hesitated to take a position that was in conflict with an earlier position" (p. 50).

When considering their revision of *Teaching High School Social Studies*, Metcalf suggested to Hunt that they rethink their Deweyan foundations in view of the criticism of his work. Ever mindful of his own commitment to "wrestle with the contradictions in one's own beliefs" (Reardon, 1990, p. 107), Metcalf cautioned that he didn't "want to become a reactionary" (L. E. Metcalf, personal communication with M. Hunt, February 24, 1964).

There was little chance, though, of anyone ever perceiving Larry Metcalf as a reactionary, but it is a credit to the man that he wished to live by the same liberal values he so strongly advocated. This, as we will see, became an issue later in his career, when he confronted the "revolutionaries" of the 1960s and 1970s and their suspicion, if not outright disdain, for the term "liberal." He was not only comfortable with the term, but was proud of his commitment to liberal thought. Furthermore, he saw the very methods of thinking that he endorsed as the perfect strategy for addressing the concerns of campus radicals.

THE ROLE OF THEORY

When first published, as well as long afterwards, *Teaching High School Social Studies* (1955) was considered to be quite different from other social studies methods textbook. Anyone comparing today's textbooks devoted to social studies methods would notice a stark difference between them and Hunt and Metcalf's (1955) first of two editions. While today's method texts refer to theory to a slight degree, Hunt and Metcalf devoted the *entire first half* of their text to elucidation of the theoretical constructs that guide their work. I daresay that, today, their approach would not lead to a contract from any leading publisher, much less sell thousands of copies. In their second edition (1968), they essentially apologized for excessive early theorizing, and revised the text accordingly.

The impetus for their theoretical emphasis is partly a result of the times—the field of teacher education was enmeshed in a unique set of circumstances. First, there were far fewer universities then, and the ones that prepared teachers tended to specialize in that area. In fact, many of those institutions had the word "teacher" in their titles (e.g., President Lyndon B. Johnson graduated from Southwest Texas State Teachers College.) The largest teacher education institutions had laboratory schools connected to their programs. Because the express intent of laboratory schools was to connect theory to practice, it stands to reason that an emphasis on theory would be among the foremost criteria when professors from such institutions selected a methods textbook.

Second, in an emerging field of study, theoretical discussion is more of a priority. Thus, it is not surprising that the need to build a theoretical base was a prime consideration of social studies pioneers.

Third, although the times were ripe for a theoretical approach to social studies methods, Metcalf was also a product of his times. He did not merely react to the emphasis on theory; he embodied it. In all of his publications, Metcalf considered theoretical issues as a central element in his arguments.

Tellingly, when responding to one of the perennial critiques of the lack of subject matter preparation in teacher education, Metcalf (1957) questioned whether the right question was even being asked: "We slip into the habit of trying to figure out how much content (subject matter) and how much methods (slick tricks) to include in teacher education without raising a more fundamental question of how much educational theory to include" (p. 277). Metcalf railed against divisions between theory and practice. He was also fond of saying that there is nothing more practical than a good theory (Metcalf, 1988).

In a general review of the research in social studies, Metcalf (1963a) harped upon the tendency to treat "technique without reference to a guiding theoretical framework" (p. 932). In his (1967) review of Oliver and Shaver's textbook (1966), despite his appreciation for the book, Metcalf was critical of the authors' "lack of theoretical clarity" (p. 172). His strongest praise was in reference to their theoretical grounding—in this case, the authors' emphasis on "feeding, expanding or contradicting the students' already existing personal theories of social reality" (Metcalf, 1967, p. 172).

REFLECTION AS A GUIDING PRINCIPLE

The theory Metcalf relied upon the most was that of reflection. He bestowed the greatest tribute to his mentor, Alan Griffin, for his application of reflective theory when he claimed, "although the fact has not been generally recognized, Griffin stands almost alone in his attempt to elaborate in practical and theoretical terms what reflective theory means for teaching history and for the subject-matter preparation of high school history teachers" (Metcalf, 1963a, p. 934). He went on to assert that Griffin's (1942) dissertation "ranks as a major intellectual achievement in social studies education within the past two decades" (Metcalf, 1963a, p. 934).

Griffin placed reflection at the core of social studies education, with students using it as a method to determine truth. Metcalf (1963a) underscored the point by pointing out how, in a democratic society, reflection must serve as the *only* method to determine truth. He was determined to place the students' intellectual processes, not the teacher or society, at the center of learning. His commitment to this most liberal of ideas is the foundation for all of Metcalf's writing and social activism.

In his own dissertation, Metcalf (1949) tested Griffin's theories in his college classrooms, comparing his discussion-oriented teaching with a control group. He found significant growth in logic as well as higher scores in thinking among subjects in the experimental group. This early experimentation served as a foundation for his lifelong devotion to student reflection.

Today's methods student may regard reflection as a given in any social studies classroom, but the idea was fraught with peril in the 1950s. The suggestion of students making up their own minds on the issues of the day was viewed as shocking (Cox, 1985, p. 61). A relatively conservative society, plagued by McCarthyism, could not be expected to accept such a radical change in social studies education. Metcalf, however, was unbowed. He argued that his methods were not a threat at all because American society was already exposing its dominant beliefs to criticism on a regular basis. He cited sociological studies that indicated that Americans tend to hold conflicting beliefs. He used technology as an example to show that Americans love new devices but worry about how they will change the society.

Metcalf (1963b) responded to his accusers with a tribute to democratic values: "Teachers are expected to inculcate right answers, right attitudes, right beliefs … an amalgam of suppression, indoctrination, distortion, manipulation, prescription, and persuasion. When this sort of thing is practiced in the Soviet Union or Red China, we call it brainwashing. Its use in this country is called patriotism" (p. 198).

His opposition to indoctrination was strong and multilayered. In addition to the ethical imperative, Metcalf stressed the practical: If students are taught the "right" answers, they are only substituting one prejudice for another. There is no opportunity for intellectual development.

Some critics claimed that Metcalf's advocacy of reflection violated Dewey's call for "experience." He responded that the accusation was yet another example of misinterpretation: "Reflection is doing; it doesn't have to be action" (Metcalf, 1963a, p. 947). He believed that a reflective approach would convince students that social studies was, indeed, relevant. "Formal coursework acquires relevance whenever it impinges upon what students believe, and whenever it has the effect of producing a pattern of belief that is well-grounded and internally consistent" (Metcalf & Hunt, 1970, p. 358.) As for the claim that some students cannot be taught to think, he replied with four words: "It was never tried" (Metcalf, 1985, p. 72).

CLOSED AREAS

Hunt and Metcalf's revolutionary contribution was not simply reflection; that credit goes to Griffin (1942). Rather, it was their concept of "closed areas" that made the biggest stir. Metcalf (1963b) believed that the *single purpose of social studies* is helping "students examine reflectively issues in closed areas of American culture" (p. 197).

Departing from the usual applications of Deweyan thought, Hunt and Metcalf urged teachers to move beyond typical problems in their problem-solving lessons. Instead, they recommended discussions focused on society's most vexing problems. Those problematic areas, which usually received unreflective thought, were deemed to be closed areas. The term "closed" indicated that problems were not discussed rationally, if they were discussed at all. They gave examples of (1) power and the law; (2) religion and morality; (3) race and minority group relations; (4) social class; (5) sex; courtship and marriage; (6) nationalism and patriotism; and (7) economics (Hunt & Metcalf, 1968, p. 27). In the 1968 edition of their book, Hunt and Metcalf changed the category of "closed areas" to "problematic areas of culture" because United States society had begun to address them to some degree. Yet, most of those categories would probably still be considered closed in today's school curriculum.

As indicated earlier, Metcalf insisted that the role of the teacher is not to coerce students toward a particular viewpoint when entering closed areas—it is to promote doubt in the student's own mind. "Without the presence of doubt," Metcalf (1952) asserted, "there is no reason for a student to think" (p. 23). Metcalf was infamous at the University of Illinois for conducting his classes with the students' beliefs at the center. He disdained syllabi and notes, which, he asserted, was not needed if the goal was to "tune in on what a student says" (Cox, 1985, p. 60).

Hunt and Metcalf (1968) believed that by keeping closed areas inaccessible, students lose any long-term interest in social science content. Even more serious was the resultant harm to mental health from not examining issues of primary importance to oneself. In making these arguments, they made numerous references to such psychologists as Horney and Jung. Metcalf was unapologetic for incorporating personal growth issues into the social studies curriculum. Regarding the study of sexual issues, for example, he was said to wonder, "how responsible educators could avoid study of a subject in which ignorance has caused so much personal misery" (Reardon, 1990, p. 107).

LINKING THE SOCIETAL AND THE PERSONAL

One of Metcalf's most under-examined contributions to social studies education was his attempt to link the societal with the personal. By making such a link, a course in social studies is not just an objective examination of societal issues, but also one of self-examination. For instance, the problem of social class could be viewed in terms of societal issues vis-a-vis health care, housing, and poverty, but could also be viewed through the lens of the student's own personal experiences with friendships and dating.

Metcalf argued that personal and social problems represent "different sides of the same coin" (Metcalf, 1985, p. 72). In a letter to C. Benjamin Cox, Metcalf wrote, "The study and discussion of any social problem results in the expression of personal belief. Likewise, personal beliefs can be shown to be at the root of all social problems" (quoted in Cox, 1985, p. 66).

Metcalf's emphasis on the personal was a significant departure from most approaches to problem solving in the social studies. More specifically, he stressed that the teacher must create a conflict of beliefs *within* students, not *between* them. "Until the problem resides in me," says Metcalf metaphorically, "there is no problem" (quoted in Cox, 1985, p. 66).

Based on the principle of linking the personal and the social, Metcalf dismissed the typical "Problems of Democracy" course. Never one to mince words, he declared that they "lacked both problems and democracy" (Metcalf, 1985, p. 72). If the student's doubt was not at the center of the controversy, there was no problem. If there was not honest reflection, there was no democracy.

By the same principle, but from a different angle, Metcalf was critical of the "life adjustment" curriculum that had become popular in the 1950s. He applauded attention to personal issues, but not at the expense of studying societal issues. Unlike other critics, however, he did not categorize the choice as an either-or proposition. Instead, as usual, he relied on Deweyan theory to link the personal and the societal. One of his credos was that each individual has a "personal responsibility for the public order" (Reardon, 1990, p. 107). His writings and personal behavior reflected that belief.

VALUES

Whether studying personal or societal issues, one's values inevitably enter the fray. In this regard, Metcalf was insistent that the affective realm belonged in the social studies curriculum. Indeed, the attitudes and beliefs of students were essential elements of his approach. He rejected the dualism between the cognitive and affective domains. He argued that it would be misleading to imply "that such separation is either desirable or possible" (Metcalf, 1971, p. ix). Years later, he cited the example of a nurse who kept her content knowledge regarding medicine in one part of her brain, while her beliefs in faith healing resided elsewhere. If the incompatibility between the cognitive and affective could not be examined, he wrote, no growth would take place (Metcalf, 1969). Reflection, of course, was one of the primary keys to unraveling that incompatibility.

Metcalf must have welcomed the 1960s surge of interest in values education, not just because he supported its goals, but also because it allowed him to address some of the issues that were plaguing the field of social studies education. In this way, Metcalf was able to critique social studies education at the same time he took on societal attitudes and behavior. He rarely separated the citizen from the scholar, and would be aghast at the suggestion that the two roles could ever be separated. Doing so, he argued, would place the teacher in the position of a "second-class citizen" (Metcalf, 1952, p. 22).

The very notion of values education was controversial because of the fear of indoctrination that was so prevalent in post-World War II America. Stories of Communist propaganda, especially in Soviet schools, made people suspicious of attempts to introduce values to the curriculum. Once again, Metcalf (1963b) called attention to the process of reflection when he offered the reminder that the goal is to "teach valuing, not values" (p. 198).

Metcalf (1963b) considered values education to be the very opposite of teacher indoctrination. "Teaching people to be good is not ... [the teachers'] province. Teaching that certain values are inconsistent with other values is within their province as logicians" (p. 198).

One of Metcalf's long-standing complaints was with courses on anticommunist education. These courses, developed during the McCarthy period of the 1950s, were usually the result of legislative interference with the curricular process. Because of their birth by statute rather than by educators' curricular processes, they remained in the schools long after the period of "Communist scares." The weakness of such courses in meeting the cognitive purposes of the schools was already evident to most educators. Metcalf's thrust was against the teaching of doctrine, as opposed to teaching students how to weigh the varying claims of Communists and anti-Communists in order to form their own opinions.

Metcalf railed at the notion of suppressing

> information about Communism if in the judgment of the school authorities such information might place Communism in a favorable light. This kind of practice, in addition to being unnecessary, is plainly dishonest. One of the ironies of education is the extent to which some teachers believe that the practice of honesty is necessary to the teaching of honest patriotism! More to the point, such practice violates the principle of academic freedom. (Metcalf, 1971, p. x)

He had similar objections to any form of indoctrination no matter the subject matter (e.g., drug education, black studies, or any other new topic or course).

TEACHER NEUTRALITY

An ongoing issue that came to the fore during the 1960s debate over values education was the role of the teacher. Metcalf had actually addressed the issue in the early 1950s when he pointed out how teachers' political activity provides students with a more "realistic understanding of the American political system" than those who avoid such activity (Metcalf, 1952, p. 23.) He argued that the objective should not be teacher neutrality, but instead a commitment to thought as a method to reach decisions and make judgments.

Metcalf (1952) believed teachers should express their opinions but also model the process of casting doubt on them. By relying on the principle that there is no single answer to significant questions, teachers would indicate their belief in the value of the process of thought versus having students reach a particular conclusion.

Twelve years later, university professor and teacher educator Raymond Muessig wrote to Metcalf regarding the consequences of teachers expressing strong opinions. In a classic reply that captures his merger of theory and practice, Metcalf wrote: "I have never tried to conceal my own position simply because I think it is a waste of a student's time to have him try to guess where I stand. He should find it easy to find me in order to spend most of his time on the infinitely harder job of finding himself." He went on to say that the "objective teacher is never neutral" (L. E. Metcalf, personal communication to R. Muessig, September 15, 1964).

PERSONAL ACTIVISM

Metcalf definitely practiced what he preached. He made no attempt to restrain his political opinions and activism, and he eagerly took on what he called "powerful undemocratic forces in American culture" (Metcalf, 1963a, p. 936). These battles took some interesting and surprising forms.

Metcalf's signature project was the World Order Models Project (WOMP). (The Institute for World Order eventually changed its name to the World Policy Institute, which is still active.) He served as Senior Fellow of the Institute for World Order (1968-1969), which organized WOMP. His involvement began when he joined Donald Oliver, James Shaver, and other social studies leaders in taking a course on the project which was taught by Saul Mendlovitz at Harvard University. The World Order Models Project leaders envisioned a series of regional meetings that brought together groups of scholars concentrating on a single issue. Metcalf worked on the World Order Models Project for 3 to 4 years in the late 1960s, meeting with other leaders three or four times each year (S. Mendlovitz, personal communication with the author, February, 2006).

Based on his commitment to reflection as the only method to discover truth, he argued that scholarly focus on the closed areas of our society would lead to solutions to the world's most vexing problems. War was selected as the initial WOMP topic, with the expectation that the study of military conflict would lead to the related issues of hunger and human rights. Metcalf was a firm believer that war could be abolished in the same way that slavery was abolished in the 19th century (S. Mendlovitz, personal communication with the author, February, 2006).

Metcalf was particularly drawn to the idea of interrelating issues of war, poverty, political instability, and the environment in the WOMP curriculum. Subsequently, he became the leader in adapting the project to the high schools.

Metcalf's dream of scholarly cooperation reflected his model of exemplary high school social studies classrooms. More specifically, his goal was to have students engage in the very same activities as the scholars, though for different purposes. The students would be developing their intellectual skills and content knowledge while the scholars would be seriously considering ways to solve the world's problems. It is not surprising that Metcalf's own undergraduate course in social studies methods was "unabashedly a course on the economic, social, political, ecological, and nuclear perils of the globe" (Cox, 1985, p. 65).

The thought of scholars deliberating over policy came to fruition in the Kennedy administration when the Harvard-educated young president attracted "the best and the brightest" to government work at the highest levels. Most would agree that the effect was disastrous in terms of war and peace, especially in relation to the United States' involvement in the Vietnam "conflict." Perhaps if they had followed Metcalf's vision of regional, multinational and multi-cultural gatherings, the outcome could have been different. It is notable that Metcalf's (1968) endorsement of a form of global studies predated the adoption of that approach by social studies theorists by about 10 years.

Despite his strong left-wing credentials, Metcalf took a stand against the campus radical movements of the late 1960s. As would be expected, he criticized the lack of reflection underlying the various radical claims. For example, he asked whether the burgeoning antiwar movement was truly antiwar or just anti-Vietnam War. Wrestling with the principle, he insisted, would clarify matters for the public and serve to educate the young activists. Further, he asked that radical alternatives be assessed against rational criteria (Metcalf, 1969).

In response to the race riots of the late 1960s in such places as Watts (Los Angeles), Newark, and Detroit, Metcalf called for changes in the high school social studies curriculum that would better address the problems of urban life. He proposed incorporating study of the conflict between environmental and ecological goals, order versus law, and local versus state versus national jurisdiction (Metcalf, 1969). It is apparent that he never wavered from his commitment to reflective study of closed areas as an instrument for addressing just about any policy issue.

In 1972, Metcalf refused to pay dues to Phi Delta Kappa, the educational honor society because of its "persistent policy of discrimination against the female sex." The reply from PDK Executive Secretary Lowell Rose was not only unapologetic, but Rose did not even acknowledge the issue. One would expect greater deference being paid to a three-time contributor to the organization's flagship journal, but the Rose letter merely described the policy for nonpayment of dues. Ultimately, PDK altered its discriminatory policies. There is no evidence that Metcalf's action alone resulted in this change; rather, it is more likely that it was a result of the criticism lodged by many, including Metcalf.

CONSTRAINTS OF A NONPOLITICAL SORT

Metcalf, while quite outspoken and well respected, was never a particularly prolific writer. His social activism with the World Order Models Project took up much of his time, as did his editing responsibilities for the journal, *Progressive Education*. According to brief references in his letters, another constraint on his time was the fluctuation in the health of his wife and children. A former student, Gerald Unks, recalls that Metcalf often came late to the office and left early due to family responsibilities. Unks characterized Metcalf as "not lazy" but also a "notorious procrastinator" who "took deadlines as a challenge." (G. Unks, personal communication with the author, January 12, 2006)

Recollections from former students and colleagues suggest that Metcalf's personality may have also served as a constraint in his career. "He was difficult to know," said Bill Lowe, a former student who became a longtime colleague and friend. (B. Lowe, personal communication with the author, October 26, 2005) Another colleague, noted social studies educator Jack Nelson, offered that Metcalf "did not suffer fools easily, and could be a curmudgeon when caught in social situations where the foolish comments outnumbered the thoughtful ones."(J. Nelson, personal communication with the author, October 21, 2005)

It appears that Metcalf's academic self merged with his personal self. Lowe recalled how Metcalf consistently challenged others. "He was especially brutal regarding economics. He forced everyone to think, and couldn't settle for anything but a forceful answer. He'd ask, 'Where's the evidence?'" (B. Lowe, personal communication with the author, October 26, 2005)

Creating an atmosphere of intense self-reflection, especially with regard to closed areas, is yet another example of Metcalf practicing what he preached. Yet, such intensity had its repercussions. Lowe noted, "Larry was never comfortable at cocktail party-type events." As a result, he was unable to engage in the interpersonal networking that helped bring one to prominence in professional organizations. Several longtime friends Nelson, Wilma Longstreet, and Lowe identified Barbara, his wife, who was stricken with polio, as the social center of Metcalf's world. At meetings of the National Council for the Social Studies, Barbara would meet and greet old friends while Metcalf would remain aloof. "She did the talking," recalls Wilma Longstreet (personal communication with the author, November 22, 2005). "He was quiet, a loner," said Lowe.

While many of his colleagues across the nation—including James Shaver, Howard Mehlinger, and Shirley Engle—ultimately became presidents of NCSS, Metcalf's service never approached those heights. His combative style combined with his predilection for controversy was not a formula for organizational success. According to Lowe, "Larry could never be elected to anything." Unks surmised that Metcalf's "revolutionary ideas about teaching were not what high school teachers wanted to hear." Unks also suggested that Metcalf was not interested in taking a leadership role in NCSS. (G. Unks, personal communication with the author, January 12, 2006)

In the classroom, his challenging style could have served as a model for those who had never experienced the Hunt-Metcalf approach as a student. His students who became teachers and/or professors could presumably apply their experiences as students in their own classrooms.

That said, the learning environment he created was oppressive. All of his former students indicated that they were terrified of him. George Wood used the term "Metcalf headaches" that resulted when Metcalf pushed and pushed in "never-ending debates, which he always won." (G. Wood, personal communication with the author, January 13, 2006.)

It may be that Metcalf was most comfortable when he was implementing his approaches to social studies. Nelson recalled a time when Metcalf was invited to address a statewide conference that he had organized: "Larry was a very serious person, and not a very dynamic speaker, and I was concerned that we would lose the interest of the audience. But the discussion period after his presentation was Metcalf at his best. He debated, elaborated, challenged, retorted, and debunked comments from all sides." (J. Nelson, personal communication with the author, October 21, 2005.) Wood noted that Metcalf's strength was his commitment to the highest levels of intellectual rigor. Thus, he always made a point of understanding his opponents' points of view. (G. Wood, personal communication with the author, January 13, 2006.)

In his later years, Metcalf was plagued by a serious case of shingles, which he believed he contracted in 1971, at the age of 55. In one letter, he described the pain as "agonizing and unrelenting" (L. E. Metcalf, personal communication with M. Hunt, 1976). The advent of that debilitating disease appears to have limited his intellectual output at a time when his contemporaries were becoming active commentators on the state of social studies education. Metcalf retired in 1986 and passed away in 1990.

THE BIOGRAPHY OF A PRIVATE MAN

Metcalf was "quiet, reserved, and modest," in the words of his daughter, Janet. He "never really discussed his childhood in depth" with his children nor did any of his closest friends and students recall any such references. (J. M. Stake, personal communication with the author, January 25, 2006) Gerald Unks, who had the honor of giving the eulogy at Metcalf's funeral, realized that he knew next to nothing about the man's background until he had to prepare his remarks. (G. Unks, personal communication with the author, January 12, 2006.) The few recollections that were provided by his children may be helpful in understanding Metcalf's professional life.

Metcalf was a physically frail individual. His son, Andy, supposes that he was about 5 foot 9 inches and about 130 pounds. While one of his former students (G. Wood, personal communication with the author, January 13, 2006) cautions against confusing physical frailty with intellectual frailty, his stature may have played a significant role in his childhood. Living a very sheltered life, "he was never allowed to go anywhere" and never learned to swim or ride a bicycle (A. Metcalf, personal communication with the author, January 18, 2006). His childhood was apparently devoted to books. He must have been quite different from the average rural Ohioan as evidenced by his 1933 high school valedictory address that discussed, of all things, the prospect of World War I reparations coming back to haunt the United States. He probably stood out as a bookworm with a propensity for challenging the status quo. He mentioned to his daughter (J. M. Stake, personal communication with the author, January 19, 2006) that he sometimes felt smarter than some of his teachers and didn't fit in well with his peers.

His daughter speculated that he may have been bullied by other children (J. M. Stake, personal communication with the author, January 25, 2006). That could account for his propensity toward issues of social justice. But it may also have been due to the times in which he lived, between the two world wars, during the Great Depression. He would be one of many societal critics that were produced by that politically vibrant era.

Despite his superior academic performance, Metcalf did not immediately go to college. Finances were probably an issue for his parents, neither of whom attended college themselves. He was "rescued from bookkeeping" when a wealthy benefactor provided funds for disadvantaged young men to attend the Ohio State University. It was there that he studied philosophy and education. He regarded that period as his "saving grace" (J. M. Stake, personal communication with the author, January 19, 2006).

He told his daughter that during his teaching career he was frequently frustrated by the schools' set ways of doing things. After his subsequent promotion to principal, he found it difficult to make changes as he was continually blocked by superintendents and school boards. It made him recognize that influencing teachers to be open-minded may best be achieved through teacher education. When he entered his doctoral program, he found the ideal mentor in Alan Griffin, whose work on reflection attempted to promote the open-mindedness that Metcalf sought in teachers.

According to the school yearbooks during Metcalf's years as a principal at Lexington High School in Ohio (1943-1944), several students from the school served and were killed during World War II. His interest in peace studies may have been influenced by that experience. He himself did not enter the Army because he failed the physical. (A. Metcalf, personal communication with the author, January 18, 2006.)

Judging by Metcalf's penchant for questioning authority, it is no surprise that he was an atheist (J. M. Stake, personal communication with the author, January 19, 2006). Gerald Unks suggested that Metcalf considered religion to be "hocus-pocus." Unks was present when, upon the announcement of Janet's engagement to be married, Metcalf jokingly supposed that the family would now have to join a church. (G. Unks, personal communication with the author, January 12, 2006.)

His love of reading was legendary. A former student recalls that Metcalf had to rebuild a wall in his house in order to support his collection of books. Metcalf was also a jazz aficionado. Perhaps his most endearing trait, however, was his "undying love for the Cleveland Indians" (G. Wood, personal communication with the author, January 13, 2006). Even though he lived in Illinois, he would regularly listen to Indians games on the radio and even took his family to Arizona to attend the team's spring training camp (A. Metcalf, personal communication with the author, January 18, 2006). Considering the Indians' consistent performance as also-rans, invariably finishing behind the Yankees in the American League standings year after year (except for 1954), Metcalf's siding with the underdog becomes more understandable.

METCALF IN A NUTSHELL

As one reviews the social studies work of Lawrence E. Metcalf, several conclusions come to mind. First is the recognition of and respect for his strength of character. Honest and forthright at a time when many academics avoided direct criticism of the nation and its policies, he was in the right place at the right time to lead social studies away from its tradition of rote memorization and indoctrination.

A second salient characteristic was his consistency. As one who lauded consistency as a goal of logical thinkers, he exemplified it in his commitment to reflective thought. While he paid tribute to scholars who altered their views, such as Dewey, Metcalf's basic philosophy was the same in 1980 as it was in 1950.

Commitment was a third quality one may associate with Metcalf. His dedication to world peace and public debate was exemplified in both his writing and public behavior. As the author of a methods text, he could have focused on the specific techniques of the social studies teacher, but he preferred to use that methods text as a springboard to develop the kind of society he believed would solve the world's problems.

In evaluating Metcalf's legacy, it would be easy to cite his textbooks and small, but influential, collection of essays as evidence of his impact on the field of social studies education. However, given the fact that most teachers did not implement his ideas (Stanley, 1988), one must look toward a different kind of legacy.

Metcalf's impact appears to have been on the thinking of leaders in the field. Because of the popularity of the Hunt and Metcalf (1955/1968) texts, most of the social studies scholars of the generation after them were weaned on their ideas. It would be difficult to find leaders in the field today, especially among advocates for teaching social issues, whose thinking has not been shaped by Metcalf's writing, whether they are aware of it or not. Due to his emphasis on thinking as a goal, Metcalf would probably be proud of such a legacy.

The reader may have recognized, in reviewing Metcalf's work, that many of his ideas are still relevant. His former student, Gerald Unks, reflected that "What he said was so important, we're still talking about them, years later." (G. Unks, personal communication with the author, January 12, 2006.) Here, too, Metcalf could proudly point out how good theories are always relevant and timeless. His principles of reflection, sowing student self-doubt, integrating the personal with the societal, teacher activism, and inclusion of the affective realm in the social studies curriculum are ones that should be heeded by all social studies educators. The durability of his ideas garner him a prestigious place on the trajectory from Dewey to "the New Social Studies" to the present.

NOTE

1. Hunt and Metcalf remained lifelong colleagues and friends. While they maintained a warm relationship via frequent mail, the physical distance between them (Hunt resided in California, while Metcalf resided in Illinois) kept them from seeing each other very often.

REFERENCES

Bruner, J. S., Goodnow, J. J., & Austin, G. A. (1956). *A study of thinking*. New York: Wiley.

Bruner, J. S. (1960). *The process of education*. Cambridge, MA: Harvard University Press.

Cox, C. B. (1985). Lawrence E. Metcalf: An annotated signature. *Indiana Social Studies Quarterly, 38*(3), 58-71.

Griffin, A. F. (1942). *A philosophical approach to the subject matter preparation of teachers of history*. Unpublished doctoral dissertation, Columbus: The Ohio State University.

Hunt, M. P., & Metcalf, L. E. (1955, 1968). *Teaching high school social studies*. New York: Harper and Row.

Metcalf, L. E. (1949). *A theory of conceptual learning and its implications for the teaching of the social studies for the purpose of clarifying social attitudes*. Abstracts of Doctoral Dissertations, no. 56. Columbus: The Ohio University Press.

Metcalf, L. E. (1952). Must teachers be "neutral?" *Educational Leadership, 10*(2), 22-25.

Metcalf, L. E. (1957). Intellectual development in modern schools. *Phi Delta Kappan, 38*(7), 277-280.

Metcalf, L. E. (1963a). Research on teaching the social studies. In N. L. Gage (Ed.), *Handbook of research on teaching* (pp. 929-966). Chicago: Rand McNally.

Metcalf, L. E.. (1963b). Some guidelines for changing social studies education. *Social Education, 37*(6), 197-201.

Metcalf, L. E. (1967). Review of *Teaching public issues in the high school*. *Harvard Educational Review, 37*(1) and *Indiana Social Studies Quarterly, 38*(3), 172.

Metcalf, L. E. (1969). Urban studies, reflectively speaking. *Social Education, 50*, 197-201.

Metcalf, L. E. (Ed.). (1971). *Values education*. Washington, DC: National Council for the Social Studies.

Metcalf, L. E. (1985). A response. *Indiana Social Studies Quarterly, 38*(3), 72.

Metcalf, L. E. (1988). An overview of the Deweyan influence on social studies education. *International Journal of Social Education, 3*(3), 50-54.

Metcalf, L. E., & Hunt, M. P. (1970). Relevance and the curriculum. *Phi Delta Kappan, 52*(7), 358-361.

Oliver, D. W. & Shaver, J. P. (1966). *Teaching public issues in the high school*. Boston: Houghton Mifflin.

Reardon, B. A. (1990). Lawrence Metcalf. *Social Education, 59*(2), 107.

Stanley, W. B. (1988). Beyond pragmatic inquiry: A critical analysis of Lawrence E. Metcalf's approach to social education. *The International Journal of Social Education, 3*(3), 63-83.

CHAPTER 14

PAUL DEHART HURD

Staying the Course for 72 Years

Barbara S. Spector

INTRODUCTION

"You are going to have to use your head instead of your feet to make a living." This was the guidance given to a first grader who broke his ankle and was plagued with subsequent infections until the advent of penicillin about 30 years later. Paul DeHart Hurd was the first grader. His mother encouraged him to think about his resulting disability (walking with a significant limp that became worse as he aged) as the stimulus for him to use his superior intellect as the vehicle for his life's work. This was his mother's gift to science education. Without this advice he might have chosen another career path. His physical misfortune spurred a lifetime of benefit for society through science education.

For his 72-year career, Paul heeded his mother's advice; used his intellectual curiosity and creativity, read profusely, stayed current with changes in science and in technology, and shared his accumulated wisdom as the

Addressing Social Issues in the Classroom and Beyond: The Pedagogical Efforts of Pioneers in the Field, 253–265
Copyright © 2007 by Information Age Publishing
All rights of reproduction in any form reserved.

consistent eloquent voice articulating calls to transform science education to make it socially relevant.

Paul DeHart Hurd is most noted for championing the cause of "scientific literacy," a phrase he introduced in 1958, as the learning of science he envisioned for all students in K-12 schools. What he meant by "scientific literacy" was "an understanding of science and its application to our social experience" (De Boer, 1991, p.174). This was and is in stark contrast to teaching science for the elite being prepared for careers as scientists, which was the norm when he was in school, and for years afterwards. Even in the national reform movement of the 1960s, the "golden age of science education," the prominent curriculum development projects did not teach science in its social context. Evidence of this legacy is still visible in beliefs and actions of too many science teachers in K-12 schools today.

Hurd advocated science education for young people that would enhance their daily lives and enable them to recognize its value to themselves and society. The phrase "science for life and living" encapsulated his idea. Sometimes he used the expression "science enlightenment" and other times "science and technology in society." It was, in fact, Hurd who established a foundation for the Science/Technology/Society (STS) Interaction movement.

The expression "hands-on minds-on," a common part of the current science teacher education lexicon, is also attributed to Hurd. It made transparent the need for science teachers to stimulate mental activity instead of just giving learners something to manipulate with their hands. Many teachers inaccurately assumed the latter alone resulted in learning the science concept under consideration.

Hurd's message was consistent throughout his career. While a variety of labels appeared in his writings, they all expressed the same fundamental message: Science should be taught in its social context as a means to enhance human life and living in this democratic nation in which the combined impact of science and technology is the primary cultural force. The express purpose in the variations and changes in language was to enhance the persuasiveness of his message as the societal context for communicating these ideas altered. His extensive knowledge of the science education enterprise, and the factors that influenced it, were valued highly by policy makers at all levels including nationally and internationally. Perhaps his most continuous and potent influence on policy was exerted through his role as senior consultant to the National Academy of Sciences (NAS) and his consultant service to the National Science Foundation (NSF). The National Science Education Standards (1996) evolved under the umbrella of the NAS and incorporated many of his beliefs. His thinking influenced the contents of the RFP's (Requests for Proposals) written by NSF's Directorate for Education and Human Resources.

Hurd's RFPs reflected his emphasis on science for *all* students including those who do not intend to be professional scientists and technologists. He also was consultant to many other federal and state organizations.

Furthermore, the varied and many honors Hurd received from multiple institutions and organizations bore ample evidence of his vital contributions to the field of science education. Such honors, for example, included the following: honorary doctoral degrees from Ball State University in 1979, Drake University in 1974, and the University of Northern Colorado in 1980; The National Science Teachers Association's 1969 Distinguished Service to Science Education Citation; the National Aeronautics and Space Agency 1970 Apollo Award; the National Science Teachers Association's 1979 Robert H. Carleton Award for National Leadership in Science Education; the National Association for Research in Science Teaching 1987 Distinguished Contribution to Science Education Research Award; and the American Association for the Advancement of Science Fellow. Honorary life memberships were also bestowed upon him by eight professional societies.

FORMATIVE YEARS

This illustrious native Coloradoan, born in 1905, obtained his K-12 education in Denver. By 1932, he had earned two degrees from the University of Northern Colorado, a bachelor's in botany and a master's in plant ecology. He said he started out in zoology but had the world's worst teacher, so he switched to botany. His professional career in Greeley went from 1929 to 1939. He taught high school biology, led the science department, and was curriculum director for K-12 science. He moved to California in 1939 to teach at Menlo High School and Junior College. He earned his doctorate at Stanford's School of Education in 1947.

He joined the faculty at Stanford University in 1951, and taught there through 1971. In addition to teaching science education courses to students working on their initial certifications to teach science in elementary and secondary schools, he also taught doctoral level science education courses. Over and above that, he also directed a summer institute for experienced high school chemistry, mathematics, and physics teachers.

Although he formally retired in 1971 as Professor Emeritus from the university, he continued writing, speaking, and influencing science education policy until his death at the age of 95.

Generous, intellectually gifted, eminent thinker, kind, wise, and persistent are words used to describe this amazing indomitable man. Individuals who spent a good deal of time with him, such as noted science educator Rodger Bybee, noticed that Hurd never voiced a negative personal comment about another person. He always accepted people as they were. When Hurd received his honorary degree from the University of Northern Colorado in 1980, Roger Bybee, Paul's academic "grandchild" and executive director of BSCS, presented this description of Paul:

> His views were not overshadowed by a need for personal recognition. Paul lived a professional life of egoless involvement. He had an unwavering mission, but his psychological glass was full, so he easily gave ideas and time to others. He saw the needs of science education as they were and put all of his energy into improving it. Spending time with Paul revealed his philosophical sense of humor. Subtly he would make a statement, with a twinkle in his eye that brought a smile to others ... he clearly and consistently expressed his views about how science education programs had not changed even though science, technology, and society had advanced. And some individuals, organizations, and agencies had to assume responsibility for what had, and had not, changed. (Bybee, 2002, p. 10)

PHILOSOPHICAL AND PEDAGOGICAL BELIEFS

Hurd argued vigorously that learning science should enable students to contribute to solving societal problems. Indeed, he believed that such thinking skills as decision-making, forming judgments, and resolving problems were critical to enable citizens to distinguish evidence from propaganda, probability from certainty, rational beliefs from superstitions, data from assertions, science from folklore, credibility from incredibility, and theory from dogma (Gibbs & Fox, 1999). He was also adamant that "The only place biology, chemistry, physics, and earth science exist as a separate discipline is in school catalogues. In the real world these disciplines interface and overlap. The stove pipe approach to the sciences may have been useful in the industrial smokestack economy, but not so in this knowledge-intensive society." Hurd's own research revealed that faux boundaries between the sciences and technology had disintegrated, and he called for dissolving such boundaries in the science taught in schools.

Hurd's most "approachable" book delineating his philosophical base for science education as a social issue is *Inventing Science Education for the New Millennium*, which was published in 1997 by Teachers College Press, Columbia University. While valuable in and of itself, it also provides an interesting synthesis of many of his ideas from his early works. Therein, Hurd explicitly states that all students need to be educated for responsible citizenship in this science and technology-oriented democracy in which we live, and that the knowledge needed for responsible citizenship is relevant to an individual's well being. Not surprisingly, he argues that science curricula should relate science and technology to students' lives, their communities, and their future. He further argues that such a curriculum should enable students to develop logical reasoning, problem solving, and decision making. In his book, Hurd also advocates "social inquiry" instead of "scientific inquiry" for K-12 science education, reflecting the shift in federal funding priority from basic science to strategic research. As Hurd (1997) put it, "Social Inquiry is related to ways of accessing scientific and technological information and its proper use in personal/social contexts, an aspect of cultural literacy" (p. 44). Social inquiry, then, depends on findings of scientific inquiry, but extends science to the world in which students live by interpreting information in qualitative terms. Social inquiry ideally leads to policies about use of scientific knowledge. Ultimately, the findings are influenced by politics, economics, laws, morals, values, risks, and personal development. The "social inquiry" approach is in stark contrast to the current and continued focus in science teaching on scientific inquiry (basic science) that addresses the way to generate new scientific theories, extend understanding of the structure of the discipline, or to verify existing knowledge of the natural world. Quantification of information is the key in scientific inquiry. (Incidentally, those educators whose pedagogical efforts are primarily scientific inquiry-driven rarely acknowledge there are many forms of inquiry in basic science research). As Hurd (1997) noted:

> Both scientific inquiry and social inquiry are impacted by race, gender, and cultural factors.... It is within these contexts that citizens are required to make decisions or form judgments and take action. Social inquiry thus becomes a process of logical or rational reasoning in terms of making science operational in human affairs. The process rests upon recognizing the reliability and validity of the knowledge to be used. In nearly all aspects of human endeavors there is a mass of superstition, myths, misconceptions, and biases to deal with. A common example of these factors is that of health as influenced by advertising, religion, and traditions.

> Social inquiry serves to generate a big picture of a problem that can be analyzed for further critical investigations. Findings tend to be correlative, a blend of science and humanities, culture, technology, and society. Social inquiry is a more difficult learning context than scientific inquiry, demanding what has come to be known as "higher order thinking skills," skills essential for the utilization of scientific knowledge in human affairs.... The skills are also those deemed essential in the world of work.... Much of social inquiry like that of strategic research in the sciences is more fruitful if carried out by teams of individuals. Team investigations are a form of shared inquiry and serve to broaden each member's insights on a problem. An outcome of social inquiry is social literacy. (p. 84)

A point Hurd made often in conversations about changing curricula in the United States is that we cannot resolve problems related to the revolutionary nature of current science and its social and economic changes by simply identifying major science concepts and restructuring existing curricula.

And yet that is exactly what is done. Although many science educators today expound theoretical constructs consistent with loosening boundaries among disciplines, the state of our enterprise indicates we still find such constructs difficult to enact. To date, our enterprise has not achieved them.

ADVOCACY

Hurd took every opportunity to forward his mission. His unique ability to articulate his knowledge and ideas made him a favorite of newspaper and media journalists, thus providing a broad platform to disseminate his views to the society at large. He also generously devoted time to learners of all ages—from elementary students through graduate students. A case in point is that on occasion those graduate students of mine who were reading his work and had questions that I felt only he could answer to their satisfaction, I handed them the phone and said, "Here is the phone number, call Dr. Hurd and find out." They were awed and sputtered a bit when I said that they should call this important man, and even more so when he took the time to talk to each of them at great length.

Hurd wrote prolifically throughout his career, right up to the last week of his life, when he submitted an article he had promised to *Biological Sciences Curriculum Study* (BSCS), a prominent and venerable United States based curriculum development organization for science education.

In addition to 11 books or monographs on the historical and philosophical aspects of science education, more than 300 articles on science education in the United States and other areas of the world, and numerous interviews and speaking engagements, Paul had another unique and long-lasting vehicle that he used to forward his belief that reform in science education should be predicated on science being taught in the context of society. That was BSCS. He became a consultant to BSCS in 1959, shortly after its inception, and remained a driving force in various capacities for 35 years.

Following Hurd's death in 2001, Rodger Bybee, the current executive director of BSCS, identified Paul DeHart Hurd's influence on BSCS during his tribute to Dr. Hurd:

Paul was the third person to join BSCS. Between 1959 and 1980, Paul contributed to BSCS as chair of the policy committee, served on the advisory board for Human and Medical Genetics, contributed to the Human Sciences Program, presented at BSCS symposia, served on the board of directors, and later was a special advisor to the board.

Always, Paul encouraged BSCS to implement his visions, and he supported the organization's mission through books, monographs, and articles about BSCS and our programs.

Paul also advised BSCS on a new program for elementary schools which we named in recognition of his "mantra," "Science for Life and Living." His concern for adolescents became an important factor in the design and development of the BSCS Program Middle School Science & Technology.

Finally, Paul's vision for a human biology program was realized with "BSCS Biology: A Human Approach." Privately, Paul expressed some sense of accomplishment and pride that we had recognized and implemented his ideas. However, to be truthful, funding priorities, publishing demands, and other realities left us with less than the ideals Paul espoused. (Bybee, 2002)

HISTORIAN/ARCHIVIST

Personally, I think of Paul DeHart Hurd as the "grandfather of science education." And in one sense, he was also the unofficial living archivist for the science education enterprise.

He "lived" much of the history of science education in the United States in the twentieth century and interacted personally with great thinkers of the past, such as John Dewey (R. Yager, personal communication with the author, 2005). Over and above that, he seemed to have an insatiable appetite for delving into the history of science education, its relationship to the history of science, and it relationship to the history of society. The latter enabled him to continuously present impressive evidence of the long (250 years) identified need for science education to change from culturally isolated science teaching to that which reflects the role of science as the driving force it is in today's society.

His role as archivist began with his analysis of science education in the first half of the twentieth century for his 1949 dissertation at Stanford University titled, *A Critical Analysis of the Trends in Secondary School Science Teaching from 1895-1948*. He later wrote a landmark report, *Biological Education in American Secondary Schools 1890-1960* (Hurd, 1961/1984), updating his analysis.

He furthered his accounting in the early 1970s when he chaired the Project Synthesis committee comprising Jane Butler Kahle, Robert Yager, and Roger Bybee whose mandate was to ascertain the status and future of biology education. Notably, in 1992, Hurd presented an accounting of the past century of science education in America at the National Science Teachers Association. He continued extending that record until his death in 2001.

ACADEMIC CULTURE

Hurd readily recognized that academic culture was resistant to change, especially when it came to altering the curriculum in any significant way. When identifying factors leading to the disappointing influence of the curricular reforms in the 1950s and 1960s on school science, he noted most science educators were excluded from the reform process. Higher education science departments in Colleges of Arts and Sciences failed to establish courses consistent with the newly developed National Science Foundation (NSF) supported curricula, and science departments in Colleges of Arts and Sciences did not acknowledge that the needs of elementary and middle school science teachers differed from those of students studying for a career in science. There has been some movement to mitigate these factors today, but certainly not enough.

SCIENCE/TECHNOLOGY/SOCIETY (STS)

It is difficult to attribute a date to the beginning of STS, because it was a grass roots movement that began quietly in many parts of the country at various levels of education simultaneously. That said, STS seemed to become a viable movement with the 1978 final report of Project Synthesis to the National Science Foundation (Harms & Kahle, 1978). Project Synthesis included a working group on science and technology led by Joseph Piel of the State University of New York at Stony Brook. That work encouraged many of us to begin sharing STS related initiatives in which we had been engaging.

It was Paul DeHart Hurd, though, who set the intellectual foundation for the now highly respected science/technology/society interaction movement in science education. That, in and of itself, was and is a remarkable accomplishment and testament to his forward-looking vision and the energy, zeal, and dedication that he put into the field of science education and the need for science education to examine the critical issues impacting our society and world. He was incredibly studious about digging out historical details (R. Yager, personal communication with the author,

2005). Indeed, it was Hurd who called for an understanding of technology to become a legitimate part of science teaching. This call was founded in his historical research documenting the way changes in technology led to changes in the kinds of questions investigated by research scientists, how the needs of research scientists stimulated development of new technologies, and how concomitant changes in society emerged. The philosophical perspectives he developed from history were intended to provide the science education enterprise with a vision of what the enterprise should be: changes in society and changes in the practice of contemporary science, moving from a reductionist approach to a more holistic approach.

Hurd was also an active member of the National Association of Science, Technology, and Society since its inception in 1985. At the latter's 1995 conference, my graduate student, Tom LaPorta, and I spoke about a five-credit course in our teacher education program that included multiple approaches we used to enable students to develop their own grounded theory of STS. Subsequently, Hurd initiated a lively discussion among the attendees by asserting that "The unique thing is that it takes time and a lot of interaction to find out that there is a relationship between science, technology, and society." This statement is characteristic of what I find profound about so many things Hurd commented upon. Such observations and pronouncements were obvious once stated, but were ones that had not been previously thought about by others. Indeed, the aforementioned statement typified his uncanny knack for making something complex look simple without losing the integrity of the idea. Finally, everything he talked about put science in a social context.

At the close of the aforementioned conference, Tom and I had the opportunity to sit and talk with Hurd for several hours in the hotel's restaurant, and at one point I asked him: "How do you deal with the frustration of seeing ideas you set forth reappearing over the years and not succeeding in revolutionizing science education?" My question reflected my own frustration as a reformer, who, granted, had been at it for considerably less time than Hurd. I was seriously questioning my ability to deal with my disappointment of continuously confronting new barriers to change. I had begun wondering whether it really was a lost cause. His answer invigorated me and will likely enable me to tolerate the slow pace of change for the rest of my life. My understanding of his answer was that of Paul DeHart Hurd as the lifelong scientist: Through each cycle of struggle, we learn something new and have another opportunity to make it work.

THE RESEARCHER

Hurd was always grounded in reality, even though his vision for science education as a social issue might have seemed like an unrealistic dream to some people. A story he told at a conference about the basis for his recommendations for educating young adolescents left me with a powerful image. Here was this well manicured, important, mild-mannered man sitting on school steps interviewing dropouts, or potential dropouts, who are hanging around outside the school. He wanted to glean ideas from them in regard to how changes in science education might mitigate the social issue of school dropouts, which was a major concern of his. These interviews corroborated his deeply held view that science teaching had to take place in a social milieu. He came to believe that matters of environmental protection and constructive uses of new technologies were among the issues in society that had potential to make science relevant to students, especially middle school students.

Hurd had the insight to recognize middle school curricula as the neglected and critical link to successful K-12 science education. In his book, *Transforming Middle School Science Education* (2000) he discussed the biological, social, and emotional needs of young adolescents that needed to be considered in order to develop meaningful science curricula and pedagogy for them.

Research into the efficacy of his suggested curricular changes and their ultimate impact on a student's knowledge base or thinking was left to those who designed and implemented curricula based on his philosophical stance. That said, the findings of various researchers, including Dr. Robert Yager and many of his colleagues such as David Kumar and others, into the impact of the STS movement as it has been implemented to date are positive.

We still do not, however, have empirical evidence of the potential impact of Hurd's vision for inventing science education, because the full scope of his recommendations have not been implemented to date. That would require more dramatic restructuring of schooling than we have been able to achieve thus far.

SOCIETAL CHANGE

Hurd's historical studies convinced him that the central feature of United States education was "amnesia." The enterprise consistently forgot what worked well and kept trying to reinvent the same things. It also forgot what did not work and kept trying them over again. He strongly believed that such societal amnesia was a major barrier to providing social relevance for science in elementary and secondary schools.

Alarms sounded in my head the first time I heard Hurd say "We can't fix science education by doing the same things that caused the problem in the first place." He was essentially echoing Albert Einstein's statement: "You cannot solve a problem by thinking in ways that caused the problem." Hurd, in turn, made me think of Thomas Kuhn's description of events that ensue before a paradigm shift finally occurs in science. Most scientists keep refining the old procedures to solve a problem they cannot overcome. It is not until someone, usually at the fringe of the enterprise, risks an entirely new approach to the problem that a useful answer emerges and the paradigm shifts.

Hurd's straightforward statement is one of the most powerful tools a teacher educator and/or staff developer can use to encourage students, current teachers, and school administrators (and even some teacher educators) to risk reconceptualizing science teaching to match today's societal paradigm.

Another principle of social change involves helping people develop ownership of an idea. Enabling a target audience to provide input to the planned change through national consensus building was a strategy used to develop the documents currently guiding reform in science education: *Science for All Americans* (SFAA) (Rutherford & Ahlgren, 1989), *Benchmarks for Science Literacy* (AAAS, 1993), both products of Project 2061, and the *National Science Education Standards* (NSES) (NRC, 1996). This consensus building strategy is burdened with tradeoffs that often leave documents stating less dramatic changes than desired by visionaries such as Hurd and his followers. The consensus process used to obtain "buy-in" from the science education enterprise cost much in terms of enacting Hurd's position. Indeed, Hurd expressed great reservations about the ability of these guides to enable science education to fully serve the social needs of the enterprise.

Hurd's indomitable drive to reform science education rubbed off on his students and their students. It should be no surprise that the development of the preceding documents were led by disciples of Paul DeHart Hurd: F. James (Jim) Rutherford, whose brainchild was Project 2061, was Hurd's student at Stanford University; Roger Bybee, who led a working group to bring *National Science Education Standards* (NSES) to publication for the National Research Council (1996), was Jim Rutherford's doctoral student at New York University. Like Hurd, taking risks and following their beliefs put both Rutherford and Bybee on atypical pathways for science educators. While they were successful professors in higher education institutions, when they wanted broader influences than they could exercise within their higher education institution's constraints, they invented new pathways to forward reform. They exemplify the impressive legacy left by Paul DeHart Hurd.

CONCLUSION

Paul DeHart Hurd died of pneumonia on December 23, 2001, in Menlo Park, California. He was 95 years old.

Following his death, a memorial resolution about Paul DeHart Hurd was presented to the Stanford Faculty Senate on May 27, 2002, by Dr. Elliot Eisner, the notable curriculum theorist who was a fellow faculty member of Hurd's at Stanford University:

> Paul was a progressive educator in spirit and in conception—developing curricula and instructional practices that teach students the reasoning skills of scientific inquiry, along with facts. His contribution to policy making, research, curriculum development, pedagogy, and teacher training extend back to his dissertation in 1948.
>
> His contributions to education are now widely acknowledged as a way to increase the meaningfulness of scientific understanding. During the 40's science was much more docile a subject.
>
> His prolific and persuasive writing stimulated the thinking of science educators throughout the nation.
>
> Paul DeHart Hurd was one of the first to recognize the need for a post-modern approach to science for pre-collegiate education in the sciences, early adolescent development, and its significance for middle grade science curriculum. His interest in closing the educational gaps between science, technology, and society was a foremost interest. What he wanted, perhaps above all, was the creation of new ways of thinking for a new age. He was persuasive. "Not just hands-on, but minds-on" was one of his memorable aphorisms. Paul DeHart Hurd was a science educator with a social vision.
>
> He aimed at what was broad and most significant in the field of science education and he will be remembered as someone who succeeded in articulating a vision that shaped much of science education during the middle of the twentieth century.

REFERENCES

American Association for the Advancement of Science. (1993). *Benchmarks for science literacy*. New York: Oxford University Press.

Bybee, R. W. (2002, Spring). Remembering Paul DeHart Hurd: A clear vision and strong voice for science education. *The Natural Selection*, pp. 9, 10.

BSCS. (2001). *The BSCS story: A history of the biological sciences curriculum study.* Colorado Springs, CO: BSCS.

De Boer, G. (1991). *History of ideas in science education: Implications for practice.* New York: Teachers College Press.

Gibbs, W. W., & Fox, G. (1999). The false crisis in science education. *Scientific American, 211*(4), 86-92.

Eisner, E. (2002). *Memorial resolution: Paul DeHart Hurd.* Stanford University.

Harms, N. C., & Kahle, J. (1978). *The status and needs of pre-college science education: Report of Project Synthesis.* (Final Report to NSF for Grant, SED 77-19001). Washington, DC: National Science Foundation.

Hurd, P. D. (1949). *A critical analysis of the trends in secondary school science teaching from 1895-1948.* Unpublished dissertation, Stanford University.

Hurd, P. D. (1984). *Biological education in American secondary schools 1890-1960.* Washington, DC: American Institute of Biological Sciences. (Original work published 1961)

Hurd, P. D. (1997). *Inventing science education for the new millennium.* New York: Teachers College Press.

Hurd, P. D. (2000). *Transforming middle school science education.* New York: Teachers College Press.

National Research Council. (1996). *National science education standards.* Washington, DC: National Academy Press.

Rutherford J., & Ahlgren, A. (1989). *Science for all Americans.* Washington, DC: American Association for the Advancement of Science.

CHAPTER 15

DONALD OLIVER

The Search for Democratic Community

Barbara Slater Stern

INTRODUCTION

In creating a plethora of materials during the 1960s under the name *Public Issues Series/Harvard Social Studies Project,* the intention of Donald Oliver and his collaborative team was to improve the teaching of history/social studies with the goal of helping students analyze and discuss persisting human dilemmas related to public issues in a democratic setting (Oliver & Newmann, 1967b). Speaking of their goal, Oliver (1978) commented as follows: "We saw the society beset by serious problems; we believed in the process of intelligent inquiry as the only decent vehicle toward their amelioration or resolution; and we believed in the constitutional process as the most reasonable means by which the individual's consent could be expressed, extended, or withdrawn" (Oliver, 1978, p. 5).

Ultimately, the materials were never widely adopted, and while some social studies teachers still implement specific instructional strategies developed by Oliver and his associates, (e.g., the jurisprudential teaching

Addressing Social Issues in the Classroom and Beyond: The Pedagogical Efforts of Pioneers in the Field, 267–289
Copyright © 2006 by Information Age Publishing
All rights of reproduction in any form reserved.

model), teaching controversial issues in the secondary classroom is not all that widespread. When one digs into Oliver's beliefs about the reasons for the latter as well as the ramifications it has for society, he seems almost prescient about the problems that beset humanity today, both in the United States and around the globe.

The focus of this chapter is on Donald Oliver's development as a curricular innovator and his retreat from social science education into process philosophy and a belief in the need for community, religion, and the creation of "space" for an affective rather than just a rational approach to solving society's problems.

DONALD OLIVER, THE PERSON

Donald Oliver died at home June 28, 2002, following a 3-month illness from brain tumors (K. Gewertz, 2002; personal communication with Polly Oliver, April 1, 2005). His obituary states that his two main philosophical interests were the development of a theory of culture and the systematic study of human experience. His concerns were for everyday life and finding a balance therein.

Questions worthy of examination are: "How and why did Oliver move from the concern with the public sphere to the private sphere, and from progressive educator to curricular reconceptualist?" and "Was Oliver searching all along for the path to a democratic community?"

Donald Oliver was born in 1929, a child of the Great Depression. According to his wife, Polly, the Depression had a huge effect on the Oliver family in that it resulted in significant financial problems for them (P. Oliver, personal communication, April 1, 2005). On a different note, Harold Berlak, a former doctoral student, observed that "Don believed his family didn't really understand him—they were small town and parochial and working class" (personal communication, August 18, 2005).

Oliver attended a one room schoolhouse in Connecticut and then Norwich Free Academy, the public high school in his hometown. He pursued his postsecondary education with a scholarship to Amherst College where he received his Bachelor's degree in psychology in 1952. Jim Shaver, a former student and later a colleague of Oliver's at Harvard University, recalls Oliver recounting his work in the dining hall at Amherst and recalling the resentment he felt at serving the "rich" students who did not seem to value their opportunities (personal communication with James Shaver, March 7, 2005). Harold Berlak and David Purpel, another doctoral student at Harvard, both commented that Oliver had a strong social class bias. More specifically, Purpel recalls that Oliver was "socially and culturally anti-elitist" but seemed to have an "antipathy to students in his class—men at Harvard who were primarily from the upper class and dressed accordingly" (personal communication with David Purpel, August 31, 2005).

Polly Oliver recalls that her husband had originally wanted to be a pediatrician, but felt he could make a bigger contribution as an educator (personal communication with Polly Oliver, April 1, 2005). Thus, he chose to pursue a doctorate at the Harvard Graduate School of Education, earning his PhD in 1956 (Gewertz, 2002) and joining the Harvard Faculty thereafter. It was at this early point in his career that Oliver worked with some of his most notable doctoral students in social studies education: Jim Shaver, Harold Berlak, and Fred Newmann, among others. Shaver and Newmann became most associated with the Public Issues series, and both (personal communications) recalled their graduate classes with Oliver. In speaking about Oliver, they describe an individual who was brilliant, distant, disaffected, insecure, confrontational, uncomfortable around others, analytic, acerbic, and a bulldog in an argument. Both recounted remembering a female student leaving class in tears although she was not the "target" in the Socratic discussion—she simply could not handle the intensity and passion of the class. It was an intensity and passion that did not wane over the years, even as Oliver mellowed slightly. It appears that Oliver's students either "loved" him or "disliked" him because of his intensity and what they viewed as a lack of support due to his critical analyses of their thinking and projects.[1] All was not roses and students did leave Don to work with other advisors" (J. Shaver, personal communication, January 3, 2006). Polly Oliver describes her husband as an "Old Testament prophet" who could be Socratic, but who could also give a "hellfire and brimstone sermon."

As Oliver "mellowed" over time, his later students saw a different side of him. Dan Proctor, one such student, recalls weekly Friday night "salons" at the house where Don would cook a large batch of soup, someone would bring bread, and students would gather around for extended conversation.

Shaver explains Oliver's transformation, in part, by citing a letter he received from Len Godfrey, a teacher and friend of Don's, after Oliver had passed away: "Don (who had told me 'if there really is a God we're in trouble') had discovered God, was attending church and singing in the choir ... " (personal communication to J. Shaver from L. Godfrey, March, 4, 2003.)

Oliver clearly was a complex individual who grew and changed in significant ways during the course of his lifetime. Indeed, the aforementioned fusion of religiosity with academic rationality is crucial in understanding his move away from public issues to the more private sphere. However, of most importance in this chapter is Oliver's involvement with the social issues approach exemplified by the Harvard Public Issues project.

OLIVER'S EARLY YEARS AS A SCHOLAR

Early in his career Oliver wrote about the tentative nature of historical knowledge, addressing such questions as: "What should be taught?"; "How do we know our facts are correct?"; and "How many perspectives are we viewing?" He was also vitally concerned about what he perceived as the inadequacy of textbooks and teachers to address controversy in the classroom, especially in a way that involved thoughtful analysis and rational problem solving (Oliver, Shaver, Berlak, & Van Seasholes, 1962).

The seeds of the Harvard Public Issues Project began in a call for the examination of the assumptions underlying the extant social studies curriculum in a 1957 *Harvard Educational Review* article. In the same article Oliver discussed the value of an inquiry approach and delineated specific instructional strategies that would nurture intellectual discussion (reprinted in Oliver, 1968). Shaver recalls that the thrust of Oliver's 1957 article (which mirrored his interactions with others) was predicated on incisive and disturbing questions. Disturbing because he hit on largely ignored issues, where answers were largely taken for granted, and in that he often used analogies that evoked unsettling examination (personal communication with J. Shaver, January 3, 2006). Such an approach is what Shaver and Newmann called rationale building. Shaver does not recall Oliver ever using that term, but says that he might have done so. Continuing, Shaver notes the following:

> What I found exciting as I first studied with Don in 1956 was that his analytical approach contrasted so sharply with the usual tendency to take the textbook-dominated history/social studies curriculum largely for granted in teacher education, and focus on how to plan lessons, get students involved in learning abstract concepts identified by scholars, find auxiliary materials, write tests, etc. I thought I'd gone to Harvard to learn to be a good teacher; Don made it clear that I was there to learn to think about being a good teacher and about a good curriculum. Don pushed us, as he did the profession in the 1957 article, to think about our often unexamined assumptions about such matters as the nature of society, especially in the context of citizenship education and deciding on desirable teaching outcomes, about how people learn, and so on in developing a rational basis for teaching and curricular decisions. Of course, such examination, a la John Dewey, was to be ongoing, not just for a class or a test. I think he instilled that bent toward analysis of assumptions and their implications in us. (Personal communication with James Shaver, January 3, 2006)

Throughout their writings about the pedagogical foundations of the Harvard Public Issues Project, Oliver, Shaver and Newmann all discuss the problems with history as traditionally taught—that is, how it is unconnected to student's lives, and uninteresting to students, and boring. They also address the need not only to enliven history/social studies but also to inject the traditional goal of social studies in United States schools (e.g., preparation of good citizens in a democratic society) with a reasonable chance of success. How this can be accomplished becomes the question.

It is clear from the literature, as well as from interviewing Newmann and Shaver, that the intellectual basis for the Public Issues series stemmed from Dewey's philosophy of education coupled with Gunnar Myrdal's groundbreaking study, *An American Dilemma*. According to Oliver (1968), Myrdal defined the American Dilemma as the "difference between what men say is right and what men actually do" (p. 32). Oliver then suggests the need to reinterpret the American Dilemma in terms of "two sets of moral standards: one which applies to the conduct of a particular group at a particular time, and one which applies to men in society at any time" (p. 32). He explains that instead of inconsistency between what people say and what they do, the real inconsistency stems from two sets of beliefs learned at different points in the education of the individual: one public and one private. The societal values are the ones stated in public, and the group values are the ones closer to actual behavior of an individual. "Thus, it only appears as if there were an inconsistency between belief and conduct. The individual, then, constantly faces two problems—the problem of group conformity and the problem of societal conformity" (Oliver, 1968, p. 32).

At this point in his career, Oliver had a "burning faith in Jeffersonian enlightenment" (Oliver, 1978, p. 595), and translating this faith into materials, issues, and procedures to be presented and discussed in schools was the goal. By Jeffersonian enlightenment Oliver is referring to fundamental American values and process as stated in the founding documents: the *Declaration of Independence*, the *Constitution*, including the *Bill of Rights*, and such supporting documents as *The Federalist Papers*, on which this nation bases its government. All of these intellectual documents are influenced by Enlightenment and infused with western humanistic traditions and values. In turn, the moral basis for the public issues series was based on the latter, and thus emphasizes the dignity and worth of the individual. This is taken as a first principle (perhaps based somewhat, but not entirely, on the Judeo-Christian Ethic or the Golden Rule). The idea is that valuing the individual leads to as much personal freedom as possible and thereby is a positive force in our society. Oliver states: "We do not intend to rationalize this value judgment; we are simply saying that this is a basic value in our society, and that we have selected it the most important one to be protected and perpetuated" (Oliver, 1968, p. 28). Myrdal refers to such normative concepts as the "American Creed" (Oliver, & Shaver, with Berlak & VanSeasholes, 1962). The "American Creed" is a foundational aspect of Oliver and Shaver's 1966 book, *Teaching Public Issues in the High School*. Their discussion of the Creed begins with a section entitled "Ethical Principles Underlying the Analysis of Controversy in a Democratic Society: A Summary." In the latter they explain how the value of human dignity and rational consent is the foundation upon which American government rests. They then go on to make the case for use of law to restrain federal and state governments thereby insuring the protection of individual rights. In this regard, Oliver and Shaver (1966) state that "a major goal of the society is to develop a public awareness that these basic values should be respected and applied as standards for making public policy … [and] that government and law should be the outgrowth of public debate. Important to this tradition is the value placed on the dignity and worth of each individual and, a corollary, the value placed on the use of reason and persuasion" (pp. 78-79).

"The American Creed" (see Myrdal, 1944; Newmann & Oliver, 1970), then, becomes the subordinate set of moral and intellectual concepts to assist students in becoming good citizens. Newmann and Oliver (1970) go on to define the Creed as a set of values to which most Americans adhere, including: the preeminent worth and dignity of the individual; equality; inalienable rights to life, liberty, property, and the pursuit of happiness; consent of the governed; majority rule; due process of law; community and national welfare; and rights to freedom, of speech, press, religion, assembly, and private association. These fundamental values are described as composing America's constitutional morality and are underpinned by such American beliefs as brotherhood, charity, mercy, nonviolence, perseverance or hard work, efficiency, competence and expertise, competition and rugged individualism, compromise, cooperation, honesty, loyalty and integrity of personal conscience (pp. 11-19). Newmann and Oliver describe these values as having historic roots in Western society including the Judeo-Christian tradition, the Enlightenment, English common law, Puritanism, the frontier, and American capitalism.

In an interesting footnote in their book, Newmann and Oliver comment on the obvious by reminding readers that the Creed is an ideal and that rarely do Americans actually enforce or even follow all these values. In fact, they comment, the actual behavior of Americans might display a greater commitment to such values as "materialism, conformity, sensationalism, hedonism, aggression and violence, and hypocrisy" (Newmann & Oliver, 1970, p. 12). Nonetheless, the case is made that the virtues listed in the Creed should serve as guidelines for public policy, implementation and enforcement rather than the negative behaviors mentioned

above. To educate students about public issues, then, would involve helping students to examine the values of the American Creed and helping
them to gain the knowledge and dispositions to become good citizens by
their striving toward meeting the ideals that all Americans agree upon in
general, abstract terms.

It is important to note that the term used by the authors is "public
issues," not social issues. Indeed, at that point in time, the authors saw
these terms as different—some issues that they perceived as private (e.g.,
abortion) were understood to be social, not public issues. And, public
issues are not simply "synonymous with 'current events.' By public issues
we mean problems or value dilemmas *persisting* [emphasis in original]
throughout history and across cultures" (Oliver & Newmann, 1967b, p. 3).
Furthermore, at no time did the authors push for action beyond an
understanding of such issues in class. In other words, the Public Issues
Series did not have the goal of sending students out onto the streets to
protest despite the time period, late 1960s and early 1970s, when protests
over issues (e.g., the Vietnam war, racism, women's rights, the pollution of
the environment) were relatively common.

The authors stressed that public issues are quite complex and often the
generality and abstraction of the values involved leads to a clash between/
among values and a need to prioritize them. Therefore, the goal of the
Public Issues Series was to assist students to, first, clarify positions, and
then to learn to rationally discuss issues where there were two or more
legitimate positions or where two or more American values clashed and
needed prioritization. Thus, teaching materials were developed and
instructional strategies were suggested to enable teachers and their students to undertake these tasks in their social studies/history classrooms.

THE PUBLIC ISSUES SERIES/
HARVARD SOCIAL STUDIES PROJECT

The Harvard Social Studies Project, piloted first at a junior high school in
Concord, Massachusetts and later at a high school in Newton, Massachusetts, was the origin of the development of many of the materials that
later became known as the Public Issues Series. These materials were conceptualized and developed as a collaborative effort by Oliver, his doctoral
candidates, and the teachers (e.g., Leonard Godfrey of the Peter Buckley
Junior High School in Concord) whose classrooms and students participated in piloting the instructional materials and strategies. While the
existing pamphlets do not credit all the authors involved, it is important
to note the collaborative nature of this project. Shaver recalls, "Don was
excellent in involving all of the project members in curricular decisions

and development. Len Godfrey remembers fondly lying on the carpet in the living room of his home with Don, me, and others developing lesson plans, particularly planning analogies to be used, during the Concord phase of the project—but, unfortunately, that didn't carry over to publication recognition" (personal communication with James Shaver, January 3, 2006).

The teaching materials used in the Public Issues Series seem very similar in format to early materials produced by Harold Rugg and his collaborative team. Like Rugg's pamphlets, the Public Issues pamphlets, each targeting a specific historical or political problem, focus on a vignette, story, film, piece of literature, picture, etc. that provides a discrepant event(s) or situation. For example, in the introduction to a civil rights topic, the vignette describes a widow who owns a boarding house and wishes to bar a "Negro" from renting a room. Here the right of equal access to fair housing clashes with the widow's right to use her property as she sees fit. Both claims are legitimate American values. Which should take precedence?

Each pamphlet (unit), then, begins with an introduction that challenges the students to ask questions and to see questions as more important than answers. A major goal, and challenge, is to make history more than a passive intake. The early booklets open with a page entitled "The Necessary Question." This page makes the case that history/social studies courses cover too many answers and include too few questions. The authors continue by explaining that this causes students to think that history **had** (bold in original) to happen just the way it did, leading to the conclusion that what happened was always the right way or the only way possible. A segue is then made to explain that this attitude is one of disempowerment causing students to believe that they cannot really understand or do anything about the "rushing stream of political, economic, and social events" (Oliver & Newmann, 1967b, p. 1).

Throughout, Oliver and Newmann continue to make the case that the past and the present are matters for Americans to think about, not merely observe and memorize. Thus, they assert, "This book grows out of a vigorous belief that each student is part of our national past and present. It is intended to take you into a **living dimension of history** [bold in original]" (Oliver & Newmann, 1967b, p.1). The introduction concludes by explaining the origin of the Harvard Social Studies Project as a research effort where scholars, teachers, and high school students were brought together to find a better way of approaching social studies. Later editions of the pamphlets (published in 1971 and 1972) do not include the "Necessary Questions" section, but still contain the explanation of the origin of the product, and then address the student (and teacher) by stating the following:

This unit, like other books in the Public Issues series, is intended to involve you as something more than a spectator; as more of a thinking, acting participant in history and modern life. It does not provide ready-made, right-and-wrong answers to social problems of the persisting questions of history. Rather it challenges you and your fellow students to develop your own positions and to resolve conflicting views that face citizens in a free society. (p. 3)

Thus, like the earlier Rugg materials, the Public Issues series sees the students as active participants in a search for understanding about the past—and, perceive the latter as a necessity for solving the problems of today. Also, like the Rugg materials, the units are interdisciplinary, drawing vignettes not only from primary sources but also from literature and statistical data and factual information from economics, sociology, and political science.

To illustrate the approach of the pamphlets, one entitled *Negro Views of America* will be discussed herein. This pamphlet opens with a discussion entitled "A Sense of Worth," which cites Michael Harrington's now classic book *The Other America* (1962), as well as Ralph Ellison, a noted African-American author. The discussion then moves to "the case" of Frederick Douglass, using primary source excerpts from *Narrative of the Life of Frederick Douglass* (1845/1966). The questions at the end of the "case" are entitled "Facts of the Case," and this is where students are to explain what they read by addressing multiple levels of Bloom's taxonomy, thus ensuring critical understanding and thinking about the reading. As the pamphlet develops, there are readings from Richard Wright's *Black Boy* (1945) and Lorraine Hansberry's *A Raisin in the Sun* (1958/1966), along with an illustration from the film version of Hansberry's play. There are several more "cases" with questions entitled "the facts of the case" for students to answer.

Then, on page 46, there is a section entitled "Persisting Questions of Modern Life." This section asks students to compare and contrast the last three cases they have read in order to come up with what they (the students in class) believe in regard to where the problems of the ghetto lies. Pages 46-49 contain statistical data from the Bureau of the Census and include a section on page 49 entitled "Using Statistics to Draw Conclusions." This section refers students specifically to this data and asks them to interpret its meaning. This is followed by a section on sociology entitled "Three Theories of Racial Difference" (p. 50) that first explains the theories and then uses a basic graphic organizer (chart) to have students use evidence to ascertain the validity of each theory. The unit then moves onto "Strategies for Change," with a discussion by a black millionaire followed by a section on "Black Nationalism and Black Power." These sections also conclude with a section entitled "Persisting Questions of Modern Life." The last two pages (62-63), which are entitled "Review, Reflection, Research," target the "general problem," have students review the readings and then consider the issues of fair housing and integration. The final part of this section is titled "Strategies for Change," and, at Bloom's evaluation and synthesis levels, asks students to consider the problem of racial prejudice in America by examining the problem from multiple perspectives. Initially, there is a quotation about legislating love and morality that leads to the conclusion that laws will not improve racial relations. The directions ask the students to react to the article. The interesting aspect here is how the authors allow for shades of gray in the student responses: "Your answers should consider whether all laws on race relations should be abolished, or whether some are justified and for what reasons" (p. 63).

Next, the topic moves to assuming that the problem is to change basic attitudes of "whites toward Negroes and of Negroes toward whites in the specific direction of mutual respect" (p. 63). Here, the students are asked to formulate specific proposals for doing this including: considering racial integration in jobs, housing, and education; interracial social affairs; giving attention to the matter in schools, homes, and churches; and efforts to breaking up the ghettoes. Students are asked not only about which proposals they think would work but also to consider how they would implement such.

The problem then moves onto a more specific economic focus involving tax dollars and public expenditures. Students are asked to consider whether there is an inherent social responsibility to help achieve equity using the tax structure along with public funds. This pits values from the American Creed of competition and rugged individualism against community and brotherhood.

Such an approach demonstrates an integrated or social studies approach to problems which were a central focus of the 1960s and 70s— and which, obviously, persist to this day in our society. That the authors consider this unit a public rather than a social issues topic points out how difficult it is to separate these terms—a fact that Newmann discussed when he explained their original thinking and how he changed his understanding of this problem over the years of his career (personal communication with Fred Newmann, March 14, 2005).

The series' pamphlets cover a variety of social studies courses (e.g., U.S. History, government, civics, sociology, law studies, and, to a lesser extent, geography and world history). Teachers were encouraged to select those that most applied to their own curriculum.

Among some of the many pamphlets directly attributing authorship to Donald W. Oliver and Fred M. Newmann of the Harvard Social Studies are:

The American Revolution: Crisis of Law and Change (1967a);
The Railroad Era (1967f);
Taking a Stand: A Guide to Clear Discussion of Public Issues (1967i);
Religious Freedom: Minority Faiths and Majority Rule (1967g);
The Rise of Organized Labor: Worker Security and Employer Rights (1967h);
The Immigrant's Experience: Cultural Variety and the Melting Pot (1967c);
Negro Views of America: The Legacy of Oppression (1967e);
Municipal Politics: Interest Groups and the Government (1967d);
The New Deal: Free Enterprise and Public Planning (1968d);
Rights of the Accused: Criminal Procedure and Public Security (1968e);
Community Change: Law, Politics, and Social Attitudes (1968b);
Communist China: Communal Progress and Individual Freedom (1968a);
Nazi Germany: Social Forces and Personal Responsibility (1968c);
20th Century Russia: Agents of the Revolution (1968f);
The Civil War: Crisis in Federalism (1969a);
Race and Education: Integration and Community Control (1969b);
Status: Achievement and Social Values (1969c);
Revolution and World Politics: The Search for National Independence (1970d);
The Limits of War: National Policy and World Conscience (1970b);
Organization Among Nations: The Search for World Order (1970c);
Diplomacy and International Law: Alternatives to War (1970a);
Privacy: The Control of Personal Information (1971c);
The Progressive Era: Abundance, Poverty, and Reform (1971d);
Population Control: Whose Right to Live (1971c); and
Jacksonian Democracy: The Common Man in American Life (1971a).

In addition to these pamphlets printed by Xerox Education Publications, several more were adapted from or linked in some specific way to the Public Issues series:

Moral Reasoning: the Value of Life (Lockwood & Cutler, 1972); and
Social Action: Dilemmas and Strategies (Oliver, Newmann, & Morrill, 1972).

More recent updates and adaptations of earlier projects published by the Public Issues Series: Social Science Education Consortium include:

The Progressive Era: The Limits of Reform (Giese, 1989);
The Railroad Era: Business Competition and the Public Interest (Greenawald 1991), and
Science and Public Policy: Uses and Control of Knowledge (Singleton, Oliver, & Newmann, 1993).

Steve Feinberg, a former graduate student of Oliver's and now a noted Holocaust educator with the United States Holocaust Memorial Museum, related that when he first began teaching the subject of the Holocaust, the best material available at the time was the pamphlet from the Public Issues series (personal communication with Steve Feinberg, October 15, 2005).

Developing pamphlet units, of course, was not a revolutionary idea, and in addition to the out-of-date Rugg pamphlets, American Education Publications was publishing materials that focused on case studies for student understanding prepared by the editors of *Current Events; Everyweek, Our Time*, and *Read Magazine*. Thus, a case study approach and preparation of individual units for teacher use were instructional strategies popular in the 1960s and 1970s and cannot be seen as groundbreaking ideas stemming from Oliver alone. However, what is striking when reviewing the titles of the Public Issues Series is how the dilemmas are established in the titles of the pamphlets and how those dilemmas relate to the values delineated by the American Creed. This was not true of pamphlets and case studies developed by other authors and organizations. The point is, Oliver and Newmann, as well as the rest of the collaborative team, remained conscious at all times of the underlying theme they were encouraging teachers and students to explore, examine, debate, and evaluate: values necessary to understanding and promoting democratic citizenship. Even more interesting was their belief that this was best done by analyzing complex murky situations where it is conceivable that all parties have legitimate value concerns.[2] Thus, unlike the aforementioned Rugg materials, the Public Issues Series spends considerable written space to providing guidance to teachers about the mechanics of leading successful analytic discussions and providing instructional strategies that lead teachers to developing the needed comfort and expertise to handle these topics in the classroom.

In one particular pamphlet, *Cases and Controversy: Guide to Teaching the Public Issues Series*, Oliver and Newmann (1967b) provide teachers with guidelines and strategies for helping students to distinguish among prescriptive, descriptive, and analytic issues and the subcategories therein (pp. 4-5). Prescriptive issues, for example, involve judgments about what should or ought to be done—they are concerned with legitimacy and "rightness" or "wrongness" of certain policies or actions. As such, they are concerned with personal beliefs and conscience, public policy, ethics, and law. Descriptive issues focus on problems of fact (describing, interpreting, and explaining, and the truth of events or conditions—did they really occur), and the relations between the events and conditions. Analytic issues focus on meaning. They ensure that everyone is viewing an issue using the same definitions for problems and terminology.

The teacher's guide also addresses, in part, the power of analogy, the value of defining terms, and the significance of making critical distinctions. The latter is followed by a description of the discussion process, including the purpose of discussion, the teacher's role, and ways to evaluate discussion. The section on instructional strategies for classroom use includes the difference between Socratic discussion and other formats, including less confrontational discussion methods for those teachers or students uncomfortable with the directness and focus of the Socratic Method.

Some of the pamphlets included games (simulations) students could undertake. *The Railroad Era*, for example, included a simulation entitled "Railroad Game (pp. 21-22). The instructions for the latter are as follows: "Railroad competition was bitter in the 1870s. Could you have met its tough demands? This 'game'—simulating a real-life business problem—puts your mettle in meeting the challenge that faced railroad managers" (p. 21). The simulation divides the class into four groups representing the managers of four railroads for successive rounds. The "Review, Reflection, Research" section of the unit integrates the "game" experience with the readings to ensure that students understand the underlying concepts of the simulation.

Another instructional strategy that was recommended was the jurisprudential or legal-ethical model of instruction discussed by Oliver and Shaver (1974). (See chapter 8, "Using a Jurisprudential Framework in the Teaching of Public Issues.") The jurisprudential, or legal-ethical, approach focuses on a contemporary issue stated in concrete terms, that is, a case that is most often a current event. The teacher then "relates the contemporary case to cases which range widely in time and space, appealing especially to historical analogies to broaden the context of the discussion" (Oliver & Shaver, 1966, p. 145). Oliver and Shaver go on to say that it is the "amalgamation of law-government, ethics, contemporary, and historical factual questions developed around perennial issues of public policy that we refer to as *jurisprudential teaching*" (emphasis in the original) (Oliver & Shaver, 1966, p. 146). The authors make a point of differentiating this instructional strategy from "critical thinking," the latter of which they define as separating fact from opinion or identifying logical fallacy. More specifically, they state that "Our approach emphasizes the clarification of two or more legitimately held points of view as they bear on a public policy question. In general, there is much less concern with rhetorical devices or the logic of deductive reasoning than with the anatomy of legitimate communication and persuasion" (Oliver & Shaver, 1966, p. 146). The focus is on dialogue: either between student and teacher or between and amongst students. As such, the role of the teacher is "complex, requiring that he think on two levels at the same time" (Oliver & Shaver,

1966, p. 146). The teacher is required to "double think" both about the issue(s) under discussion and the intellectual process(es) by which the issue(s) can be clarified or resolved. This can be accomplished either through discussion or through a simulation such as a "mock trial." In either case, as an instructional strategy, the jurisprudential model of teaching requires that the teacher lead students through a series of eight steps which can be summarized as follows: (1) Abstracting General Values from Concrete Situations; (2) Using General Value Concepts as Dimensional Constructs; (3) Identifying Conflicts Between Value Constructs; (4) Identifying a Class of Value Conflict Situations; (5) Discovering or Creating Value Conflict Situations Which are Analogous to the Problem Under Consideration; (6) Working Toward a Qualified Position; (7) Testing the Factual Assumptions Behind a Qualified Value Position; and (8) Testing the Relevance of Statements (Oliver & Shaver, 1966, pp. 160-164).

In concluding their discussion of the jurisprudential model of teaching, Oliver and Shaver (1966) delineate their underlying assumptions about creating a social studies curriculum based on political controversy:

1.   It is useful to distinguish facts from values.
2.   It is useful to describe political controversy in terms of values rather than simply in terms of specific controversial cases.
3.   It is useful to differentiate the general values of the Creed from the ultimate concern of a democratic society, the dignity of man.
4.   The process of using comparative cases or analogies has the value of clarifying one's value positions and leading one toward an empirical statement of political disagreement.
5.   The methods of history, journalism, and the social sciences are appropriate ways of dealing with empirical disagreements.
     (pp. 164-165)

Over the years, Oliver and Shaver published multiple articles on the assessment of teacher-pupil interaction (Oliver & Shaver, 1963a), using content analysis of oral discussion to evaluate political education (Oliver & Shaver, 1963b), and the effect of teaching methods and interaction on learning to think critically (Shaver & Oliver, 1968). From the beginning, then, in addition to the development of content materials that would be challenging and interesting to students, a major concern of Oliver and Shaver was the development of a pedagogy to help effect change in the social studies classroom.

On a related but different note, in order to facilitate the use of the public issues materials in different courses, Oliver and Newmann (1967b, p. 8) presented ways in which teachers could integrate the pamphlets using an historical topic approach, a chronological-historical approach, a social science approach, a values-or issue oriented approach, a current problems approach or a simplicity-complexity dimension. Thus, while considerable leeway was given to the teacher for independent action, structures were provided to make implementation of the materials more accessible.

Tellingly, Newmann recounts that:

> As we thought about disseminating the materials to teachers, we imagined three groups: (1) those who would never agree to or would not understand this approach even with significant staff development; (2) those who would be sympathetic or interested but would need significant staff development to succeed; (3) those highly committed to the approach and able to implement it if only they had adequate instructional materials with modest teacher guides since they were unprepared to launch a major staff development effort. [Ultimately,] we decided to publish the series to serve mainly group three. (Personal communication with Fred Newmann, December 29, 2005)

In retrospect, the failure to implement the Public Issues series widely in the schools probably is due to several key reasons. Teacher resistance to such radically different material should not be underestimated nor should the resistance of school boards, administrations, and/or parents to the introduction of such controversial materials in the classroom. There are a considerable number of interest groups (both then and now) who do not accept the premise that history, especially American history, is open to question and interpretation or that the correct, that is, the most just path might not have been followed in all cases. And, while the authors clearly stated, as did Rugg concerning his materials, that the final perspective is open to student interpretation, the "Facts of the Case," the "Persistent Questions of Modern History" and the "Review, Reflection, Research" question sections all have an undeniably liberal bent. This might also be part of the reason why the fate of the Rugg, Oliver, Shaver and Newmann materials was similar.

Furthermore, the reality was that both the federal funding in the form of grants dried up and some of the principal writers were not really interested in teacher development (serious in-service, workshops, etc.) at that point in their careers.[3] Thus despite the excellence of the materials, they were never widely implemented. Concomitantly, as the various authors completed their studies, or obtained their doctoral degrees and, as in the case of Berlak, Shaver, and Newmann, moved onto the next stage of their careers, there was a geographic distance that was problematic. This problem was heightened by the fact that it appears Oliver was an individual who needed to engage face-to-face with his collaborators. Over and above that, he was notorious for neither opening his mail nor returning telephone messages. Shaver refers to this as an "out of sight, out of mind problem" (personal communication with James Shaver, January 3, 2005). Finally, and possibly most significantly, the principal author's interests diverged.

A CHANGE OF HEART:
PHILOSOPHY, EDUCATION, HOME, AND COMMUNITY

Throughout the period of the Harvard First Studies Project Oliver is reported to have been very unhappy in his marriage. He had three young children at home and by all accounts provided most of the childcare and did the majority of the household chores for 20 years. As early as 1967, Newmann and Oliver published an article titled *Education and Community*, and followed it up with *A Proposal for Education in Community* in 1975. Reading between the lines, it is clear that Oliver was searching for something missing from his life and it was not going to be remedied through rational discussion.

According to Polly Oliver, student unrest at Harvard in 1968 also had a deep impact on Oliver (personal communication with Polly Oliver, April 1, 2005). During the period, he lost respect for authority and for hierarchical organizations. He saw the 1960s as a revolution—a time when students rejected obedience and awe of authority—and he came to see that as real learning. Communal schools teaching nonviolent protest (e.g., the Highlander School) were preparing individuals such as Rosa Parks to stand up for their individual rights against the system. Some of the Highlander people became Oliver's students, and through his contact with them he became more interested in rural and adult education.

Shaver sees both of the above concerns as "a strong continuity between Don's thinking underlying the Harvard Project work and his later rejection of public schooling. Both reflect his strong drive, first laid out publicly in the 1957 article, to relentlessly examine assumptions, his own as well as those of others, and push to the logical end of that examination in his own conclusions about education" (personal communication with James Shaver, January 3, 2005).

It was after his divorce and subsequent happy marriage to Polly Oliver that references to singing, the importance of the religion through the church (Unitarian), and the affective aspects of life began to appear. Oliver's 1976 book, *Education and Community: A Radical Critique of Innovative Schooling* is seen by Newmann as Oliver's most important (and most difficult) work. The preface of this volume provides a solid sense of the change in Oliver's thinking at the time:

The initial premise of this book is that there is a crisis of will in the education professions, as well as the helping professions generally, because of a loss of faith in the liberal vision of the modern democratic society. Traditionally these professions have been built on psychological theories which provide guides for the improvement, correction, or growth of individual human beings. The theories have been (and are being) applied to curriculum reform, teacher training, the upgrading and humanization of supervisors and the process of supervision, the process of administration and the like. They run all the way from mechanistic statements about the nature of man (e.g., Skinner) to humane and sentimental statements stressing personal autonomy and self actualization (e.g., Rogers and Maslow). Beneath the application of these theories, however, is a technological model of progress. One creates a model of change; one applies it to individuals or institutions; one evaluates it to establish a "data base"; one then corrects the model and goes through the process a second time (the "double loop") etc. It is a straightforward research and development paradigm borrowed from the industrial revolution.

With this approach to social change, one does not usually look at the society as a whole, or the community, or the neighborhood. One looks at individual humans (i.e., clients) and the corporate institutions within which they behave and are managed. One assumes through gradual increments of behavior change managed by scientists and technicians some diffuse whole called "society" will get better and better.

We [sic] believe that the inability of the helping professions to act constitutes a loss of faith in this model of social change.

This theory is wrong-headed because it assumes that various primitive aspects of man's nature can be successfully extinguished or reconstructed. These aspects include, for example:

1. The need for small communities (bands, tribes, neighborhoods, etc.) as sources of support which stand midway between the intimate and volatile nuclear family and the work-oriented corporation;
2. The need for a concrete (and perhaps magical) religio-philosophical meaning system which explains the various mundane requirements of life; and
3. The need for validation and acceptance of the broad diversity of types (in age, sex, temperament, status, etc.) commonly found in human communities. (Oliver, 1976, p. vii-viii)

Oliver goes on to explain that the thesis of the book is the need to move to an understanding of how to create balance between primal and modern aspects of human community, thought systems, and personality. Doing so, he states, includes "creating a balance between efforts to maximize the potential development of each individual and recognizing the necessity and value of diversity among humans, even in such sensitive areas as intelligence, motivation, and social responsibility" (Oliver, 1976, p. ix). He closes the preface stating: "It is our [sic] hope that the book might provide a new conceptual basis for a social studies and humanities curriculum" (p. x).

As the years passed, Oliver studied more deeply the works of Alfred North Whitehead and became engaged in process philosophy. While he continued his interest in discussion, he was fundamentally a critic—an analyzer of society willing to follow questions to their logical/illogical conclusion not only about the United States but all societies and cultures. The contents of Part IV of *Education and Community* is illustrative of such a change (e.g., On the Kibbutz: A Modern Secular Community; The Hutterites: A Modern Religious Community; Marathon House: A Therapeutic Community; Highlander Folk School: A Social Action Community; Japanese-Americans: A Modern Ethnic Community; and The Peasant Village: Education to Encourage Cooperative Communal Attitudes).

Polly Oliver states that her husband frightened a lot of people by questioning assumptions that they did not even know they had! (Personal communication with Polly Oliver, April 1, 2005).

Gradually Oliver moved to a more holistic, affective place in his life. At the same time, in terms of the curriculum in general, and the social studies curriculum specifically, Oliver lost faith in the school system as a way of educating people as well as in purely rational discussion in classrooms as a means to improving citizenship. In his later writings, which actually begin in the 1970s, Oliver relates that he had been naïve. More specifically, he asserts that belief in Jeffersonian Enlightenment was not sufficient for creating a democratic community. In a review of Carbone's book on Rugg, Oliver (1978) writes: "The awareness of the ideological immaturity represented both in Rugg's work and my own … leads one less to personal embarrassment than to the search for a deeper and more realistic grounding of one's idealism" (p. 595). He continues in the review to indict all educational progressives for a failure to deal with the tension between morality and power. This fits with what Dan Proctor, a later graduate student and friend of Oliver's, said about Oliver moving to a more "systems" understanding and approach to life and its problems (personal communication, April 1, 2005). Proctor states that Oliver had set up and conceptualized the Harvard Social Studies Project before he had asked all the questions. He hadn't paid any attention to the economic system as a system. He had accepted a dichotomy between the moral and systems approach. But as time went on, Oliver no longer accepted a difference between public issues and social issues—they became, to his way of thinking, one and the same. Continuing, Proctor explained that to Oliver's way of thinking humanity is unconscious of fundamental systems. How else, he thought, can humanity destroy the planet? In moving to this new way of thinking, Oliver lived what he believed—he continued to financially support his extended family (ex-wife) and to include everyone in his and Polly's family in holidays, occasions, and so on. He rode a bike, walked, or took public transportation; and drove a car as little as possible. He sang in the church choir. He invited students to large meals on Friday nights for friendship and conversation. Tellingly, his last book is dedicated to "the domicile at 18 Willow Street," his home address.

Thus, in the end, Oliver no longer believed you could educate in formal schools. He took a sabbatical from Harvard and went to barber school because he began to believe that the best learning could be done in hair shops and coffee houses. He had a daughter who became an artist and he, too, studied art.

Oliver, as previous stated, was an intense individual who lived deeply and passionately. All the individuals interviewed for this chapter mentioned that although he was passionate, he was also intensely private. And, while a later graduate student felt that Oliver was supportive of their projects no matter what his personal opinion of them (personal communication with Steve Feinberg, October 15, 2005), Oliver did not really share his feelings with most of his early doctoral students.[4]

In the final analysis, it is not simple to "peg" Oliver. There is always the contradictory side of the man who continued to love Socratic confrontation, the man who loved the word "ambiguity" and used it often in his speech, the man who loved questions, but once he had found his answers, was no longer interested in pursuing that topic. The man who put people and community at the forefront of his philosophy, but who did not stay in touch with those who left his immediate environment, even when they made the effort to continue the relationship.

Oliver stopped focusing on the problem solving approach of the Public Issues Series as he became convinced that people could discuss things *ad infinitum*, but it wouldn't really change anything because people do not really listen to each other. He no longer believed in the secular state as a solution to social problems. Rather, he believed that people need community, spirituality, and religious institutions with their moral codes to provide structure. He no longer believed that the adherence to an abstract set of values, such as The American Creed, was workable. Human beings as a species, he sensed, simply aren't all that rational.

Of course it is interesting, almost prescient, to follow the trajectory of Oliver's work. His last books are dense, abstruse reconceptualist works focusing on community and personal solutions to social problems. It is as if he could foresee the melding of the issues he once so clearly separated as public and social, be they abortion, euthanasia, civil rights, or prayer in school. It makes one remember an old line from the Feminist movement of the 1960s: "the personal is political."

Oliver certainly continued to see a society beset by serious problems, but he no longer believed that the constitutional process as defined and taught by the new social studies materials would be the solution to the problem. In the end, Oliver would probably have us all living in small communities rather than large cities. He spent most of his adult life in the Cambridge area, and while he enjoyed day trips, he was not one to travel to academic conferences. He enjoyed the pleasures of home, hearth, and neighborhood. He would probably embrace the small schools movement as well as vouchers to give people power and choice over their own and their children's educations. He would look with favor on schools without walls and on de-schooling society in order for real learning to occur. He would not approve of the standards and high stakes testing so prevalent today, but he would find a quieter, gentler path to ensure that "no child be left behind" and that the society, and therefore the world, become a better, more inhabitable place. When all is said and done, it seems that Oliver's life, thought, and work was an ongoing search for a truly democratic community.

NOTES

1. James Shaver stated that the lasting influence Oliver had on his own life was "the importance of the examination of one's assumptions and their consistency with one another and with one's other beliefs and behavior" (personal communication with James Shaver, January 3, 2005).

2. In today's "you are with us or against us" mind-set, the idea of compromise and prioritizing values claims and recognizing the legitimacy of multiple perspectives seems long forgotten, and teachers seem to shy away from controversial issues, possibly due to a lack of expertise in handling these issues in the classroom.

3. Shaver, alone, did continue to work with staff development and inservice for teachers on these and similar materials he developed in Utah, and did so as late as 1993.

4. Be that as it may, Oliver had a tremendous impact on many of his students, and it must not go without saying that a large number of his doctoral students became major contributors to their academic fields—particularly in social studies—and dedicated to improving teaching and learning.

REFERENCES

Douglass, F. (1966). *Narrative of the life of frederick Douglass: An American slave.* New York: Crowell. (Original work published 1845)

Hansberry, L. (1966). *A raisin in the sun*. New York: New American Library. (Original work published 1958)

Harrington, M. (1962). *The other America: Poverty in the United States*. New York: Macmillan.

Gewertz, K. (2002, July 18). GSE Professor Donald Oliver is dead at 73. [electronic version]. *Harvard University Gazette*, pp. 1-2.

Giese, J. R. (1989). *The progressive era: The limits of reform*. Boulder, CO: Social Science Education Consortium.

Greenawald, D. G. (1991). *The railroad era: Business competition and the public interest*. Boulder, CO: Science Education Consortium.

Lockwood, A. & Cutler, C. L. (1972). *Moral reasonning: The value of life*. Columbus, OH: American Education Publications.

Myrdal, G. (1944). *An American dilemma: The Negro problem and modern democracy*. New York: Harper & Brothers.

Newmann, F. M., & Oliver, D. W. (1967). *Education and community*. [Social Studies]. Retrieved March 1, 2005, from the ERIC database.

Newmann, F. M., & Oliver, D. W. (1970). *Clarifying public controversy: An approach to teaching social studies*. [Social Studies]. Retrieved March 1, 2005, from the ERIC database.

Newmann, F. M., & Oliver, D. W. (1975). A proposal for education in community. [Social Studies]. *National Elementary Principal, 54*(3), 48-49. Retrieved March 1, 2005, from the ERIC database.

Oliver, D. W. (1968). The selection of content in the social studies. In J. P. Shaver & H. Berlak (Eds.), *Democracy, pluralism, and the social studies, readings and commentaries: An approach to curriculum decisions in the social studies* (pp. 17-42). Boston: Houghton Mifflin.

Oliver, D. W. (1976). *Education and community: A radical critique of innovative schooling*. Berkeley, CA: McCutchan.

Oliver, D. W. (1978). Reflections on Peter Carbone's *The social and educational thought of Harold Rugg*. [Social Studies]. Retrieved March 1, 2005, from the ERIC database, 593-597.

Oliver, D. W., & Newmann, F. M. (1967a). *The American revolution: Crisis of law and change*. Public Issues Series/Harvard Social Studies Project. Middletown, CT: American Education Publications.

Oliver, D. W., & Newmann, F. M. (1967b). *Cases and controversy: Guide to teaching the public issues series*/Harvard Social Studies Project and Supplement. [Social Studies]. Retrieved March 1, 2005, from the ERIC database.

Oliver, D. W., & Newmann, F. M. (1967c). *The immigrant's experience: Cultural variety and the "melting pot."* Public Issues Series/Harvard Social Studies Project. Middletown, CT: American Education Publications.

Oliver, D. W., & Newmann, F. M. (1967d). *Municipal politics: Interest groups and the government*. Public Issues Series/Harvard Social Studies Project. Middletown, CT: American Education Publications.

Oliver, D. W., & Newmann, F. M. (1967e). *Negro views of America: The legacy of oppression*. Public Issues Series/Harvard social studies project. [Social Studies]. Middletown, CT: American Education Publications. Retrieved March 1, 2005, from the ERIC database.

Oliver, D. W., & Newmann, F. M. (1967f). *The railroad era: Business competition and the public interest.* Public Issues Series/Harvard Social Studies Project. Middletown, CT: American Education Publications.

Oliver, D. W., & Newmann, F. M. (1967g). *Religious freedom: Minority faiths and majority rule.* Public Issues Series/Harvard Social Studies Project. Middletown, CT: American Education Publications.

Oliver, D. W., & Newmann, F. M. (1967h). *The rise of organized labor: Worker security and employer rights.* Public Issues Series/Harvard Social Studies Project. Middletown, CT: American Education Publications.

Oliver, D. W., & Newmann, F. M. (1967i). *Taking a stand: A guide to clear discussion of public issues.* Public Issues Series/Harvard Social Studies Project. Middletown, CT: American Education Publications.

Oliver, D. W., & Newmann, F. M. (1968a). *Communist China: Communal progress and individual freedom.* Public Issues Series/Harvard Social Studies Project. Middletown, CT: American Education Publications.

Oliver, D. W., & Newmann, F. M. (1968b). *Community change: Law, politics, and social attitudes.* Public Issues Series/Harvard Social Studies Project. Middletown, CT: American Education Publications.

Oliver, D. W., & Newmann, F. M. (1968c). *Nazi Germany: Social forces and personal responsibility.* Public Issues Series/Harvard Social Studies Project. Middletown, CT: American Education Publications.

Oliver, D. W., & Newmann, F. M. (1968d). *The new deal: Free enterprise and public planning.* Public Issues Series/Harvard Social Studies Project. Middletown, CT: American Education Publications.

Oliver, D. W., & Newmann, F. M. (1968e). *Rights of the accused: Criminal procedure and publics security.* Public Issues Series/Harvard Social Studies Project. Middletown, CT: American Education Publications.

Oliver, D. W., & Newmann, F. M. (1968f). *20th century Russia: Agents of revolution.* Public Issues Series/Harvard Social Studies Project. Middletown, CT: American Education Publications.

Oliver, D. W., & Newmann, F. M. (1969a). *The civil war: Crisis in federalism.* Public Issues Series/Harvard Social Studies Project. Middletown, CT: American Education Publications.

Oliver, D. W., & Newmann, F. M. (1969b). *Race and education: Integration and community control.* Public Issues Series/Harvard Social Studies Project. Middletown, CT: American Education Publications.

Oliver, D. W., & Newmann, F. M. (1969c). *Status: Achievement and social values.* Public Issues Series/Harvard Social Studies Project. Middletown, CT: American Education Publications.

Oliver, D. W., & Newmann, F. M. (1970a). *Diplomacy and international law: Alternatives to war.* Public Issues Series/Harvard Social Studies Project. Middletown, CT: American Education Publications.

Oliver, D. W., & Newmann, F. M. (1970b). *The limits of war: National policy and world conscience.* Public Issues Series/Harvard Social Studies Project. Middletown, CT: American Education Publications.

Oliver, D. W., & Newmann, F. M. (1970c). *Organizations among nations: The search for world order.* Public Issues Series/Harvard Social Studies Project. Middletown, CT: American Education Publications.

Oliver, D. W., & Newmann, F. M. (1970d). *Revolution and world politics: The search for national independence.* Public Issues Series/Harvard Social Studies Project. Middletown, CT: American Education Publications.

Oliver, D. W., & Newmann, F. M. (1971a). *Jacksonian democracy: The common man in American life.* Middletown, CT: American Education Publications.

Oliver, D. W., & Newmann, F. M. (1971b). *Population control: Whose right to live.* Middletown, CT: American Education Publications.

Oliver, D. W., & Newmann, F. M. (1971c). *Privacy: The control of personal information.* Middletown, CT: American Education Publications.

Oliver, D. W., & Newmann, F. M. (1971d). *The progressive era: Abundance, poverty, and reform.* Middletown, CT: American Education Publications.

Oliver, D. W., Newmann, F. M., & Bane, M. J. (1967). *Cases and controversy: Guide to teaching the public issues series*/Harvard Social Studies Project and Supplement. [Social Studies]. Retrieved March 1, 2005, from the ERIC database.

Oliver, D. W., Newmann, F. M., & Morrill, G. (1972). *Social Action: Dilemmas and strategies.* Middletown, CT: Xerox Corp.

Oliver, D. W., & Shaver, J. P. (1963a, February 15). *The development of a multidimensional observational system for the analysis of pupil-teacher interaction.* [Social Studies]. Retrieved March 1, 2005, from the ERIC database.

Oliver, D. W., & Shaver, J. P. (1963b, February 15). *The use of content analysis of oral discussion as a method of evaluating political education.* [Social Studies]. Retrieved March 1, 2005, from the ERIC database.

Oliver, D. W., & Shaver, J. P. (1966). *Teaching public issues in the high school.* Boston: Houghton Mifflin.

Oliver, D. W., & Shaver, J. P. (1974). Using a jurisprudential framework in the teaching of public issues. In D. W. Oliver & J. P. Shaver *Teaching Public issues in the High School* (pp. 145-169). Logan: Utah State University Press.

Oliver, D. W., & Shaver, J. P. (1996). Using a jurisprudential framework in the teaching of public issues. In W. C. Parker (Ed.), *Educating the democratic mind* (pp. 145-168). Albany: State University of New York Press.

Oliver, D. W., & Shaver, J. P., with Berlak, H., & Van Seasholes, E. (1962). *The analysis of public controversy: A study in citizenship education.* Boston: Harvard Graduate School of Education.

Shaver, J. P., & Oliver, D. W. (1968, February 9). *The effect of student characteristic-teaching method interactions on learning to think critically.* [Social Studies]. Retrieved March 1, 2005, from the ERIC database.

Singleton, L. R., Oliver, D. W., & Newmann, F. M. (1993). Science and public policy: Uses and control of knowledge. Boulder, CO: Social Science Education Consortium.

Wright, R. (1945). *Black boy: A record of childhood and youth.* New York: Harper & Row.

CHAPTER 16

E. JOSEPH PIEL

The Making of a Risk Taker in Academia

Barbara S. Spector

INTRODUCTION

Place: South Pacific
Scene: A marine dive-bomber cruises the beautiful blue sky
over lush green jungles
Sound: Ack-Ack-Ack Ack-Ack-Ack
Speaker: There you are! I've got you now
Sound: Whiz Boom!

This scene was enacted numerous times for 3 years as E. Joseph Piel, marine pilot, deliberately drew fire from antiaircraft guns "buried" in the jungles on places with legendary names like Guadalcanal, Bougainville, and the Solomon Islands. The anti-aircraft installations guarding enemy airfields during World War II were so well camouflaged there was no way

Addressing Social Issues in the Classroom and Beyond: The Pedagogical Efforts of Pioneers in the Field, 291–305
Copyright © 2007 by Information Age Publishing
All rights of reproduction in any form reserved.

to locate them except to hope the guns would fire at his plane. During what he described as his "government-sponsored vacation in the South Pacific" it was Piel's job to take out such installations so other planes could bomb the airfields. Piel was doing what he loved to do, flying airplanes.

Before going to Navy Flight School, Piel did a 6-month stint as an air controller for the Federal Aviation Administration (FAA), a job for which he had to have the proverbial "nerves of steel." It is easy to understand why taking, what most in academia would call "risks," led Piel to assert: "Maybe it was because of my experience during the war, I ended up not being afraid of taking chances.... Curriculum problems didn't really bother me that much" (J. Piel, personal interview with author, December 20, 2005). And take academic risks he did!

LIFE CHRONOLOGY

Emil Joseph Piel was born April 17, 1918 in Fairview, New Jersey. Piel's father, born in New York City, was an engineer with the Alcoa Aluminum Company in Edgewater, New Jersey. While working and raising a family, Piel's father earned his degree from the International Correspondence School. Piel's mother, born in Cheshire, Connecticut, married at 16. She was 20 years old when Piel was born. Piel, the youngest of three children, was encouraged to go to college, while his two sisters went directly into the work force.

Piel and his family moved to Edgewater, New Jersey, where Piel entered the second grade. Piel recalled an event from those early years that still has an impact on him today. While telling him he was "writing with the wrong hand," the second grade teacher took the pencil out of his left hand and put it in his right. When he told his mother, she said, "Well, if that's what the teacher said, that's what it is." He attributes his poor handwriting to this switch.

The Edgewater neighborhood in which Piel grew up comprised working-class families. Only a few people had cars. During the Depression, Piel's father retained his job—one of the lucky few who did so. Because of this, Piel does not recall being especially affected by the uncertainty of growing up during the Great Depression. In fact, he didn't know his family was poor. He does remember, however, that he had to learn to eat everything on his plate.

Piel recalls another event that occurred when he was 9 years of age. His uncle taught him how to drive a Model T Ford using all three pedals on the floor—one each for the gas, the brake and reverse. (This early experience stimulated his interest in automobiles, which has continued throughout his career.) Piel also became active in the Boy Scouts of America, becoming a Life Scout, and eventually an assistant scoutmaster. It was during these early years that his lifetime involvement with church groups began with the Young People's Fellowship in Fort Lee.

Piel excelled in school and was especially interested in science and mathematics. Early on in his education he was placed in the college preparatory track in the Fort Lee secondary school he attended. Although academically inclined, he also had an interest in athletics. He went out for football, but football was canceled because too few students participated. Having a desire to be involved in extracurricular activities, he turned his attention to band and became student director of the orchestra, the drum major, and the twirler. The band marched in Memorial Day and Fourth of July parades and other town celebrations. In order to earn extra money, Piel learned to play the drums in secondary school and was in a "filler Big Band trio"—playing when the regular band was taking a 10 or 15 minute break—in the Catskills mountain hotels. Eventually, Piel did get to play football and participate in track when he became a student at Montclair College in 1936. Prior to his decision to attend Montclair College, Piel was offered a scholarship at Stevens College, but the award was not sufficient to cover the entire cost of tuition. Thus, instead of going to school, he went to work at Alcoa as a laborer making boxes in which aluminum was packed and then later worked in the rolling mills where they rolled ingots of aluminum into thin sheets of aluminum. Of this period, he has written:

> I couldn't go to college, even though I had the scholarship; we just didn't have the money for me to go to [college], especially to Stevens, where it was expensive. Well, I was invited by the band director at Montclair State, [who] knew the band director from Fort Lee High School, and he said, "We have a band, but we don't have anybody to lead the band. We don't have a drum major. We don't have the twirler," and this fellow, Charlie Grohl, said, "Oh, I know somebody," and I was working in the factory at the time.... So, he encouraged me to go to Montclair to lead the band, even though I was working in the factory.... To get to Montclair, I went to New York and took a train to Montclair, and then, from downtown Montclair, I took a bus up to the college, and so, I got introduced to Montclair State at that time.... This band director said, "Gee, would you like to come to Montclair?" I said, "Yes," and he said, "Well, I'll see if I can get you a scholarship." So, we met with the director of music at Montclair State, Dr. McKeeken, a very large and imposing woman, and he told her that I'd been leading the band and I was going to come to Montclair and he wondered if I might get a music scholarship.... She looked at me and she waved her arm imperiously ... toward the piano and said, "Play," and I said, "I don't play the piano." (Laughter.) I said, "I play the drums," and she never said another word to me, but she ate him out right in front of me, saying, "What are you doing, bringing this idiot here for a scholarship?" but I went anyway (laughter)

because I enjoyed science and they had an outstanding science department. (Illingworth & Whitman, 2005)

In Piel's junior year of college the government offered no-cost pilot training through a civil pilot training program. He jumped at the opportunity to learn to fly and continued in that flight program through 1942, even though he graduated from college in 1940. He earned both a private pilot's license and a commercial license. The latter, however, was short lived. In September 1941, he had to make a cross-country flight when he was getting his instructor's license and flew over the White House by mistake. The Federal Aviation Authority (FAA) revoked his commercial license immediately. Shortly thereafter, ironically, the FAA recruited him on December 1, 1941, to be an associate air traffic controller in Jacksonville, Florida. It took 6 months for him to find a way to get out of that "seat job" and back to flying. He enthusiastically volunteered for military flight training, graduating a year later as a second lieutenant marine pilot. Within a relatively short time, he was deployed to the South Pacific as a combat pilot.

Piel married in 1945. Compliments of the GI Bill, he subsequently earned his Master's degree from Montclair State University in 1947. He taught high school physics from 1948 to 1952 at Caldwell High School in New Jersey. With his Bachelor's and Master's degrees, he was qualified to teach all the science courses and all the mathematics courses in a high school. These qualifications provided the context for his next career move in 1952, which was as chair of the Science Department at East Orange High School in New Jersey. He remained there until 1960 while simultaneously earning a doctoral degree in Supervision and Curriculum in 1960 from Rutgers University.

For his dissertation, he documented what he recently described as the horrible situation in physics teaching.

> It was a sterile subject and not many people would take the course.... All one did was learn a series of laws that have no use to them personally. Students had no picture of what it was good for.... Those that did take the course usually hated it. (J. Piel personal interview with the author, December 20, 2005).

The textbooks physics teachers studied in college and used in their own classrooms at that time had all the physics to be taught in the beginning of the chapter. A few paragraphs at the end of the chapter might have offered applications of how a principle worked. According to Piel, such textbooks did not include what he thought was most important. More specifically, he was clear that physics needed to be made interesting by relating it to the real world. Teachers, he felt, therefore, needed to get industry experience. In his dissertation, Piel included a plan for the reeducation of New Jersey's physics teachers and the numerous people returning from World War II service going into teaching. As Chair of the Science Department in East Orange High School, he ensured that all of his colleagues had invitations to work at Bell Laboratories, do public service, or work at the local electrical company for a couple of weeks during the academic year or in the summer.

In 1961, Piel became principal of West Essex High School, and remained in that position until he left in 1966 to begin a faculty career in higher education. While in public education, Dr. Piel took full advantage of the K-12 public school calendar by using his summers to contribute to the science education enterprise. For example, during the summers of 1956 to 1960, while he was science department chair, he joined the Physical Science Study Committee (PSSC), a group of university and high-school educators established at the Massachusetts Institute of Technology (MIT) to develop a new high-school physics course, *PSSC Physics* (which was published in 1960). F. James Rutherford (founder of Project 2061 and chief education officer of the American Association for the Advancement of Science), better known as Jim, was among the leaders of this *PSSC Physics* initiative. It was a landmark in science education in that it was the first of what was to become a series of major NSF-funded curriculum reform projects, the so-called "alphabet curricula" of the 1960s and early 1970s.

Piel was pleased with the originality of the laboratory experiments in *PSSC Physics*. Indeed, he thought that the activities and experiments were a good start for students to experience "hands-on" physics research for which they could not find the answers in the textbook. However, Piel also was disappointed that *PSSC Physics* fell short by not relating the physics content to the problems of society.

During the summer of 1965 Piel had a unique experience working full time for Bell Laboratories. This experience helped solidify his belief that all science teachers need opportunities to learn about science and technology in the workplace in order to make science relevant to learners. He was also convinced that teaching basic physics without simultaneously focusing directly on its applications in the world beyond the classroom was not productive.

When he returned to Bell Laboratories, he explored more concrete avenues involving technology and its interaction with society. Ed David, Director of Computers at Bell Laboratories, and John Truxal, Chair of Electrical Engineering at Brooklyn Polytechnic Institute, agreed with Piel that they needed to look at how technology affects society and how society affects technology. Thus began the talk of a radically different curriculum project for high school science, *The Man Made World* (TMMW) (1971).[1]

Piel accepted a position in 1966 at The Brooklyn Polytechnic Institute, (whose name was later changed to Polytechnic University of New York in Brooklyn), and remained there until 1972. He also served as the Executive Director of the Engineering Concepts Curriculum Project (ECCP), a National Science Foundation (NSF)-funded project which was responsible for the development of the high school curriculum entitled *The Man Made World* (TMMW). At the latter, Piel worked closely with the Co-Directors of ECCP, John Truxal and Ed David.

In 1972, Piel and two accomplished colleagues who shared his vision and attitude toward risk-taking joined forces with John Truxal to go to the State University of New York at Stony Brook on Long Island. Truxal went to Stony Brook as the Dean of the College of Engineering, Piel as a tenured full professor to develop the Department of Technology and Society in the College of Engineering; and Tom Liao as faculty appointee in the latter department. They finished writing *TMMW* at Stony Brook and published it in 1972.

A recurring theme among those who know him well is Piel's devotion to people. He cared greatly about his colleagues, students, family, and his church. When the move from Brooklyn Polytechnic Institute to Stony Brook took place, Piel elected to remain living in his home in New Jersey, because it meant his wife could continue working with her church. This is remarkable when one realizes it meant Piel spent at least two hours driving to Stony Brook on Long Island and two hours back to New Jersey every day. It is no wonder he often-used concepts related to the automobile to illustrate Science/Technology/Society (STS) issues (J. Truxal, personal interview with author, February 23, 2006).

The Department of Technology and Society at Stony Brook flourishes to this day and is a leading resource for the science/technology/society (STS) interaction movement worldwide. STS is the umbrella label for the reform of science education that became prominent after 1982 when a media blitz, orchestrated by the National Academy of Sciences, informed the world there was a serious crisis in science and mathematics education.[2]

In 1985 Piel was also a vital actor in the development of the National Association of Science Technology and Society (NASTS), now the *International* Association of Science Technology and Society (IASTS). NASTS was the brainchild of Rustum Roy, Professor of Solid State, Geochemistry, and Science/Technology Society at The Pennsylvania State University and John Truxal, but they encouraged Piel to take a major role in forming the association.

In the second half of the twentieth century, while Piel's career was expanding, two major initiatives were undertaken that created visions for what science education should be in the United States. They were *Project*

Synthesis (1980) and *Project 2061* (Johnson, 1989 and 1993). Norris Harms, director of *Project Synthesis*, invited Piel to chair one of the six committees developing data bases for the project titled The Science/Technology and Society (STS) Committee. Significantly, chapter 11 in the *Project Synthesis Final Report* to NSF described the desired state for school science relating to STS. Knowing Piel from the PSSC Physics days, as well as Piel's work on *Project Synthesis*, Jim Rutherford invited Piel to participate in one of *Project 2061's* five committees whose charge was to describe an ideal vision of science education. In essence, *Project 2061* is a second-generation spin off of *Project Synthesis*. As a result, Piel's beliefs about the role of science, technology, and society in science education became a vision embraced by AAAS.

Piel became Professor Emeritus in 1987 when he formally retired from Stony Brook. However, he continued working through 2002 as a consultant with the Department of Technology and Society he had helped to create.

Today, Piel directs his talents to working with his church, enjoying his family, his second marriage, and traveling. He plans to return to the Solomon Islands for the first time since WWII on a pleasure cruise in March and April 2006.

INTRODUCING SOCIAL ISSUES
INTO THE CURRICULUM

A major venture into teaching applied physics, or what is today frequently labeled "problem-based learning," beckoned when Piel returned from military service. A major goal of his was to make physics interesting for students.

Piel's love of planes led to his fascination with the connection between humans and machines and, ultimately, to his including the connection in his curriculum. Inspiration for including this relationship in his teaching also came from an article he read in a science teacher's journal around 1955 by an author from Purdue University.

Piel also created and taught an entire course around the automobile, building on teenagers notorious love for cars. All the physics principles being taught in this physics course were actually principles that were used in automobile systems (e.g., how Archimedes' principle is manifested in the "float" in the carburetor; the spraying of gasoline and air mixture into the engine is a clear example of Bernoulli's principle; and the forces that move the pistons up and down in the engine demonstrates Boyles and Charles' laws). Piel even had a surplus helicopter engine set up in his classroom so he could teach about engines.

From such experiences, Piel became interested in other areas of social interactions of science and technology. Since so many of his students enjoyed music, he also chose to use music to teach physics.

At one National Science Teachers Association (NSTA) conference in which Piel was showcasing the teaching of physics through the automobile, someone said "but how do you get kids into college if you have been teaching physics through the automobile?" Piel replied: "I'll tell you about one kid I taught. He managed to get into MIT and his big problem was he never got out of MIT, because he ended up as president. That was Paul Gray. He was also President of AAAS."

LIFE AS FODDER FOR CURRICULA

Piel used his own daily life experiences and those of his students as sources of real world problems for teaching. When he was at a workshop in Wichita, Kansas, in the early 1970s, he discovered that the yellow and the red streetlights in the city came on almost simultaneously. As a result, a driver would end up going through the red light and get fined and, in fact, this happened to Piel. This experience and the discovery resulted in Piel addressing how long it takes a car going at the speed limit to stop after the driver sees a yellow light and knows that he or she has to stop. It became clear the law did not take into account technology, and thus it was not possible for a driver to comply with the law. Piel was not the only victim of getting a traffic summons for going through the light. One of the teachers with whom he worked had a similar experience. The teacher wrote a letter complete with charts to the court showing it was impossible to stop in the length of time he was given. This street light incident illustrated why Piel insisted learners understand that there is a need to have a balance between technology, law, and education.

Another example of "real life" as fodder for the curriculum came with the emergence of cell phones in the early to mid-1980s. Piel asked his students to investigate the interaction between cell phones and society. They learned that there were many associated societal problems. Among some of the many were as follows: communities wanted the service, but did not want the cell phone towers to be built in their communities; towers were built in the migratory pathway of birds, and as a result thousands of birds flew directly into cell phone towers; and at certain frequencies there was an effect on the problem-solving abilities of a person using the phone.

When reminiscing about how he used his experience in air traffic control as a frame of reference for STS teaching, Joe indicated the following: "Keeping planes on a particular schedule so they don't run into another airplane on a different schedule going to the same airport is actually a mathematical problem that is a technology/society problem."

A point Piel often made about STS was for every technical problem there is a solution that is forthright, simple, direct, and … wrong. Without deliberate education, people often look at the obvious facets of a problem and make decisions with negative spinoffs, many of which could have been anticipated, mitigated, if not prevented.

THE MAN-MADE WORLD

When asked what his most significant contribution to science education was, Piel responds without hesitation, *The Man Made World* (TMMW)—the seeds of which were sown when he returned to summer work at Bell Laboratories after working with the PSSC Physics group. The keys to Piel's beliefs about science education are found in this product. Making science teaching relevant and meaningful to learners can be done by using real world societal problems and studying the embedded science and technology necessary to solve such problems.

It was clear to Piel that the interface of technology, science, and society was best addressed through engineering principles. Engineering is about solving problems based on principles of decision-making, optimization, feedback, stability, and so forth. To solve societal problems, therefore, people have to know something about engineering principles. In this regard, Piel notes that:

> When we wrote the *TMMW*, we started with the principles of engineering as we were solving the problems. Physics is a perfect medium for analysis, if done the right way. Our approach was here are some problems and here we need to learn the physics to solve the problems. What are the systems you can use to solve the problem? What are the society/technology interactions? The problem solving here involves a technological solution, or a political solution such as a law, or education, (e.g., educating the public as to why they should be saving water or energy, etc.). (J. Piel personal interview by the author, December 20, 2005)

Tellingly Piel likens the writing of a chapter for the study of physics to writing a mystery story, which, in turn, enables the learner to experience the intrigue that drives scientists and technologists. He noted that when authors write mystery stories, "They start with the murder. They don't start with how the police organization works. They eventually get around to explaining how the system works to solve the problem. It should be the same way with science, technology, and society" (J. Piel personal interview by the author, December 20, 2005).

TMMW targeted high school students somewhere between their sophomore science courses and junior physics courses. Physics was not a prerequisite for students to take the *TMMW* course. When the "back to basics movement" started in the 1970s, Piel was vocal that *TMMW* was as basic as the three R's. *TMMW* enjoyed about a decade of publication and distribution by the book publisher McGraw Hill, and it also served as a point of departure for spinoffs, such as a college liberal arts curriculum titled *Technology: Handle with Care* (1975); *People, Technology, Society*, for middle school students; and a video tape series, *You and Me and Technology* by M. Galey (1981) of the University of Denver, for which Piel was the content specialist.

IMPLEMENTATION OF THE MAN MADE WORLD

Because *TMMW* was a huge contrast to all other physics courses taught in a high school at that time, or any other science course for that matter, it required special attention for implementation. More specifically, people had to spend significant time learning how to teach it. It also required educators with outstanding teaching skills and a disposition to be risk takers. Indeed, one needed to be willing to take chances to teach the course. For about 10 years (1970-1980) NSF and *The Sloan Foundation* supported summer institutes designed to enable teachers to become adept at using *TMMW*. The Sloan Foundation also supported workshops for science supervisors and for university faculty, many of whom would eventually educate future teachers and encourage minorities to go into engineering.

Piel used teacher centers in Houston, Texas; San Diego, California; and Lakewood, Colorado, for his summer institutes. Humor was a key teaching tool expertly used by Piel. An interchange that occurred frequently when learners weren't as productive as they might have been looked like this: *Student*: "But I'm really trying very hard." *Piel*: (with a perfectly straight face), "Well, sometimes you are more trying than others" (T. Liao, personal communication with the author, February 23, 2006). Over and above the summer institutes, *TMMW* was ultimately translated into Japanese by Japanese educators who were looking for something to improve their science program and found *TMMW* much to their liking.

CHALLENGES TO CHANGE

Around the time *TMMW* was being implemented, *Man a Course of Study* (*MACOS*) (Education Development Center, 1979), a social studies program, was also being implemented across the nation. *MACOS* examined societies, one of which was the Eskimos. One aspect of the Eskimo society described in *MACOS* was the cultural practice of older Eskimos being set afloat on an iceberg where they could die peacefully. This generated a public outcry against the use of *MACOS*. In many people's minds, *MACOS* and *TMMW* were lumped together, and that created political problems for TMMW.

Another challenge faced by *TMMW* emerged from the need for teachers to be educated to implement it. *TMMW* was not something teachers were able to simply pick up like a textbook and follow. Another problem centered around the fact that pioneer cadres of teachers and supervisors who went through the summer institutes were of such high quality that they were frequently offered opportunities to expand their careers out of the classroom. And finally, as a result of cutbacks in support for the summer institutes, there were few people with *TMMW* experience left in the schools to teach it. The latter resulted in a constant need for more people to be educated but that need could not be adequately met. As a result, when some schools ran out of appropriately educated teachers, those who actually ended up teaching *TMMW* were not competent to teach it. In addition, schools saw that less able students were capable of benefitting from the course; and thus, as *TMMW* began to be used with less academically capable kids it gradually begun to be perceived as a "dumbed" down physics course.

Another obstacle to wide dissemination of *TMMW* was the stovepipe organization of disciplines (a commonly used term to represent the separation of the science disciplines into biology, chemistry, physics, and earth science) in both high schools and college. Overcoming past conservative curriculum management in schools became a serious frustration for Piel. *TMMW* did not fit in a traditional niche in educational institutions, because it was not biology, chemistry, physics, or earth science. As a result, its acceptability was questioned by college admission officers. Piel frequently had to write letters describing the course before it would be accepted as a serious college preparatory science course. Each time he did so, though, the higher education institutions accepted it.

Vestiges of *TMMW's* impact remained imbedded in STS in many school science courses in K-16, but it did not succeed in mitigating the barrier presented by the organization of the traditional disciplines. The concepts behind *TMMW* are now being taught in physics, chemistry, and biology around the country as part of the STS movement. Still, *TMMW* was instrumental in launching the STS movement, and the significance of Piel's contribution should not be underestimated.

Throughout his career Piel wrote instructional programs, textbooks, videos, and computer programs. He also pioneered the use of the unique capacities of the computer to create programs enabling learners to construct an understanding of science and engineering concepts that had been difficult for students to comprehend using other materials. A favorite is the animated computer simulation to teach about optics and the persistence of vision.

LESSON LEARNED IN REGARD TO SURVIVING UNIVERSITY POLITICS

Piel's situation is a classic example of some of the positive benefits of having tenure in order to be free enough to concentrate on being a serious innovator. A key to that freedom, of course, is also having administrators with the vision to support the innovators. The President of Stony Brook, Dr. Marberger, and the Dean of the college in which Piel's department resided, Dr. Truxal, were enthusiastic supporters of STS. In fact, Truxal retired as dean after about 5 years and joined the department where he focused on STS. Both of these gentlemen and their ongoing support greatly benefitted Piel.

The "publish or perish" syndrome demands great amounts of time being devoted to writing journal articles for science education or engineering education journals, or discipline-specific science or engineering journals. Interestingly, due to his unique and innovative work, Piel was not pressured by his administrators to play the "publish or perish game" that has led so many newer faculty to giving new names to old ideas. As a result, Piel was able to channel his creative energies into the research and development of innovative curricular materials. He did whatever research was necessary to inform the ongoing development of materials, but did not publish these findings in refereed journals. Rather, the department published them for use internally or when funding was being sought.

It is quite clear that this dive-bomber with nerves of steel used his disciplined military background to facilitate a productive career. But his ability to engage others in his mission and get the most out of the people he worked with came from his flexibility, devotion, wonderful sense of humor, good heart, and excellent people skills. Piel's leadership style was such that people just soaked up the wisdom he had. He never pushed it on anyone (T. Liao, personal communication with the author, February 23, 2006). "Joe was flexible and easy to work with regardless of one's position, and he knew how to get things done.... Piel led by example and was never afraid to try something new" (T. Liao, personal communication with the author, February 23, 2006).

Piel, who has been described as the "grandfather" of *TMMW*, has had a tremendous impact on science education throughout his life, and his legacy continues today through all those he mentored.

NOTE

1. The use of sexist language in science education was still acceptable at the time. This curriculum will be discussed in more detail later in this chapter.
2. There are multiple understandings of what the STS movement engenders, and because of this the following explanation is included to assist individuals to more deeply appreciate how STS is both understood and misunderstood by educators:

> Some equate STS to a curriculum organizer, others equate it to topics to be studied, and still others equate it to a particular instructional strategy. It helps me to place the interpretations on a continuum: On the left of the continuum people use the traditional textbook, which is organized around the structure of a discipline. They consider themselves to be teaching STS, because there is a paragraph or section at the end of each chapter identifying a specific application of the scientific principle in that chapter to a technology used in society. These teachers' goal is usually to cover information in the textbook. The intended outcome is for students to pass a test that allows them to go to the next grade level for science.
>
> Moving to the right on the continuum, people use STS as the label for teaching through themes that cut across all the sciences. For example, energy, or cause and effect, are used to talk about things as diverse as plate tectonics and the human digestive system.
>
> Continuing to the right on the continuum are those who consider teaching STS to be addressing topics comprising identifiable components of science, technology, and [the latter's] impact [on] society. Effecting a change in society, even in the smallest way, is enough to be classified as teaching STS. It would be as simple as talking about cautions in home canning of fruit in a unit on microorganism and disease, or the use of moving walkways to facilitate passage in airports. They often use existing technology as the context to interest students in learning science principles inherent in technology (e.g., physics principles inherent in a toy).
>
> Further to the right on the continuum, people insist there must be a problematic issue, something for which there is no single solution, if teaching is to be labeled STS. Their position is STS requires risk assessment, cost/benefit analysis, environmental impact analysis, tradeoffs, and decision-making. The needs of individuals and diverse groups with vested interests are considered in [the] decision-making. The interaction of moral and ethical values people hold

derived from ways of knowing other than science—such as religion, philosophy, or aesthetics—become part of the data to explicitly consider in the decision-making process. The scientific enterprise is portrayed as a dynamic human endeavor; a part of society in which changes in science and technology effect decisions people make, and decisions people make effect further scientific and technological developments and the future of our planet.

On the right hand of the continuum, people interpret STS as a synonym for constructivist (one makes sense of new data by adding, deleting, or rearranging information in one's idiosyncratic cognitive framework) epistemology, learning theory, and teaching/learning approaches. The intended outcome for students is to learn how to learn, so they are capable and inclined to make reasoned decisions in our science and technology driven society. Learners become scientifically and technologically literate through systematically inquiring into STS events, which are multifaceted issues that challenge society and the future of the planet. STS is used as an organizer of the entire curriculum, integrating many disciplines. (Spector, 2005, pp. 193-194)

The people functioning at the right-hand end of the continuum assume that knowledge developed in individual disciplines needs to be reorganized when it is taught in schools.

REFERENCES

Education Development Center. (1970). *Man: A course of study*. Washington, DC: Curriculum Development Associates.

Engineering Concepts Curriculum Project. (1971). *The man-made world*. New York: McGraw-Hill.

Galey, M. (1981). *You, me, technology*. [Film Series] Boulder: University of Colorado.

Harms, N. (1980). *Synthesis: An interpretive consolidation of research identifying needs in natural science education*. [Final Report]. NSF-SED-80-003.

Illingworth, S., & Whitman, D. (2005). *Oral history of Joseph Piel*. Retrieved April, 29, 2005 from http://fasHistory.rutgers.edu/oralhistory/Interviews/Piel_emil.html

Johnson, J. R. (1989). *Technology: Report of the 2061 Phase Technology Panel*. Washington, DC: American Association for the Advancement of Science.

Liao, T., & Piel, E. J. (1970). Let's get relevant. *The Physics Teacher 8*(2), 74-82.

Light, K., Tallon, L., Clark, B., Lobis, F., Disbrow, J., & Patton, J. (1988). *You, me, and technology*. Bloomington, IN: Agency for Instructional Technology.

Physical Science Study Committee. (1960). *PSSC Physics*. Boston: D. C. Heath.

Piel, E. J. & Truxal, J. G. (1975). *Technology, handle with care*. New York: McGraw-Hill.

Spector, B. S. (2005). Serendipity: A paradigm shifter's friend in academia. In S. Totten & J. E. Pedersen (Eds.), *Researching and teaching social issues: The per-*

sonal stories and pedagogical efforts of professors of education (pp. 181-206). Lanham, MD: Lexington Books.

CHAPTER 17

MAXINE GREENE

"Wide-Awakeness" as a Prerequisite for Moral Vigilance and Action

Samuel Totten

For me, education must have to do with what is to be, what is not yet, even as it has to do with keeping something alive. It has to do with empowering, with releasing, with developing—in diverse ways—critical and creative capacities. It has to do with enabling persons to become different from the way they have been, to become courageous enough to renew what they have come to hold in common, to imagine things, especially insufficient things, being otherwise than they are. (Greene, 1982, p. 1)

INTRODUCTION

In my mind's eye, whenever I think about Maxine Greene I see her reddish brown hair, aged but lively countenance, and bright eyes behind large lensed spectacles. I hear her gravelly voice (a result, no doubt, of her Brooklyn accent grated on by years of smoking cigarettes), and the ever-present words and phrases she uses in her lectures, essays, books, and

Addressing Social Issues in the Classroom and Beyond: The Pedagogical Efforts of Pioneers in the Field, 307–324
Copyright © 2006 by Information Age Publishing
All rights of reproduction in any form reserved.

conversations (at least with her students and colleagues). Such words and phrases as: "mindfulness"; "wide-awakeness"; "to challenge the taken-for-granted"; "the capacity to surpass the given and look at things as if they could be otherwise"; "to choose" and "critical self-reflectiveness."[1]

One could easily write a "lexiographic biography" of Maxine Greene, and in doing so illuminate her deepest passions and commitments. While the aforementioned words and phrases are those of a philosopher; they are those of a unique philosopher—one who is committed to not only examining ontological and existential questions but who deeply cares about how "lived lives" are played out and impact one another, education, and society. Indeed, she is one who wrestles with and inquires into what it takes to create a better, more just, and more equitable life for one and all.

As an existential phenomenologist, Maxine's focus has, in her own words, been "concerned with human individuality in the most radical sense, with subjectivity, with authenticity, with learning as a process of self-identification or as a pursuit of Being," and "in consciousness and the ways in which the world is grasped by human beings born into cultures, into social contexts, trying to interpret the world as perceived, the world as imagined, the world as known" (Greene, 1982, p. 3).

Interestingly, almost every one of the aforementioned words or phrases—in reality, many are key concepts—is germane to thinking about, teaching about, and acting upon critical social issues facing society. For example, take "to challenge the taken-for-granted." In many of her works Maxine challenges her readers to think about how the general populace—if not they, the readers, themselves—view the following: the homeless; the build-up of nuclear weapons; the extant curriculum. In regard to the homeless, for example she prods one to reflect on whether one accepts the homeless as a fact of life, worthless people, or a "problem" to be dealt with by city officials. At one and the same time she prods, cajoles and encourages one to posit and then probe such questions as: Why are people homeless? Are there factors in our society that contribute to and/or cause homelessness? Are there remedies to homelessness that one can help implement?

Or take the concept "critical self-reflectiveness." In part, Maxine suggests that critical reflectivness should assist one to posit questions about one's lived life, beliefs, and actions. As one of her former students, I can attest to the fact that I constantly strive for critical reflectiveness as I go about life— and in good part that is due to Maxine Greene's tutelage. For example, among the questions I constantly ask myself are: "What can I do to ameliorate, for example, human rights wrongs?" or "Am I part of the solution or part of the problem when it comes to racism in the world today?" or "Am I steward of the environment or do I contribute to gross consumption and waste?" or "Is what I am teaching my students truly valuable; and if so, how and why?"

Maxine is incredibly well read and a lover of the arts. Indeed, she is passionate about reading, visiting art museums, and the role that fiction, poetry, drama, painting, and other arts can and should play in one's education and life and within in the larger community. It is no wonder that her essays, books, lectures, and daily conversations are peppered with references to a wide array of philosophers, novelists, poets, and artists and/or their works—if not a rich and thought-provoking commentary on such. Among the philosophers she frequently mentions, quotes, and/or comments on are: Hannah Arendt, Albert Camus, John Dewey, Merleau-Ponty, Herbert Marcuse, John Paul Sartre, Alfred Schutz. Among the novelists and short story writers: James Baldwin, Jorge Borges, Kate Chopin, Joseph Conrad, Flaubert, Milan Kundera, Hemingway, Herman Melville, Toni Morrison, Andre Malraux, Tillie Olsen, Grace Paley, John Steinbeck, Mark Twain, Elie Wiesel, Alice Walker, Virgina Woolf. The poets: Baudelaire, William Blake, Emily Dickinson, T. S. Eliot, Denise Levertov, Wallace Stevens. The artists: Mary Cassatt, Cézanne, Delacroix, Goya, Edward Hopper, Henri Matisse, Georgia O'Keefe, Picasso, Art Spiegelman, van Gogh. The essayists: Jonathan Kozol, Richard Rodriquez, Henry David Thoreau. Educational theorists: Michael Apple, Carol Gilligan, Dwayne Huebner, Lawrence Kohlberg. And that is only a partial listing within each category. Indeed, only an infinitesimal listing of each.

Some may think, "She has a propensity for showing off, overtly displaying her erudition, how wide-read she is, and how well educated." That is not the case at all. Indeed, those who are inclined to making such assumptions are dead wrong. The use of such phrases, concepts, and allusions are second-nature to her. To use a cliché, they seem as comfortable and "common" to her as an old pair of favorite shoes. They are a good fit, not showy, but a daily part of her life and how she moves in it.

All of this brings to mind, for me, at least, Maxine Greene's unique blend of scholarship (philosophical, pedagogical, literary, artistic) and ardent commitment to addressing social issues in her own life, the classroom, the university, the city, state, nation, and across the globe.

SO, WHO IS MAXINE GREENE?

For a start, Maxine is now a woman of 80 plus years. A white, Jewish, woman. Well educated (a BA from Barnard College, Columbia University, 1938, an MA, 1949, and a PhD, 1955, from New York University), who is a voracious reader and synthesizer, and one who has a flair for engaging others in fascinating "conversation"—face to face, in the classroom, in her speeches, and in her writing. She's an intellectual and a scholar who fluidly crosses over and into various disciplines. She is at home in the world of intellectuals, teachers, as well as the "common person." She is a philosopher who specializes in the philosophy of education. A unique philosopher who ponders how individuals go about living their lives ("lived lives"), and contemplates and writes about and acts on what can be versus what is. She was a longtime (and highly respected and beloved) professor of philosophy of education at Teachers College, Columbia University— one in a long line of luminaries (John Dewey, George Counts, Harold Rugg, among others) who "came at" social issues in vastly different ways.

Of her philosophical approach to curriculum development, teaching, and, one might say, life, she has said:

> Like many other philosophers, I was deeply struck by Richard Rorty's (1979) new interest in "edifying philosophy," the point of which is "to keep the conversation going rather than to find objective truth" (p. 377). Rejecting dependable rational frameworks and "universal commensuration," Rorty chooses to turn away from systems in the way the "great edifying, peripheral thinkers (namely Dewey, Wittgenstein, and Heidegger) did" (p. 386) and try the modes of hermeneutics or interpretation. This introduces, of course, ideas of vantage point, perspective, and multiple discourses.

> It [is] the kind of space in which persons [can] pursue themselves as distinctive beings because they [are] participants in an ongoing conversation, because they [are] aware of social insufficiencies, because they [are] committed to transforming [action]. To me, that is the consummation of a view of curriculum rooted in a concept of "self." Text, content, discipline, multiplicity, laughter—and, in time, the constitution of a truly human world. (Greene, 1990, pp. 76, 78)

For close to 40 years (from 1965 to 2000), she taught at Teachers College, Columbia University, serving as an Associate Professor of English, Professor of English, Professor of Philosophy and Education and then the William F. Russell Professor in the Foundations of Education (1975-2000). From 1966 to 1973, she also served as the editor of the highly regarded journal *Teachers College Record*.

She is an ardent advocate of the arts and arts in education, and since 1976 she has served as the Director of Teachers College-Lincoln Center Project in the Arts and Humanities: "Philosopher in Residence," Lincoln Center Institute for the Arts in Education.

Her life of the mind involves a rich exploration of the past, present, and future but she strives to live in the present—and to be present to the present. She is a person who thrives on probing into the "whys" of life, and constantly writes and speaks—and no doubt thinks—about what it means to be (or not to be) "wide-awake" in a world where far too many are engulfed, in Virginia Woolf's phrase, "the cotton wool of daily life." She is one who perceives herself as "incomplete" and constantly in the process of "becoming." In this regard, she has said: "Like Dewey, I believe that 'the self is not something ready-made, but something in continuous formation through choice of action …' and I would emphasize the importance of action. I believe that singularity is best expressed through the ways in which a person conducts himself, through his interests, through his identification with work or study or political activity or social cause" (Greene, 1975, p. 10).

EARLY YEARS

Maxine was born in and grew up in Brooklyn, where her father owned a factory. Maxine notes that she came to a consciousness about social issues early in life. More specifically, she states that "I became so ashamed about it [the fact that her father owned a factory], really ashamed…. He was paternalistic to his workers and, of course, hated unions" (Weiss, Systra, & Slater, 1998, p. 26). Later, while studying at Barnard College, Columbia University, she notes that she came into contact with "radicals" who corroborated her thinking and feelings vis-a-vis workers' rights and the oppression the latter frequently experienced at the hands of owners, managers, and bosses.

As a young adult, she became active on a number of fronts that addressed various social issues. She asserts that "Among the high moments of my life was the time the *SS Bremen* came in from Germany [in the mid to late-1930s], and many young people marched to the harbor, where some climbed the mast to try to pull down the Nazi flag. I wanted desperately to do that, but I could not climb" (Weiss, Systra, & Slater, 1998, p. 26). Around the same period of time, she says, "[P]robably with the same people, I [picketed] some stores on Fulton Street in Brooklyn because they would not hire black cashiers—and that was in Bedford-Stuyvesant. I was arrested for picketing" (Weiss, Systra, & Slater, 1998, p. 26).

Later, she "joined something called the Workers' Alliance, which specialized in taking furniture back after evictions…. I was pregnant and we were having a meeting at this Workers' Alliance thing, and a man came up with a pail and threw lye in the chairman's eyes, blinding him" (Weiss, Systra, & Slater, 1998, p. 26).

She also had a great affinity for those who fought in Spain against the right-wing Fascist dictatorship of Franco:

When I was a junior [in college], my father let me go to Europe with a classmate. He gave me a list of tasks to perform for his business that I did not understand. On the boat, I met some men going to fight in Spain with the Abraham Lincoln brigade, and I wanted to go to Spain. Obviously, I couldn't, but eventually I got to Paris and found a job with the Loyalist Embassy. It was the year of Guernica [the bombing of the town of Guernica by Germany, the latter of which was memorialized in Picasso's famous painting entitled "Guernica"], and of a World's Fair. I met people I thought were noble people—Constancia de la Mora, Louis Aragon. (Weiss, Systra, & Slater, 1998, p. 26)

Continuing, she says that "When Barcelona fell, I thought I would commit suicide, that it meant the death of all our hopes because the Fascists had won in Spain" (Weiss, Systra, & Slater, 1998, p. 25).

In 1939 or 1940, she began working with the American Labor Party and went to the New School part-time. At the New School, she wrote a paper on what was then referred to as "collective security," a situation in which "the United States would join the Soviets and others; I suppose, it meant, in a common front" (Weiss, Systra, & Slater, 1998, p. 25). Her professors, who she describes as "old German social democrats," refused to give her credit for the paper, and the New School dismissed her. "They said I wasn't scholarly, was too radical. That is how I know what they were then. They were the ones, after all, who allowed the Nazis in and then they got kicked out [of Nazi Germany]" (Weiss, Systra, & Slater, 1998, p. 25).

Following her graduation from college, Maxine aspired to be a writer. She, in fact, wrote what she describes as two and a half unsuccessful novels. One was a 700-page "very 'subversive' novel about a folk singer during the American Revolution who tacked his songs to trees" (Weiss, Systra, & Slater, 1998, p. 24). It also encompassed the "Jeffersonian period, and the Alien and Sedition Acts under which people were set to jail for their sympathies with the French Revolution … Little, Brown thought it was too left-wing or something" (Weiss, Systra, & Slater, 1998, p. 24). Her second novel was about a mulatto woman, but when the publisher asked her to rewrite it in the first person, Maxine found she couldn't do it. Her next novel was about "a daughter of someone like John Dewey, who had maybe yes or maybe no squealed on somebody to the Un-American Activities Committee. She is looking in a quarry at the start, wondering if her father committed suicide. My own father committed suicide almost right after I wrote that, and it scared the living hell out of me. I never again wrote any kind of fiction" (Weiss, Systra, & Slater, 1998, p. 24).

In the aftermath of World War II, she has remarked that, "it was a little difficult to be an authentic activist. [Here, she doesn't provide an explanation, but one can, with some confidence, surmise that it was likely due to the conservatism of the period, the Cold War and the rise of McCarthyism.] I thought, [however] I could incorporate somehow some of my ideas into teaching" (quoted in Weiss, Systra, & Slater, 1998, p. 23).

MIDDLE YEARS

After getting divorced and remarried, her husband suggested that she go back to school. Even though she had a daughter, Linda, who was in elementary school at the time, Maxine decided to follow through on her husband's suggestion. While in school at New York University (NYU), she had another baby, a boy, Tim. She has stated that one of her strongest memories of those years of study and child-raising was "one of propping up a huge book on eighteenth-century philosophy while feeding Tiny Tim from a bottle."

At NYU Maxine studied under such notables as George Axtelle, Theodore Bramweld, and Adolphe Meyer. It was actually Axtelle, a "Deweyite," who over lunch one day suggested that she pursue a PhD in philosophy of education. In their article, "The Foundation of Professionalism: Fifty Years of the Philosophy of Education Society [PES] in Respect," Giarelli and Chambliss (1991) report that:

> [T]he importance of philosophy of education naturally resulting from Dewey's influence made the development of professional training programs in philosophy of education unstoppable. Already by the 1930's and early 1940's, the second and third generations of people trained by Dewey and his followers at Teachers College [Columbia University] were taking positions at outposts of higher education across the country and developing a professional conception of philosophy of education. (p. 266)

In a matter of years, Maxine Greene's own students and the students of the latter would be described in terms of "first, second, and third generations."

Recalling her student days at NYU, a point in time just after she had her second child, she tells about having to leave a philosophy seminar "with a careful explanation that the baby-sitter was leaving—and seeing the aged and dignified William Heard Kilpatrick get up as well, calling, 'Take me with you'" (cited in TC Today, 2001, n. p.).

Maxine was awarded her PhD in 1955. By this time, though, she had already begun teaching courses in Philosophy of Education at NYU but when Axtelle left the institution, Maxine was left "to fend for herself with a dean, 'an awful guy,' who thought she was 'too literary'" (Kohli, 1998, p. 12). The latter criticism would plague her for a long, long time.

Actually, being "too literary" was only one of the many problems she faced in the academy. Another was that her approach to philosophy flew in the face of what was deemed "the" approach—the analytic tradition. An equally thorny problem was that the field of philosophy—and, in particular, philosophy of education—was dominated by white males who held patriarchal views of a woman's "place" in the world.

In regard to the aforementioned concerns, Kohli (1998) notes that:

> By the late 1950s and early 1960s, the period when Maxine Greene was entering the academic world as a philosopher of education, the primary source of philosophical legitimation came from the Anglo-American analytic traditions.

> In addition to the hegemony of linguistic and logical analysis in PES [Philosophy of Education Society], which did not provide a hospitable environment for a literary existential phenomenologist like Maxine, she had to face an almost all-male organization. Mary Leach, in an illuminating feminist reading of the society, found that "in 1961, for example, there was a lone female listed on the program, though a formidable one—Maxine Greene."

> Things did not improve much until the late 1970s or early 1980s. Even then, it remained a predominately male enterprise to present at PES—[and] the discursive practices that shaped the meetings were decidedly masculinist.

> Maxine's decision to draw on continental philosophy, the arts, and literature was often met with skepticism, even disdain, by many of her (male) peers who, steeped in a more Anglo-analytic tradition, thought her work "unintelligible" and certainly "un-philosophical." (pp. 14, 15, 20)

Tellingly, as late as 1998, Maxine observed that "In academe, I see competition and, still, white man elitism" (quoted in Weiss, Systra, & Slater, 1998, p. 22).

Maxine once commented that:

> I can't exactly remember becoming a feminist—only reacting to slights along the way, believing the men who treated me as soft and darling and willing to type all the membership cards, someone who had a baby before anyone else and was always making excuses about absent sitters and colds and nauseas.... Trouble was, having been reared with Daddy's view as the The Right View, the view from Nowhere, as it was, I figured they were right; and I had to be the best male philosopher in a way—although the stubbornness in me (which I did not associate with feminism)—made me insist on the existential view and the literary material and the contingency on perspec-

tive and the frailty of the human being whoever she or he was. (Quoted in Hollingsworth, 1998, p. 76)

Speaking of sexism, Maxine writes as follows:

Sexism, to me, is emblematic of constrains and closures. It canels personal possibility.… Existentialists have talked a great deal about the ways in which "othering" affects people—about the tensions experienced when individuals are seen as "types" or as objects. (Greene, 1978, pp. 244,248)

Despite the naysayers, Maxine was committed to her belief of the power of art and literature to help individuals become more reflective about their lived lives. And for this reason, no doubt, she voraciously took in all she could about the arts and continued to read about and comment on a broad range of eclectic artists and authors. Speaking of the value of the arts, she has said: "Engagement with the arts opens conversations to deeper levels. Politically, the more we can encourage communication about things that are important to us and the people around us, the more we feel ourselves to be individual beings" (Inside TC Staff, 2002, n.p.). And, educational researcher Jean Anyon (1998) has noted, Maxine "often uses the arts as a lens through which to view the social forces impinging on schools and students" (p. 219)—and, one might add, society.

In 1956, finding NYU not to be the friendliest of places, Maxine accepted a position as an Assistant Professor to teach English at Montclair State Teachers College in New Jersey. She says that it was through teaching a course on world literature during her year (1956-1957) at Montclair that she began to really learn about literature as she had no "formal training in English, maybe one course, once" (cited in Kohli, 1998, p. 14). Ultimately, she returned to NYU for several years as a part-time instructor. In 1962, she accepted a tenure-track position as an Associate Professor of Education at Brooklyn College of the City University of New York, where she taught "foundations of education." In 1965, Maxine took a job at Teachers College, Columbia University as an Associate Professor of English and editor of *Teachers College Record*. Kohli (1998) reports that the new job, though, was "nothing less than bittersweet" (p. 14). More specifically,

Although Lawrence Cremin, the chair of the Department of Philosophy and Social Sciences, wanted her on the faculty, she was forced to come in through the backdoor as editor of *Teachers College Record*. Hindsight suggests apparent sexist resistance to her appointment within the department; they had yet to ever hire a woman. It was only after first teaching for several years in the English Department that she was finally "allowed in" and a given a proper appointment in Philosophy of Education. (p. 15)

Maxine's gumption eventually paid off, but it was not without a lot of anxiety, hurt-feelings, and pain. Eventually, in 1967, she was elected to serve as the president of the Philosophy of Education Society (PES); and then, in 1975, she was appointed to the William F. Russell Professor in the Foundations of Education.

"DOING PHILOSOPHY"

> What might it mean to pose distinctive kinds of questions with respect to our own practice and our lived situations, the kinds of questions that make us more than "accidental tourists," more than clerks or bureaucrats or functionaries? (Greene quoted in Ayers, 1998, p. 4)

Maxine is committed to "doing philosophy" and teaching about "doing philosophy"—as opposed to "simply" reading it, analyzing positions of philosophers, or searching for meaning in what others have written. In her syllabus for "Modern Philosophies of Education," which I took in the fall of 1982, Maxine explained her concept of "doing philosophy" in the following way:

> We are going to "do" philosophy, not study various points of view. I think about it as a verb in a way, as Dewey thought about "mind." "Mind," he said, "is primarily a verb. It denotes all the ways in which we deal consciously and expressly with the situations in which we find ourselves.... Mind denotes every mode of interest in and concern for things: practical, intellectual, and emotional.... Mind is care in the sense of solicitude—an active looking after things that need to be tended to...." Philosophy is mindfulness: it is a mode of cognitive action, a way of questing—I hope a way towards wide-awakeness.... [M]y interest is in philosophizing with respect to education—posing distinctive kinds of questions with respect to our projects, our practices, our language—questions that provoke us to think about our own thinking, not only about the concepts we use in sense-making, but about the languages which we use and the ways in which the contradictions and tensions of our society affect us. I do think a critical awareness may follow from such questioning, as it may follow from taking a different standpoint on what has been taken for granted—and on major premises we may never have examined before.... Questions like these are called for when there is a need to clarify, to overcome fragmentation, to build interpretive frameworks, to make our experience more coherent, to think in terms of what ought to be. (p. 2)

"Doing philosophy," then, is integrally tied to becoming and being conscious of the world in which one lives. In part, that involves making a true effort of being aware of and informed about that which is fair versus unfair, just versus unjust, humane versus inhumane, right versus wrong. In this regard, Maxine has written:

> I think we have an obligation to learners to enable them to recognize how ideas are cooked up and who makes them and why. I think, similarly, we have an obligation to help them recognize why we are so prone to see the phenomena of the world around—the extremes of wealth and poverty, for instance, the consumerism, the violence, the injustices—as so normal, so built into the every day.... Aware of incompleteness, and open possibility, our students may—as we ourselves may—become aware of and responsive to lacks and insufficiencies, come together in the light of shared perceptions, shared interpretations—and to choose, in their ensembles, to repair. (Greene, 1982, pp. 5, 14)

Ultimately, then, "doing philosophy," means that one needs to ponder one's "relationship" to such matters, and move from reflection to action. Inherent in it as well is, obviously, the concept of "tikkun" or the repair of the world.

TYING TEACHING, CONVERSING, AND WRITING TO ACTION

In almost every essay, book chapter, and book Maxine Greene has written since 1978 she has addressed an eclectic range of social issues in regard to either (1) how they impact the lives and education of the young, and/or (2) the critical need for each and every person to become aware of, reflect upon, conversant with, and hopefully, willing to address those issues that impact them, their community(ies), and the world. In many of the same works she has also addressed why it is significant for teachers and their students to be conversant with such issues.

A mere listing of the social issues that she has addressed in her writing, talks, and courses would, literally, take pages. For the sake of brevity, some of the issues that seem to have most greatly engaged her interest and/or concern are: sexism, discrimination against women and minorities, poverty, racism, elitism, antisemitism, and the danger of nuclear weapons. Many of these issues have been lifelong concerns of Maxine.

In an interview in 2002 she tellingly said: "As a Jewish woman reflecting on anti-Semitism, one can never say, "We are all right now" (quoted in Inside TC, n. p.).

As for her primary focus today, Maxine notes that she mainly focuses on current politics: "It is something in this society which moves people to make other people 'other.'" (Inside TC Staff, 2002).

Unlike most educators represented in this book, Maxine never designed a particular strategy or program for addressing social issues;

rather, her "project," to use a term she is fond of, is to assist one to think deeply about one's own "lived life"—that is, to move toward a disposition in which one truly examines, as a regular way of life, the unexamined life and the world (family, locally, nationally, globally) in which one lives. Part and parcel of that is to take a critical stance in which one reflects on the "taken-for-granted," and to examine one's beliefs and actions accordingly. Last but not least, Maxine encourages her readers and students to move beyond the "taken for granted," and, in concert with others, to work in positive and humane ways to transform one's lived life, society, schools, nation, and the world. The latter, of course, involves thinking and pondering, deeply and reflectively, about how one treats others; cares or does not care for the welfare of one's fellow human beings, the environment, the larger world; and one's philosophical, political, and pedagogical stance in relation to how one interacts with others and addresses (or neglects to address) critical issues in one's life and world. All of this, she argues, and convincingly, requires the nurturing of a wide-awakeness in order to acknowledge and face the fact that the ways of the world (the injustices, the unfairness, the transgressions, the hurtfulness) are not givens and can, if there is a collective effort and will, be altered in order to make life fairer and more humane. The latter inherently involves making a Herculean effort to overcome one's own ignorance of the world in order to delve as deeply as possible into one's own thoughts, feelings, and actions—or lack thereof—regarding key issues that impact one and/or one's society. She, then, is a philosopher who believes in—and strives toward in her own life and teaching—praxis.

Significantly, and this is germane to being a reflective human being who is committed to the common good, "Maxine's interpretations of freedom, justice, community, democracy, and imagination always reflect the changing historical, economic, social, cultural, and political situations in which they are embedded" (Kohli, 1998, p. 17).

Those who reflect upon and choose to incorporate into their own lived lives aspects of Maxine Greene's philosophical and pedagogical approaches will, it seems, over time, begin to develop and nurture habits of the mind and heart that almost invariably lead to a commitment to address social issues—and to do so with the aim of bringing about the most just, fair, equitable, and humane world possible.

PASSION, COMMITMENT, AND PRAXIS

"Passion" is a word that informs Maxine's philosophy, life, teaching, writing, and conversations. Based on what has been said thus far it should be obvious that Maxine is passionate about a lot, including but not limited to: being reflective about her lived life; learning; reading; the arts; doing philosophy; the world around her; sharing rich conversations with friends, colleagues, students, and teachers; her own teaching; others' teaching and learning (education); and the concept of "tikkun."

She has long had an ardent commitment to young people, to opening new horizons to them so that they can "become what they are not yet, to be free, to explore, to discover." She is equally passionate about teachers becoming reflective practitioners and moving beyond the taken for granted, be it in relationship to: the extant curriculum; the standardized test-driven way of teaching that many schools and teachers have "adopted"; the stultifying constraints teachers often allow standardized testing to place upon them; that which constitutes "leadership" in today's schools; the emphasis on "training" in many schools versus rich, deep (or authentic) education; the perception that "arts" are an "add-on" versus an integral part of anyone's education; and unfair and unjust practices that are "passed on" from one generation to the next as a result of the negative systemic aspects of schooling.

In her essay, "Reflection and Passion in Teaching," Maxine writes:

> [I]f we are the kinds of educators who want to provoke, to motivate persons to move and become challengers, I believe we have to reconceive. And to stir ourselves, to disturb, to transform. An emotion, a passion can be a transformation of the world. It can break through the fixities; it can open to the power of possibility. It may even render practice more reflective. (Greene, 1986, p. 81)

And in regard to the issues of passion and social issues, she has written that:

> [T]o be concerned ... is to be conscious of a web of possibilities; to experience passion is to be invested in what might or might not be.... The ability to reach beyond, to envisage a wider span of understanding and a better order of things enables persons to perceive the deficiencies in what exists, to become capable of indignation or even outrage.... In outrage (at "man" corrupting everything, at homelessness, at burned-out buildings, at child abuse, at arms buildups, at neglect), there may be efforts to reach out with others to do something, to repair. (Greene, 1986 pp. 74, 79)

ABIDING PASSIONS:
THE ARTS, IMAGINATION, SOCIAL ISSUES

As alluded to earlier, Maxine's lectures, writings, and conversations are peppered with allusions to literature, art, music, drama, and dance.

Indeed, she has a deep affinity for the arts and believes that a deep understanding of them is integral to becoming a "wide-awake" human being/citizen. More specifically, she believes that:

> [A]rt works or engagement with art works demand a break with submergence, with the taken-for-granted, with nonbeing. They provide vistas out of the actual. They make it possible to imagine things being other than they are. "Art cannot change the world, but it can contribute to changing the consciousness and drives of the men and women who could change the world," Marcuse said.

> [I]ndeed, the arts and humanities cannot but open new possibilities for anyone who engages with them—new possibilities in experience, new possibilities of perspective, new possibility of being in the world.... New vantage points open, new projects become conceivable; and things begin to seem less petrified, less finished, less complete.

> Awareness of incompleteness, yes, and open possibility, our students may—as we ourselves may—become aware of and responsive to lacks and insufficiencies, to shattered networks and torn webs. We may be able to empower our students to come together in the light of shared perceptions, shared interpretations—and to choose, in their ensembles, to repair. (Greene, 1975, pp. 12, 13, 14)

Maxine does not "simply" write and speak about the arts. In fact, for close to 30 years she has been "the philosopher in residence" at the Lincoln Art Center in New York City. In that role, she was instrumental in establishing The Center for Aesthetic Education. Of this program and her goals, she says:

> For all of these years I have been trying to talk about imagination and perception, and the always shifting meanings of art. [We have] artists work with teachers and teachers are awakened to the languages of art, and to the opening—and this is what's so important to me—of new perspectives and new possibilities and experience. I guess I have always thought of the Lincoln Center Institute as involved with the awakening of teachers and the sort of stirring of teachers to move beyond the banal, often repetitive habit-ridden into which many of them have been forced to live.

> I have hopes always that if teachers are awakened, if teachers become more imaginative, if teachers face the darkness and the ambiguities of their own lives, something about what they have become may become contagious when they are in the classroom, when they are working with artists, or when they are working with performances. (Quoted in Taylor, 2000, n.p.)

Continuing, she says:

I think, and you may argue this point, artists and teachers are very different. Their causes are different. The job of the artist, as Conrad said, and so many others, is to make us see, to make us feel, to make us understand. To make us penetrate something that we could not conceivably imagine without, say, the *Ninth Symphony*, without *King Lear*, without *The Colour Purple*. There was a marvelous article the other day in *The New York Times* talking about what art does is bring you in touch with something that otherwise would be forever submerged. And to me, that is the job of the arts. The job of the teacher is to release other people to learn to learn. To use whatever enriches her or his life in order to move them to reach out.... To move them to go beyond where they are.... To move them as, Dewey said, "to become different" ...

And the more wide-awake we are, the more wide-awakeness we can develop [art and education], the better chance that we have that children will wake up and rebel against dullness and boredom and repetitiveness and the mechanical life, and what Dewey called, "the opposite." I always liked this, and I always say it, "The opposite of the aesthetic is the anesthetic!" I like to spend my life fighting the anesthetic. You know, the numbness, the dullness, the refusal to respond. (Quoted in Taylor, 2000)

Maxine has more energy and passion than many half her age. And this is evident in the fact that she is never content that she has done enough, tried hard enough to reach, teach, and assist people to become more reflective human beings and to lead richer lives than they might otherwise. This concern and passion is particularly deep as it relates to the state of schooling today. It is no surprise that her passion has led her, despite her advanced age, to create a new project that fuses her passions of imagination, the arts, and social justice. In this regard she says: "I am ... obsessive about imagination, and about the neglect of imagination in some of the reports that have come in the name of school reform.... And partly because of that obsession, and partly because of a long interest in social transformation, I have been trying to nurture a center for social imagination at Teachers' College" (Maxine Greene quoted in Taylor, 2000).

Such concern resulted in Maxine founding the Center for Social Imagination, the Arts, and Education at Teachers College, Columbia University. As the founder and director of the center, she notes that the center

["i]s committed to the development of alternative modes of inventing, creating, and interpreting." Through these endeavors of the imagination, and through its series of interdisciplinary programs, the Center seeks to shape visions of "a lovelier world," embracing, in all its diverse cultural richness, one humanity. Working in the tradition of John Dewey, William James, and the Existentialists, the Center brings school children, artists, academics, and social activists together in conferences and workshops to explore possibilities of reform and transformation in schools and social communities. By sponsoring monthly "salons," the Center attempts to generate dialogue and research projects that open new perspectives in the arts, humanities, and the human sciences. The Center is also in the process of developing networks that bring together art institutions, public schools, and Teachers College, Columbia University, in order "to investigate, document, and articulate just what role encounters with the arts—including the quintessential 20th century art forms of film and video—might play in inspiring social visions and, by consequence, in effectuating vibrant, moral communities." The Center, in its desire "to enlarge the conversation, to try for clarity, to persuade," publishes occasional essays, in both belles letters and position paper formats, reflecting imaginative thinking and advocacy in these areas of concern. (From the Center's Purpose of Statement)

The beauty of such a center and program is that with Maxine behind it it will not simply be a forum for scholars and intellectuals to present their ideas, but a place that is welcoming, receptive to, and the nurturing of classroom teachers and all that they and their students face on a day-to-day basis as they attempt to make sense of the world in which they live as well as their "lived lives."

CONCLUSION

Hopefully, this essay about Maxine Greene does not appear to be little more than a hagiography. That said, I will be the first to admit that I was and am honored that I was a student of Maxine Greene's. I also readily admit that I find most of her books, essays, and other writings to be some of the most thought-provoking I've read in the field of education and social issues. Be that as it may, I do hope that I've provided the reader with a sense as to who Maxine Greene is, her philosophy, thoughts, and passions. If nothing else, I hope this essay at least encourages others to seek out her writings and ponder her insights in regard to how teachers can wrestle with, and help their students wrestle with, many of the enduring questions that have captivated humanity over the ages—and not only the latter, as significant as they are, but also those social issues that impinge upon our, and/or others', daily "lived lives."

NOTE

1. Among some of the many other words and phrases that come to mind are: "choosing"; "humane choosing"; "to arouse"; "glimpses of possibility to what is not yet, to what ought to be"; "the tasks of knowledge and action";

"a field of multiplicities"; "constantly becoming"; "humane freedom"; "social commitment"; "to take an initiative"; "to provoke"; "multiple perspectives"; "lived lives"; "to do philosophy"; "to identify [oneself/themselves] by means of significant projects"; "activation of imagination"; "not freedom from but freedom to"; "to cultivate multiple ways of seeing"; "critical consciousness"; "come awake to deception, to mystification, to distortion"; "positive freedom"; "overcome passivity"; "the tasks of knowledge and action"; "constantly becoming"; "to refuse stasis and the flatness of ordinary life"; and "to awaken them [the young] to their situations and enable them to make sense of and to name their worlds."

REFERENCES

Anyon, J. (1998). The social context of educational reform. In W. C. Ayers & J. L. Miller (Eds.), *Maxine Greene: A light in dark times and the unfinished conversation* (pp. 219-228). New York: Teachers College Press.

Ayers, W. (1998). Doing philosophy: Maxine Greene and the pedagogy of possibility. In W. C. Ayers & J. L. Miller (Eds.), *Maxine Greene: A light in dark times and the unfinished conversation* (pp. 3-10). New York: Teachers College Press.

Giarelli, J. M., & Chambliss, J. J. (1991). The foundation of professionalism: Fifty years of the philosophy of education society in respect. *Educational Theory, 41*(3), 265-274.

Greene, M. (1975, February 23). *Education, freedom, and possibility.* Inaugural Lecture as William F. Russell Professor of Educational Foundations, Teachers College, Columbia University.

Greene, M. (1978). Sexism in schools. In M. Greene (Ed.) *Landscapes of learning,* (pp. 244-255). New York: Teachers College Press.

Greene, M. (1982). *Syllabus - Modern philosophies of education.* Teachers College, Columbia University.

Greene, M. (1982). *Wide-awakeness in dark times.* Speech delivered at Teachers College, Columbia University.

Greene, M. (1986). Reflection and passion in teaching. *Journal of Curriculum and Supervision, 2*(1), 68-81.

Greene, M. (1990). Interpretation and re-vision: Toward another story. In J. T. Sears & J. D. Marshall (Eds.), *Teaching and thinking about curriculum: Critical inquiries* (pp. 75-78). New York: Teachers College Press.

Hollingsworth, S. (1998). Social responsibility and imagination: Lessons and letters. In W. C. Ayers & J. L. Miller (Eds.), *A light in dark times: Maxine Greene and the unfinished conversation* (pp. 71-77). New York: Teachers College Press.

Inside TC Staff. (2002, March 1). Book talking with Maxine Greene. *Inside TC, 7*(6), n.p.

Kohli, W. (1998). Philosopher of/for freedom. In W. C. Ayers & J. L. Miller (Eds.), *Maxine Greene: A light in dark times and the unfinished conversation* (pp. 11-21). New York: Teachers College Press.

Miller, J. L. (1998). Autobiography and the necessary incompleteness of teachers' stories. In W. C. Ayers & J. L. Miller (Eds.), *Maxine Greene: A light in dark times and the unfinished conversation* (pp. 145-154). New York: Teachers College Press.

Rorty, R. (1979). *Philosophy and the mirror of nature*. Princeton, NJ: Princeton University Press.

Taylor, P. (2000). An informal conversation with Maxine Greene: The power of aesthetic partnerships. *Applied Theatre Researcher*, No. 1, Art. 5, n.p.

TC Today Staff. (2001, January 1). Flunking retirement: A chat with Maxine Greene. *TC Today, 25*(2)n.p.

Weiss, M., Systra, C., & Slater, S. (1998). Dinner with Maxine. In W. C. Ayers & J. L. Miller (Eds.), *Maxine Greene: A light in dark times and the unfinished conversation* (pp. 22-32). New York: Teachers College Press.

NOTABLE PUBLICATIONS BY THE PIONEERS OF THE STUDY OF SOCIAL ISSUES

Theodore Brameld

Brameld, T. (1947). An inductive approach to intercultural values. *Journal of Educational Sociology, 21*(1), 4-11.

Brameld, T. (1950a). Conceptualizing human relations. *Journal of Educational Sociology, 23*(6), 315-328.

Brameld, T. (1950b). *Ends and means in education: A midcentury appraisal.* Westport, CT: Greenwood Press.

Brameld, T. (1950c). *Education for the emerging age.* New York: Harper & Row.

Brameld, T. (1951). Human relations—A "field of forces." *Journal of Educational Sociology, 24*(6), 329-334.

Brameld, T. (1955). Culture and education. *The Journal of Higher Education, 26*(2), 59-68, 111.

Brameld, T. (1956). *Toward a reconstructed philosophy of education.* New York: Dryden Press.

Brameld, T. (1965). *The use of explosive ideas in education: Culture, class, and evolution.* Pittsburgh, PA: University of Pittsburgh Press.

Brameld, T. (1968, July). The changing American people: Are we deteriorating or improving? *Annals of the American Academy of Political and Social Science, 378,* 75-82.

Brameld, T. (1971). *Patterns of educational philosophy.* New York: Hart, Rinehart, and Winston.

Brameld, T., & Fish, E. (1946, March). School administration and intercultural relations. *Annals of the American Academy of Political and Social Science, 244*, 26-33.

Brameld, T., & Sullivan, E. B. (1961, February). Anthropology and education. *Review of Educational Research, 31*(1), 70-79.

George S. Counts

Counts, G. S. (1929). *Secondary education and industrialism*. Cambridge, MA: Harvard University Press.

Counts, G. S. (1930). *The American road to culture: A social interpretation of education in the United States*. New York: John Day.

Counts, G. S. (1931). *The Soviet challenge to America*. New York: John Day.

Counts, G. S. (1932, April 9). Dare progressive education be progressive? *Progressive Education*, pp. 257-63.

Counts, G. S. (1932). *Dare the school build a new social order?* New York: John Day.

Counts, G. S. (1934). *The social foundations of education*. New York: Charles Scribner's Sons.

Counts, G. S. (1938). *The prospects of American democracy*. New York: John Day.

Counts, G. S. (1946). *Education and the promise of America*. New York: Macmillan.

Counts, G. S. (1952). *Education and American civilization*. New York: Teachers College Press.

Counts, G. S. (1957). *The challenge of Soviet education*. New York: McGraw-Hill.

Counts, G. S. (1971). A humble autobiography. In R. J. Havighurst (Ed.), *Leaders in American education: The seventieth yearbook of the National Society for the Study of Education* (pp 151-174). Chicago: University of Chicago Press.

Counts, G. S., & Childs, J. (1943). *America, Russia, and the communist party in the postwar world*. New York: John Day.

John Dewey

Dewey, J. (1899). *The school and society*. Chicago: University of Chicago Press.

Dewey, J. (1910). *How we think*. Lexington, MA: D. C. Heath.

Dewey, J. (1916). *Democracy and education*. New York: Macmillan.

Dewey, J. (1920). *Reconstruction in philosophy*. New York: Henry Holt.

Dewey, J. (1922). *Human nature and conduct*. New York: Henry Holt.

Dewey, J. (1925). *Experience and nature*. Chicago: Open Court.

Dewey, J. (1927). *The public and its problems*. New York: Henry Holt.

Dewey, J. (1935). *Liberalism and social action*. New York: G. P. Putnam's Sons.

Dewey, J. (1938). *Experience and education*. New York: Macmillan.

Dewey, J. (1939). *Freedom and culture*. New York: G. P. Putnam's Sons.

Rachel Davis DuBois

DuBois, R. D. (1936, March). Developing sympathetic attitudes toward peoples. *Journal of Educational Sociology, 9*(7), 387-396.

DuBois, R. D. (1938, November). Can we help to create an American renaissance? *English Journal, 27*(9), 733-740.

DuBois, R. D. (1942). *National unity through intercultural education.* Washington, DC: The U.S. Office of Education, Education and National Defense Series, Pamphlet No. 10.

DuBois, R. D. (1943). *Get together Americans: Friendly approaches to racial and cultural conflicts through the neighborhood-home festival.* New York: Harper & Brothers.

DuBois, R. D. (1950). *Neighbors in action: A manual for local leaders in intergroup relations.* New York: Harper & Brothers.

DuBois, R. D., & Li, M. S. (1963). *The art of group conversation: A new breakthrough in social communication.* New York: Association Press.

DuBois, R. D., & Li, M. S. (1971). *Reducing social tension and conflict through the group conversation method.* New York: Association Press.

DuBois, R. D., & Schweppe, E. (Eds.). (1935). *The Jews in American life.* New York: T. Nelson.

DuBois, R. D., & Schweppe, E. (Eds.). (1972, 1936). *Germans in American life.* Freeport, NY: Books for Libraries Press.

DuBois, R.D., with Okorodudu, C. (1984). *All this and something more: Pioneering in intercultural education.* Bryn Mawr, PA: Dorrance.

Shirely H. Engle

Engle, S. H. (1947). Factors in the teaching of our persistent modern problems. *Social Education, 9*(4),167-169.

Engle, S. H. (1951). The potential of the secondary school in achieving a desirable public opinion. In J. C. Payne (Ed.), *The teaching of contemporary affairs: 21st Yearbook* (pp. 76-85). Washington, DC: National Council for the Social Studies.

Engle, S. H. (1960). Decision making: The heart of social studies instruction. *Social Education, 24*(7), 301-304, 306.

Engle, S. H. (1965). Objectives of the social studies. In B. G. Massialas & F. R. Smith (Eds.), *New challenges in the social studies* (pp. 1-19). Belmont, CA: Wadsworth.

Engle, S. H. (1970). The future of social studies education and NCSS. *Social Education, 34*(7), 778-781, 795.

Engle, S. H. (1980). *Defining the social studies: What is the problem?* Paper presented at the meeting of the National Council for the Social Studies, New Orleans, LA. ERIC Document ED 204 200.

Engle, S. H. (1986). Late night thoughts about the new social studies. *Social Education, 50*(1), 20-22.

Engle, S. H. (1993). Foreword. In R. W. Evans & D. W. Saxe (Eds.), *Handbook on teaching social issues. NCSS Bulletin 93*. Washington, DC: National Council for the Social Studies.

Engle, S. H., & Longstreet, W. L. (1972). *A design for social education in the open curriculum*. New York: Harper & Row.

Engle, S. H., & Ochoa, A. S. (1988). *Education for democratic citizenship: Decision making in the social studies*. New York: Teachers College Press

Maxine Greene

Greene, M. (1963). *The public school and the private vision*. New York: Random House.

Greene, M. (1967). *Existential encounters for teachers*. New York: Random House.

Greene, M. (1973). *Teacher as stranger: Educational philosophy in the modern age*. Belmont, CA: Wadsworth.

Greene, M. (1978). *Landscapes of learning*. New York: Teachers College Press.

Greene, M. (1988). *The dialectics of freedom*. New York: Teachers College Press.

Greene, M. (1995). *Releasing the imagination: Essays on education, the arts, and social change*. San Francisco: Jossey Bass.

Books About Maxine Greene

Ayers, W. C., & Miller, J. (Eds.). (1998). *Maxine Greene and the unfinished conversation. A light in dark times*. New York: Teachers College Press.

Pinar, W. (1998). *The passionate mind of Maxine Greene: "Am … not yet."* New York: Falmer Press.

A Film About Maxine Greene

Exclusions and Awakenings: The Life of Maxine Greene. (Directed by Markie Hancock and produced by Kathryn Gregorio. Available from: University of California Extension, Center for Media & Independent Learning, 2000 Center Street, 4th Floor, Berkeley, CA 94704.) "Weaving through the past and present, 'Exclusions and Awakenings' captures the hurdles and triumphs that Greene faced as philosopher, mother, professor, wife, and leader-from her childhood in Brooklyn to the balancing act of school, motherhood, and marriage."

Alan F. Griffin

Griffin, A. F. (1940). *Freedom American style*. New York: Henry Holt.

Griffin, A. F. (1940). *Our freedom*. Columbus OH: School and College Service.

Griffin, A. F. (1942). *A philosophical approach to the subject matter preparation of teachers of history.* Unpublished doctoral dissertation, Ohio State University, Columbus.

Griffin, A. F. (1952, October). The teacher as citizen. *Educational Leadership, X*(1), 4-9.

Griffin, A. F. (1953). Community pressures and education. In H. G. Hullfish (Ed.), *Educational freedom in an age of anxiety* (pp. 149-166). New York: Harper and Brothers.

Griffin, A. F. (1963, October). Revising the social studies. *Social Education, 27*(6), 534.

Richard E. Gross

Gross, R. E. (1948). Teaching controversial issues can be fun. *Social Education, 12*(6), 259-260.

Gross, R. E. (1951). Controversial issues and educational freedom. *The Social Studies, 42*(5), 195-198.

Gross, R. E. (1953). Aims for American history in an era of crisis. *Social Education, 17*(6), 257-260.

Gross, R. E. (1964). *How to handle controversial issues. How to do it series no. 14.* Washington, DC: National Council for the Social Studies.

Gross, R. E. (1967). The curriculum: Research, development, and revision. In J. S. Gibson (Ed.), *New frontiers in the social studies: Action and analysis* (pp. 32-49). New York: Citation Press.

Gross, R. E. (1996). World history and issues-centered instruction. In R. W. Evans & D. W. Saxe (Eds.), *Handbook on teaching social issues* (pp. 161-163). NCSS Bulletin 93. Washington, DC: National Council for the Social Studies.

Gross, R. E., & Dynneson, T. L. (1991). *Social science perspectives on citizenship education.* New York: Teachers College Press.

Gross, R. E., & Muessig, R. H. (Eds.). (1971). *Problem-centered social studies instruction: Approaches to reflective teaching. Curriculum series, number fourteen.* Washington, DC: National Council for the Social Studies.

Gross, R. E., Messick, R., Chapin, J. R., & Sutherland, J. (1978). *Social studies for our times.* New York: John Wiley & Sons.

Gross, R. E., & Zeleny, L. D. (1958). *Educating citizens for democracy: Curriculum and instruction in secondary social studies.* New York: Oxford University Press.

H. Gordon Hullfish

Hullfish, H. G. (1932). Educational confusion. *Educational Research Bulletin, 11*(5), 113-119.

Hullfish, H. G. (1942). Education and postwar economics. *Educational Research Bulletin, 21*(1), 1-4.

Hullfish, H. G. (1944). *Philosophy and education in interaction*. Conference on Democracy and Education. Columbus, Ohio State University.

Hullfish, H. G. (1947). What kind of education? *Educational Research Bulletin*, *26*(5), 113-122.

Hullfish, H. G. (1950). The nature and function of democratic administration. In H. Benjamin (Ed.), *Democracy in the administration of higher education* (pp. 48-62). New York: Harper & Brothers.

Hullfish, H. G. (Ed). (1953). *Educational freedom in an age of anxiety: Twelfth yearbook of the John Dewey Society*. New York: Harper & Brothers.

Hullfish, H. G. (1953). *Keeping our schools free: Public affairs pamphlet no. 199*. New York: The Public Affairs Committee.

Hullfish, H. G., & Klein, A. J. (1940). Further development of the college program: The relation to democratic culture. *Educational Research Bulletin*, *19*(18), 507-522.

Hullfish, H. G., & Smith, P. G. (1961). *Reflective thinking: The method of education*. New York: Dodd, Mead.

Maurice Hunt

Bigge, M. L., & Hunt, M. P. (1980). *Psychological foundations of education: An introduction to human motivation, development, and learning* (3rd ed.). New York: Harper & Row.

Hunt, M. P. (1948). *The teaching of economics in the American high school*. Unpublished doctoral dissertation. Columbus: Ohio State University.

Hunt, M. P. (1969). Some views on situational morality. *Phi Delta Kappan, 50*(8), 452-456.

Hunt, M. P. (1974). Taxonomizing educational objectives: Some questions about the approach of Benjamin Bloom. *Proceedings, Twenty-Second Annual Meeting of the Far Western Philosophy of Education Society* (pp.127ff). Tempe: Arizona State University.

Hunt, M. P. (1975). *Foundations of education: Social and cultural perspectives*. New York: Holt, Rinehart, and Winston.

Hunt, M. P., & Metcalf, L. E. (1955 & 1968). *Teaching high school social studies*. New York: Harper and Row.

Metcalf, L. E., & Hunt, M. P. (1970). Relevance and the curriculum. *Phi Delta Kappan, 51*(7), 358-361.

Hunt, M. P., & Metcalf, L. E. (1996). Rational inquiry on society's closed areas. In W. C. Parker (Ed.), *Educating the democratic mind* (pp. 97-116). Albany: State University of New York Press.

Paul deHart Hurd

Hurd, P. D. (1949). *A critical analysis of the trends in secondary school science teaching from 1895-1948*. Unpublished dissertation, Stanford University.

Hurd, P. D. (1958). Science literacy: Its meaning for American schools. *Educational Leadership, 16*(1), 13-52

Hurd, P. D. (1961,1984). *Biological education in American secondary schools 1890-1960*. Washington, DC: American Institute of Biological Sciences.

Hurd, P. D. (1969). *New directions in teaching secondary school science*. New York: Rand McNally.

Hurd, P. D. (1983). An overview of science education in the United States and selected foreign countries. Commissioned paper in the National Commission on Excellence in Education (Eds.), *A nation at risk: The imperative for educational reform—An open letter to the American people. A Report to the Nation and the Secretary of Education*. Washington, DC: U.S. Superintendent of Documents.

Hurd, P. D. (1989). Accomplishing curricular changes-implementation. In W. G. Rosen (Ed.), *High school biology today and tomorrow* (pp. 289-336). Washington, DC: National Academy Press.

Hurd, P. D. (1989). Science education and the nation's economy. In A. B. Champagne (Ed.), *This year in school science 1989: Scientific literacy* (pp. 15-40). Washington, DC: American Association for the Advancement of Science.

Hurd, P. D. (1990). *Fulfilling the promise: Biology education in the nation's schools*. Washington. DC: National Academies Press.

Hurd, P. D. (1997). *Inventing science education for the new millennium*. New York: Teachers College Press.

Hurd, P. D. (1998). Scientific literacy: New minds for a changing world. *Science Education, 82*, 407-416.

Hurd, P. D. (2000). Science education for the 21st century. *School Science and Mathematics, 100*(6), 282-289.

Hurd, P. D. (2000). *Transforming middle school science education*. New York: Teachers College Press.

Hurd, P. D., & Gallagher, J. J. (1968). *New directions in elementary science teaching*. Belmont, CA: Wadsworth.

Lawrence Metcalf

Hunt, M. P., & Metcalf, L. E. (1955). *Teaching high school social studies*. New York: Harper and Row.

Metcalf, L. E. (1949). *A theory of conceptual learning and its implications for the teaching of the social studies for the purpose of clarifying social attitudes*. Abstracts of Doctoral Dissertations, No. 56. Columbus: The Ohio State University Press.

Metcalf, L. E. (1952). Must teachers be "neutral"? *Educational Leadership, 10*(2), 22-25.

Metcalf, L. E. (1957). Intellectual development in modern schools. *Phi Delta Kappan, 38*(7), 277-280.

Metcalf, L. E. (1963). Some guidelines for changing social studies education. *Social Education, 37*(6), 197-201.

Metcalf, L. E. (1967). Review of teaching public issues in the high school. *Harvard Educational Review, 37*(1), and *Indiana Social Studies Quarterly, 38*(3), 72.

Metcalf, L. E. (1969). Urban studies, reflectively speaking. *Social Education, 50*, 197-201.

Metcalf, L. E. (Ed.). (1971). *Values education*. Washington, DC: National Council for the Social Studies.

Metcalf, L. E. (1988). An overview of the Deweyan influence on social studies education. *International Journal of Social Education, 3*(3), 50-54.

Metcalf, L. E., & Hunt, M. P. (1970). Relevance and the curriculum. *Phi Delta Kappan, 52*(7), 358-361.

Alice Miel

Koopman, G. R., Miel, A., Avery, E. V., & Oakes, E. C. (1933). *Helping children experience the realities of the social order: Social studies in the public schools of Ann Arbor, Michigan*. New York: Appleton-Century.

Koppman, G. R., Miel, A., & Misner, P. (1943). *Democracy in school administration*. New York: D. Appleton-Century.

Lewis, A., & Miel, A. (1972). *Supervision for improved instruction: New challenges, new responses*. Belmont, CA: Wadsworth.

Miel, A., & Berman, L. (1970). *In the minds of men: Educating the young people of the world*. Washington, DC: Association for Curriculum Supervision and Development.

Miel, A., & Brogan, P. (1957). *More than social studies: A view of social learning in the elementary school*. Englewood Cliffs, NJ: Prentice-Hall.

Miel, A., with Kiester, E., Jr. (1967). *The shortchanged children of suburbia: What schools don't teach about human differences and what can be done about it*. New York: Institute of Human Relations Press.

Jesse Newlon

Newlon, J. H. (1932). Can the high school stimulate the intellectual interests of American youth? *Junior-Senior High School Clearing House, 7*(1), 21-25.

Newlon, J. H. (1933). Need for new social science materials. *The Clearing House, 8*(2), 73-74.

Newlon, J. H. (1934, February). *The role of leadership in the reconstruction of education*. Paper presented at the meeting of the Society for Curriculum Study, Cleveland, OH. Box 5, file folder 6, Jesse H. Newlon Collection, Special Collections & Archives, Penrose Library, University of Denver, Denver, CO.

Newlon, J. H. (1936, February). *Shall the school curriculum seek to improve the type of society which maintains it?* Paper presented at the meeting of the Department of Superintendence, St. Louis, MO. Box 5, file folder 7, Jesse H. Newlon Collection, Special Collections & Archives, Penrose Library, University of Denver, Denver, CO.

Newlon, J. H. (1937a). Democracy and education in our time. *Progressive Education, 14*(8), 589-594.

Newlon, J. H. (1937b). Freedom and teaching. In W. H. Kilpatrick (Ed.), *The teacher and society. First yearbook of the John Dewey Society* (pp. 256-282). New York: D. Appleton-Century.

Newlon, J. H. (1938). Public support for a social studies program. *Teachers College Record, 39*(6), 453-458.

Newlon, J. H. (1939). *Education for democracy in our time.* New York: McGraw-Hill.

Newlon, J. H. (1940, October). Teachers and politics—1940. *Frontiers of Democracy, 7,* 22-24.

Newlon, J. H. (1941a). The curriculum and the crisis in democracy. *Curriculum Journal, 12*(5), 200-204.

Newlon, J. H. (1941b, April). Democracy or super-patriotism? *Frontiers of Democracy, 7,* 208-211.

Donald Oliver

Oliver, D. W. (1957). The selection of content in the social sciences. *Harvard Education Review, 27*(4), 271-300.

Oliver, D. W. (1968). The selection of content in the social studies. In J. P. Shaver & H. Berlak (Eds.), *Democracy, pluralism, and the social studies, readings and commentaries: An approach to curriculum decisions in the social studies* (pp. 17-42). Boston: Houghton Mifflin.

Oliver, D. W. (1976). *Education and community: A radical critique of innovative schooling.* Berkeley, CA: McCutchan.

Oliver, D., & Newmann, F. (1967). *Taking a stand: A guide to clear discussion of public issues.* Middletown, CT: Xerox Corporation/American Education Publications.

Oliver, D., & Newmann, F. (1991). *Public issues series.* Boulder, CO: Social Science Education Consortium.

Oliver, D. W., Newmann, F. M., & Singleton, L. R. (1992, May/June). Teaching public issues in the secondary classroom. *The Social Studies, 83*(3), 100-103.

Oliver, D. W., & Shaver, J. P. (1966). *Teaching public issues in the high school.* Boston: Houghton Mifflin.

Oliver, D. W., & Shaver, J. P. (1996). Using a jurisprudential framework in the teaching of public issues. In W. C. Parker (Ed.), *Educating the democratic mind* (pp. 145-168). Albany: State University of New York Press.

Oliver, D. W., & Shaver, J. P., with Berlak, H., & Van Seasholes, E. (1962). *The analysis of public controversy: A study in citizenship education.* Boston: Harvard Graduate School of Education.

Joseph Piel

Engineering Concepts Curriculum Project. (1971). *The man-made world.* New York: McGraw-Hill.

Galey, M., & Piel, E. J. (1987). Technology prepares teachers in STS. *Bulletin of Science Technology and Society, 7*(5-6), 930-931.

Galey, M., Piel, E. J., & Trilling, L. (1987). Definition of STS—Foundation for the "you, me, and technology curriculum." *Bulletin of Science Technology and Society, 7*(1-2), 178-183.

Liao, T., & Piel, E. J. (1970). Let's get relevant. *The Physics Teacher, 8*(2), 74-82.

Piel, J. (1979). Teaching about science, technology, and society in the social studies. *Social Education, 43*(6), 446-448, 455.

Piel, E. J., & Truxal, J. G. (1973). *Man and his technology: Problems and issues.* New York: McGraw-Hill.

Piel, E. J., & Truxal, J. G. (1975). *Technology, handle with care.* New York: McGraw Hill.

UNESCO. (1971). *UNESCO source book for science teaching* (rev. & enlarged, 2nd ed.). Paris: Author.

Harold Rugg

Rugg, H. O. (1922-1926). *Social science pamphlets.* New York: Teachers College.

Rugg, H. O. (Ed.). (1923). The social studies in the elementary and secondary school. *Twenty-Second Yearbook, National Society for the Study of Education, Part II.* (See the chapters authored by Rugg.)

Rugg, H. O. (1926). A preface to the reconstruction of the American school curriculum. *Teachers College Record, 27*(7), 600-616.

Rugg, H. O. (1929-1940). *Man and his changing society.* Boston: Ginn. (The Rugg social science textbooks.)

Rugg, H. O. (1931). *Culture and education in America.* New York: Harcourt, Brace.

Rugg, H. O. (1933). *The great technology: Social chaos and the public mind.* New York: John Day.

Rugg, H. O. (1939). The social studies: What I believe. In J. A. Michener (Ed.), *The future of the social studies.* Washington, DC: National Council for the Social Studies.

Rugg, H. O. (1941). *That men may understand: An American in the long armistice.* New York: Doubleday, Doran.

Rugg, H. O. (1947). *Foundations for American education.* Yonkers-on-Hudson: World Book.

Rugg, H. O. (1963). *Imagination.* New York: Harper and Row.

ABOUT THE EDITORS AND CONTRIBUTORS

ABOUT THE EDITORS

Samuel Totten is professor of curriculum and instruction at the University of Arkansas, Fayetteville. Prior to entering academia he was an English and social studies teacher in Australia, California, the Walworth Barbour American School in Israel, the U.S. House of Representatives Page School in Washington, DC, and served as a K-8 principal at Esparto Elementary in Esparto, California.

While earning his doctorate in curriculum and instruction at Teachers College, Columbia University, he studied with Maxine Greene, Dwayne Huebner, Lawrence Cremin, Ann Lieberman, and Karen Kepler Zumwalt.

His long-time interest in the teaching of social issues has resulted in the following publications: *Social Issues in the English Classroom*; *Social Issues and Service at the Middle Level*; *Guidelines for Teaching About the Holocaust* (with William S. Parsons); Special issue ("Teaching About Genocide") of *Social Education*, the official journal of the National Council for the Social Studies; Special issue ("Teaching About the Holocaust") of *Social Education*; *Teaching and Studying About the Holocaust*; *Teaching Holocaust Literature*; *Holocaust Education: Issues and Approaches*; *Teaching About Genocide: Issues, Approaches, Resources*; and *Researching and Teaching Social Issues: The Personal Stories and Pedagogical Efforts of Professors of Education*.

Among the publications he has authored, co-authored, edited, or co-edited on key social issues are: *First-Person Accounts of Genocidal Acts Committed in the Twentieth Century*; *Genocide in the Twentieth Century: Critical*

Essays and Eyewitness Accounts (co-edited with William S. Parsons and Israel W. Charny); *Genocide in Darfur: Investigating Atrocities in the Sudan*; and *The Prevention and Intervention of Genocide: An Annotated Bibliography.*

Totten is a member of the Council of the Institute on the Holocaust and Genocide (Jerusalem, Israel), an associate of the Centre for the Comparative Study of Genocide (Sydney, New South Wales, Australia), and has served as an educational consultant to the United States Holocaust Memorial Museum in Washington, DC.

Jon E. Pedersen is a professor of instructional leadership and academic curriculum and currently holds the position of associate dean for research and graduate studies in the College of Education at the University of Oklahoma. Pedersen earned a BS in agriculture (biochemistry and nutrition) (1982), MEd in administration, curriculum & instruction (science education) (1988), and a PhD in administration, curriculum & instruction (science education) (1990) at the University of Nebraska-Lincoln. He began his teaching career as a secondary school science teacher and taught high school chemistry and physics.

Pedersen is active in several national organizations including: the National Association for Research in Science Teaching, Association for the Education of Teachers of Science, and National Science Teachers Association. He is the author of over 75 publications on science teaching (many of which address teaching about social issues). He has edited four books and authored a teacher manual for robotics. During his tenure in higher education, Pedersen has been primary investigator and co-investigator of numerous grants and supported projects on science curricula development, science in-service education, middle level education, and international education totaling well over one and a half million dollars.

Pedersen has also directed numerous programs in education and science education in Bolivia, South America and has worked in over a half-a-dozen countries around the world.

ABOUT THE CONTRIBUTORS

Chara Haeussler Bohan is an assistant professor in the School of Education at Baylor University. She earned her doctoral degree at The University of Texas at Austin, her master's degree at Teachers College, Columbia University, and her bachelor's degree at Cornell University. She has authored a recent book titled, *Go to the Sources: Lucy Maynard Salmon and the Teaching of History.*

Mark David Dietz is the coordinator for information technology planning and programs at Texas State University—San Marcos. Also a doctoral student in curriculum studies at The University of Texas at Austin, he plans a dissertation that will focus on John Dewey's responses to the writings of English literary and social critic Matthew Arnold.

O. L. Davis, Jr. is the Catherine Mae Parker Centennial Professor of Curriculum and Instruction at The University of Texas at Austin. A former president of the Association for Supervision and Curriculum Development and a leader in other professional and scholarly groups, his career interests have focused on curriculum practice and theory, curriculum history, and social studies education. For 12 years, he served as editor of the *Journal of Curriculum and Supervision*. He has received, among others, the Distinguished Career Research in Social Studies Education Award from the National Council for the Social Studies, the AERA (Division B) Lifetime Achievement Award for Outstanding Research in Curriculum Studies, and the University of Texas (Austin) College of Education Dean's Distinguished Faculty Award.

Ron Evans, a professor of social studies education in the School of Teacher Education at San Diego State University, is a longtime advocate of issues-centered approaches to social studies. He served as a founding member of the Issues-Centered Education Special Interest Group of the National Council for the Social Studies and as the group's first executive secretary. He is author of *The Social Studies Wars: What Should We Teach the Children?* Also, he served as first editor of the *Handbook on Teaching Social Issues*. He has published widely in social studies journals and is currently working on a biographical account of the life and work of Harold Rugg.

Sherry L. Field is a professor of social studies education/curriculum studies and Fellow, Lee Hage Jamail Regents Chair in Education at The University of Texas at Austin. She has served as chair of the College and University Faculty Assembly (CUFA) of the National Council for the Social Studies and on its executive board, chair of the Research in Social Studies Special Interest Group of the American Education Research Association (AERA), and president of the Society for the Study of Curriculum History. She was the recipient of the Glickman Faculty Fellow Award at the University of Georgia in 2000. She has also been the editor of *Social Studies and the Young Learner* from 1996-2006. Field's research focuses on elementary social studies curriculum and instruction and its historical foundations, preservice teacher's thinking about citizenship education, and teaching about civil society and human rights. She is the author of numerous research articles published in journals such as *Theory and Research in Social Education, Social Education, The Social Studies, Journal of Curriculum and Supervision,* and *Educational Forum.* She has recently co-authored a social studies textbook series, Harcourt Horizons, and three books: *They Led by Teaching, Explorations in Curriculum History,* and *Real World Investigations for Social Studies: Inquiries for Middle and High School Students.*

William R. Fernekes is the supervisor of social studies, at Hunterdon Central Regional High School, Flemington, New Jersey. Fernekes has published widely in social studies and related publications dealing with issues-based curriculum and instruction. He served as the editor for the "Materials and Resources" section of the National Council for the Social Studies (NCSS) publication *Handbook on Teaching Social Issues* (1996) edited by Ronald W. Evans and David Warren Saxe. He is also the co-author (with Beverly C. Edmonds) of *Children's Rights: A Reference Handbook,* and the author of *The Oryx Holocaust Sourcebook,* the latter of which was recognized as an outstanding reference work by *Choice* magazine in 2003. Fernekes is a member of the NCSS Special Interest Group on Issues-Centered Education, and is the co-director (with Rutgers University Archivist Thomas J. Frusciano) of the award-winning website *Electronic New Jersey: A Digital Archive of New Jersey History,* located at www.scc.rutgers.edu/njh.

Alan W. Garrett is professor of education foundations at Eastern New Mexico University. His areas of scholarly interest include curriculum history, educational history, and curriculum studies.

Gerald L. Gutek is professor emeritus of education and a former dean of the School of Education at Loyola University, Chicago. He earned his PhD in education at the University of Illinois (Urbana), with a specialization in the history of education. Gutek has written two books on George S. Counts: *The Educational Theory of George S. Counts* and *George S. Counts and American Civilization.* Gutek's most recent publications are: *Philosophical and Ideological Voices in Education; Historical and Philosophical Foundations of Education: A Biographical Introduction; The Montessori Method: The Origins of an Educational Innovation;* and *American Education in a Global Society: International and Comparative Perspectives.* He is currently working on a history of the social ideas of American educators.

Murray Nelson, one of Richard Gross's many doctoral students, has taught at Penn State University for 30 years. He is a professor of education and American studies. He is a past member of the board of directors of the National Council for the Social Studies (NCSS) and is a former president of the Pennsylvania Council for the Social Studies. He was the editor of *The Future of the Social Studies* and "The Social Studies in Secondary Education-A Reprint of the Seminal 1916 Report with Annotations and Commentaries." He also authored three editions of *Children and Social Studies*.

Jeff Passe, professor of social studies education at the University of North Carolina at Charlotte, currently serves as president of the National Council for the Social Studies (NCSS). He is a long-time member of the NCSS Social Issues Special Interest Group (SIG). He was co-author (with Ron Evans) of the chapter on "discussion leadership" in *The Handbook on Teaching Social Issues*. Passe is the author of five books, including *When Students Choose Content* and *Elementary School Curriculum*.

Mark A. Previte is in his third year as assistant professor of secondary education at the University of Pittsburgh at Johnstown. He teaches courses in elementary social studies methods, secondary social studies methods, and general methods. He is also a university supervisor for the secondary education student teaching program. Prior to coming to Pitt-Johnstown, Previte was a secondary social studies teacher for 28 years at Northern Cambria High School in Northern Cambria, Pennsylvania. For the last 10 years, Previte has been the program chair for the NCSS Issues Centered Education Special Interest Group. Previte's publications include: *The NCSS Presidential Addresses: Perspectives on the Social Studies: 1936-1969, Volume 1* (with J. J. Sheehan); *The NCSS Presidential Addresses: Perspectives on the Social Studies: 1970-2000, Volume 2.* (With J. J. Sheehan); and "Seeing the Whole Board: A Presidential Decision Making Activity" in *The Journal: Wisconsin Council for the Social Studies*.

Karen Riley is distinguished research professor and distinguished teaching professor at Auburn University, Montgomery, Alabama. Her research interests include the history of education, the politics of education, and curriculum history. She is also a consultant to the movie industry on the topic of the Holocaust, and the author of *Schools Behind Barbed Wire: The Untold Story of Wartime Internment and the Children of Arrested Enemy Aliens*.

Susan Robertson is a doctoral candidate at The University of Texas at Austin in curriculum and instruction with an emphasis on curriculum studies and elementary social studies. She serves as a teaching assistant and supervisor of student interns and apprentices in the UTEACH-Liberal Arts certification program. Her research interests include elementary social studies, social justice in social studies teaching and learning, high-stakes testing, and issues and policies affecting second language learners.

Robertson received her BA and MA degrees from the University of San Francisco. Prior to her return to graduate school as a fulltime student, Susan taught elementary school for 10 years in California, Massachusetts, Georgia, and Texas. Robertson regularly volunteers at the Austin Children's Shelter and serves as an executive officer of the Shelter Guild.

Paul Robinson, one of Richard Gross's many teacher-preparation and doctoral students, is currently an associate professor of teaching and teacher education at the University of Arizona. His scholarly interests revolve around the history and teaching of the social studies curriculum. Among his publications are: a chapter on Arizona's social studies curriculum in *Curriculum History 2005*; a chapter on Ruth West in *Building a Legacy: Women in Social Education 1784-1984*; a chapter on the future of social studies certification in *The Future of the Social Studies*; editor of *Great Ideas in American Schooling: Continuing the Quest*; and a chapter (with Joseph Kirman) on the place of history instruction within the social studies, *Social Studies and Social Sciences: A Fifty-Year Perspective*. Recently he served on the board of directors of the National Council for the Social Studies (NCSS), and was the recipient of the Wilbur Murra Lifetime Achievement Award from the Arizona Council for the Social Studies.

Mindy Spearman is an assistant professor of elementary social studies education at Clemson University. She received a PhD from The University of Texas at Austin with emphases in social studies education and the historical foundations of education. Prior to her work at Clemson, she taught second grade in a semi-rural school district south of Austin, Texas. Her research interests include archaeology education for elementary students, preservice teacher education in the social studies, primary source research and historical thinking. She is also interested in American Educational History, especially the history of teacher education, early educational periodicals, and historical research methods.

Barbara Spector is professor of science education in the College of Education at the University of South Florida (USF) and director of the Center for Ocean Science Education Excellence-Florida (COSEE-FL) in the College of Marine Science at USF. COSEE-FL is one of 10 National Science Foundation-funded centers comprising the National COSEE Network. She has taught qualitative research methods and uses grounded theory for her own research. Her research umbrella has always focused on how change occurs in education. She is well known for her focus on the continuum from preservice through inservice science teacher education and factors contributing to educators' abilities to shift paradigms from traditional didactic teaching to holistic approaches consistent with current national standards in various disciplines. The research and development cycle she enacts involves turning theory into practice, including 9 years of a transdisciplinary residential program for middle school youngsters ("World of Water at USF"), and the USF Graduate Program of Excellence for Mathematics and Science Teachers. Spector was a pioneer in the use of social issues to teach science when she was a high school biology teacher in Syracuse, New York and continues focusing on social issues as a professor, teaching preservice and inservice science teachers. The science/technology/society interaction (STS) program she developed and teaches at USF was honored in Robert E. Yager (Ed.) (2005) *Exemplary Science: Best Practices in Professional Development*, with a chapter titled, "Hey! What, are Ya Thinking?: Developing Teachers as Reflective Practitioners." An overview of her work ("Serendipity: A Paradigm Shifter's Friend in Academia") appears in Samuel Totten and Jon E. Pederson (Eds.) (2005) *Researching and Teaching Social Issues: The Personal Stories and Pedagogical Efforts of Professors of Education*.

Beginning with her STS course 7 years ago, Spector developed a unique format for modeling constructivist teaching using the computer for distance learning courses. Her most recent innovation with distance learning is using a "live access classroom" constructed from open source software to simultaneously teach synchronously and asynchronously. Her latest venture is using social issues as the focus for teaching scientists and educators working in informal science education institutions (e.g., museums and aquaria) in a four course certificate program for marine and environmental educators.

Barbara Slater Stern is an associate professor in the Department of Middle, Secondary, and Math Education at James Madison University. She teaches curriculum theory; general methods for middle and secondary education; teaching, learning and curriculum; and internship seminar in the undergraduate, MAT and MEd programs. In addition, she supervises student teachers. Her research interests include curriculum, the history of teaching social studies/history, and integrating technology into social studies. She is the author of *Social Studies: Standards, Meaning, and Understanding*. She is also the editor of *Curriculum and Teaching Dialogue*, the journal of the American Association of Teaching and Curriculum. In addition she serves on the editorial review board for the *Kappa Delta Pi Forum* and for SAGE publications. She is currently working on an edited book entitled *The New Social Studies: People, Politics, and Perspectives*.

Mary Lee Webeck is an assistant professor of social studies education and curriculum studies at The University of Texas at Austin. She serves as chair of the Research in Social Studies Special Interest Group of the

American Education Research Association (AERA) and on the Editorial Board of *Social Studies and the Young Learner.* She is a National Board Certified Teacher and a recipient of the Milken Educator Award in 2000. She is active in creating and implementing professional development opportunities for teachers through her work with the Center for Civic Education, Texas Law Related Education and the Holocaust Museum Houston. She has also served as the director of state and national institutes for We the People: The Citizen and the Constitution. She currently serves on the advisory board of the Holocaust Museum Houston. Webeck's research encompasses teacher development in social studies. She is especially interested in middle grade students, social studies learning and instruction, and in preservice teachers' thinking about democracy in a civil society. Webeck has recently published articles on the representation of the Holocaust and the role of art in promoting dialogue among members of communities. Her work appears in *Social Studies and the Young Learner, Kappa Delta Pi Record, The Arts and Learning Research Journal,* and *Educational Measurement: Issues and Practice.*

INDEX

Printed in the United States
216313BV00004B/1/A

9 781593 115661